JOHN HELLMAN is a member of the Department of History at McGill University.

One of the earliest and most imaginative and influential attempts to reconcile Roman Catholicism and Marxism was the movement known as personalism. Founded by Emmanuel Mounier, and articulated in the journal *Esprit*, personalism was in part responsible for the theological renewal of the Roman Catholic Church within a broad political, social, and intellectual context in France and elsewhere and was an important influence on the Second Vatican Council.

Professor Hellman outlines the difficulties faced by Mounier in reconciling his desire to be both seriously Christian and politically revolutionary. His oscillations from discipleship of Jacques Maritain to flirtation with the fascists, from support for Vichy to co-operation with the French Communist party, illustrate the dilemma of many French Catholics who broke with the traditional politics of their Church, and the drama behind the emergence of a militant Catholic left in France after the Second World War.

Drawing on a variety of sources, including interviews, unpublished correspondence, and diary entries, the author relates Mounier and the *Esprit* group to French and Belgian politics and intellectual life. He reveals previously unknown links between French and Belgian personalists and leftwing national socialists in Germany as well as with the fascist left of Italy. He discusses the volatile relationship between communists and personalists, describing the influence on personalism of Bergson, Maritain, Péguy, Berdyaev, Scheler, Heidegger, Nietzsche, Marx, and Mounier himself. In addition, new light is shed on the innovative Catholicism evident at Vatican II and the conflict between it and the traditional faction in the Roman Catholic Church.

This book will be of particular interest to students of the intellectual and political life of modern France and of modern religious thought, theology, and the modern Roman Catholic Church.

JOHN HELLMAN

Emmanuel Mounier and the New Catholic Left 1930–1950

UNIVERSITY OF TORONTO PRESS

Toronto Buffalo London

© University of Toronto Press 1981
Toronto Buffalo London
Printed in Canada
ISBN 0-8020-2399-1

Canadian Cataloguing in Publication Data

Hellman, John, 1940–
    Emmanuel Mounier and the new Catholic left 1930–1950

Bibliography: p.
Includes index.
ISBN 0-8020-2399-1

1. Mounier, Emmanuel, 1905–1950.   2. Personalism.
I. Title.

B2430.M694H44   194   c81-094105-8

The photograph of Emmanuel Mounier on which the cover of this book is based appeared in the September 1970 issue of *Planète Plus*, which was prepared by Marc de Smedt *et al.*

This book has been published with the help of a grant from the Canadian Federation for the Humanities, using funds provided by the Social Sciences and Humanities Research Council of Canada.

To Odile

Contents

EMMANUEL MOUNIER AND
THE NEW CATHOLIC LEFT 1930–1950

1

Introduction

Any picture of the French literary scene in the post-war period usually includes little clusters of deracinated youth, filling Boul' Mich' cafés with earnest talk of fashionably gloomy existentialism. Such a picture is, in fact, accurate, as far as it goes, but there were other cafés beside the Deux Magots and a formidable ideological rival equally capable of seducing the café savants. The fact that the literary and philosophical works of existentialists Sartre, Camus, Marcel, and Merleau-Ponty remain the most popular French intellectual products of that period in Anglo-Saxon countries leads many to read too much of that popularity back into the period. It is doubtful if the influence of Sartre and his friends' review *Les temps modernes*, for example, equalled that of Emmanuel Mounier's Personalist review, *Esprit*, the only new review of the 1930s to survive the war. In the opinion of Jacques Ellul, 'the *Esprit* effort was fundamental for the French intellectuals of 1930. An essential shift took place and all that generation, which is now in its sixties, has been influenced by that movement (more essential in my view than Sartrian existentialism!), as much the Protestants as the Catholics.'[1] Even Sartre himself told Denis de Rougemont one day in New York City towards the end of World War II, 'You Personalists have won ... everybody in France calls himself Personalist.'[2]

What, then, was this 'personalism' and why has it proved as ephemeral as existentialism proved marketable? The latter question is tied to the former, for one reason why personalism did not seem easily exportable is that no one seems to be very clear about what it was. According to one great historian, the sympathetic Henri Marrou, it was 'a sort of handy label or rallying-cry, which was never technically elaborated.'[3] Despite the considerable efforts at definition by such well-known intellectuals as Maurice Nedoncelle, Teilhard de Chardin, Mounier himself, and Nicholas Berdyaev, we are left with the formula of the personalist and philosopher Jean Lacroix, who recently 'defined' personalism as an 'anti-ideology.'[4] Mounier's philosophical heir, Paul Ricœur, provided little help when he condemned even the effort to define personalism as a 'philosophy.'[5] According to the former editor of *Esprit*, Jean-Marie Domenach, personalism is best understood as 'a method for thinking and living.'[6] It is easy to see why a philosophy that was not a philosophy did not speedily find its way from high academics into Kerouac novels.

While the most prominent personalists could do no better than to call for the affirmation of the 'absolute value of the human person,' this very affirmation has been described as one of the most dominant and widespread 'new commonplaces,' or clichés, in western Europe. The personalist orientation has influenced business enterprises, Sunday sermons, cosmetic advertisements, the vocabulary of the newspaper *Le Monde*, and a range of Left Christian political rhetoric.[7] The personalist movement never crossed the Atlantic as spectacularly as did existentialism; it did not stimulate safaris into the misty realm of Being and Nothingness, or provide the catch-phrases for beatniks unraveling the absurdity of the universe in Ivy League coffee houses.

Personalism was better equipped to produce a form of theology and for many North Americans theology has little clout in the real world. It exists in an intellectual limbo, beyond (below?) the purview of the social critic or the historian. Although theologians are influenced by secular thought currents such as personalism, their work is often considered totally distinct, in another order, as if the same form of historical evaluation does not apply to it. In this case, a number of France's most prominent theologians – Jean Daniélou, M.-D. Chenu, Yves Congar, Henri de Lubac – were involved, to varying degrees, with the personalist movement, but the effect on their theologizing, Vatican II, and Christian spirituality in the Americas has yet to be analysed.

In France the most important statement of the personalist option was given by Emmanuel Mounier and the review *Esprit*. Although educated Frenchmen are still unsure what *Esprit* meant to say, the fact that it was something new, intense, and influential is widely accepted. North American students of French intellectual life have had difficulty in placing Mounier's 'left-wing Catholicism,' but despite his consistent hostility to the United States, those who have devoted specialized study to

Mounier and/or personalism are largely enthusiastic.[8] They have sided with Mounier's personalism against Christian democracy in general and Jacques Maritain in particular.[9] *Cross Currents*, which has pioneered in introducing new European theological reflection on this side of the Atlantic, christened its first issue in 1950 with a Mounier call for a vigorous, committed Christianity. A certain direction began to be taken by some Catholic intellectuals in North America, a generation after the 'personalist' turn had been taken in France.

So, personalism is widely acknowledged to be somehow 'significant,' both in France and abroad but, finally, what was – or is – it? It can be defined as a statement of concern for the human person, the human being considered in all his dimensions, launched in the early nineteen-thirties. It can also be less charitably defined as 'a flotilla of abstractions, a fleet of capital letters' (Paul Nizan) among which 'Person' and 'Community' were the most recurrent.[10] But the assertion of the 'absolute value of the human person' was not simply an abstract affirmation of human dignity but rather a movement of defence against two antithetical threats: individualism, and its manifestation, liberal capitalism, and communalism, and its manifestation, communism. It mirrored the desperate effort of intellectuals in the early nineteen-thirties to navigate a 'third way' between capitalism and communism.[11] Thus it was a philosophical enterprise at once vague in what exactly it would like to set up and precise in what it did *not* want to occur, that represented a strong longing not unfamiliar now. *Esprit* and the personalist movement have been described as Catholic-Christian and leftist from their origins.[12] But this results from making Mounier, a self-conscious Catholic, the founder of *Esprit* and the personalist movement – he was, strictly speaking, 'the founder' of neither – and equating the post-war *Esprit* with the pre-war *Esprit*, which refused to be considered either Catholic or leftist.

Most of the earliest and most important articulations of personalism were by German-educated, militantly anti-communist Russians, Germans, and Belgians, who were Russian Orthodox, Jewish, or non-believers.[13] Despite the pre-eminence of Mounier, personalism was hardly a French Catholic creation. There was rather, as Maurras said about Marxism, 'something German and Jewish about it,' and the defence of the person, at the outset, was rooted in Bergson and Nietzsche more than in the gospels. 'Spiritual man' was defended against the threats of the Left and of the Right and an élite 'of the Spirit,' whatever their religious affiliation or non-affiliation, were invited to rally behind the banner of *Esprit*.

The first personalists at *Esprit* in 1933 formed their own small review and became known by its name – *Ordre Nouveau*. These talented young men – Robert Aron, Arnaud Dandieu, Henri Daniel-Rops, Alexandre Marc, and Denis de Rougemont – included two who soon converted to Catholicism, but none was Catholic when they first brought personalism to *Esprit*.[14] Arnaud Dandieu, who died in 1933, has been described as the most original personalist. He drew his inspiration from Nietzsche and Husserl. Though he was cool to religion, Dandieu's claim to be the founder of personalism seems stronger than that of Mounier.[15]

The *Ordre Nouveau* group had appropriately well-developed contacts with Germany, particularly with 'left-wing' or 'dissident' National Socialists dissatisfied with Hitler's leadership of that Worker's party movement in the early 1930s. The founder of *Ordre Nouveau*, Alexandre Marc, organized meetings between young French intellectuals interested in a 'spiritual' revolution and the National Socialist 'left wing' – the *Opponent* of Harro Schulze-Boysen and Otto Abetz and the *Black Front* of Dr Otto Strasser – and some of the earliest issues of Mounier's *Esprit* ran long articles by Strasser, one of Hitler's best-known rivals.[16] Dandieu, for his part, was known to be sympathetic to the Nazi movement but not to Hitler, who was faulted by the 'oppositionists' in this period when he was pretending moderation and manoeuvering his way to the chancellorship for being 'soft on capitalism.'

The earliest articulations of personalism were violently attacked from both the Right and the Left. Jacques Maritain privately, but harshly, reproached Mounier and his Catholic friends for having anything to do with the 'goose-stepping philosophy' of Dandieu, Marc, and company.[17] Prominent Christian Democrats criticized *Esprit*'s rejection of elective democracy, which *Esprit* considered 'individualistic,' in favour of a vague, but clearly anti-democratic, program.[18] Leading French communist intellectuals condemned *Esprit* as an effort to articulte a distinctive French national socialism 'by distilling the thick foreign currents' to fit the French situation (Nizan). *Izvestia*, for its part, singled out Denis de Rougemont – the link between *Esprit* and *Ordre Nouveau*, the one intellectual who always worked at both reviews – as a 'leader of the French fascist intelligentsia.'[19] The consistent, violent condemnations of personalism by French communist and Soviet observers contrasted with the approbation accorded the movement by German observers after Hitler came to power. Otto Abetz, Joachim von Ribbentrop's adviser on French affairs, published a sample of Mounier's writing with an introductory note in his *Deutsch-Französische Monatshefte (Cahiers Franco-Allemands)*.[20] Abetz was always on the look-out for 'signs of health' in decadent 'capitalist and liberal' Europe, and his review sometimes had kind words for the personalists in France, Belgium, or Holland.[21] Both personalism and the theological speculations of Teilhard de Chardin met approval across the Rhine in the late nineteen-thirties.[22] French theologians, in turn, were much influenced by the elaboration of the theory of the Mystical Body of Christ by German theologians such as Karl Adam, which was proclaimed a doctrine of the Church in 1943.

Several French Marxists who had accused personalism of working towards a distinctive French fascist or national socialist theory dropped the charge and courted personalist favour during the Popular Front period (1935–7); the charge was only revived, by the communists, during the Vichy period. Two recent books indicate that first-rate historians can evaluate *Esprit* and the personalists in this period and draw diametrically opposed conclusions. For those French scholars sympathetic to personalists – Jean-Louis Loubet del Bayle, François Goguel, and Michel Winock – the personalists' reactions to the Italian invasion of Ethiopia, the Popular Front, the Spanish Civil War, and Munich were sound, and situated *Esprit* neatly in the avant-garde of the Left, at the heart of the Resistance.[23] To a Swiss critic of the review, Pierre de Senarclens, on the other hand, the reactions of *Esprit* to these same events were ambiguous and waffling, which helps explain the co-operation of some personalists with the Révolution Nationale of Marshal Pétain.[24] American critics all champion the personalists, tending to go along with the interpretations of the movement by French sympathizers.

America's leading experts on France during the German occupation are not particularly helpful in providing a balanced view of personalism's role in that tragic period. Robert Paxton ignores its role in the Resistance but exhumes quotations from several controversial articles in *Esprit* during the few months it was allowed to publish under Vichy and portrays Vichy's youth absorbing an exalted form of personalism around camp-fires.[25] Stanley Hoffmann, on the other hand, admits that there was a good deal of personalist rhetoric in the air at Vichy, but cautions that it is not to be confused with the 'pure Personalism of Mounier and Lacroix.'[26]

The role of *Esprit*, Mounier, and personalism after the war is far clearer than its role before the war. *Esprit* was fairly clearly defined as a review of the 'Catholic avant-garde in France,' part of a general opening of the Left in French Catholicism that included worker priests, Chrétiens progressistes, and those caught up in enthusiasm for Pierre Teilhard de Chardin's cosmic speculations.[27] Although a young French historian and member of the *Esprit* group has faulted his colleagues for naïveté in this period regarding the realities of Stalin's activities in the Gulag and eastern Europe – *Esprit* was a strong critic of the Marshall Plan, defended the communist régime in Poland, justified the incarceration of Mindszenty – most historians have found the Personalist opposition to Christian Democracy 'from the Left' to have been salutory and justified.[28] Most say that there was a certain scale of 'generosity,' 'openness,' and 'concern for social justice' among French Catholics in that period and the personalists were 'furthest along,' 'more advanced,' and hence on the extreme Left.

Certain right-wing critics of the personalists have blamed them considerably for the Marxisization of contemporary Catholic theology and spirituality.[29] There is some truth in that analysis, but it is more accurate to say that the sense of the sacredness of the 'person' and the importance of 'community' as essential dimensions of Christian spirituality grew up, in Europe at least, as part of the personalist effort to create an *alternative* to revolutionary movements inspired by Marxism, not Marxism itself.[30] It would dissipate many confusions if we could understand how the historical origins of phenomena such as personalism which are behind the modern mutation in Catholic theology and spirituality were the work of men, not only of the Holy Spirit.

EMMANUEL MOUNIER 1905–50

Historians may have short-changed personalism but no such fate has befallen Emmanuel Mounier. On the contrary, he has had a series of extravagant claims made for him. The former editor of the review *Esprit* has been called a 'maître à penser' for our times, 'an authentic prophet,' 'an original political thinker who knew how to harmoniously integrate ... anarchism and Marxism,' a man who was 'almost alone in opposing ... a coherent doctrine to communism,' 'a seminal figure in today's Christian-Marxist dialogue,' 'the only one who has given a virile response to the theses of atheistic existentialism,' the thinker who, with Jacques Maritain, did 'the most since the First World War in teaching French Catholic intellectuals to understand their place in modern times.'[31] As if these impressive intellectual kudos were not enough, Mounier is also described as a Resistance hero and 'a leader of the maquis of Vercors.'[32] Absurdist playwright Eugène Ionesco has regularly claimed him as a formative influence and called him 'more of a philosopher than Camus; he disassociated, distinguished, integrated everything.'[33] Finally, François Mauriac trumps them all by saying that Mounier was 'an authentic saint.'[34]

Mounier has come to be regarded as an important transformer of the French Roman Catholic Church from engaging in rearguard reaction to being in the vanguard of theological renewal and New Left activism – from the Church of Charles Maurras, the Action Française, and Philippe Pétain to that of Teilhard de Chardin, the worker priests, and Pope John XXIII. Mounier as a stolid, isolated, left-wing Catholic before the war, then Resistance hero, then post-war pioneer in Christian-Marxist dialogue helps to explain, and reflects, the extraordinary disparity between pre-war and present-day French Catholicism. But this legendary Mounier, as we shall see, was largely invented.

Viewed through the prism of his post-war writings (as he almost always is) Mounier may indeed give the impression of having been an original, unwavering, consistent man of the Left. But he was a peculiar mixture of violent language and private timidity, full of ringing exhortations to political commitment while wrestling with a deep aversion to politics. He was sometimes hot-headed and unjust, often confusing, and has compounded misunderstanding by rewriting his personal history at every turn. He seldom admitted mistakes, fashioning an image of decisiveness and consistency from a morass of hesitations and contradictions while, in complete good faith, castigating the mass of his contemporaries for their lack of resolution and lucidity.

Mounier was always a serious Christian, but he wanted to be a social revolutionary, too. As editor of *Esprit* from 1932 until his death in 1950, Mounier tried to marry black France with red France, the priests with the Jacobins, and create a transcendent synthesis. His whole life was spent in that effort.

For generations, devout religious believers and left-wing political activists had seemed inevitable antagonists in France. Mounier's attempt to combine these two traditions led him to be denounced as an apostate and praised as a reformer, to be seen as the hope of the Catholic Church in France and as a sign of its final dissolution. Although he died over a decade before John XXIII began to 'open the windows of the Church,' Mounier is still considered a 'progressive' Catholic because in many respects he was born before his time. As a herald of the new course that the Catholic Church has taken since the Second Vatican Council, this complex French intellectual confronted many of the issues that have faced the Church in our own day.

However, Mounier's intellectual and political evolution and the relationship between the values he proclaimed and his concrete activities were different from what many of his contemporary disciples seem to imagine. He was a deeply spiritual young man who began a small-circulation review in 1932, was interested in forming a religious community for laymen, but became more and more interested in revolutionary politics. He flirted with anarchism and fascism in the late nineteen-thirties, and, then, in 1940, was suddenly catapulted from obscurity by the defeat of France to a position of some importance in Vichy's abortive National Revolution, only to emerge, in an extraordinary metamorphosis, as a prominent 'Left Catholic' after the war. Mounier's story is also that of a generation of avant-garde Catholics in France.

It is a central contention of this book that no aspect of twentieth-century French history has been more misrepresented than the story of the 'theological renewal' in the Christian churches or the emergence of left-wing Christian political activism. Mounier's generation of avant-garde religious thinkers in France have, in effect, written their own reviews and achieved almost saintly stature among their readers in other lands. Mounier's friends, active in the intellectual background to the Second Vatican Council, have tended to believe themselves instruments of the Holy Spirit, which has not led to a lucid, historical analysis of their activities. This book places the origins of the theological and spiritual transformation brought by the Second Vatican Council in a broader context than individual redemption. The intellectual evolution of modern European religious thinkers must be set against the background of the rise of Nazism and fascism in a new way if our understanding of the European Christian experience in the twentieth century is to be enlarged. The understandable need for 'saints' and the appeal of one-dimensional answers must both be sacrificed to historical truth.

Much of this book concerns France during the controversial Vichy period. Close associates of Emmanuel Mounier or other personalists have been among the most influential historians of that régime (eg, Robert Aron) and of the years preceding its installation (eg, François Goguel). Perhaps because a remarkably large number of French historians and other influential academic, political, and journalistic figures were nurtured by Personalism, the more questionable aspects of the movement's role under the Pétain government have never been clarified. The Vichy period has proved a painful one to re-examine for those who lived through it, and it remains a vital factor in ideological and political strife in France.[35] Since, for Mounier and some of his closest comrades, personalism overlapped religious convictions, an obscuring of personalism's history occurred, sometimes from altruistic motives. Mounier and personalism need to be placed in a balanced focus so that we may better understand the experience of his generation and the factors behind the evolution of some of Europe's most influential modern Christian intellectuals.

One thing is clear: Mounier was not a Christian like the others. He violently challenged the lukewarm of his faith:

These crooked beings who go forward in life only sidelong with downcast eyes, these ungainly souls, these weighers-up of virtues, these dominical victims, these pious cowards, these lymphatic heroes, these colourless virgins, these vessels of ennui, these bags of syllogisms, these shadows of shadows, are they the vanguard of Daniel marching against the Beast?

To effect completely so many depressing visions, ten faces of monks lost in the silence of a monastery suffice; or the recollection of that Spanish peasant woman whom I glimpsed one day in the darkest corner of a small church in Toledo, her arms stretched wide in a sovereign gesture, rigid as a queen upon her knees. Must we then search the monasteries and chapels of Castile in order to gather up the dying reflections of a fire that would consume the world?

As a young man Mounier did search the monasteries and chapels of Castile in his study of a sixteenth-century Spanish mystic. He soon abandoned that to join some of the most intelligent and altruistic young men of his generation in a movement to rekindle the fire of Christianity and gave himself to it, heart and soul.

Perhaps nothing so clearly illustrates the problem Mounier faced in bridging the gap between religion and politics as this book itself. Few readers will correspond to Mounier's ideal and read texts devoted to both areas with equal interest. Accordingly, those whose major interest lies in Mounier's politics may pass quickly through chapters 1 and 2, which treat Mounier's spiritual evolution in some detail and presumably would be of minor interest to the political specialist. I feel obligated, however, to Mounier himself to point out that he would not have approved.

2

Those Years 'Too Happy, Too Calm'

When Emmanuel Mounier became a well-known intellectual he described himself as of mountain peasant stock, from the glacier-ringed valleys whose streams ran down onto the Grenoble plain. This was only marginally true. He was always very close to his father, a humble Grenoble pharmacist, and to his mother, who took him to confession on Saturday nights. But by his later twenties, when he became a severe critic of the kind of urban middle class milieu into which he had been born in 1905, he took a romantic pride in his four peasant grandparents. When encountering pretentious intellectualism he could 'feel a grandfather react in me, his health run in my veins, the air of his fields purify my lungs.'[1] His grandparents always helped him feel close to 'the people' and rural ways.[2]

The affectionate, doting Paul Mounier took his son to Grenoble's concerts and lectures and encouraged his ambition to be a country doctor. The boy was rather serious and timid. Illness left him deaf in one ear, nearly blind in one eye, severely wall-eyed, and set back a year in school.[3] Despite his success in lycée literature and philosophy courses, he enrolled in the Faculty of Sciences in the fall of 1923 to prepare for medical school. There his unhappiness with science studies soon led him into 'despair to the point of suicide.' By March he was no longer eating and enrolled in a closed retreat preached by a priest active in the youth branch of the French Catholic Action movement.[4]

When the newly religious Emmanuel abandoned his pre-medical studies his father introduced him to a young Grenoble philosophy professor, Jacques Chevalier, considered 'safe' for students of strong Catholic backgrounds, explaining that the boy wanted 'to do philosophy as a form of the apostolate.'[5] Chevalier was initially unimpressed with this 'large blond boy with blue eyes and a pale complexion. He looks at me intensely without fixing on me (because of a slight defect in vision). He seems very intimidated in my presence, listens quietly, says practically nothing. When he speaks it is in a precipitous rush.'[6] But Chevalier was trying to form a young Catholic intellectual élite in Grenoble, so he took him under his wing.

Chevalier was a militant Catholic frustrated by his confinement to the intellectual backwoods of Grenoble, where his relations with his colleagues were strained.[7] He was a passionate disciple of Henri Bergson and was studying religious perceptions in an effort to form a new philosophy of the individual. He warned Mounier about the 'modern idealism' of the Sorbonne, where Léon Brunschvicq, historian of science and a Jew, was a bitter critic of 'irrational vitalism' in philosophy. Chevalier also described the prominent anti-religious sociologist Emile Durkheim and the anticlerical philosopher 'Alain' (Emile-Auguste Chartier) as the proponents of the 'manifest errors' with a mysterious power for diffusing them.[8]

Chevalier, despite his lack of sympathy for the Republic, was professedly apolitical, but he was rethinking his Catholicism in the light of Bergson and this set him off against the rigidly orthodox Action Française Catholics.[9] Thus Mounier's new *maître* was isolated from the French philosophical establishment for his ardent Catholicism and from the Right for his modernist connections.

When Mounier first met Chevalier, religious integralism and Thomist philosophy were basking in the victory caused by Pius x's condemnations of Alfred Loisy's doctrines and the pope's anathematizing of the general effort to 'twist unalterable truth to suit modern thought.'[10] Bergson's writings had been placed on the Index of Forbidden Books in 1914 and the theories of some of his followers were condemned, while others, such as Maurice Blondel, were in frequent doctrinal difficulty with Rome. The Church was troubled by the loose Bergsonian definition of spiritual experience: the emphasis on 'living experiences' (Laberthonnière), the interior life, as divine communication with the human. Chevalier taught Mounier that the 'modernism of Loisy' had been essentially distinct from Blondel's ideas, but, as we shall see, the 'philosophical' formation Chevalier provided him was obviously influenced by the modernist spirit.[11]

In the fall of 1924 Mounier was producing an essay on 'Psychology and Metaphysics' for Chevalier, and the following May the diary of Jacques Rivière 'dazzled' him.[12] 'It was first of all to understand, that I became Christian,' wrote Rivière, as he sought to clarify his 'conversation' with God, his certitude of God's 'presence,' through an analysis of his interior life which enthralled Mounier.[13] This latter advised his sister Madeleine, who was trying to convert a friend to Catholicism at this time, to take Rivière's correspondence with Claudel and 'put them someplace in your room where Mlle B. will see them ... nothing is better than what Blondel calls the method of immanence: take the souls where they are ... and if Mlle B. can ... follow .. that is worth more than all the philosophical treatises. Because one *lives* a conversion.'[14] Chevalier, during the fall of 1925, encouraged Mounier to examine his 'interior life': to read a little, then profoundly meditate on what he read, in a small seminar room at the Université de Grenoble with a selected 100 to 150 books in it.[15] And he joined Chevalier's private seminar for future professors, which had a unique rule for participation: 'the continuous sentiment of the presence of God.'[16]

Chevalier required an openness from his students in religious matters not unlike that demanded by a Jesuit master of novices. Mounier, who had been recuperating from his depression for a year, was soon completely taken up in these sessions, as he effusively wrote his maître in December 1925:

I feel myself penetrate deeper into the interior life of our group; it seems that I am more intimately yours. The grandeur of the goal to achieve summons and stimulates me. It seems to me that in participating in this common ideal I become larger than myself: I am shouldered up by those who have come, carried by the common spirit and will of all ... you lead us towards the infinite: we ought to ... have the ambition to go the highest possible without fixing any other limit than that which the events guided by Providence will impose. God will do the rest.[17]

While individuals organizing around common spiritual ideals are an ancient Christian tradition, Chevalier promoted 'a common spirit and will' to 'go the highest possible,' to approach 'the infinite' as a group. Although this exploration of fresh analyses of the 'inner life,' from Jacques Rivière's to Bergson's, strayed from the mainstream of Catholic practice, Mounier found it a purer form of Catholic orthodoxy: 'At the beginning ... I did not realize how much your spirit, that of your group, was in agreement with my most intimate aspirations, the most delicate nuances of *my* Catholicism – I could also say of true Catholicism, because you have seized the very essence of it.'[18] Mounier described himself to his sister as having undergone a sort of religious conversion:

You see, my dear Madeleine ... we all have one or several conversions to make. And the passage from a traditionalist and bourgeois pietism to a truly Christian life ... is at least as difficult as that from atheism to faith. Because those who believe in nothing and are searching have a hundred times more value than those who are sleeping in exterior practice ... the bourgeois of the faith must be brought back from the dead.[19]

Mounier's 'conversion' quickly set him off from his fellow Catholics through a disdain for the slack spirituality of the French middle class among whom he had grown up.

Soon Chevalier's devotion to Bergson was matched by the twenty-year-old Mounier's adulation of Chevalier, whom he described lecturing in Grenoble:[20]

Five. The vast hall of fifteen hundred seats grows silent. But the silence is heavy with attention. This dissimilar crowd, freed for an hour from its distractions, seems to form a unity of fervent souls in a prayer devoted to the truth. ... Below, the lecturer. His face still suffused by the glow of youth; the image of a force in full maturity ... all his diverse themes converge .. as if a cathedral of ideas were being constructed before us ... the dialogue of a musician and his instrument. ... At the end spontaneous applause of the crowd ... ineffable visions were awakened in the centre of every heart.[21]

In September 1926 Mounier's Diplôme d'Etudes Supérieures (Master's degree) subject was decided upon: 'The Double Movement, Theocentric and Anthropocentric, in the Philosophers of the Eighteenth Century,' a subject inspired by the analyses in Abbé Henri Bremond's ten-volume *Histoire littéraire du sentiment religieux en France*, appearing at that time.[22] In the new term Mounier was Jacques Chevalier's unofficial secretary: correcting proofs of his *Bergson*, or transcribing the discussions which followed his lectures.[23] Chevalier found Mounier a 'docile, fervent, transparent soul,' 'expected very much' of him, and he decided to hold special weekly sessions for Mounier and a few others to divulge the contents of his own research on mysticism and conversations with Bergson.[24]

Chevalier, although a jealous *maître*, encouraged contact with Father Emile Guerry, a dynamic figure in the activist wing of Catholic Action, and particularly in the Grenoble branch of the Association Catholique de la Jeunesse Française.[25] Guerry competed with the Action Française for influence among Catholic youth and bitterly attacked Maurras' organization.[26] Mounier, 'a straight, young provincial,' ignorant not only of fashionable literature – Valéry, Cocteau, *Dada*, and so on – but even of Action Française philosophers such as Jacques Maritain, became a Catholic Action enthusiast.[27] Mounier's local bishop also supported the ACJF and in 1927 vigorously enforced the Church's new ban on membership in the Action Française.[28] Mounier, at twenty-one, had no interest in politics and spent his time in Bergsonian introspection; he was still, in his own words, an innocent and devout 'blue-eyed boy.'

In late 1926 Mounier was shocked by Action Française attacks on Pius XI as an unworthy pope.[29] (Pius XI's predecessor, Pius X, had pleased Maurras by condemning the Christian democracy of Marc Sangnier's *Sillon* as linked to 'Modernism.')[30] French Catholic youth leader Georges Bidault complained that Maurras' movement hampered Catholic Action recruitment, while the Action Française criticized the new pope's support for the conciliatory policies of French Foreign Minister Briand which revived Sangnier's pacifist ideas. The young Thomist philosopher Jacques Maritain helped produce a carefully reasoned reply to Catholic criticisms of the Action Française, which described its political doctrine as close to the metaphysics of Thomas Aquinas.[31] It was opposed, it said, by 'jealous Christian Democrats and revengeful Modernists smarting at their defeats under Pius X.'[32] A de facto condemnation of the League soon traumatized many French Catholics who had fused their Christian and patriotic sentiments, such as the eleven of France's seventeen archbishops and cardinals who were favourable to it.[33]

On 15 December, Mounier recalled a friend's interrogation by Jacques Chevalier on the friend's visit to a troubled Jacques Maritain:

RIONDET I have the impression of a man who loves the truth, and with neither *a priori* idea nor sentiment, goes to it by his reason alone.

CHEVALIER With no *a priori* idea? But isn't Saint Thomas for him the very expression of the truth?

RIONDET The closest expression that is. ... But Maritain admits that St Thomas is amendable.

CHEVALIER, MOUNIER [AND THE OTHERS] Only on details.

CHEVALIER Maritain has retained ... an intellectual pride that takes this form in his doctrine...

RIONDET That is impossible to believe by anyone who knows his ascetic life.

CHEVALIER That doesn't matter at all ... there exists in Maritain an unconscious and involuntary pride. ... the same milieu are faithful to both the Action

Française and integral orthodoxy. The idea common to both is that what is living and solid in Christianity is the Greco-Roman law.[34]

Chevalier told Mounier and his friends that Maritain had rejected Bergson for an Action Française ideology that was 'without question the greatest modern heresy.'[35] He blamed Maritain for failing to understand 'that God is an educator, that He gave a rudimentary revelation to the first Jews ... which Christ perfected ... at the end of Greco-Roman civilization, when humanity arrived at the age of reason,' and that Bergson now had an important role to play.[36] Chevalier informed Mounier that there was a divine pattern in modern intellectual development, a profoundly evolutionary view of history shared by few French Catholics at the time.[37] He condemned the League for the initiatives in Rome against Bergson and Bergsonians.[38] Chevalier convinced Mounier that Christian thought was 'going somewhere' and that despite the pernicious efforts of reactionaries, the Christian intellectual avant-garde would make an important contribution to mankind in the twentieth century.

When Chevalier spoke of the seventeenth century in Mounier's courses he enjoyed juxtaposing Descartes and Pascal, and Mounier ended his own DES thesis comparing the sense of God in the two thinkers. Mounier suggested that religious perception was the most important aspect of a philosopher's effort, and thus Pascal was a more important 'philosopher' than the founder of rationalism.[39] Chevalier confided that 'rather than giving my students a system, I give them a *spirit* [esprit] and a method.'[40] In a May 1927 session Chevalier described the premises of his efforts:

We have abandoned the study of the individual to novelists and mystics. ... There is much more psychology in Proust, even more in Saint Theresa, than in the two volumes of Dumas.[41] Because the possibility of ecstasy in a man reveals to us ... a power which enters into his very definition....

A science of the individual necessarily implies that one can have a knowledge of miracle ... one comes closer to God in studying one sole being all his life than in studying the totality of the sciences. ... Maine de Biran, who studied himself all of his life, renewed philosophy much more profoundly than did Kant.[42]

Chevalier inspired the young Mounier to read modern mystics and perceive figures such as Maine de Biran as pioneers in analysis of the psychology of the unconscious.[43]

Paris was the intellectual testing ground for bright young men from the provinces and Chevalier decided to send Mounier to follow the best of his students, such as Jean Lacroix and Jean Guitton, who had been successful in the *agrégation*[44] in philosophy. On 28 October 1927, following Mounier's departure that day for Paris, Chevalier privately noted that his teaching had had an 'exceptional resonance' in that 'soul of a rare quality, completely interior, completely concentrated on itself....' He also lamented 'a certain lack of simplicity... in ... expressing his thought,' Mounier's temptation to feel himself 'invested with a mission,' to 'persist in errors, as well as in truths, once he had defended them.'[45] L. Maggiani, who had studied in 'Brunschvicq's Sorbonne' before joining Chevalier's study group, feared that Mounier, moulded by three years of Chevalier, was going to be 'burned.'[46] But Chevalier had close friends, such as Father Pouget and Jean Guitton, who would look after his protégé in the big city.

On arrival Mounier sought out the gentle and aesthetic Guitton, a new *agrégé* with a coveted scholarship from the Fondation Thiers to study 'Time and Eternity in Plotinus and Saint Augustine,' who did his best to acclimatize him to his new setting.[47] But Mounier quickly felt a 'horror' of the Sorbonne.[48] He described Brunschvicq to his sister Madeleine as 'among the phoneys; something very bourgeois, very established about him.' He was only attracted by intelligence, he wrote her,' 'to the extent that it contributes more light on the interior life.'[49] However, the Ecole Normale Supérieure promoted the intellectual qualities valued by Léon Brunschvicq, not Jacques Chevalier, and soon Mounier became painfully self-conscious, in his words, 'a dreamer ... afraid of the noise of his own words, of the imprudence of his interventions....'[50]

In November Guitton introduced Mounier to the eighty-year-old theologian Father Pouget, and for the next six years the two joined the future theologian Jean Daniélou, and a few others, in studying with Pouget two afternoons each week.[51] The priest spoke of Bergson's research into mysticism, and scripture, offering what Daniélou later described as 'philosophical reflections on theology' along with explorations of the mystics.[52] Pouget, like his friends Loisy and Bergson, innovatively applied the latest advances of modern thought to biblical exegesis. The 'cell' around this master sought to develop the interior life, not simply the intelligence as in the courses of Brunschvicq.[53] Mounier was 'buoyed up' by it as by the Chevalier group in Grenoble, and wrote Chevalier that when he was in Pouget's presence, 'it seems to me that I am confronting the truth itself....'[54]

The emotional support Mounier received from the Pouget sessions seemed more than offset by the sudden death of his closest childhood friend, Georges Barthélémy. He described Barthélémy as the only friend of his age group 'who advanced profoundly into my intimacy, to whom I opened certain sanctuaries ... we were united, without a declaration, by the discovery ... of our souls.'[55] Mounier had begun to analyse his personal relationships in great detail,[56] and in January 1928, in a small café on the rue Gay-Lussac, Mounier reread Barthélémy's letters:

in the middle of those nameless people, brains filled with some folding money, a lipstick, an evening's bridge game or tomorow's flirtation! The more one lives, the closer one lives to Pascal: the divine disquiet of unsatisfied souls, that is the only thing which counts. Oh! The circumscribed minds, the men seated in the chairs, on the rostrum, in their armchairs the satisfied people, the intelligentsia, the u-n-i-v-e-r-s-i-t-a-i-r-e-s![57]

Barthélémy's death encouraged Mounier's tendency to consider himself an Israelite in the land of the Egyptians, to immerse himself in Pascal and to wear a cloak of moral superiority to shield himself against the intimidating lucidity of the Ecole Normale Supérieure. Nonetheless, he threw himself into study after this shock and his devotion to Chevalier seemed unflagging in his letter of 25 May:

I think that now you can have confidence in me. I consider myself forever immune to the poison of the Sorbonne ... it is dangerous above all, for those who ... have no other concern than the development (and I specify: academic) of their intellect. I am certainly incapable of that objective attitude of those young men who place themselves before problems as if in front of a piece of anatomy...

When I had the crisis, in January, those people .. would have ... disgusted me with philosophy if there had not been you, and my past, and true philosophy....[58]

He also wrote to his sister that his Chevalier years had been 'too happy, too calm.'

On 16 July 1928, Mounier dined with Chevalier and Father Pouget on the eve of submitting to the final examinations of the *agrégation* in philosophy.[60] He was already of the educated élite with a *baccalauréat* (secondary school-leaving certificate) at a time when only twelve thousand were granted per year in a population of over forty million.[61] Yet this young provincial of undistinguished background went on to hold his own at the ENS among the likes of Jean-Paul Sartre, Simone de Beauvoir, Paul

Nizan, Jean Daniélou, and Raymond Aron, despite the peculiarly narrow sort of education he had received. At the end of July, Mounier, to the astonishment of his colleagues and himself, not only passed but ranked second behind Aron, while Sartre failed and passed the next year with de Beauvoir.[62] Maggiani, who had predicted disaster for the Chevalier disciple, admitted that he 'conceived a lively respect, in fact a certain awe, for such an admirable – or shocking – adaptability' on Mounier's part.[63]

Mounier's success did not lessen his old resentments against the intellectual establishment. During his August vacation near the mountain village of Uriage above Grenoble, he wrote Guitton that: 'For a time I almost fell into the "mentality" of the university machinery ... now I shudder as over a narrow escape.' He was reading the *Correspondance de Rivière et de Fournier*, and it was clear that his dazzling feat in the *agrégation* did not divert his preoccupation with the inner life.[64]

In the fall of 1928 Chevalier found Mounier a place in the Maison de la Jeunesse which Daniélou directed on the Boulevard Saint-Germain. Guitton found a part-time teaching job for him, while the quick and polished Daniélou, a new *agrégé* in grammar and a 'Bergsonian,' introduced him into one of the most sophisticated grand bourgeois Catholic circles in Paris.[65] Daniélou was the son of Charles Daniélou, a prominent radical socialist politician close to Briand, and Madeleine, first in the *agrégation* in literature in 1903, director of the Catholic Collège Sainte-Marie in the elegant suburb of Neuilly. Daniélou's brother Alain was an expert on eastern religions, his father a staunch anticlerical, his mother and he at the centre of French Catholic intellectual life.[66]

Mounier wrote of his timidity and feelings of inadequacy to a friend on 10 November: 'It is difficult to move in the world of souls with the maladroitness of our bodies. What is absurd is not to feel myself on an equal footing with men, but tiny among men, impotent each time when faced with the realization of a project.' His concerns were more and more religious ('and if I were not cowardly I know where that would take me'), and he bridled against Chevalier's insistence that he settle on his thesis: 'If I made myself a paradise, I would like to philosophize there like a bird sings,' he confided to Guitton.[67]

Chevalier had, in Jean Lacroix's words, 'a confused and bastardized method of teaching,' and Mounier's close friend H.-I. Marrou later blamed him for deflecting Mounier's undoubted literary talent into some confused philosophical writing. Chevalier's method had been extremely narrow, even for a period in which a philosophy *agrégé* had good training in classical languages but little economics, sociology, and political theory: it even avoided the critics of 'spiritualism' such as Durkheim, Brunschvicq, or the Radical philosopher so important for many of his fellow *agrégés*, 'Alain.' Mounier was burrowing deeper into the rock of his faith; he testified to direct perception of the presence of God and came to be indifferent towards thinkers who did not help him prune, deepen, enrich that experience. Like a contemplative monk, he became uninterested in intellectual effort unrelated to his spiritual life.

Even contemporaries of Mounier who were experts on medieval thought such as Jacques Maritain and Etienne Gilson had wider interests in 'non-spiritual' subjects than the Chevalier circle. Curiously, however, as well as Mounier, Chevalier also trained two of the most famous Catholic thinkers of that generation, Lacroix and Guitton.

Besides Father Pouget's 'cell,' Jean Daniélou also frequented another high-powered intellectual 'chapel' with a prestigious membership. By the end of 1928 Mounier, too, was being invited to the Sunday afternoon discussions in the Maritain bungalow in the little middle-class suburb of Meudon to the west of Paris.[68] Maritain was Chevalier's age (forty-six in 1928), and soon to become one of the most influential Catholic intellectuals for Mounier and his entire generation. Though not a personalist, an understanding of Maritain is essential to an understanding of personalism and Mounier.

CONVERTS: JACQUES AND RAISSA MARITAIN

Jacques Maritain's mother, who was separated from her husband, was the daughter of one of the founders of the Third Republic, Jules Favre, and though a 'non-believer,' she had her son baptized Protestant out of fidelity to the Republican tradition.[69] Jacques grew up with an uncompromising demand for intellectual certitude which, at sixteen, led him to hurl himself in despair on the rug in his room. At the Sorbonne he met a kindred spirit in Raïssa Oumansoff, a frail but iron-willed Russian Jewess who had entered university at sixteen. Frustrated with the positivism and relativist metaphysics of the faculty, the two young people agreed to commit suicide if they did not discover the absolute certitude they demanded.[70]

One day in 1903, Charles Péguy, another bitter critic of the Sorbonne, took them to Bergson's famous lecture series at the Collège de France, which, in Raïssa's words, assured them 'that we are capable of truly knowing reality, that through intuition we may attain to the absolute....'[71]

While these lectures inspired the engineer Georges Sorel to plan the restoration of archaic and heroic values and his anticlerical friend Péguy to celebrate St Joan of Arc, the Maritains soon found them 'too flimsy a refuge.' Soon they sought out the eccentric novelist and prophet Léon Bloy in his hovel on the hill of Montmartre. In Raïssa's words:

June 25, 1905, two children of 20 mounted the eternal stairway which leads up to Sacré-Cœur. They carried in themselves that distress which is the only serious product of modern culture. ... They were going towards a strange beggar who, distrusting all philosophy, cried divine truth from the housetops, and who ... condemned his time ... with far more liberty than all the revolutionaries in the world.
    ...he was a fire-stained and blackened cathedral. The whiteness was within, in the depth of the Tabernacle. ... One knew, or one guessed, that only one sorrow existed here – 'not to be of the saints.' And all the rest receded into the twilight.[72]

Bloy lived in terrible poverty, and as an 'ungrateful beggar' borrowed money from all of his friends because he considered charity 'a grandeur for those who give.' Maritain later recalled an incident in church revealing much about Bloy's character: 'A woman usher arrived in front of him with the collection plate precisely at the moment of the elevation of the host. Furious, he turned his enormous terrible eyes, and pointing his finger, hissed "On your knees, brigand!" The poor woman, flabbergasted, fell to her knees in worship.'[73] On 11 June 1906, Jacques and Raïssa Maritain were baptized Roman Catholics, having experienced what Raïssa called 'the rude shock of conversion.'[74] Jacques had become, as he told Jean Cocteau in 1926: 'A convert. A man God has turned inside out like a glove.'[75]
    Bloy's absolute certitude helped convert the Maritains, but to better understand their own belief they soon began to read the *Summa Theologica* of Aquinas and live in 'an atmosphere of intellectual strictness, and of spiritual rectitude, thanks to St Thomas.'[76] The thought of the rigidly logical 'Angelic Doctor' helped stimulate their interest in the ideas of Charles Maurras, whose contempt for the modern world and defence of Roman Catholicism against the 'individualism' of the Reformation and the 'irrationalism' of Rousseau placed their new Thomism in a political perspective. The modern world seemed to require a revival of Aristotelian political principles.[77]
    Jacques Maritain's new Thomism led him to reverse his earlier

sympathy for the Bergsonian criticism of the intellect. In 1914 he lambasted 'weak philosophers and superficial theologians' who spread a 'cheap Bergsonism' among young people, with a 'sentimentality disguised as "intuition."' This, in turn, posed 'a mortal danger for the intellect.'[78] That same year, to the chagrin of Catholic Bergsonians such as Jacques Chevalier, Bergson's major writings were placed on the Index of Forbidden Books in Rome.

After the war Maritain published a series of works which established him as a major philosopher of the Action Française school. He helped create the *Revue Universelle* with the royalists Jacques Bainville and Henri Massis and a publication series, in which Mounier published his first book, to rival the *Nouvelle Revue Française* of Gide and Rivière.[79] Although Maritain never joined the League, he encouraged his friends Massis and Psichari to join.[80]

When Mounier first visited Meudon, in the fall of 1928, Maritain had just shocked his friends again by declaring that a Catholic had to reject the Action Française's position of 'Politics first' to affirm 'the spiritual first.'[81] Maritain did not completely change his intellectual perspective overnight and still thought, like Maurras, that the Protestant Reformation and the doctrine of progress were important sources of the West's spiritual decadence.[82] But he was also, in retrospect, at a turning point in his intellectual evolution: helping guide away from Maurras young Catholic intellectuals shaken by the condemnation of the League. In December 1928 Mounier began transcribing important conversations at the Maritains' into his diary.[83]

ACADEMIC DIFFICULTIES AND 'SPIRITUAL FRIENDSHIP'

When Mounier first came to know the Maritain circle he was far more interested in the Pouget sessions and seemed a self-absorbed, Catholic, young Werther: 'There are days where I like to be young, gay, simple, idyllic and others where I feel a need to immerse myself in the grandeur of the tragic. ... When I am taken by the former, I condemn the latter, and the inverse; but at bottom both are rich, both are necessary.'[84] He still felt confident he would win a Fondation Thiers scholarship by the summer of 1930, but what thesis subject was compatible with his concentration on his inner life?[85] The Ecole Normale had not significantly expanded those intellectual boundaries which had been set in Grenoble.

Mounier then discovered the writings of Charles Péguy. Daniélou suggested that Mounier speak on Péguy in May in a series of religious conferences which included Jacques Chevalier. 'Since Péguy,' Mounier soon wrote his sister, 'I am possessed by Joan of Arc.' On 11 May, her feast, he went to Orléans for a march of thirty thousand 'with a sentiment of devotion for her, while many were only thinking of ... the Action Française, Jeunesses Patriotes or Woman's Suffrage,' and when he returned to Paris he was moved to tears by the performance of *Saint Joan* of George Bernard Shaw.[86]

Devotion to Joan of Arc had been fostered by the eccentric sculptor Réal del Sarte before the World War I and now she became something of a national warrior saint. But Mounier, as he explained to Chevalier, was moved by Péguy's distinctive vision of Joan:

I am always under your sign and your inspiration. The spirit that you blew into me germinates and grows ... in watching that reawakening, the day before yesterday in Orléans, I saw in a glance the family forming in me under your patriarchy, Bergson, Péguy, Joan of Arc. ... You have guided me with a continual presence....[87]

In later years Mounier said Péguy seduced him away from a promising academic career and the influence of Chevalier.[88] But in fact Mounier first read Péguy with an interest stimulated by Chevalier's research into mysticism.

The evening after Mounier's conference on Péguy, Chevalier explained that philosophers could talk of mysticism because it had 'some sort of natural basis,' because it was a 'gift.' (But this 'gift' had to be transformed by grace or it did not bear fruit.') Mounier recorded the discussion on 'natural mysticism':

JACQUES CHEVALIER The mystic does not entirely renounce the self ... but he renounces egoism to rediscover the 'one' of pure nature where he rejoins God. Then he is carried by a free gift into the supernatural....
MADAME DANIÉLOU And the contents of that natural mystical state?
JACQUES CHEVALIER It is rather a movement, something like metaphysical intuition.
MADAME DANIÉLOU It is necessary to mark the difference. Father de Grand-maison said that mysticism is the abnegation of all egoism much more than an intellectual state.[89]

Chevalier's 'immanentist' doctrine of a 'natural mysticism' was criticized by others for failing to appreciate that Christian mystical perceptions were 'supernatural.' But, as Mounier correctly noted, all Chevalier's analyses countered that distinction.[90] In fact his conception of a natural mysticism encouraged exaltation in the Chevalier or Pouget study groups. It explains the peculiar complexity and intimacy of Mounier's relationship with a man who saw himself less as an academic adviser than as a spiritual director helping his students to perceive God Himself.

It was not surprising that Mounier found that arch-enemy of the Sorbonne, Charles Péguy, so attractive at this point. On 19 June he approached the Abbé Bremond, but the distinguished historian was astonished at his thesis interests: 'Where did you come from? You are really *agrégé* in philosophy? ... *On Mysticism?*'[91] Bremond described the Bergsonian philosopher Blondel as 'very close to the mystics,' but said 'Chevalier knows them less well, I think. A very good man, but an eclecticism with very jarring rhetoric.'[92] Even Bremond, hardly part of Brunschvicq's Sorbonne, found Mounier's approach bizarre and after a year of searching he was still without a thesis director or topic. In July, his request for a Fondation Thiers fellowship was refused.

Mounier began to resent an academic establishment which seemed to have little place for devout Catholics. One had to produce theses palatable to a Brunschvicq or a Durkheim to achieve academic success and renounce one's religious training and approach to the subject. The influence of Protestant, Jewish, and non-believing academics in the French educational system, far out of proportion to their representation in the population, rankled Catholic academics like Chevalier relegated to the provinces while 'secularizers' held prestigious chairs in Paris and formed new professors for the provinces. Mounier's presence in Paris mirrored the fact that the Catholics were beginning to fight back on several fronts.

Several of Chevalier's former students were involved with the Davidées, an organization founded by Marie Silve, a primary schoolteacher in the mountain village of Saint-Pons. ('Davidée' Birot was a heroine in a novel by the conservative Catholic novelist René Bazin.)[93] The Davidées 'lay apostolate' brought their members together for mutual spiritual development, to share pedagogical methods, and to challenge the premises of the French primary school system.[94] Mounier's monthly essays from January 1929 for Mlle Silve's journal *Après ma classe* had titles such as 'The Idea of the Irrational' and 'Bergsonian Intuition.'[95] In 1931, under a pseudonym, he defended Mlle Silve's group against the charge that it was a sectarian pressure group. He insisted it was primarily a 'spiritual friendship' for the young women involved.[96]

In July 1929 Mounier went to Saint-Pons to help formulate a

'spirituality' for the Davidées and experienced 'the most beautiful hours of my life' with Guitton and 'the incomparable Mlle Silve,' who had also felt humiliated by her teachers for her religious convictions.[97] He confided that he found:

> The spirit of Mlle Silve that of Joan of Arc. ... You could never believe my joy there. How many times have I agonized over the alternatives: to remain a scholar ... or to act ... and sacrifice precious meditation for agitation and rhetoric. Here is a first opportunity for action without the bruises....[98]

Mounier decided to help Mlle Silve form 'élites' to open the primary schools of France to the spiritual dimension.[99] Mounier spoke to the movement on Péguy, to young women 'devoid of false mysticism, free of earthly pride, without duplicity.'[100]

Mounier advocated a 'spiritualist' teaching method in *Aux Davidées*:

> Mademoiselle ...
> ... I want to show you how ... the philosophical spirit is the inseparable union of a certain attitude of life and a certain method of spirit ... a certain passionate curiosity for the interior life, our own and that of things. A detachment from the agitated surface of ourselves ... a withdrawal towards the secret region where life is unravelling and history is flowing....[101]

He promised the young teachers that if they sought God in others, no matter how cold or hostile they were, they would be sure to find 'souvenirs' of themselves later.[102] This aided the movement's effort to teach isolated village schoolmistresses the possibilities for measuring their students' natural mysticism. Marie Silve, in turn, regularly visited Maurice Blondel in Aix-en-Provence for advice in using this method of 'imminence' in teaching. The Davidées wanted to transform the state school system from within, but political affiliation was not allowed to those engaged in this 'purely spiritual work.' Mounier admired this feature and later adopted it in his own movement.[103]

In the fall of 1929 Madame Daniélou brought Mounier to Neuilly to, in his words, teach 'High Society in pinafores.'[104] At the Collège Sainte-Marie Mounier was said to be a Bergsonian and although the girls did not know exactly what that meant, they thought it was 'something new and intense.' But Mounier's lectures seemed abstract and impersonal; he was timid, 'a rather clumsy tall blond boy,' hampered by what Jean Lacroix later called the 'confused and bastard conception of teaching' he had acquired in Grenoble.[105]

In November, Jean Daniélou decided to enter the Jesuits, closed the Maison de la Jeunesse, and abandoned his plan to co-author a book with Mounier to popularize the thought of the still unknown Péguy. Daniélou did, however, send his brother-in-law, Georges Izard, as a replacement and Mounier persuaded Péguy's son, Marcel, to collaborate on the project as well.[106] Izard was a powerful and dynamic personality who greatly influenced Mounier.

Mounier returned to Paris in the fall of 1929 with a thesis subject suggested by Chevalier in mind: John of the Angels (1536–1609), a relatively unknown Spanish mystic. He saw Professor Jean Baruzi, expert on St John of the Cross, who explained to Mounier that he would have to master Spanish to examine the primary texts.[107] In December he complained that each professor he saw 'demolished' his thesis projects. Even Professor Jean Laporte, a young Catholic hostile to Durkheim and Alain who had given him his highest marks on the *agrégation*, offered telling criticism: the only thing Mounier would find in the mystics was an inability to describe their experiences.[108] But Mounier was determined to press on. The more resistance Mounier encountered at the Sorbonne, the more his bitterness against the French academic establishment and the more he visited Jacques Maritain.

MARITAIN: THE BLIND AND LUMINOUS FISH

In the summer of 1929 a bitter struggle erupted over an election to a vacant chair in the Collège de France. The pre-election favourite, sociologist Marcel Mauss, disciple of Durkheim and intellectual mentor of anthropologist Claude Levi-Strauss, was attacked as a 'wily little Jew' by some Catholics and nationalists who favoured the candidacy of Chevalier. One elector, the distinguished Arabic scholar Louis Massignon, recalled the voting day to Mounier: 'One side glared at the other with bloodshot eyes. And that poor old man who came from his deathbed to save France!' A Catholic told him that voting for Chevalier took precedence over his conscience's notion of who was the most qualified candidate. Massignon saw Chevalier orchestrating these pressures and thereby destroying the Chevalier candidacy; the Thomist historian of philosophy Etienne Gilson, busy establishing medieval studies at the University of Toronto, was attracting more and more support.[109]

Chevalier's difficulties in the Collège de France were accompanied by a crisis in his student group in Grenoble which Chevalier, with tears in his eyes, described to Mounier in September. Some individuals in the group had accused Chevalier of wanting to dominate them, and wanted more time for their intellectual careers. This, said Chevalier, was a heresy: 'I do not want to ignore God until the moment when, thanks to that, one succeeds. With Laporte, Gilson, Gouhier, whatever they say now, there is something impure: not to have said it before. I would not want to be in their place.'[110] Only Guitton and Mounier, Chevalier lamented, seemed to understand him.[111]

In the forest of Tronçais, not far from Paris, was 'François I's reserve,' a woodlot set aside by Colbert centuries before. There Chevalier's father had cut majestic trunks to build ferries for the American troops in the Great War and his sister, in meditating, had found her vocation as a nun. In November 1929 the master took Mounier where only Guitton, among the students, had been invited. Chevalier did not suspect that 'the other Jacques' would soon come between them.[112]

The memories of a whole generation of Christian intellectuals – Daniélou, Mounier, Jacques Madaule, Maritain, Gabriel Marcel, Nicholas Berdyaev – return to the discussions in the early nineteen-thirties at the Maritains'. Historian Madaule later recalled the scene:

At Meudon, a bit lower than the plateau, in a region where the houses almost, but not quite, touched one another, Jacques and Raïssa Maritain lived in a house where they had visitors Sunday afternoon. ... Maritain spoke in a very soft, almost inaudible, voice which did not at all resemble his style, which was assertive and sometimes violent – cutting to be exact. One had to cut off the false, to prune, to prune....

Pale, a bit swollen, with something cat-like in the skull and shoulders which he always covered with a carelessly fixed muffler, Jacques Maritain had the physique of his voice rather than that of his style. Nevertheless his eyes, a bit globular and very clear, which seemed to observe nothing or no one – they were fixed on the infinite – gave away the gentle, but inflexible intransigence of the Thomist philosopher.

...one of the intellectual chapels of Paris. There are the young – younger than I – who speak. They seem, themselves, initiated. From time to time, one or the other noiselessly left the salon and went up to the next floor where the Chapel, the true one, was.

...the most furtive allusion was sufficient for those sprightly spirits. It was in fact a communion. It was the reflection in light, brilliant, self-effacing words of the silence above, on the first floor.

Certainly the atmosphere of Meudon was a bit rarefied. Perhaps that came from the *mariage blanc* of Jacques and Raissa. They were imitated by a few other couples. It was like a convent with walls of dazzling whiteness, where all was of an irreproachable and audacious good taste.[113]

The conversations ranged over aesthetics, political theory, and music and were dominated by Maritain, Marcel, and Berdyaev. The younger listeners were to dominate Christian thought and art in France for a generation.

After Jean Daniélou's departure for the seminary, Mounier continued the Sunday afternoons in Meudon, which he viewed with a cool detachment contrasting to his emotional experiences at the Davidées. One such afternoon in December 1929 was recorded in Mounier's diary:

> There was there, at Meudon, Maritain who looks small against the mantle-piece between his mother and the speaker. DuBos prepares his elegant senten-ces. Gabriel Marcel, eternal sulky child, has found 'his just place' [sic] on one end of the couch near the door. Some pianists. A Russian Count who was conseil-ler d'Empire. Ghéon, whose least thoughts are reflected on his face, etc. – Nabokoff speaks of 'the phenomenon of Inspiration in music.'
> ...the conversation trails off. Maritain talks to me for a moment on my Péguy: 'The difficulty is to present him in the light and truth, without however deforming him and shocking his non-believing friends'...[114]

Despite Chevalier's warnings, Mounier began to seek Maritain's advice on his study of Péguy.[115] Maritain had serious reservations about Péguy's Joan of Arc:

> He was too exclusively dominated by Joan of Arc, who had a temporal mission. I often think about the problem in relation to Philip II. That was a moment in history when an all-powerful Catholic monarch could have imposed the true religion on Europe. The Armada: God permitted a storm to destroy it. God neglects temporal means. Christ never employed them. Péguy, who did not understand the monastic life, did not see that very well. Hauviette, who repre-sented the option of pure prayer, is superceded by Joan of Arc. He seemed in this way to ... head towards a sort of 'temporal first.' I see that tendency in all the men of his generation: Maurras, Massis....[116]

Péguy had even told Maritain, after the latter's conversion, that he would make a good Hauviette, a spokesman for prayer without action.[117]

Maritain also pointed to Péguy's tendency to consider 'philosophies as cultures more than as systems of ideas, and their worth ... in what they brought along with them':[118]

through Bergson he came to understand that ... truth came more from intuition than an expressible knowledge. As a result he perhaps retained the idea that diverse systems, even the most opposed, were in communication via a certain basis of intuition, that they were all true ... that would be very false if one wanted to say that all systems ought to be respected equally ... that one cannot say without being grotesque that one is 'right' and the others are 'wrong.'[119]

Maritain, singling out faults in Péguy, hit on certain tendencies in Mounier: the personification of ideologies in individuals, the abandonment of any conception of absolute truth among conflicting philosophies, the respect for all systems based on strong intuitional conviction. Mounier was laying his own Bergsonism open to criticism and, inevitably, reconsidering his long apprenticeship to Chevalier. Mounier's letters and conversations with Maritain were spare, logical, carefully structured, and tightly reasoned. After six years of tenderminded spiritual direction, Maritain's whip-like intellect was bracing.

In March 1930, Mounier confided to Massignon that he had 'discovered Maritain person to person.' The Arabist remarked that Maritain communicated better in conversations than in books: 'Cocteau defined him very well: a blind and luminous fish. He is occupied with doctrines and pays no attention to persons. That explains why he can be so astonishingly indulgent for our judgment at times, and so hard other times....' Maritain, Massignon said, was clearly superior as a philosopher to Chevalier, whose awkward mixture of Cartesianism and Bergsonianism with Christianity was 'an apologetical deformation of history.'[120] Mounier was moved by the combination of intellectual discipline and spirituality displayed by both Maritain and Massignon. He recorded an 'unforgettable' visit with the latter in which, after dismissing the Chevalier system, Massignon described Bergsonism as 'a useful stage for a soul ... but hardly a body of doctrine to build one's life upon.'[121]

Maritain seemed ignorant of Mounier's discipleship to Chevalier, and Mounier in this period, under a pseudonym, published another eulogy of Chevalier.[122] In March 1930 Mounier's new scholarship application proposed to explore new ground 'at the heart of mystical psychology ... follow the moral fecundity of that experience (all the great mystics having been the founders of orders, or of religions, or of new spiritualities)....'[123] Then he travelled in Spain, ostensibly to explore John of the Angels, and filled his diary with landscapes and faces and gave a lecture in French on Péguy at the University of Salamanca.[124]

MOUNIER'S PÉGUY

In May 1930, Mounier confided that Péguy reached 'miraculous regions' of his heart.[125] In January he had interviewed Péguy's old mother, whose earthy, picturesque qualities he described for the Davidées.[126] On 22 May he returned to Orléans for a bust unveiling, in the company of Daniel Halévy, Henri Massis, the Tharaud brothers, Péguy's sons, and a few others in a private chapel and noted, watching them, 'behind the grill, some peasants, with their rough leathery and wrinkled skin, and thick moustaches.'[127]

Mounier's long essay on Péguy, which appeared in 1931, displayed Mounier's Bergsonism and new sensitivity to the social and political implications of the 'spiritual.' Péguy seemed the direct opposite of both Brunschvicq's Sorbonne and Mounier's previous absorption in his inner life. Péguy's 'instinct,' Mounier wrote,

told him that thought ... took place in the heart of the people. The philosopher ... is an echo as well as a guide. And since 'the people' was ... a spontaneous state of spirit, a plenitude of soul which wells up everywhere in the race, he thought humanly through the natural movement of his humanity.[128]

Péguy, wrote Mounier, had decided to introduce 'a new resonance' into Bergson's thought because he appreciated 'a climate more than a doctrine....'[129] For Mounier, Péguy, too, brought a climate, an original mystique, that counted as more than a system.

For Mounier, Péguy's socialism 'was simply the transposition of the proletarian and popular love of work well done' that Péguy had learned while caning chairs in Orléans. The caners didn't work for their salaries, their employer, or the clients, but simply to do their job well. Quoting Péguy:

'A tradition, coming, welling up from the profoundest depths of the race ... demanded that that chair leg be well made. Every part in the chair that one could not see was exactly as perfectly made as that which was visible. That is the very principle of the Cathedrals.' It was a handsome continual sport, and yet more: 'They said while laughing, and to annoy the curés, that *to work is to pray*, and they did not realize how well they put it.'[130]

Mounier admired Péguy's notion of the spiritual impetus at the heart of socialism, of the irrelevance of elections and politicians:

he warned those of his friends who thought they could achieve the operation with a few electoral manoeuvers ... only a mystique, one of the same grandeur, can surmount another mystique. ... What makes a revolution is not some intrigues in the court or parliament. ... The politician ... harbours a sort of horror of fecundity ... like those sterile old men who detest childhood.[131]

Until this point in his life Mounier had seemed indifferent to politics despite the Wall Street crash and the Nazis on the move in Germany. He had conceived of mystics as strictly apolitical, 'the founders of orders, of religions, of new spiritualities.' But now Mounier discovered in Péguy that mystics were to be the great movers of men on the political level as well.

Mounier also learned to see Christianity as a certain 'mystique.' He celebrated the 'anti-theologism' of Péguy: 'Péguy was a man of faith ... he felt no need for the certitudes of theology. ... The possibility that Joan of Arc could have doubted her voices would have seemed absurd to him.'[132] Maritain condemned the irrationalism of Luther and Rousseau, but seemed to admire the 'prophetism' of Léon Bloy and the young Mounier. Mounier never took theology too seriously or worried much about the legitimacy of his 'voices.'

Péguy's prose writings helped Mounier fuse Bergson, socialism, his anti-theological Christianity and hatred of the Sorbonne into the 'spiritual revolution.' In 1929 Mounier's lights were Bergson, Péguy, and Joan of Arc. The essay on Péguy articulated the synthesis:

Péguy learned the law of the Christian in the school of Joan of Arc. She was the exclusive model of all saintliness for him; he always thought of that exact fidelity in the human task, of that miraculous absence of miracles in her mission. Bergson, on his side, taught him that it is by the wedge of action that the spiritual penetrates the material. ... He always seemed on the point of writing: temporal first. But he was not insensitive to the fact ... that human action decays very quickly into politics if it does not ceaselessly revive itself in the sources of its mystique. ... To push the action to the end, out of loyalty, and then leave the result to God: the Péguyiste code of the good fight.[133]

Péguy's socialism of cathedral builders, rather than auto-workers, somehow touched the romantic peasant side of Mounier. Péguy reinforced his interest in spiritual writers and his research proposals. Péguy's soldier-saint Christianity demonstrated that mystics, seemingly isolated and irrelevant, were, in fact, the great movers of men; politicians were mere tools of the mystics.

When Mounier developed his admiration for Péguy, France was still predominantly agricultural, and Péguy spoke for the peasantry and chair-caners against the paganism, anonymity, and 'world of money' that was replacing rural life. For Péguy the peasants were an eternal source of hope: 'For fifty years the foreign soldier stole the grain, burned the churches: but each year the peasant sows his field, rebuilds his steeple. He maintains all, he saves all.'[134] Mounier seemed oblivious to other thinkers also claiming to represent the eternal values of their particular races appearing in Europe at this time. In 1931 the former Jesuit novice Martin Heidegger wondered if the Nazis embodied the peasant values of his natal village in the Black Forest, and the Christian mystic Codreanu founded his Iron Guard in Rumania, glorifying ancient Rumanian peasant culture. In 1932, the Catholic youth leader Léon Degrelle launched the 'rexiste' movement in Belgium and Antonio Salazar began to practise Catholic social teachings as president of the Council in Portugal. Péguy, Degrelle, Heidegger, and Salazar shared Roman Catholic backgrounds and affection for pre-capitalist virtues against those of the modern bourgeoisie. But it would be difficult to lump all of these men together as representing 'fascist' movements and not simply religious revivalism or peasant reactions against modern economic pressures. No one had clear definitions of fascism or mysticism in the nineteen-thirties, which led to loose use of language.

When his Thiers application was turned down a second time, Mounier blamed the authorities' misgivings about the Péguy project. Indeed, the director of the Fondation thought Mounier 'a fuzzy-minded dreamer.'[135] While Maritain offered sympathy and help to find a job, Mounier was still, two years after his *agrégation*, without a thesis topic or financial support for his studies.[136] After several days in mid-summer with Guitton and Mlle Silve, Mounier promised Chevalier to spend the winter on his thesis.[137] But the scholarship refusal had been a serious blow and it was then, as Chevalier later lamented, that 'the other Jacques' 'traced a grandiose, urgent mission for him,' which 'accentuated some of these faults that I had fought against the most energetically.'[138]

After *Esprit* came to be considered a revival of Péguy's *Cahiers de la*

Quinzaine, the Mounier legend pictured him as a hardy peasant who threw over an unusually promising academic career to fight for social justice. In fact, Mounier came from a middle class background and his difficulties with academia were rooted in the spiritual interests of Chevalier rather than the social concerns of Péguy. Chevalier demanded that Mounier place the spiritual before his material interests, comfort, politics, career, or development of his analytical powers.

Péguy, Claudel, and the Maritains, who converted to Christianity in the early nineteen-hundreds, had become Catholics at a time when, in French intellectual circles, that implied anti-republicanism and anti-intellectualism. Mounier was born into a later generation and a Catholic milieu in which belief preoccupied many of the most liberal and creative minds. Like Péguy, the young Emmanuel, who corresponded with his sister Madeleine for the mutual progress of their 'interior lives,' was seen as 'precociously serious about all his concerns.'[139] But after discovering Chevalier, Mounier described his adolescent 'conversion' as having been 'at least as painful as that from atheism to faith.'[140]

Mounier soon began to acquire intellectual stimulus outside the mainstream of Catholic intellectual life, devoid of structured theological formation or traditional metaphysical analysis. Nor did Chevalier expose his students to the sociology of Durkheim, neo-Kantian ethics, Marxism, and other 'secular' phenomena. His teaching seemed narrow even to the Thomists, who would have directed Mounier more to epistemological or ontological problems. Chevalier was in that distinctive tradition of French Catholic moralists that runs from Pascal through Péguy to Mounier himself. The *Pensées*, bedside reading for the young Mounier, were a good introduction to Chevalier.[141]

As Pascal juxtaposed the rhetoric with the conduct of the Jesuits, Chevalier contrasted the impressive intellectual structure of Thomism with the barren 'interior life' of the Thomists and gave Mounier a Jansenist distrust of rational analysis. In summarizing Chevalier's influence, Henri Marrou remarked: 'Philosophically speaking, it was bad luck for Mounier to have been initiated to philosophy by that mediocrity.'[142] By a slow, painful process Mounier himself eventually came to share that cruel judgment.

While Maritain and Claudel had earlier fought the 'mandarins' of Paris with logic and syllogistic argumentation, Mounier faulted his teachers for their lack of spiritual depth to counterbalance their intellectual breadth. Many young intellectuals of his generation, dissatisfied with their Catholic backgrounds but frustrated by the university's alternatives, turned to new, activist, innovative styles of Catholicism.

Mounier accused French Catholic parents of producing oversensitive adolescents unprepared to face the harsh realities of adulthood.[143] Although always close to his own parents, Mounier's attacks on the softness and sentimentality of the Catholic family, on the 'spiritualist evasions' of the interior life, seemed an effort to exorcise vulnerabilities in his own personality. Marrou wrote of his friend:

Mounier ... very quickly sensed what had been contingent and perhaps ... cruel in the first orientation imposed on his youth (what in the naïveté of his twenty years and the patois of the milieu he called 'to do philosophy as a form of the apostolate'): if he had been born elsewhere than in a sector of the most humble provincial petite bourgeoisie, if he had grown up elsewhere than in that Grenoble ... where people took César Franck for musical composition and Jacques Chevalier for a thinker, if he had encountered Paris and measured himself sooner against the values prevalent there, false or true (the trained ear recognizes some resentment in his diatribes against the university), we would certainly have had a completely different Mounier...[144]

Mounier's growing antagonism towards middle class Catholics set him off from the prominent converts of the older generation. Rather than attack the godless, he turned more and more against the Catholics with whom he had been raised. His sensitivity to the debilitating effects of 'false Christianity' convinced him that the bark of Peter would have to be rerigged and change course before it could set off again under full sail. For Maritain, Massis, Claudel, and the other new Catholic converts, it had been enough merely to get aboard.

Soon Mounier began to publish his own review, and project his distinctive view of the crisis of his culture to a larger audience. What began as an attempt to exorcise private demons soon became a common effort to save an entire civilization. His concern with the purification of his soul soon evolved towards a tightly organized communal effort to purify an entire society.

3

The Founding of *Esprit*

TOWARDS A CATHOLIC 'NOUVELLE REVUE FRANÇAISE'

Despite later legends that Mounier and his friends were devout men forced into worldly concerns by the gravity of the political crises of their day, there was little indication that Mounier's deepest concerns were anything but religious and aesthetic in the period of his review's founding. *Esprit*, rather than born of the new political concerns of pious men, seemed to grow out of a single-minded attention to the spiritual dimension of existence. Mounier described faces, landscapes, paintings, theological discussions, and the spiritual qualities of his comrades in his diaries but ignored France's political crises, including the Great Depression. He felt himself at the margin of a pagan and materialistic society whose political élites and economic fluctuations were matters of secondary importance. Neither with the Chevalier group in Grenoble, the Davidées, the sessions with Father Pouget, nor even in the Meudon discussions, were day-to-day French politics the focus. Mounier found his small and rarefied world, much like that of the Carthusians in the valley above Grenoble, at the heart of the true drama of the universe. Their discussions, like Gregorian chant, were timelessly relevant.

Mounier's turn towards politics began when he began to see much of his collaborator on the Péguy book, George Izard, in the fall of 1930. Izard, son of the director of a primary school in Hérault, was polished, sociable, and dynamic. After he failed the examination for entry to the Ecole Normale Supérieure, he had served as the chief of staff for his friend Jean Daniélou's father, the Radical deputy. He married Daniélou's sister, Catherine, in 1929 and came to share several passionate concerns with Mounier and the Daniélous.

Mounier also spent time with Izard's best friend, André Déléage, a young man noted for winning scholastic prizes while organizing rowdy demonstrations among the boarding students at Louis-le-Grand. Déléage was also given to showy displays of physical courage – in one instance, slashing his thumb with a knife. Though his father was an anticlerical director of a state primary school, once in Paris Déléage became a fervent, 'quasi-medieval' Catholic who would leave his room at the Cité Universitaire at midnight and walk across the city to pray in Sacré-Cœur. Once president of the Protestant student association at Louis-le-Grand, Izard had been taken one day by Déléage to the church of Saint-Etienne-du Mont and emerged converted to Catholicism. Izard and Déléage were a formidable twosome.

His schoolmates considered Déléage to be 'a scholar, an apostle, a leader of men, a hero.' But Déléage, too, had to abandon plans to enter the Ecole Normale Supérieure, though in his case, due to illness. Instead he became a librarian at the University of Toulouse while pursuing an interest in the Middle Ages through his dissertation, directed by Marc Bloch, which later earned him a doctorate in this field. Déléage, like Izard, was instinctively an activist. Both were frustrated by the academic establishment and remained ardent Catholics devoted to Péguy. Izard had admired the Action Française at one point and Déléage, with his contempt for democracy, rowdiness, and medieval religiosity might have joined Maurras' league if that option had not been closed by a papal condemnation. Both rejected 'bourgeois culture,' and sought a radical alternative in Péguy, an alternative at once spiritual and political. Izard and Déléage touched Mounier because he too was driven, since discovering Péguy and Joan of Arc, to make use somehow of his spiritual resources.[1] In December 1930, Mounier described spiritual men as suffocating in the times.[2]

There were, however, hopeful signs emerging. Maritain was willing to try again to start a review which would compete with the *Nouvelle Revue Française*. Several of his friends in the new generation, such as the young novelist and critic Marcel Arland, winner of the Prix Goncourt, seemed interested in such a project, and it certainly seemed easier than restoring Aquinas to the centre of the Sorbonne.[3] In early December 1930, Mounier and Izard, returning from a discussion at the Berdyaevs', discussed undertaking such a review. Mounier confided to his friend: 'I am disgusted with teaching as the French state plans it for me. ... I see myself called to greater things. ... I do not think we have a crazy idea ... you give it all the solidity in the world.'[4] Mounier, as Jean Daniélou later recalled, soon revealed 'a very strong will, under his rather fragile outward appearance.'[5] During that winter of 1930–1 Mounier still felt constrained to assure Chevalier that his new friend Izard was a Chevalier admirer.[6] For several months, Mounier spoke to his mentor only of his thesis, not the proposed review. Maritain had told Mounier that the meetings formulating the review's guidelines were 'reserved to a very narrow circle of friends.'[7] Chevalier could not be included.

In February 1931 Mounier confided that his studies were languishing and that he was 'not resigned to wasting his youth in erudition.'[8] The Mounier known to Daniélou was finally emerging, and Mounier was fully conscious of it: '[I have] given rein to that explosive pressure which accumulated under what was only a calm surface to the eyes of friends. Some days I am ... astounded with that boldness despite my timidity and insufficiencies. Unknown, without a penny, am I really taking this path?'[9] The result of this upheaval is mirrored in Mounier's Péguy study, which reflected a new generation's search for responses to the economic and political crises. Mounier joined Izard and Déléage quite successfully in crossing the bridge to the real world. The only sour note was a contemptuous review by Péguy's old friend Henri Massis in the *Revue Universelle*. Mounier confided his own bitterness to Chevalier. 'Because I put sanctity before heroism, he accuses me of pious exegesis, of inventing a 'Péguy for démocrates populaires.' ... I am going to ... disassociate us once and for all from those people ... blow my chances for the prize of the Académie....'[10] Mounier answered Massis sharply in the *Revue Universelle* and made a lifelong enemy.

In April Mounier revealed the review project to Chevalier but described it as proceeding from ideals Chevalier had championed:

Some people independent of Thomism have asked me ... if I could not ... bring the support of your name and our friends to the common task. I thought that this was a unique opportunity for the group ... so I spoke to Maritain, who ... would be delighted to work in common with other Catholic forces.

Evidently the review will not call itself Catholic, and will even ask for the collaboration of certain non-Catholics who are interested in the cause of the spiritual. ... If I refuse the affair will fall into the hands of either the Thomists or the literary types. ... I have not revealed myself on this to anyone at this point save to Guitton and to P. Pouget, who press me to accept; Guitton because of the group....[11]

He urged Chevalier to destroy the letter, which 'should not fall into other hands,' and said he would feel fulfilled if 'I could be one of the rivulets for the generous élan that you bear....'[12]

Mounier may well have thought himself working for the ideas of Chevalier, but it was the 'other Jacques' who collared potential contributors and vetoed others.[13] Maritain also edited the prospectus which Mounier prepared, and, with Gabriel Marcel, helped persuade the Desclée de Brouwer house to offer administrative services, inexpensive printing, and 50,000F a year, with a target of 10,000 copies a month by 1934.[14] The older men contributed their names, contacts, financial support, and advice while the younger contingent – Mounier, Izard, and Déléage – handled the practical details. The first prospectus promised regular contributions from a panoply of writers.[15]

In the spring and summer of 1931, as France sank into the Depression, Mounier crisscrossed France trying to sell shares in the review to Chevalier's group, the Davidées, Berdyaev's fellow Russian exiles, and Maritain's acquaintances, including several ecclesiastics. Madame Daniélou's circle was left to Izard.[16] Not surprisingly, Mounier's hope for funds for a full-time director of the review faded, so he decided to teach at St Omer, near the Belgian border, and commute to Paris.[17]

BELGIAN RESPONSE AND RUSSIAN INSPIRATION

The July prospectus proclaimed: 'we feel ourselves united ... by a fundamental concern for the ... spirit ... against the usurpations of matter and the dissolution of the person.' This proclamation prompted a letter from a Bruxellois who promised to sacrifice his own review for Mounier's, and enclosed a cheque for 1,000F and a list of potential supporters.[18] Jacques Lefrancq, administrator in the Royal Museum in Brussels, had simultaneously discovered Mounier, Péguy, and Christianity. His small review, *Equilibres*, promoted the 'spiritual socialism' of the Belgian Henri de Man, but he was enthusiastic about Mounier's lecture in Brussels. For his part, Mounier immediately liked Lefrancq and his student associate in the museum, Paulette Leclercq, 'une jeune enfant claire et décidée' and the future Mme Mounier. He began to spend more and more time with them. (Soon Mlle Leclercq, the effervescent and idealistic daughter of a middle class liberal Belgian family, became a Catholic, and, in July 1935, Madame Emmanuel Mounier. The Mouniers lived in an apartment in Lefrancq's house in Brussels until the outbreak of the war.)[19]

Another significant development was taking place in the mind of Jacques Maritain, who was making curiously sympathethic remarks about

Soviet communism in the Meudon discussions: 'what would we put in its place? After all, they made a serious house cleaning...'; that régime's effort to do completely without God had a certain 'grandeur.'[20] Once he confessed that 'if communism was not so radically atheistic, and if it maintained that minimum of individual property necessary to man, I could see no reason for not adhering,' and, with Raïssa, defended the altruism of the Bolshevik leaders.[21] All of this was a bit heady for the Meudon group, except for the Russian Berdyaev.[22] The two men differed on several philosophical issues but shared a very 'advanced' perspective on communism for Christians of the time. Maritain left it to Berdyaev to muse on 'The Truths and Lies in Communism' and thus, Maritain hoped, 'situate the review very precisely' on a vital issue.[23] A short look at Berdyaev is therefore essential.

Nicholas Berdyaev was among the most original and, as Alexandre Solzhenitsyn has recently recalled, courageous, intellectuals of his generation.[24] Born in Kiev in 1874 into a family of the military aristocracy, he was nonetheless attracted by liberal and revolutionary ideas. Expelled from the university, he was exiled to the north of Russia until authorized to continue studying at Heidelberg. There he was strongly influenced by romantic philosophy. Once back in his homeland he became a devout Christian and, while committed to social reform, more and more critical of Marxism. Under order of expulsion again in 1917 for attacking the subservience of the Orthodox hierarchy, Berdyaev naturally welcomed the Bolshevik victory and was named professor of philosophy at the University of Moscow. However, he persisted in his religious activism and was finally expelled from Russia in 1922 with a host of prominent intellectuals. He settled in a small house in Clamart, near Paris, in 1924, where he conducted an intellectual salon that overlapped the Maritains.'

Berdyaev's *A New Middle Ages* (*Un nouveau Moyen-Age*, Paris: Plon 1927) announced the end of the humanism of the Renaissance and Reformation and the defeat of the rationalism and scientism of the late nineteenth and early twentieth centuries. He saw in Russian communism, and then in Italian fascism, the first signs of a new, but different, middle ages. Religion would no longer be private, as among the bourgeoisie, but would fuse the individual and the society in a common faith and respect for the same spiritual reality.[25] Berdyaev's analysis of the positive aspects in Soviet experience impressed the backers of the review among whom Mounier circulated it.[26]

BIRTH OF A MOVEMENT

Mounier wanted major essays for his review from prominent Bergsonians such as Maurice Blondel, Bremond, and Chevalier.[27] Madame Daniélou backed him in this, since she thought 'Pascal, Bergson, brought much more to us than all that theology' of Maritain.[28] She believed the cultivation of Christian spiritual resources far more vital than politics. Christians should form the élite whose vision would, in time, inspire the people. She disapproved of 'going to fish for a few individuals among the people.'[29] She thought society was moved in deep and mysterious ways by spiritual élites and mystics more than by social theorists. She cautioned Mounier to 'be careful of Maritain,' 'he is a delicious soul, with a charming spirituality, but he often has bad judgment. He has often been wrong about people.'[30]

Nonetheless the 'Catholicism' of the review was soon downplayed by some of the young men interested in it. Izard hoped Briand's peace cause would unite Christians and non-Christians. Izard was in his own words 'a political animal,' interested in the 'spiritualist socialism' of Henri de Man, who felt that Catholicism inspired a love for the people not found in the French Socialist party.[31] His friend Déléage held several exotic monarchist and anti-intellectualist positions, in what Mounier called his 'fluid Bergsonism.'[32] According to the maverick left-wing writer Ramon Fernandez, the review could join the Christians and all 'revolutionaries' against the 'rationalists.'[33] The young novelist and historian Henri Daniel-Rops hoped it would draw the non-Catholic 'spirituals' away from the NRF; he observed that his students had a new sense of the 'mystical value of ideas' and were ready for a new kind of literature.[34]

Mounier brought young Catholic *agrégés* such as fellow Chevalier product Jean Lacroix, Thomist Etienne Borne, and medieval scholar and Christian trade unionist Paul Vignaux to the review.[35] Izard and Déléage brought more politicized young men such as André Ulmann, secretary to the journalist Charles Dulot at L'Information sociale, and the colourful Georges Duveau, surrealist habitué. The latter, an historian and writer for *Paris-Soir*, was an expert on the anarchism of Pierre-Joseph Proudhon.[36]

Mounier recorded the discussions of late 1931 in his diary: 'Déléage ... in a perpetual explosion of bewildering ideas, of ingenious sophisms, throws his sparks over everything. ... He excites all of us. Izard brings the warm passion of the Southerner. ... My role, in general, is to recall the mystical point of view, or rigour in ideas.'[37] Mounier had preferred the title 'La révolution spirituelle,' for the review but thought Madame Daniélou's suggestion – 'Esprit' – remarkably forthright, analogous to a Communist review which called itself *Matter*.[38] The discussions seemed to proceed far beyond Maritain's guidelines. 'A movement was being born,' one participant recalled. Worldly types were less impressed. One cynic said the group should hold a séance and chant in unison, 'Esprit, are you there? If so, knock once.'[39]

The new shape of the review project quickly caused Chevalier to lose interest.[40] Mounier turned earnestly to Maritain for support: 'Would you, from today, promise to never hide your opinion, on whatever subject? ... It would be a security for me to feel that transparency of our friendship, that nakedness of your affection.'[41] Jacques Madaule, a young *agrégé* in history and geography from Réalmont in the southwest, met Mounier at this time at Meudon and recalled him as 'a bit dull, painstaking, contrasted with the brio of Izard. A philosopher strayed into politics, I thought. But ... the solidity, the calm, of the man attracted me, with ... that seriousness that he seemed to put into everything he said.'[42]

Maritain helped Mounier by ensuring that from January 1932 *Esprit* was given two rooms and free secretarial help in the offices of Desclée de Brouwer on the Rue des Saints-Pères. At the same time Maritain warned against downplaying the 'Catholicism' of the review: 'If you were to adopt the method of the minimum ... you would find yourselves barren in the face of a Ramakrishna who, with all his mysticism, would be superior to the minimum.'[43] Mounier asked for money from Catholic manufacturers in Grenoble and Lyon, the Russian artist Marc Chagall and his friends, and French Catholic bishops noted for their social concerns.[44] But the new prospectus for the review did not read like a document likely to seduce the Catholic establishment:

How can we not be in a permanent revolution against the tyrannies of this period? ... Everywhere systems and institutions which neglect man are imposed on him: he destroys himself in conforming to them.

We want to save him in rendering to him the consciousness of what he is. Our principal task is the rediscovery of the true concept of man. ... We find ourselves all agreed to establish him on the supremacy of the spirit ...

...our hostility is as vivid against capitalism, in its present practice ... as against Marxism or Bolshevism. Capitalism reduces ... to a state of servitude irreconcilable with the dignity of man; it orients all classes and the whole personality towards the possession of money; the single desire which chokes the modern soul. Marxism is a rebel son of capitalism from which it has received the faith in the material. ... Bolshevism ... reaches a breadth of doctrine and a heroism which are at the level of history. But ... with means which only reflect the tyranny of the material.

It is up to us to discover a society attentive to his temporal interests, but which subordinate them out of a concern to assure the development of man....[45]

Mounier had trouble in early 1932 justifying this new rhetoric to all but the most adventurous Catholics. The prominent Catholic social activist Robert Garric, a professor in Madame Daniélou's College, publicly ridiculed *Esprit*'s condescending and ineffectual revolutionary verbalism.[46] Marcel Primard, head of a philanthropic group of Catholic businessmen solicited for financial support, informed Mounier that the review did not even seem particularly Christian.[47] Even Jean Guitton, Mounier's closest friend, wrote of his own 'crisis of discouragement and doubt about *Esprit*.'[48]

Mounier wrote Garric that it was necessary for 'a few of us to live in the Absolute, level the condemnations that no one dares level, proclaim the impossible ... and, if they are Christians, not allow themselves once more to be bypassed by history with their petit-bourgeois solutions...'[49] In response to Primard, Mounier outlined a notion of 'spiritual action' that was decidedly Christian: 'We do not know the plans of God. ... But as long as we feel a mission that interior signs confirm ... we could never turn back. ... I believe that our worldly success will develop to the exact degree with which we will pursue ... that deepening, that interior purification, from where all fecundity bursts forth....'[50] Mounier reiterated this to Izard: 'We have the first duty ... to affirm, to purify, to supernaturalize our spiritual life,' but characteristically he added an attack on his fellow intellectuals for too often refusing worldly commitment.[51]

In early 1932 Mounier began to study the problem of 'property': in St Thomas Aquinas; in the papal encyclical *Quadragesimo Anno*, published a few months earlier; and in Maritain.[52] He wanted to aid *Esprit* by sketching the social and political implications of that 'interior purification' essential to any success.

In this attempt Mounier drew upon André Déléage, calling him 'exciting to all of us' with his call for 'social doctrines which will ... create, in work and in recreation, that state of poetry which is the complete liberation of the soul....'[53] Péguy, too, was essential as 'the mediator of Bergson' for Mounier thought Henri Bergson's own researches into the relationship between action and contemplation were also stimulating to him.[54] Early in 1932 Bergson's new *Les deux sources de la morale et de la religion* put him into a state of 'intense vibration.' Mounier and Izard assembled their friends and, ignoring dinner, read it to them until four in the morning.[55]

In *Les deux sources* Bergson condemned 'closed morality' – traditional, varying from country to country – in contrast to what he envisaged as an 'open' morality, founded on the highest feeling of the Good, applicable to all humanity. Men were to transcend their 'frénésie industrielle,' rediscover the 'frénésie d'ascétisme' of the Middle Ages and the inspiration of heroes and of saints, and help the universe become 'a machine to make gods.' Existing religion, for Bergson, seemed 'static,' and he called for a new 'dynamic' religion, in communion with the universal élan, Love, the pure essence of God. Mystics' efforts were to help spark a renaissance of the spiritual to redefine the limits of human aspirations. Bergson sought a new science of the spirit, of the vast unexplored regions of the subconscious, of the interior life.

Bergson had vindicated Chevalier and Pouget by turning towards Catholicism, proclaiming his 'moral adherence' in his 1937 *Testament*.[56] Mounier explained to his students at St Omer how Bergson had articulated the same distinction between a 'closed' morality and an 'open' morality towards which Mounier himself had been working.[57] Indeed Mounier began to see the common élan of the *Esprit* group transcending all the old 'closed' moralities of the past: even non-believers could proclaim the 'primacy of the spiritual.'

This union of Catholics, Protestants, Russian Orthodox, Jews, and non-believers in the 'spirit' soon began to trouble other Catholics.[58] For behind *Esprit*'s ecumenism there was Mounier's notion that a variety of mystical experience was common to those who chose to live 'in the Absolute,' religious or not. With this the authority of Roman Catholicism inevitably came into question; for, as Maritain had pointed out, who would defend the uniqueness of Christian mystical experience against the distinguished non-Christian mystic?

Les deux sources de la morale et de la religion was quickly put on the Index of Forbidden Books by Rome, in a period when, as the Action Française had learned, that meant something. The papal nuncio soon warned the archbishopric of Paris of modernist tendencies in Mounier's review.[59] There were internal problems with the journal as well. Déléage, as a later member of the *Esprit* group gently put it, had 'a "fascist" temperament': 'Over and above his military ways, his taste for discipline, a certain fascination with violence, he employed a totalitarian vocabulary.'[60]

Mounier had already confessed in his personal journal to finding 'too much roughness in Izard, not enough faith in the invisible.' Nevertheless, like a good Bergsonian, he decided that all was well 'as long as the same élan carries us along.'[61] But Déléage wanted a 'soviet' to direct the review and a party 'organized dictatorially like the society which it ought to promote.'[62] Mounier then surprised his friends by standing up to Déléage, attacking his 'Hitlerite language,' and insisting that the *Esprit* circle exhibit its 'difference from the parties.'[63] He demanded priority for work groups producing ideas; an extraparliamentary party could follow from that.

In April 1932 Mounier explained to a friend that *Esprit* would involve 'a circuit of active friendships ... intellectual collaboration. ... In as many cities as I can, I am trying to create little work groups, which will receive the résumé of the meetings of the central committee, exchange suggestions with it, discuss, take initiatives, propose, hold lectures, talk, promulgate, contradict ... many things.'[64] Beyond his base of *agrégés* in French provincial lycées, Mounier sought a contact in a foreign city for every two in France, and thus to make *Esprit* an international review and movement concerned with the problems of an entire civilization.[65]

On 2 June the new editor explained the unique character of his review to the Christian Democrat publicist Francisque Gay: 'the spirit has another calling today ... if it is to ... direct the renewals still possible. ... It was not yesterday that philosophy discovered the primacy of the spiritual. ... It is precisely because it forgot it a little too much and a little too long that we want to resuscitate the miracle....'[66] But by early July Mounier was forced to recognize that there were two currents dividing *Esprit*. On one side were 'activists, the lawyers engrossed with the movement' and on the other those like himself who were convinced the New Left group was 'not yet mature.'[67]

Maritain returned from Toronto in the spring of 1932 to urge that Mounier firmly direct *Esprit* and not let it be influenced by 'a nameless movement sending you czarist edicts from the provinces. We must absolutely assure your permanence and your rights.' Mounier rejoiced at 'a new infusion of friendship' into their similarity of views.[68] Maritain pushed Meudon regulars – Marcel Arland, the painter Georges Rouault, Gabriel Marcel, de Monléon, and the composer Nicolai Nabokoff – as contributors to make an 'interesting ensemble' with Berdyaev.[69] At the same time Maritain opposed any input by the volatile librarian in Toulouse:

The most serious ruptures would be better than letting 'Esprit' become the 'organ' of a political movement. That would be to turn things upside down. It is the spirit which directs the organs in sound philosophy! Always the old quarrel of the 'mystique' and the 'politique.' It is essential that you be absolutely firm on that principle.[70]

Maritain's promise to break with *Esprit* if Déléage's movement won out was a death threat for the review. In time it was Maritain's views that prevailed.

As *Esprit* developed it came to embody, for Maritain and some of France's other leading Christian intellectuals, the hope of an option not bound to a flourishing Right. Talented young rightists like Thierry Maulnier, Jean de Fabrègues, and Jean-Pierre Maxence, a Thomist who had frequented Meudon, were simultaneously launching reviews – *Réaction* (1930–2), *La Revue du Siècle* (1933–4), which departed from Action Française orthodoxy but seemed to announce a new and imaginative 'Young Right.'[71] *Je suis partout* (1930–44), a right-wing alternative to *Esprit*, drew young Maurrassians (Maulnier, Pierre Gaxotte, Lucien Rebatet, Georges Blond, Claude Roy), and soon became what its sub-editor Robert Brasillach called 'something like the official organ of international fascism.'[72]

In sum, most lively reviews drawing young Catholic intellectuals in 1932 seemed committed to right-wing positions. The only alternative seemed to be to work with the clerical reviews like *La Vie Intellectuelle* of the Dominicans or join the older Christian Democrats at *L'Aube* or in the Jeune République. Maritain wanted a solid new initiative, tied to Berdyaev's name, to seduce the new generation of Catholic intellectuals. As he had hoped, *Esprit* soon attracted young 'spiritual revolutionaries' such as the young Russian Alexandre Marc. Young dissidents from Marc Sangnier's Jeune République proposed a union of the 'new forces of the Left' with the *Esprit* group on a common anti-war platform. Similarly, the journalist Jean Luchaire, another admirer of Briand, seemed to envisage these two groups, with his journal *Notre Temps*, as the nucleus of a 'New Left.' In July a sort of provisional federation united the three groups. The unstable nature of such a union of free spirits became apparent all too soon. In July, a lavish meal was planned but Mounier became angry when Luchaire sat a prostitute at the table of honour, and, with the young Christian Democrats, broke with him.[73] All this worried Maritain, who considered this Catholic 'New Left' a fragile growth and easily compromised by immature elements.[74] The subterranean currents around *Esprit* would again surface at its founding meeting in August 1932.

FONT-ROMEU

The ethereal setting for the founding congress of *Esprit* must have seemed rather ominous to Déléage, who was pushing for an organ for new forms of Catholic political commitment. Madame Daniélou's isolated and romantic villas, Saint-Paul and Sainte-Marie, were in a pine forest on the outskirts of the small mountaintop village of Font-Romeu, high in the Pyrénées near the tiny republic of Andorra. The eight days for the twenty-odd friends of *Esprit*, who met there on 15 August (six from Paris, six with Déléage from Toulouse), began with a mass outside under the pines, with Basque hymns, the bells of village churches echoing in the distance, and a sermon on the Holy Spirit. The entire scene and the brightly coloured clothes of the girls reminded Mounier of a Courbet painting.[75]

The bucolic mood quickly passed as the imperious Déléage pressed intensely for doctrinal elaboration. The discussions were quickly dominated by Izard, Déléage, and Mounier.[76] Although in later years much was made of this 'founding congress of *Esprit*,' most big names behind it were not there, and many of the bright young men who joined *Esprit* before the war were not yet associated with it.[77]

The first *Esprit* congress had young historians, librarians, journalists, lawyers, and priests. That Déléage envisioned such a gathering to be the birth of an 'international worker's party' tells us much about his romanticism. Only Pierre Doat, the elder of the group at forty, whom Déléage had brought along from Toulouse, seemed to have had political experience (in Georges Valois' Faisceau).

Mounier described the motley assembly in his journal: Déléage 'a revolutionary temperament reinforced by that of a violent poet. ... With his follies, he guarantees us against complacency....'; Izard 'in top form' with 'no head for philosophy,' drawn 'towards direct and passionate action, towards contact with men'; architecture graduate L.-E. Galey, 'strongly revolutionary ... rough and refined, sensual as the devil, a lady-killer with a faithful attachment to the family,' but with no grasp of philosophy either. Georges Duveau, Mounier recalled, was 'the joy of the gathering,' a 'great heart,' 'interested in all the ladies, but with a lot of ... Christian purity despite his frequenting of the surrealists.'[78] Bouyx, a faithful disciple of Jacques Chevalier, was soon disappointed with the discussions and cynically proposed for the review's cover, under its title, the slogan 'Embrace the carnal.' The Dominican Maxime Gorce proposed various radical ideas such as the abolition of seminaries.[79] The Abbé

Boucraut, since he hardly said a word, for several days was taken by Déléage to be a police spy. Things were going in several directions at once. None of those at the Font-Romeu congress who stayed with the review later, except Mounier, were particularly 'Catholic' and Izard tried to dissuade Mounier from making *Esprit* 'too Catholic.'[80] These young men of middle class small-town backgrounds, often unemployed or unhappy with their jobs, all wanted to launch 'a revolution inspired by the spiritual' but the distinctively Catholic concerns of Mounier, Madame Daniélou, and Maritain did not seem to interest them. This was not the most likely group to create a Catholic *Nouvelle Revue Française*, or spiritual New Left. The 'politicals,' though, were delighted with the meeting: Duveau left, the last day, with joyful tears in his eyes; Izard 'let himself go and sang at the top of his lungs'; Déléage held every phrase in the meeting's reports to be sacred.[81] Mounier registered some doubts in his *journal* and left

a bit befuddled by these eight days of tension, that uproarious atmosphere which corresponds so well to my ideas and so little to my temperament. ... I seek only silence. ... What will the future bring? Surely much of that was knit together there, but how long will these heterogeneous pieces hold together? We have to be rather strong and pure to digest them....[82]

Izard experienced no such doubt. He thought the group left the congress 'more united than ever....' and years later, when he was a famous lawyer and member of the Académie Française, he boasted that he had never deviated from the ideals of Font-Romeu.[83] Mounier remained less sanguine and two days after the close of the congress complained to Izard of the theory of 'integral collectivization' in the congress reports.[84] Déléage and Izard thought they had introduced a new communal dimension into *Esprit*'s spiritual revolution, and founded a movement in which Mounier had a secondary role. Déléage's expectations for the next summer's congress included a rosy picture of a group of forty giving reports from a variety of study groups, before a subjugated and humbled Mounier.[85]

In fact Mounier, not Izard and Déléage, set the doctrinal orientation of *Esprit* – with an effusive and romantic panegyric to the 'spiritual' – while he complained to Izard that the reports of the Congress did not explain 'what it all signified in daily life.'[86] He sent the group's report on economics to several individuals for comment, including the spiritualist socialists Georges Valois and Henri de Man.[87]

Not surprisingly, the Font-Romeu congress disquieted both Chevalier and Maritain, although Mounier made an effort to persuade Chevalier that the project was still inspired by his old group:

the effort at constant revision and interior rigour that you have taught me has led me to refine my conception of the defence of the spiritual. ... We will only save the spirit ... in courageously separating it from ... historical alliances where it only compromises its purity. ... We are heading, I think, towards a second Renaissance, which must be preceded by a liquidation of the individual and the restoration of the person. ... It is necessary to purify the revelation of collectivism and not blindly oppose it. The theory of the Mystical Body is there to support us.[88]

This concern with the 'person' as opposed to the 'individual' was in the earlier writings of both Chevalier and Maritain. Mounier decided that the new phenomenon of 'collectivism' could also involve the 'defence of the spiritual,' and here the Roman Catholic theological theory of the Mystical Body of Christ was to the point with its notion that spiritual communities could be living embodiments of the Son of God.[89]

Evidently Mounier had come to see more Grace, more of the Spirit, more 'purity,' in his comrades like Galey, Duveau, and Ulmann – non-believers grouped together in *Esprit* – than in most of his fellow Christians. This ecumenism towards non-believers was consistent with his reading of Bergson. Bergson's Catholic mystics, conversing with one another from mountain peak to mountain peak across the valleys of the centuries, much like Nietzsche's supermen, seemed to have more in common with non-Christian mystics than with their plodding and superstitious fellow Catholics. Mounier simply annexed non-believers sensitive to 'the spiritual' who radiated that 'new Renaissance' of collectivism, and bound them to a Catholic élite.

Mounier's interest in the theory of the Mystical Body of Christ revealed his ties to the 'theological renewal' then germinating in the French Catholic Church. German Catholic theologican Karl Adam's book on ecclesiology, published in France as *Le Vrai Visage du Catholicisme*, was acclaimed by the influential Dominican theologian Yves Congar, of Saulchoir in Belgium. Writing in *La Vie Intellectuelle* in April 1932, Congar described the Mystical Body of Christ as a doctrine stimulating a 'communitarian spirituality' which negated religious individualism.[90]

A leftist application of such a view was popular in Mounier's circle. The theory of the Mystical Body helped Mounier explain the 'unity in the spirit' he enjoyed with his friends. *Esprit*'s supporters at Saulchoir were the theologians who most promoted this new conception in France, and the most influential pre-war elucidation of this doctrine in France was also by an early friend of *Esprit*, the Jesuit Henri de Lubac.[91] (His *Catholicisme*, published in 1938, stressed the social dimensions of the sacraments and showed the influence of the 'personnalisme communautaire' of *Esprit*.) Soon Mounier, too, demonstrated that this concept had far-reaching implications.

Mounier's first *Esprit* essays shocked some of his friends. Maritain, shaken by their tone, asked Mounier pointblank if he had any 'commitments to the movement' and charged that the review seemed even less 'Catholic' than the *Nouvelle Revue Française*. Mounier agreed that they could not 'hide Christ' but privately noted that Maritain, for all his efforts, had attracted few non-Catholic authors for the monograph series he directed.[92]

In short, on the eve of launching his review, Mounier had to face scepticism from several quarters. But, for his part, he was convinced that he was an instrument of something greater. On 9 October 1932, the day he received the first printed issue of *Esprit*, he recorded such a feeling in his *journal*:

This morning, at the nine-thirty Mass at Saint-Sulpice ... I experienced an effusion of joy and prayer until tears came to my eyes, as I have not felt since Lourdes. The grandeur of this day, something that I didn't think I would experience until the morning of my marriage. ... Do I have a destiny? ... I deeply felt ... timidity, *gaucheries*, pettinesses, 'all the faults of a delicate soul.' And my sins, dull-minded, insipid sins. But all the splendour which was pouring down on me! From the altar, the light of the stained glass windows, the light of the Eucharist which is truly the glory of the morning; the light of the expression of that young priest, conscientious and contemplative in his reading of the Mass...

My God ... if some fame comes to us, let men think of us as You will think of us yourself the day of judgment. ... That You alone put some spark in us....

...let them know that all the rest is Your doing. My decision two years ago is the culmination of what You have wrought in me ... since the morning of my first Communion. ... Lord I want You to be so much a part of the work that You would shatter it Yourself from the inside if it is not Your will.

...*Esprit*, here it finally is in my hand.[93]

At twenty-seven Mounier felt himself 'invested with a mission' and that a divine spark had been planted in the *Esprit* group as a whole. He had always recorded signs of contemplative religiosity with sensitivity and artistry in his diaries, but now his meditations began to make less reference to the scriptures or the life of Jesus and more to the Spirit working in men. *Esprit* now forced him into an active, public, high-profile career 'against his temperament,' despite his possessing 'all the faults of a delicate soul.'

The origins of *Esprit* were marked by the peculiar relationship between the religious and the political in the circle around Mounier. Déléage fused fascist tendencies with a devout and serious Catholic spirituality. Mounier, for all his concentration on his spiritual life, seemed more and more fascinated by politics. The nascent review did not merely propose a new politics in France; its concerns were far too religious for that. But the review's 'revolutionary' rhetoric also set it apart from the religious literature of the day. Some simply dismissed Mounier's vague gropings for a doctrine and his spiritual élitism as 'fascist.' But could one condemn several centuries of Catholic religious orders for the same 'fascist' characteristics? Mounier's determinedly orthodox Catholicism soon set him apart from most of the other 'spiritualists' of his day, but his new politics also set him off from his fellow Catholics.

Esprit seemed to be suggesting something new – and controversial. Its first issues excited much of the younger generation of intellectuals in France. The degree to which it was as yet unfocused did not count against it, for the times themselves were unfocused. The appeal was obvious: the journal was at once traditional, in its Catholicism, and revolutionary, in its call for action, and, moreover, *Esprit* seemed indisputably French. Born of Bergsonians, Péguyists, and so on, *Esprit* was the stepchild of many schools. None could afford to ignore it.

4

Esprit Launched

REBUILDING THE RENAISSANCE

When *Esprit* became a famous review, associated with some of France's most important philosophers, its humbler origins and extravagant early rhetoric were forgotten. But the origins of personalism should not be tied to a few powerful and prestigious figures deciding one day to publish a review to air their common ideas. Personalism was very much more the creature of unknown and frustrated young men. The Depression had touched several of them: some were unemployed, or had had academic difficulties and were supporting themselves with odious occupations.[1] Others had been relegated to lycées in the provinces.[2] Even those with excellent academic credentials had dim prospects for advancement within the 'establishment.'[3] Most of the *Esprit* circle believed that as devout Catholics, academic drop-outs, or unknowns from the provinces they could never get far in the detested 'system.' Like many Parisian intellectuals in the 1930s they thought France, or her political leaders, to be rotten and corrupt.[4] In some ways *Esprit* seemed just another review lambasting what it called the 'established disorder,' and, in fact, its appearance was not widely noted in the press.[5]

To the close observer *Esprit* was distinguishable from other new publications on the basis of format alone: by its high quality paper and typography, its large size (200 pages), and the subtitle 'Revue internationale, édition française' – this latter at the suggestion of a Russian exile friend, Alexandre Marc.[6] Although the first contributions came from a nucleus of young Frenchmen, the most widely noted was written by a Russian, and in subsequent issues contributions from Belgians and Germans were prominent.[7] And the first issue had little that was comfortably Catholic about it either. *Esprit* seemed international, non-confessional, and not easily situated on the French religious or political spectra.[8]

Mounier began by calling for the 'rebuilding of the Renaissance':

> We say: Primacy of the spiritual. ... On the Right they are trying hard to weld together the bloc: property-family-country-religion. ... Most of the new forces, in contrast are on the Left....
>
> The first duty is therefore clear: to disassociate the spiritual from politics and more particularly ... from the Right....
>
> ... Our final goal is not the happiness, the comfort, the prosperity of the city, but the spiritual flowering of man. ... Marxism is ... the concrete representation of our deficiency. We must join to it a philosophy of our own fabrication. We will work at doing that....
>
> We are ... revolutionaries, but in the name of the spirit.
>
> It is not force which makes revolutions, it is light.
>
> ... a first abstract humanism was constituted in the Renaissance, dominated by the mystique of the individual; a second humanism every bit as abstract and no less inhuman is being constituted today in the USSR, dominated by the collectivist mystique. The gigantic struggle which is taking shape before our eyes ... opposes the first Renaissance which is collapsing to the second which is in preparation. The tragedy of the battle is that man is in the two camps, and if one destroys the other, he loses an integral part of himself ...
>
> The West defends structure, the East, communion. We must certainly integrate the two....[9]

Interestingly enough *Esprit* seemed to hold more hope for the Renaissance of the West in Germany than in France. While the review did not even mention French politics, Jean Lacroix's note treated the national-socialist movement which he saw trying to synthesize 'the nationalist thesis and the communist anti-thesis.'[10] Déléage described German cinema as representative of 'a country which is prodigiously alive ... the fertile soil where almost everything that is young in Europe is being created, the land of hungry bellies and the most audacious dreams, of billy clubs and of thought.'[11] Thus from the first issue *Esprit* called attention to the possibility of a spiritual revolution across the Rhine.

In December 1932, *Esprit*'s call for a 'spiritual revolution' was placed with the other 'demands' of the young when the NRF published a whole collection, a Cahier de Revendications, assembled by the Swiss writer Denis de Rougemont, one of Mounier's new comrades. Twelve essays, representing new reviews, all demanded 'revolution' of a sort: some called for a 'personalist' revolution (Robert Aron, Arnaud Dandieu, Alexandre

Marc for *Ordre Nouveau*, and Thierry Maulnier for *Réaction*), others for a 'spiritual revolution' (*Esprit*), still others for a Marxist revolution (Henri Lefebvre and Paul Nizan). Mounier described the kind of change he thought the most urgent:

A more serious burden than temporal misery oppresses certain of us.
Deaf to the purest teachings of our Faith, of our Church. ... We have allowed the primacy of the material to become an historical fact.
When we say: primacy of the spiritual, we are not signifying primacy of bourgeois thought, which we execrate ... we are in the first rank of its accusers, Marxists further along than them, because for us it is ... a poison which sterilizes our souls ... a sin. We are not a final defence, a more subtle camouflage. We refuse all kinship with the faults of the modern world....
We want revolutionaries to understand that we do not fear the consequences of our ideas either for our possessions, or for ourselves. ... They should also accept that the spiritual life ... is an unalterable interior dimension which is our reason for being and our reason for acting.[12]

Mounier in later years was embarrassed by these early essays, but through the extravagant prose some abiding *Esprit* themes were already discernible: mankind was passing from one inhumanity, capitalism, into another, communism.[13] Neither the right-wing nor left-wing responses was acceptable; only the spiritual dimension could inspire a viable alternative. Mounier never abandoned this view.

At the time, Mounier assumed that he had much in common with both the 'New Right' and young Marxists, as the Cahiers de Revendications suggested a similar attitude towards the crisis in France. Denis de Rougemont concluded that 'the peril has created a unity among us ... a unity of refusal. Groups such as Ordre Nouveau, Combat, Esprit, Plans, Réaction ... by their constructive demands, are perhaps revealing ... the first outlines of a new French revolution.'[14] While the early *Esprit* had only been commented on by the *Action Française* (unfavourably) and a Christian Democratic publication (favourably), the Cahiers de Revendications brought new notoriety.[15] Paul Nizan, comrade of Jean-Paul Sartre at the Ecole Normale, pious Catholic turned communist, moved quickly to avoid joining his 'revendications' to those of the others. In the next *Europe*, he rejected the claim that a call for spiritual revolution characterized the new generation:

There is the Spirit, Being, Spiritual Conceptions, the Soul, the Possession of all

of life, Contemplation, the Sword of the Intelligence: a flotilla of Ideas advances, with full sails, a fleet of capital letters. ... The new champions of the Spirit come with their noble anguish, their eloquent protestations....
... I read elsewhere that the spiritual life is 'an unalterable interior dimension.' ... They want to live richly, these large-souled men. Declining capitalism only bores them ... There are so many beautiful gifts which it isn't employing. ... The Spirit demands power: it wants certitudes, it has had enough of the 'mediocre' life, it wants the adventures of action. ... Bourgeois thought, they say, '... We execrate it ...' ... They will accomplish the spiritual revolution ... it's a question of soul: 'It's not force which makes revolutions, it's light....'

But Nizan did not thereby conclude that this 'revolution' was unimportant:

Let no one say that those groups are insignificant. ... They still lack a social base ... troops could follow them tomorrow. We are in a country which loves sytems. ... Italian fascism acts first, there were killings of workers and then doctrinal elaboration. Here the killings of workers will come after the ideas and the noble systems. Our new adversaries ... do not yet have a very precise and very clear fascist consciousness. ...

Nizan went on to envision merely a more Gallican fascism:

they criticize fascism to the degree that it is weakened by certain survivals of outmoded bourgeois positions: the French are much more 'intelligent' than the Italians and the Germans. We very well know that they decant, purify, and perfect the thick foreign currents; they bring the experiences to fruition: French national socialism will simply be more artful than the others....[16]

In January, Marc, Ulmann, and Mounier all attacked Nizan's insensitivity to the 'liberation of the whole man.'[17] Mounier argued that Nizan's insistence that revolutionaries confine their demands to those of the proletariat was narrow and limiting; *Esprit* challenged the inertia or cupidity of the proletarian masses as well as that of the bourgeoisie. No one bothered to deny Nizan's contention that French spiritual revolutionaries drew some inspiration from Germany, or that the *Réaction, Ordre Nouveau*, and *Esprit* groups were similar in inspiration.[18]

Mounier did not seem to take the criticism of Nizan very seriously. He was, like many a zealous founder of a religious movement, uncalculating, open-hearted, and too willing to sacrifice his material interests for his ideals. He was more often accused of being politically impractical, muddleheaded, and vague than he was of masking cynical and self-serving political impulses. He was far more sensitive, in any case, to the religious scruples of Maritain than to Nizan's polemical accusations of protonazism.

ORDRE NOUVEAU: LEFT-WING NATIONAL SOCIALISTS AND
NIETZSCHEAN PERSONALISM

In order to understand Nizan's fear of an *Esprit* role in a French national socialism as well as the review's interest in Germany, one must recall that at this time many of Germany's unemployed were joining Sturm-Abteilung (SA, the brown-shirted 'storm-troopers,' a private army of 300,000 men) and the large academic proletariat – students without job prospects or regular sources of income – were helping this movement make particularly rapid headway in the universities.[19] In this period dissidents were still challenging Hitler's control of the National Socialist party and invoking the original socialist Twenty-Five Points, proclaimed at its founding in 1920.[20] Dissident leaders Gregor and Otto Strasser had the support of several radical intellectuals, such as the young Dr Joseph Goebbels, a party functionary in Rhineland, who saw the 'Strasser wing' as representative of the hopes of a 'proletarian socialism' against the more conservative party leaders in Munich.[21] There was at least a rhetorical similarity to the 'revendications' in France.

After rebellious SA men stormed party headquarters in Berlin in August 1930, Hitler's black-uniformed personal bodyguard, the SS ('Security Guards,' under Heinrich Himmler) expelled several hundred of them from the city and they then joined the 'Black Front,' the revolutionary National Socialists, of Dr Otto Strasser, who was advocating a 'German socialism.'[22]

By the end of 1931 the National Socialist party seemed the party of the new generation – thirty-eight per cent of its members were under thirty! – and in the elections of July 1932 it became by far the strongest in parliament. In November 1932, however, extremist elements of the National Socialists again escaped Hitler's control when during the Berlin transport workers' strike the communists and 'Brown Shirts' joined in attacking the police, damaging rails, and knocking down high-tension wires. Hitler blamed the subsequent National Socialist electoral defeat on the 'undermining and sabotage' of the radical Strasser clique.[23]

Two months later, Hitler's prudent tactics paid off when he was made chancellor of Germany. In the following spring and summer the opposition parties, including the 'fascists,' were dismantled or dissolved, books burned, and the first measures taken against Jews in the professions. Hitler dealt with the sa and his 'left-wing' National Socialist rivals during the 'night of the long knives' (30 June 1934): surprised sa leaders, and Gregor Strasser, were shot without trial by the loyal ss, thus liquidating the National Socialist 'opposition.'

All of this ties into the birth of personalism because *Esprit* was linked with the National Socialist dissidents through the Ordre Nouveau group – the title came from Marc's manifesto calling for a 'New Order' in 1930. At a time when most Frenchmen dismissed National Socialism as merely a form of exaggerated nationalism, *Esprit* had contacts with the 'Strasser clique,' and the German-linked Ordre Nouveau group played an important role in formulating *Esprit*'s philosophy and in the review's difficulties with Jacques Maritain.[24] Central to the personalist link with the Nazi left, however, was Alexandre Marc himself.

Mounier had discussed *Esprit* with 'Marc' since early 1932. Then in his late twenties, Marc, born Lipiansky, was a short, dark, dynamic figure with a colourful past and little visible means of financial support. Born in Odessa into a Jewish family, he had narrowly escaped execution as a revolutionary socialist during the October Revolution. He then studied in Germany under the phenomenologist Edmund Husserl at Freiburg-im-Breisgau, and later, at the Ecole libre des Sciences politiques in Paris, where he led regular, animated discussions in a restaurant on the rue du Moulin-Vert or in the apartment of the young right-wing writer René Gillouin. Here he introduced his comrades from 'Sciences Po' René Dupuis and Jean Jardin, and Denis de Rougemont, to the phenomenology of Husserl and the 'existentialism' of Husserl's student Martin Heidegger.[25] Marc's tastes were anything but lightweight.

Marc also collaborated on *Plans*, an elegant and imaginative review launched in 1931 by a young lawyer, Philippe Lamour. Lamour had been a militant 'Blue Shirt' in Georges Valois' Faisceau before trying to found his own French Parti fasciste révolutionnaire.[26] When that failed, Lamour published *Plans* to bring together all the 'new' scientific, economic, political, and artistic tendencies of the period. There were contributions from Arthur Honegger, Fernand Léger, Claude Autant-Lara and René Clair, and – on special art paper – the plans for the 'Cité radieuse' by the brilliant young architect Le Corbusier, another former Faisceau – along with romantic pictures of Hitler and Mussolini. Political articles were written by Lamour himself, Hubert Lagardelle, the well-known *syndicaliste* who had introduced Mussolini to the ideas of Georges Sorel, the Swiss Aldo Dami, former secretary of Valois' Librairie nationale and future essayist for *Esprit*, and Marc, de Rougemont, and Dupuis, all of Ordre Nouveau.[27]

Marc had attended meetings with young Germans at the Sohlberg camp in 1930, which had been organized on the French side by the pacifist journalists Pierre Brossolette and Jean Luchaire, and where he met a dynamic young German design teacher named Otto Abetz, a leader in promoting contacts between German and French youth. Marc's friend Dupuis wrote a manifesto for a Front unique de la jeunesse européenne which called for a common revolutionary struggle of the youth of the two countries, for a 'return to the real man,' 'federalism,' 'elaboration of a European plan.'[28]

In August 1931 Marc and his Ordre Nouveau friends aided journalists Luchaire and Brossolette to organize a meeting at Rethel, in the Ardennes. The organizer on the German side, Abetz, had joined Baldur von Shirach in forming Reichsbanner, an organization seeking a 'third way' between the Communists and the Nazis. Also at the meeting were representatives of *Die Tat* – national, non-Marxist communists – and Otto Strasser, in the uniform of his 'Black Front' (Strasser's ideas were later published in *Plans* and *Esprit*).[29]

'Personalism' was the new term characterizing the distinctive ON-*Plans* orientations. In *Décadence de la nation française* (1931), ON's Robert Aron and Arnaud Dandieu had attacked the 'perverted' individualism of liberalism. Philippe Lamour soon proclaimed that they were all 'anti-individualists' because they were 'personalists.'[30]

The February 1932 Franco-German Youth Congress at Frankfurt-am-Main drew one hundred participants, including Otto Strasser, Abetz, and a left-wing national socialist close to Marc named Harro Schulze-Boysen, director of the review *Planen*, the German counterpart of *Plans*.[31] Lamour wanted to smuggle arms into Germany to some of their friends but the *Ordre Nouveau* group dissuaded him from doing so.

Plans' circulation attained eight thousand copies for subscribers in fifteen different countries, four or five times more than *Esprit*. Cercles d'Amis de Plans were created in France, Germany, and other countries and held meetings and lectures in Berlin, Cologne, Hamburg, Brussels, Zurich, and Geneva. But from March 1932 there were financial difficulties and Lamour's effort to continue with a more modest format gradually failed.[32] Marc and the Ordre Nouveau group then published in *Mouve-*

ments, a review which disapproved of the group's German ties and, after
Marc began working with Mounier, of its 'flagrant rallying to Catholic
spirituality.'[33]

During the summer of 1932 Mounier told Marc that he and Izard
wanted 'to found a review like *Plans*, inspired by ideas close to Ordre
Nouveau's – but Catholic.'[34] ON then proposed to merge with *Esprit*, and
bring 150 German groups along with them.[35] Marc was given an office
across from Mounier's at Desclée de Brouwer and began to assist him,
particularly with the review's international development. *Esprit*, Marc
thought, would be merely a sort of literary organ for the Ordre Nouveau
group.[36]

Marc and his friends were working towards an ideology, 'personalism,'
for their Front unique de la jeunesse. Arnaud Dandieu contributed what
was most original and distinctive to the effort, and his interest in Nietzsche
and the phenomenologists Husserl and Max Scheler complemented those
of Marc. Marc and Dandieu worked out a 'personnalisme créateur' which
offered an alternative to the 'French decadence' and 'American cancer'
they perceived in Europe.[37]

Marc and Dandieu defined the essential characteristics of the person as
'conflict, struggle, act, creation, and domination'; philosophy was a
'battle,' intelligence a 'sword': 'Intellectual truth ... recaptures its purity at
the summit of human aggressivity, in the literal sense, at the point of the
sword. In each armed conflict .. the intelligence ... rediscovers itself ... in
the firm fullness of virility....'[38] The ON group were no strangers to *Esprit* –
the philosophers Gabriel Marcel and Jean Lacroix, among others, had
attended their meetings. On 18 October 1932, Marc took *Esprit*'s editor to
meet ON's chief philosopher at the court of entry of the Bibliothèque
Nationale. Mounier found the alleged 'enemy of intellectuals,' 'an
intellectual to the fingertips,' and the personalism of Ordre Nouveau
vague. But from the fall of 1932 he seemed more and more impressed by
several themes, particularly as interpreted by Marc. Marc had become
interested in Péguy, and in fact joined the Catholic Church in October
1933; he saw his task as 'Christianizing' the new philosophy of personalism. Mounier thought it difficult to orient Dandieu's thought in
this direction:

His 'personalism' ... is a fundamental affirmation of the creative power of the
human person, Nietzschean in a sense, he admits.... In God, he literally sees
an opposition to human creation....

A. Marc saves things with his Catholic vision of the universe where God is a person living in the Christ and, through his Mystical Body, in ourselves. He believes thereby to rejoin both God and Dandieu. Dandieu... admits that the Catholicism of A. Marc expresses his thought, but he refuses to consider it orthodox. I accept the orthodoxy, but refuse the fidelity of Marc's interpretation to the thought of Dandieu....[39]

What could Mounier find attractive in Dandieu's exaltation of the human person, his 'intelligence-sword,' and what Mounier called his 'open sympathies for certain Hitlerite themes'?[40] Here Marc's effort to catholicize Dandieu's doctrine was important. Marc was holding serious discussions with men from different traditions inspired by a conception of the Spirit even broader than that of Mounier. He helped inspire a certain ecumenical movement in France decades before it became fashionable.[41]

The second *Esprit* contained Marc's call for a 'revolutionary federalism' and 'a new order,' and soon this 'personalist' orientation precipitated serious discord at the review. Maritain was troubled by Mounier's association with irreligious self-styled revolutionaries. Mounier proposed a special issue on Christianity but Maritain was not satisfied and pressed Mounier to have a Catholic-Christian core at *Esprit* characterized by 'purity, disinterested loyalty, fraternal friendship.'[42] Maritain was unsettled by the new directions:

There is something dangerous and equivocal at the origin of the review concerning your position in regard to Catholicism. ... You are not a *neutral* review, and you are lost if you permit ... the least germ of neutrality or inter-confessionalism to take root in you. Your only true strength ... is the Faith and the Gospel and that must be seen, known, and said. ... God or Atheism ... a true parting of the waters. ... If those things are not said ... a vital logic will draw you, in spite of yourself, where you do not want to go.
... for the love of God, look out and be firm![43]

Mounier sent Maritain an example of Dandieu-Marc's 'personalism' and Maritain's response was prompt and bitter:

My dear friend,
I am returning the manuscript that you have sent to me. I severely condemn it both as to content ... and tone ... it goes against your most cherished values. ... One does not have the right to confuse souls. And then that goose-stepping philosophy! It has an impossible tone....[44]

The November *Esprit* also irritated him, as he found one of Mounier's articles almost anti-Catholic:

a condemnation of *Catholics* by men whose first criterion is the *revolution* ... a cruel confirmation of my fears that in spite of your loyalty ... the internal logic of the positions taken leads you, in practice, to place the revolution (spiritual first of all, as you wish, but finally the revolution, a human, a 'cultural' entity) *before Christ....*[45]

Mounier promised to be open to Maritain's arguments but in the privacy of his diary he was dubious:

My heart says he is entirely right: Christianity should be proclaimed as soon as possible ... but he thinks like a hermit ... we have to draw our public from all quarters and a flaunting of Catholicism would discredit us in the eyes of many, as long as we have not yet given proof that one could be integrally Catholic and sincerely revolutionary at the same time.[46]

Maritain insisted that the review make clear that it held to 'Christianity' more than to 'revolution' and have 'someone on your *editorial council* who is your age and who represents not ... a more or less vague spirituality, but ... philosophical and theological rigour.'[47] Mounier, after a discussion with Ulmann and Izard, agreed to all Maritain's demands.[48]

The December 1932 *Esprit* published a 'Programme for 1933' which seemed responsive to Maritain's objections, assuring its readers, '*the revolution is not the primary value ... we are of the party of the spirit before being of the party of the revolution....*' But Mounier's 'party of the spirit' still seemed different from Maritain's. Mounier described the Spirit as:

an absolute ... for all of us. But it reveals itself differently. ... One recognizes it in the summons of a hero, or in an anonymous purity, an infallible generosity, or again in the justice which wells up in the heart of the people. Many others ... in a personal God. ... We are a certain number who confess the Christ and find in Him the very meaning and the strength of our gathering. ... Thus, our diversity....

Esprit, then, held to its 'unity with the Spirit' despite Maritain's warnings. In this same issue of *Esprit*, historian Edouard Dolléans heartily endorsed the revival of the historic 'spiritual revolutionary' current in France.[49] Another essay proposed an order for men committed to the spiritual revolution.[50] Izard also announced that *Esprit*'s 'movement' was interested in the 'young radicals' led by Gaston Bergery who, it was hoped, would launch a 'new formation.'[51] Obviously *Esprit* was still appealing to a broad spectrum of religious views.

When Mounier returned to Grenoble in December there was whistling and fighting at his lecture. Jacques Chevalier publicly disavowed the new review's 'Briandist' attitude towards Germany.[52] But one of Chevalier's brightest ex-students, Jean Lacroix, formerly sympathetic to the *Action Française*, was becoming an important, and faithful, contributor, along with other young provincials with right-wing backgrounds such as Edmond Humeau, an unemployed ex-seminarian and poet, and Pierre-Henri Simon, a former *normalien* leader of the Jeunesses Patriotes, now teaching in a Catholic school in Lille.[53] Soon a steady stream of talented intellectuals was joining *Esprit*.[54]

In December, Maritain sailed for the University of Toronto, having left an essay for the January *Esprit* which supplied the *Esprit* movement with a rigorous definition of spirituality: authentic spiritualization depended on 'a subsistent Love with whom one can unite more and more while aiming towards sanctity....'[55] True spirituality was neither a response to the 'call of a hero' nor the feeling of 'generosity,' but was necessarily directed towards a unity in love, towards sanctity. Other 'élans,' however edifying, stirring, or attractive, were simply not the same thing. This seemed a direct refutation of Mounier's broader definition. Maritain also rebutted Dandieu's 'personalism,' with its vague spiritualism, which was finding more and more space in *Esprit*. Maritain simply stood this anti-Christian philosophy on its historical head: not only 'the notion of the Person,' but also the 'consciousness of his value' had developed in the early Church. Dandieu's idea that the personality could only thrive without God was thus absurd, as it was the Christian sense of God that had fostered the very notion of the human person.[56] Against Marc and Dupuis' determination to root the 'person' in his particular regional, racial, and cultural milieu – with a sort of *Völkisch* federalism incorporating Péguy's notion of a distinctive French peasant-Christian culture – Maritain argued that Christianity's roots were 'fully universal, supra-racial, supra-national, supra-cultural.'[57] Here again Maritain's Catholicism ran up against some of the new ideas in Mounier's review.

One of the major factors behind Maritain's reservations about *Esprit* was the left-wing national socialist influence that persisted in it. A week after Hitler came to power, the February 1933 *Esprit* provided its subscribers with a portrait of a weak and indecisive Hitler, unable to seize power, the 'Kerensky of our revolution' (Otto Strasser), slowly leading the national socialist movement to ruin' (Alexandre Marc).[58] Strasser denounced the Nazis as 'not sufficiently revolutionary,' called for the collectivization of key industries and the reconstitution of the middle classes (the *Mittelstand*) and the small farmers to stabilize the country.

Marc saw a political situation in Germany in which 'non-conformists,' fragmented in small groups whose number grew every day, had concerns similar to *Esprit*'s. While young Marxists had to contend with 'the spiritual deficiency of Marxist socialism' and 'the dogmatism of Moscow,' Marc described the young Nazis as in an equally frustrating situation:

The national-socialist party is doubtlessly *a party of the young*: that particularity constitutes the most attractive aspect of that movement which the Führer, Adolf Hitler, is slowly leading to ruin. To become a national socialist was, for a young German, to demonstrate independence from the established disorder.[59] It was to condemn a world without grandeur, given over to the cowardly compromises of liberalism and the materialist temptation. It was to nobly affirm the virtues of a freely accepted discipline in a corrupt and degenerate world. The young national socialists were moved by a sincere need for spiritual grandeur which, moreover, found itself in contradiction with the primacy of the race.

... *Today, the best of them have lost confidence* ... the young national socialists constitute an eminently favourable field of propaganda for the 'non-conformists.'[60]

Marc praised the 'Black Front's' fidelity to original national socialism, to corporatist ideals and a hierarchical organization of the economy, although he regretted that a few of Strasser's collaborators sometimes displayed 'a rather confused *biological mysticism* incompatible with our conception of the spiritual.' Marc praised 'non-conformist' Harro Schulze-Boysen for working with analogous Swiss, Dutch, and French movements; and Schulze-Boysen himself, in the same spirit, called upon French youth to '*live and prepare your revolution!*'[61]

Despite its silence on French politics, *Esprit* supported political groups in Germany, apparently because the 'spiritual revolution' was more advanced there. Mounier's former comrade at the Ecole Normale, Raymond Aron, did send a warning on the Nazis to *Esprit*.[62] But the 'oppositionists' supported by *Esprit* were more worried about the faults of the Weimar Republic, big capitalism, and parliamentary régimes.[63] They attacked Hitler for his moderation – on the very eve of his savage consolidation of power!

The early *Esprit*'s notion of an anti-Hitler national socialism seemed much influenced by Otto Strasser, whose program spoke of a Reich corporative chamber and guilds, of hereditary fiefs and the re-agrarianization of Germany, as well as a splitting up of large estates, profit participation, and a 'people's state.'[64] Relative to Hitler's Strasser's socialism was, in historian Ernst Nolte's words, 'much more durable and much more carefully thought out.' Although Marx would have called it petit bourgeois, 'on the whole it was a genuinely socialist program.'[65]

Maritain's opposition to the Ordre Nouveau group did not prevent him from working for *Esprit* in certain milieux. He confided to Mounier that 'living in Canada one realizes that the British empire and Anglo-American protestantism are truly the heart (if such a word can be used!) of capitalism'; he found it 'a bitter and disgusting experience' and thought *Esprit* would find support in French and English Canada, and eventually publish an American edition.[66] Apparently Maritain had come to see *Esprit*'s value as stimulating young Christians into rethinking their faith. After Mounier curbed the immature elements which had destroyed its chances of becoming a new NRF, it could serve this purpose at least.

Despite Maritain's reservations, however, the ON group continued to publish in *Esprit*: Dandieu called for 'the personalist and spiritual revolution' in July, and Mounier confided to Izard that he saw 'nothing basically contradictory' between the ON and *Esprit* groups.[67] When Maritain returned in May he found Izard's political wing and the spectre of ecclesiastical condemnation even more serious threats to *Esprit* than the earlier philosophical aberrations.

In retrospect we can see that, contrary to what was later alleged in *Esprit* and histories of philosophy, the review's personalism was not created by Mounier and his 'Left Catholic' friends but rather by non-Christian intellectuals with German philosophical formations. Maritain was a bitter critic of Ordre Nouveau, but Mounier always seemed to consider it an extremely original movement of thought. Mounier forgave Dandieu his sympathy for 'certain Hitlerite themes' and swallowed Maritain's attack on 'Nietzschean Personalism's' philosophical merits, partly because of the Ordre Nouveau group's German contacts. Mounier seemed to assume a certain importance for the anti-capitalism of the Strassers' left-wing national socialism in Germany, and to hope that the Nazi movement would display its positive aspects after Hitler's leadership was broken. *Esprit* was accused by a handful of French Stalinist intellectuals of playing the Nazis' game, but a later historian has argued that these young personalists were best described as 'non-conformists,' as in Alexandre

Marc's formula. Paul Nizan's charge that personalism had to be seen in the larger context of the rise of Nazism was not taken very seriously: in 1932 Otto Strasser was planning a great 'anti-fascist congress' (which included many of Mounier's new friends), hardly a crypto-Hitlerite undertaking. Nevertheless both Maritain and the Marxists continued to weigh personalist rhetoric and ideals against personalist actions.

THE 'THIRD FORCE': TROUBLES WITH THE CHURCH

To grasp the practical implications of *Esprit*'s early positions we must study the two movements in the review's orbit, Marc's Ordre Nouveau and Izard's Third Force. The former was heavy in theory and light on action. The latter was ready for action, but prepared to leave most of the theorizing to *Esprit*.

In November 1932, Izard, Galey, and Duveau decided to call *Esprit*'s movement a 'Third Force' relative to capitalism and communism. They called a meeting in a cob-walled shed at 110 rue de Sèvres lit only by two oil lamps and charcoal heaters whose red reflections on the frosted window panes gave a surrealistic impression worthy of a theatre set. The speakers, 'violently daubed in red by a nearby lamp,' gave dramatic orations – for example, 'Messieurs, we are in 1788' – after which a young German and a French friend of 'the new Right' in Germany shared the stage. Mounier concluded from the discussion that German youth was 'further along than us....'[68]

Mounier, however, still had reservations about this Third Force which he expressed in his diary: especially that 'the spiritual and Christian' aspect of *Esprit* bothered them.[69] One night, at a Parisian intersection, one Third Force militant 'very politely ... almost affectionately,' said to him, 'We are leaving, go and make your spiritual meditations.'[70] Mounier, although troubled by their 'ambitious, sensual, adventurous, violent' qualities, also conceded regretting his own aversion towards political action, the gentleness of his upbringing, and his 'excessively prolonged adolescence.'[71]

At least partly to meet Maritain's objection that *Esprit* did not seem particularly Christian, Mounier published a special issue on Christianity, 'Rupture entre l'ordre chétien et le désordre établi,' which drew contributions from Denis de Rougemont and 'Christian socialist' André Philip for the Protestant side, Berdyaev for the Orthodox, and Charles Dulot for the non-believers. Mounier set the theme with a violent attack on the 'treasons' of Christians. He pictured the Catholic politicians in many countries as allied to a bourgeoisie which was 'born against the Christian spirit, in the sixteenth century,' drew its 'metaphysics from Voltaireanism,' and elaborated its 'code of the perfect egotist' with the Declaration of the Rights of Man during the French Revolution. He explained that given 'the compromises of Christianity with the world' 'one cannot be totally Christian, today ... without being a rebel.' He denounced liberalism, Christian Democrats, and the bourgeoisie as having lost 'the sense of Being,' love, the meaning of the Cross, and so on. The authentic Christian has to break totally from the Christian bourgeoisie.[72]

Mounier denied that his essay could be classified as either of the 'Right' or of the 'Left,' but some of his critics saw him playing the game of the former, others of the latter.[73] Paul Archambault, prominent theorist of the small Christian Democratic party in France, found the review's lack of precise political commitments and frequent recourse to the word 'revolution' irresponsible.[74] Robert Garric, occupied with social action projects, found the word 'revolution' being dishonoured by Mounier and his friends and wondered what they actually hoped to accomplish.[75] As the political line of the review became clearer, Archambault also faulted its disturbing tendency to attack liberal and democratic values.

Another veteran of the Sillon, François Mauriac, charged that *Esprit* was playing into the hands of the communists! On the front page of the conservative *L'Echo de Paris* on 25 March, he rapped the knuckles of 'les jeunes bourgeois révolutionnaires':

What stupidity to mingle the hangman and the victim, the capitalist system and the middle class in the same hatred! ... the French middle class has been the crucible in which the genius of our people of peasants and workers has come to fruition: engineers, doctors, scholars, philosophers, painters, poets – and the very saints. (Theresa of the Child Jesus, Theresa Martin, [was a] petite-bourgeoise who, on simple paintings, is depicted holding the hand of M. Martin, in frockcoat and top hat ...). The rebellious themselves, Baudelaire, Rimbaud, only existed thanks to that middle class they denounced, but of which they were sons. Charles Péguy is the only one who was not at all middle class; he was an isolated miracle that you will not recreate: perhaps the weakness of your movement is in wanting to recreate péguyisme without Péguy....

Somewhat ominously he added: 'God only grant that the country not pay the costs, and that the children of light are not clearing the path for the power of darkness.'

Father Henri du Passage, director of the Jesuit review *Etudes*, attacked

Esprit's 'intellectual bolshevism,' and the controversy extended to the daily *La Croix* and to the Catholic press in Switzerland and Belgium.[76] On 19 April, Luigi Maglione, papal nuncio in France, wrote confidentially to Canon Dupin, Vicar General of Paris, that there were some 'excellent articles' in *Esprit* alongside 'other articles which merit not only disapproval but condemnation.' The nuncio enclosed a theologian's report on *Esprit* which the canon was to present to the archbishop of Paris along with the problem of assigning an 'authorized counsel' to the review's direction.[77]

Esprit's movement, the 'Third Force,' aggravated its difficulties with the Church when it began working with 'the neo-communism' of Gaston Bergery.[78] The Third Force had only a few hundred adherents, but Bergery was a nationally known deputy, a leader of the Young Turks in the Radical party, who in March 1933 launched a widely publicized Common Front against Fascism to transcend the old political parties. Izard had helped draft the Front's manifesto for the dashing Bergery, a militant anti-communist married to the daughter of the Soviet ambassador to Paris. Bergery hoped to draw the whole non-communist Left into his movement. Although both the socialists and communists forbade their members to join, Bergery's new, disciplined, vigorous, anti-capitalist politics did appeal to a few left-wing politicians, as well as to Georges Izard and the novelist Drieu la Rochelle.[79] This involved *Esprit* in a movement which used Marxist rhetoric and whose manifesto described Christianity as 'an ideology several centuries old, dépassée economically....'[80]

In the April and May issues of *Esprit* Mounier defied Mauriac to specify how *Esprit*'s doctrines were Marxist. He told Garric that commitment to revolution was 'our profound spiritual exigency,' and even if the revolution they were advocating did not occur, 'a great witness is not wasted.'[81] But Mounier's depiction of *Esprit* as above politics and spiritually inspired was undermined by Izard's language. Maritain reacted angrily to Izard's note in the May 1933 *Esprit*, which laid claim to much that was beyond the province of religion:

The 'Third Force' ... refuses fascism, a consolidation of capitalism.... In communism it deplores the substitution of the slavery of statism for the slavery of capitalism. It is a new ideal. It may first make the collectivist revolution with communism; but that revolution will be a simple destruction, an elimination of profiteers. Afterwards it will effect the personalist revolution and that revolution will be the veritable construction, the edification of a new world on the personal development of each man.

On 18 May Maritain outlined his view of the danger:

that paragraph of the 'chronicle of the Third Force' is completely intolerable; you should not allow that to happen. Perfect 'Kerenskyist' foolishness. To make a revolution in two stages ... is idiotic and betrays the spiritual values that those young people have given themselves the mission of defending....

... grave equivocation will only be cleared away the day when you will have posed the question 'of the true nature and true dimensions of the 'spiritual revolution,' and then ... of the purification of the means implied by it. So long as you have not done that, you will in fact be in the wake of the other revolution and you will not have achieved your specific character. After serious reflection on the matter, one is led to infer a total inversion of current ideas and values ... a 'resistance strength' and active patience, like those which Gandhi's example has provided, should come to the fore....

I shall not always be able ... to write a long letter like this to you. I am a bit tired of these 'remonstrances' that my friendship obliges me to send to you, my dear Emmanuel, and which you accept, I know, with an equal friendship.... The root of the question is that your enterprise requires souls oriented towards sanctity, of the intelligence as well as of the heart. You know this, but most of your collaborators only have a very vague idea of this. This is your cross....[82]

Maritain demanded that *Esprit* publish a letter from him which Mounier thought would amount to rebuke from official Catholicism.[83] Mounier also learned that the Conseil de Vigilance of the archdiocese of Paris was about to meet concerning *Esprit*. Mounier's 'ecumenism' seemed about to lead to a fatal break with the Church.

In response to the papal nuncio, Cardinal Verdier noted official misgivings about *Esprit*: its collaboration with the non-Catholics seemed based upon 'a common and closed doctrine, a synthesis alongside the Catholic synthesis'; its Third Force 'a curious sort of fascist movement with an extreme Left style'; its unconcern for the positions of the Church.[84] Jean Plaquevent, a priest active in student circles in the Latin Quarter, was asked to report on it. But Plaquevent was a friend who had warned Mounier about the group's 'union in the spirit' and confided what he knew of the discussions of *Esprit* in the Church hierarchy.[85] Mounier also had the support of the writers Maurice Brillant, who was asked to write an opinion for the Conseil, and Georges Coquelle-Viance, who promised to intercede with the nuncio.[86] Maritain admitted that the Church's reservations were sound: 'It seems unlikely to me that a theologian would not feel himself conscience-bound to judge dangerous for Catholics ... formulas where, under the pretext of spiritual revolution, one puts them little by little in connivance with simply "the revolution...."'[87]

Mounier recognized that the publication of Maritain's letter would be a 'catastrophe' for *Esprit* in the circumstances. On the other hand he felt he only needed more time to 'spiritualize' Izard's friends:

to break with the 'Third Force' would be to send them to nothingness, while my duty, that of *Esprit*, is to ... strip them of their 'Leftist mystique' ... to accomplish the same work of discrimination on the Left that we have on the Right.

That would be easy if I had the men; but it is devilishly difficult to find competence and vigour of spirit united to true spirituality ... they must be given a habit of light so that they can keep something after the rupture ... more time is needed for that....[88]

On 23 May Plaquevent told Cardinal Verdier and the Conseil de Vigilance that the *Esprit* group was not dangerous. It was made up of unemployed young people, several highly intelligent young teachers rebelling against their professors, and had the support of Maritain and other Catholic leaders. He said that Mounier wanted the review to be a meeting ground between socialists and Catholics, and that while Izard and a few others had socialist tendencies, one could count on the Catholic orthodoxy of Mounier. This satisfied Cardinal Verdier, the 'Red Archbishop,' known for his sympathy for audacious youth movements, who suggested that *Esprit* might well play 'the role of avant-garde of the Christian apostolate' and be better served by 'counsellors' than 'censors,' who would scare off non-Catholics.[89] Maritain then told Mounier that he would drop his disavowal letter if Mounier renounced publishing 'the program and ideological manifestations of the Third Force in *Esprit*.[90] Mounier privately regretted that there was 'so much timidity on the side of the meditative types, so little competence' but concluded that 'one group must be played off against the other,' and he promised Maritain that the questionable 'activists' would be cited, in the future, only in a pluralistic context.[91]

On 13 June the nuncio was assured that Mounier had separated from Izard and that Vicar General Beaussart and Father Plaquevent had been assigned to censor the review *Esprit* and counsel its directors. Cardinal Verdier would allow it to continue for the time being, although it would be condemned if it became dangerous to the faith of its readers.[92]

On 30 June the De Brouwer publishing house informed Mounier that it was being reorganized and could no longer provide services for *Esprit*. Since the review was already in financial straits, Mounier thought that this was a pretext to put an end to it: he asked Madame Daniélou and Maritain for help in finding a job so that *Esprit* could continue.[93]

By the summer of 1933 *Esprit* represented opposing tendencies which seemed too antagonistic to be transcended by the common attachment to the spirit. From this time on, to mollify Maritain, *Esprit* simply 'reported' the activities of the Ordre Nouveau and the Third Force. But the two currents nevertheless continued alive and well in the pages of *Esprit*. To counter the threats to his work Mounier elaborated a distinctive doctrine compatible with Catholic orthodoxy – a 'personalism' for *Esprit*.

In later years, Mounier and subsequent historians of his movement tried to downplay his difficulties with the tiny groups of intellectuals around Ordre Nouveau and the Third Force. But the effort to interest France's Christian intellectuals in an extraparliamentary, international, 'spiritual revolution' remained central to the *Esprit* enterprise. Both these movements, as well as Jacques Maritain, had an important influence on Mounier's synthesis, as will become clear. *Esprit*'s personalism emerged in the effort to reconcile some of the basically contradictory influences on a generation of Frenchmen.

5

The Fascist Challenge

THE EARLY 'ESPRIT'S' MARXIST CRITICS

The revolutionary language of the new *Esprit* and the youth movements which orbited around it troubled the orthodox – not only Catholics, but communists as well. Young Stalinist intellectuals soon saw the review as a serious threat and their critique of it offers a different view of the origins of personalism from that of Mounier and his friends.

In July 1933 the review *Commune* was founded by the Association des écrivains et artistes révolutionnaires (which included various Communist intellectuals – Henri Barbusse, Paul Vaillant-Couturier, Louis Aragon, Paul Nizan) to combat the growing temptation of fascism for French intellectuals. Although at the time *Esprit* was publishing only three or four thousand issues, *Commune* warned that Mounier's review – despite its 'lack of political influence or popular base,' 'terribly vague doctrines,' and 'imprecise program' – was extremely dangerous.[1] It described *Esprit*, the Third Force, the *Ordre Nouveau* group, *La Revue Française* (of Thierry Maulnier, Jean-Pierre Maxence, and Robert Francis) as united in fostering the very conceptions advocated by fascism ('primacy of the spiritual,' 'personalism,' and so on) which *Commune* had been founded to fight.[2]

According to *Commune*, most of these young intellectuals were petit bourgeois, unemployed, and enviously critical of big capital. A few were 'ambitious' young engineers, especially at *Ordre Nouveau*; others were unsuccessful novelists – Nizan cited Maxence and Daniel-Rops – 'like Joseph Goebbels'; or academic drop-outs and déclassés. They served as 'intellectual guard dogs' for the grande bourgeoisie, who subsidized their review.[3] *Commune*'s writers perceived a sort of closet Catholicism, especially at *Esprit*, but attributed the common philosophical orientation more to the neo-Hegelian tradition and the sinister influences of Heidegger, 'a leading philosopher of Hitlerism,' and the 'aesthetic' wing of National Socialism, represented by Goebbels.

Commune sneered at Mounier's Catholicism ('that bestial slave religion'), what they called his abuse of the word 'revolution,' and 'the naïve belief that the Catholic Church could take part in any condemnation of capitalism.' *Commune* described the practical proposals of the Third Force in their organ *Front Social* as 'likely sooner or later to dispose the adherents of the "Third Force" to join the ranks of fascism.'[4] The Marxists insisted that the personalism in *Esprit*, *La Revue Française*, and *Ordre Nouveau* was rooted in romantic individualism, and that it was Nietzschean and élitist, despite its claims of being 'neither Right nor Left.' Nizan noted that Goebbels had described Nazism's doctrine as centred on 'the personality.'[5] He noted further that the *La Revue Française* group – Maulnier, Francis, and Maxence – was already 'notoriously fascist,' while *Ordre Noveau* favoured 'pre-fascist ideological movements analogous to *Esprit* and *Ordre Nouveau*: the reviews *Die Tat* and *Der Gegner* – movements rapidly absorbed by National Socialism.'[6] Nizan saw a 'federalism' similar to 'the little artisan's universe ... in the system of M. Heidegger, official philosopher of National Socialism.' Jacques Bartoli described *Esprit* as 'pre-fascist' not 'fascist,' but predicted that many of the group would quickly pass to an 'acknowledged fascism.'[7] According to Gérald Servèze, both *Esprit* and *Front Social* favoured 'the ulterior recruitment of fascism ...,' but *Front Social* was more dangerous because it was beyond all semblance of religiousness and tried to establish a popular base.[8]

Nizan ridiculed Mauriac's charge that *Esprit* was dangerously anti-bourgeois, arguing that the contrary was the case:

> The development of the person ... is finally the development, in new forms, of the very person of the bourgeois ... to save the individuality to which he has clung historically....
>
> M. Mauriac asks: 'Who will make that revolution ...' ... Will 'the children of light prepare the way for the power of darkness?' M. Mauriac should be reassured ... M. Mauriac will greet with joy ... the defenders of the Person, in fascist uniforms ... the children of Light.[9]

How valid was *Commune*'s harsh dismissal of the early *Esprit* group as déclassé and disreputable? While several jobless young men were involved, there were soon over forty agrégés around the review.

Daniel-Rops, Marrou, Dolléans, Duveau, François Goguel, and Madaule may have been frustrated novelists but they all became well-known historians. Maritain, Marcel, and Berdyaev are usually counted among the most important Christian thinkers of the twentieth century. Nizan had been on firmer ground when he portrayed the *Esprit* group as a middle-class intellectual élite 'distilling thick foreign philosophical currents.' Academic drop-outs they were not.

The Marxist critics seemed to make little distinction between fascism and National Socialism, even after Hitler clapped German 'fascists' in prison. The left-wing current in National Socialism was not recognized any more than the Nazis' ability to attract the masses. The same sort of perplexity was reflected in *Commune*'s analysis of *Esprit*. *Commune* never quite called *Esprit* 'fascist,' but the review was described as surrounded by dubious individuals, abortive movements, suspect ideas, and ominous foreign connections.

French communist intellectuals seemed to devote considerable attention to *Esprit* beause of its originality and the interest it generated among intellectuals. *Commune* offered little analysis of the programs of the large conservative Catholic organizations, such as the Fédération Nationale Catholique or the Christian Trade Union, because there were analogous initiatives already present at the time of Marx and Engels. *Esprit* seemed to fall somewhere between the Catholic and the fascist camps: 'Catholic' and 'revolutionary,' advocating spiritual revolution and anti-fascism. While some French Marxists simply dismissed *Esprit* as 'Catholic' or 'fascist,' Paul Nizan, an unusually sensitive critic of Catholicism, portrayed the review as locking itself into a posture in which inevitably it would be torn between fascism and Catholicism. He also suggested that this peculiar dilemma might one day become the drama of French Catholics in general. In this Nizan was remarkably prophetic.

The 'fascist' reputation of the personalists was enhanced, when, in the spring of 1933, Alexandre Marc began to publish a review for the elaboration of an Ordre Nouveau ideology. It drew contributions from several budding 'technocrats,' notably Jean Jardin, a young executive at the SNCF (French National Railway System), and Robert Loustau and Robert Gibrat, who belonged to the Centre Polytechnicien d'Etudes Economiques as well as to its mysterious planning group, X-Crise. Denis de Rougemont, for one, found, *Ordre Nouveau* much more 'revolutionary' than *Esprit*.[10]

The fifth issue of *Ordre Nouveau* began with a salutation to the führer: 'Monsieur le Chancelier, we believe truly that with you Germany will, or is able to, achieve the maximum. We believe that in the spiritual origins ... of the national socialist movement are found the germs of a new and necessary revolutionary position.' Still, after citing 'national socialist victories,' the journal reiterated the perennial objections it shared with the national socialist 'oppositionists' – that Hitler compromised with capitalism, promoted statism over regional differences, and so on.[11] The journal also clearly foresaw the dangers of the war. Members of the ON had said all this before; what was new and widely observed was the review's new deference towards Hitler's achievements.

One sympathetic subscriber to *Ordre Nouveau* was the German ambassador to Great Britain, Joachim von Ribbentrop, a late-comer to the Nazi party, joining in 1932.[12] In the summer of 1934, Marc's oppositionist contact, Otto Abetz, met Ribbentrop, who became Abetz's patron. Abetz was named delegate of the Reich's head office for youth affairs in 1934, and charged to organize the meetings of French and German veterans under the patronage of the Deutsch-Französische Gesellschaft.[13] Abetz launched the bilingual, elegant *Deutsch-Französische Monatshefte/Cahiers Franco-Allemands*, which printed sympathetic reports on interesting revolutionary movements in other European countries, including personalist initiatives. Ribbentrop became Hitler's chief, if unofficial, adviser on foreign relations, and after 1934 Abetz was Ribbentrop's expert on France.

Since Marc's and Mounier's reviews were joined in their readers' mind, the 'Letter to Hitler' clearly implicated *Esprit*.[14] French intellectual Georges Friedmann even charged that *Esprit* and *Ordre Nouveau* were 'preparing the theory of a French national socialism.'[15]

'ESPRIT': ANTI-FASCIST

Ordre Nouveau was not alone in France in seeking new political initiatives. Since the 1932 elections, groups of radicals and centrists had succeeded one another in France without offering firm and coherent leadership, and finally a bond scandal which implicated government officials, the 'Stavisky affair,' occasioned an extreme Right offensive against the régime. On 9 January 1934, there was rioting in the streets of Paris, as the right-wing press called for an insurrection and *L'Humanité* violently denounced both the fascists and 'la République pourrie.' The unrest culminated in massive riots in February.

Esprit brought out a special issue on fascism in January. At first glance, Mounier's lead-off critique of 'fascist spiritual pseudo-values' set the personalists against the Right.[16] For, although he granted fascism's 'apparent resurrection of the spirit,' its 'youth, health, will, unanimity, authority, fervour, reconstituted social organism, clean houses, zealous functionaries, ardent crowds,' he also squarely confronted what was objectionable in extant fascisms:

> We in no way deny that fascisms bring, in contrast to the régimes they displace, an element of health and an elevation of tone which are not energies to be scorned. We recognize the considerable differences that distinguish one from the other. ... But it is a question here of isolating their essence, not their modalities.
>
> We must call fascism on the political, social, and economic plane, a defensive reaction....

Mounier went on to describe how 'reactionary' fascism preserved capitalism within the cult of the 'party-State.' Despite appearances, fascism was an enemy of true spirituality:

> more profoundly we denounce fascism as a type of human attitude, the most dangerous seduction which is proposed to us today. Pseudohumanism, pseudospiritualism which bends man under the tyranny of the most clumsy 'spiritualities' and the most ambiguous 'mystique': the cult of race, of the nation, of the State, of the will to power, of anonymous discipline of the leader, of athletic successes and economic conquests. In the last analysis, a new materialism....

Earlier, Mounier had condemned the essence of capitalism, 'individualism' and of communism, 'materialism.' The essence of fascism for Mussolini, he admitted, was 'a spiritualist conception of life' which seemed, in theory, close to *Esprit*'s aspirations. But in fact fascism, he charged, fell into a host of clumsy, materialistic 'mystiques.'

Mounier glibly passed over fascism's élitism, cult of violence, irrationalism, and denial of democracy and liberty. In fact, he admitted that there was something seductive about fascism when juxtaposed to the 'decadent' liberal democracies:

> one does not combat a mystique with a mystique on an inferior level. One does not combat fascism with maudlin democratic fidelities, with elections. ... Today there is a fascist temptation in the whole world. A temptation of facility ... how easy it is to put the whole works in the hands of a man, to await commands, and to blindly obey in the intoxication of heroic speeches! But a

temptation of grandeur also: everything in disorder, disgust everywhere – suddenly cleanliness, energy, some dignity, order.

Was Mounier sympathetic or unsympathetic to the rise of fascism? Quotations from his writings in this period could support contradictory conclusions. Mounier was a true Péguyiste in the sense that like his hero he offered what Maritain called 'a host of mutually contradictory affirmations.'[17] Only about capitalism did Mounier never have anything favourable to say, save an odd sympathetic remark for certain nineteenth-century robber-baron types. Nor did he find in liberalism those virtues he perceived in the different fascisms. The year 1933 witnessed the Estado Novo in Portugal and the Falange in Spain. The previous year Sir Oswald Mosley had founded the British Union of Fascists and Léon Degrelle the Rexist movement in Belgium. Dollfuss was trying to transform Austria along the lines suggested by Quadragesimo Anno. Most of Mounier's negativism seems directly aimed at Mussolini, less directed at the German National Socialists, and barely applicable to the movements of Salazar or José Antonio.

Was Mounier 'decanting, purifying, and perfecting the thick foreign currents,' seeking a 'more artful' form of 'national socialism'? He ridiculed this charge and argued that his personalism was anti-fascist, something fresh and unprecedented, without parallels in other countries, except perhaps in Belgium around the 'neo-socialist' theorist Henri de Man.

Reflecting pressure from Maritain to separate from the *Ordre Nouveau* group, Mounier concluded his abnegation of fascism with criticism of them: 'Just after your letter [to Hitler] appeared, *Le Figaro, Le Temps*, that is the newspapers of salons and cannon merchants, covered you with praise. ... Don't you feel the threat to your integrity? Don't you know that the funds are ready, and waiting for you if you adapt to a revolution not too nasty and sufficiently aristocratic?'[18] Hitler had just received the support of large industrial magnates in January 1932, and when Mounier wrote this, Hitler's power was not yet completely consolidated. Mounier criticized *Ordre Nouveau*'s flattery of Hitler as 'conservative' behaviour – hardly the quality at *Ordre Nouveau* which troubled Maritain. Besides Mounier's, several of the other essays in the special *Esprit* on fascism strongly criticized it.[19] One stressed the difference between the German national socialist movement and the Hitler cult, saying Nietzsche might well have endorsed the former, but never the latter.[20] Another called attention to the marriage between 'the social revolutionary element and the national traditionalist element,' and to the genuine 'socialist movement' in Nazism.[21] In addition, *Esprit* exhumed – for the first time in French – the original twenty-five points of the National Socialist program. Eugène Mèves, a young Belgian friend of Otto Strasser, in presenting them, lamented 'the promises of social revolution ... forgotten since Hitler's accession to power.'[22] There followed Strasser's long denunciation of Hitler's 'weakness and indecision,' and another young German's violent attack on the Hitlerite régime's fanaticism and abrogation of individual liberties.[23] In the succeeding *Esprit*, Strasser attacked imperialistic political power. Each 'Volk' was 'an organism created by God and bearing well-defined physical, spiritual, and moral characteristics. ... The idea of a people (and its realization: nationalism) is contrary to all forms of imperialism, all interference of one people in the life of another people. ...' He argued that mainstream national socialism was essentially anti-colonialist and anti-statist: the movement had been perverted by the influence of the Vatican and fascist Italy, by Hitler's 'weakness, impatience, lack of clarity' and his recent 'deification.' There was now an 'abyss' between Hitler and national socialism.[24] Strasser portrayed German youth identifying with 'the family of the Western peoples' and wishing France well.[25]

While *Esprit*'s opposition to fascism and Hitler were often restated in early 1934, the review still seemed to distil more positive values from 'pure' national socialism than did most Paris-based reviews.

6 FEBRUARY: SPIRITUAL PRINCIPLES AND RIOTING IN THE STREETS

On the night of 6 February 1934 several large, disciplined organizations – the Croix de Feu, Pierre Taittinger's Jeunesses Patriotes, the Camelots du Roi – joined by a few communists and forty militants from the Third Force led by André Déléage, converged on the Palais Bourbon shouting 'down with the crooks.' The demonstrators, according to several witnesses, almost succeeded in their assault on the Chamber of Deputies, and in succeeding days the counter-demonstrations of the socialists and communists prolonged the atmosphere of tension and violence.

Up to this point, *Esprit* had been internationalist: pushing one minority political line in Germany, and then, by publishing the Plan de Travail of Henri de Man, another in Belgium, but overlooking politics in France. When Mounier's denunciation of 'the system' was echoed in the streets of Paris by young men determined to overthrow the Republic and seize power, his reaction was ambiguous.[26] Christian Democrat Paul Archambault, on the eve of the February riots, had attacked Mounier for dismissing democracy as 'a mystique on an inferior level' to fascism, and deplored his calls for the revolutionary overthrow of the democratic Republic.[27] In *L'Aube* two weeks after the 'events,' Mounier declared that 'the *political* principles of modern democracy – sovereignty of the people, equality, individual liberty' were not 'absolutes' for the *Esprit* group but were 'evaluated in the light of our conception of man ... of the Community which completes him.' The thrust of Mounier's argument was that the Christian Democrats foolishly held to an old mystique; *Esprit*, too, was on the side of democracy; but 'future democracy,' the democracy that 'had not yet been realized.'[28]

On which side of the barricades did this place Mounier? In his editorial on the events of February, his first on a contemporary political event, he attacked the 'lies' and 'myths' propagated by both sides: rejecting the 'myth' of the Republicans that 6 February was a fascist plot, and the 'myth' of the Right that the Stavisky affair had revealed profound corruption in the régime. How many who protested against the rottenness of the régime, he asked, had effected their own 'revolution against the reign of money' as they would demand of the government?

Mounier considered the situation in France still pre-revolutionary: *If there is a revolution now,*' he said, '*it will not be ours.*' The 6 February riots seemed to convince him of the weakness of the truly revolutionary forces in his country, and encouraged him to defend the purity of the spiritual revolution against the 'false mystiques.'[29]

Was this defensible posture at a time when political thugs were trying to bring down the government through street riots? The *Esprit* movement refused to be judged in political terms. Mounier steadfastly envisioned his comrades' efforts in the same dimension of history as the great spiritual insurrections of the past. One could dismiss such a 'spiritual revolution' as quixotic and hopelessly unrealistic were it not for the successes of figures like Gandhi and Joan of Arc. However, events were taking a turn that would force Mounier to 'politicize' these noble sallies; and attacks from right and left compelled him to articulate personalism with a new – and overdue – clarity.

THE ARTICULATION OF PERSONALISM

By early 1934, in addition to the attacks on *Esprit* by Marxists and Democrats, there was a new threat which endangered the very life of the review. In September 1933 Mounier had confided that he believed 'more and more that we will be condemned by the Church.'[30] Nervously, he complained to Georges Izard that this was because of an absurd misunderstanding: 'A philosophy of the person is the exact opposite of Communist philosophies,' and if *Esprit*'s personalism was once articulated Catholic objects to it would disappear because 'there is no way that it can be glued on to Marxism.'

Whatever this philosophy of the person was, it was certainly in the air in the circles Mounier frequented. Several contributors to *Plans* or *Ordre Nouveau* defended the 'human Person' or 'spiritual man,' whom they saw threatened by both dollar-chasers and bolsheviks. The Young Right wanted to assure the victory of heroism, saintliness, and art over the material. For some the 'person' was Nietzschean in inspiration; others filtered the Nietzschean inspiration through Husserl and Heidegger and 'Christianized' it. All opposed the crude individual, the atomistic society fostered by capitalism, the Third Republic, and standard liberalism. All idealized multidimensional man, the 'higher type' struggling for heroic virtues and aesthetic standards against the mass. While Marxists saw the personalists defending bourgeois individualism, the personalists saw themselves fighting against the enslavement of man to an economic system, the machine, a party, or the state.

Mounier's affinity for the 'person' grew from his studies with Chevalier, his reading of Bergson, and his fascination with the phenomenon of 'spirituality,' broadly defined. His strong Catholic background set him against 'individualism': the 'egoism' of the Renaissance, the 'arrogance' of the reformers, and the 'secularizing' liberalism of the Third Republic. The idea of the person was a handy way for a Bergsonian Catholic to define what he stood for against both the Third Republic and the Marxists. He could see no reason why the Church should take umbrage at his formulation.

In the same fashion that church disapproval affected *Esprit*, so too Maritain's criticism led to greater independence from *Ordre Nouveau*, the Third Force, and then from Maritain himself. Only hours after Maritain's friends at Desclée de Brouwer had excluded Mounier from their offices, Georges Zerapha, a Jewish wallpaper manufacturer who had been impressed with strong denunciations of Hitlerite anti-semitism in *Esprit*, offered to provide the review with a free office and secretary.[31] Zerapha liked the ecumenical thrust of *Esprit* and the sense of spiritual brotherhood. Like his co-religionists Robert Aron and Paul-Louis Landsberg, he wrote sympathetically about Christian spirituality in *Esprit* – although unlike Alexandre Marc, Jacques Ellul, and Philippe Wolf, he did not convert.[32] His financial support allowed *Esprit* more independence from the agents of Catholic orthodoxy.

In the summer and fall of 1933 *Esprit* restated its determination to have an autonomous philosophical base. The July issue announced that *Esprit's* 'friends' were to gather, wherever people were interested in the review, four times each year. The groups, like the old Amis de *Plans* of Philippe Lamour, were to be an international network for the solicitation and spread of new ideas.[33] Soon Mounier proudly announced that *Esprit* had work groups or sympathizers in all the large cities of France and in fifteen foreign countries, and that 'those of us who are trying to be Christians have declared ... our determination to break with the established disorder.' 'This is the first time,' he claimed, 'that the revolutionary power of Christianity has been proclaimed, by such a group, in our times....' He declared that 'the time has come to clarify the review's ideas.'[34] In this vein, Arnaud Dandieu published the first of a projected series of doctrinal essays on personalism intended to distinguish *Esprit's* spiritual revolution from the 'neo-communism' of Gaston Bergery and the Third Force. When Dandieu died suddenly in August, Mounier lost a possible source for a distinctive, anti-Marxist *Esprit* ideology.[35]

One reason why *Esprit* needed a sophisticated anti-Marxist critique was because Georges Izard's flirtation with Marxism had caused much of *Esprit's* difficulties with Catholicism. Mounier himself was not interested in Marx, although he confided that he hoped to study him some day.[36] From Dandieu, Mounier inherited an interest in the thought of the German phenomenologist Max Scheler, who reinforced Mounier's conviction that *Esprit's* philosophy had to be antithetical to all 'communist philosophies.' Thereafter Mounier insisted to Izard that there was 'no true spirituality without hierarchy, and a constant purification of the inferior levels....'[37] Catholic religious orders were vertically structured, tightly regulated communities, with an abbot and/or general on the top and humble lay brothers on the bottom. Their models of holiness were saints, a spiritual élite. In the October 1933 *Esprit*, Mounier envisaged his ideal future society as one vast monastery in which the rule of money and the material would come to an end. Scheler's analysis led Mounier to suggest that men could be united by their interior lives into a community of persons that would itself become a Person, and in November he moved to divorce this conception of the person clearly from that of *Ordre Nouveau*.[38] Apparently in response to Maritain's pressures, Mounier sought a more 'spiritualized' personalism than that of Marc and his friends.

A week after the February 1934 riots Mounier explained the urgency of a new personalism to Berdyaev: 'Either I, or Maritain ... will explain the 'Ordre Nouveau' conflict to you. The movement is obviously becoming oriented towards an anti-worker fascism ... that we cannot accept.' In order to help create a distinctive *Esprit* ideology, Mounier organized study groups with Paul-Louis Landsberg, a student of Max Scheler exiled in Paris, to define 'the personalist-communitarian philosophy of our movement.'[39] At the same time, he promised Berdyaev that *Esprit* would make a special effort to recruit more 'revolutionary Christians.'[40]

Esprit's efforts in early 1934 to distinguish its personalism from that of *Ordre Nouveau* was not appreciated by that group.[41] Mounier, however, reiterated that defining the person as a 'pure act,' 'creative aggressivity,' or 'spiritual violence' was extremely dangerous, and that Arnaud Dandieu, despite his openness to certain 'central tendencies of Hitlerism,' would never have gone along with the differential tone of their 'Letter to Hitler.'[42]

On 11 May 1934 thirty people, many newcomers to *Esprit*, assembled in the little café À Saint Sulpice in the heart of the Latin Quarter. They were quickly divided into study groups on the problems of the corporation and business, on the state and federalism, on Marxist studies, and on colonialism. On 14 May a 'philosophers group' was subdivided into groups to 'define means of spiritual efficacity,' to study Marx with the aid of Marcel Moré, and to study 'our metaphysics of the Person and the Community.'[43]

The long overdue definition of personalism was to be a great common effort which Mounier was to catalyze and co-ordinate. By the end of 1934 Maritain, Berdyaev, P.-L. Landsberg, Gabriel Marcel, Jean Wahl, and Georges Gurvitch were participating in the 'philosophy group' in Paris. Many young men in the provinces, with important careers ahead of them, followed this work in the pages of *Esprit*. Berdyaev and Landsberg soon emerged as the most influential thinkers in the group.[44] Ironically, the effort to create an *Esprit* personalism was spearheaded by foreigners with German philosophical formations, who were respectively Orthodox and Jewish – despite Personalism's decisive influence on a generation of French Catholics.

The fruits of all this labour emerged throughout 1934 as Mounier published position papers in *Esprit* on 'property,' 'communism,' 'Christian politics,' 'anti-capitalism,' 'work,' and 'art.'[45] In late 1934 and early 1935 he made direct attempts to clarify his 'communitarian personalism' in a set of essays subsequently published as *Révolution personnaliste et communautaire* (Paris 1935). Finally, the next year, just after the French Popular Front came to power, he hammered out his *Personalist Manifesto*, a useful distillation of major themes for the use of the *Esprit* groups in France and abroad.[46]

Mounier's first expositions of personalism were notable in their new concern for 'community,' a need to form 'collective persons,' 'persons of persons' inspired by a 'living poverty' or 'generous simplicity.'[47] He also hailed the 'immense renewal' of Christianity which could come from the 'communitarian theology of the Mystical Body' and a new grasp of the 'collective vocation of the Christian.'[48] Here at the heart of *Esprit*'s anti-capitalism was the recognition that the person could only fulfil himself in 'organic communities.'[49] Capitalism denied man 'his true daily bread: the development of an interior life in the heart of communitarian life.' Such a life, as Mounier saw it, would initiate aesthetic improvements as well:

Art must become once again mixed in with the day-to-day life of everyone, as it was in the Church, in dances and popular holidays, as it ought to be in the factory, the countryside, the home, in public buildings. That the peasants renew their desire to celebrate the feasts of the land, with dances, songs and plays; that the workers ... create handsome factories, that the faith rid itself of ... a decadent piety and learn again to sing in images.[50]

In sum, Mounier's personalism, unlike that of *Ordre Nouveau*, became more communitarian. For Mounier, the 'community of persons' came to be romantic and creative, with a supernatural dimension.

TOWARDS 'COMMUNITARIAN PERSONALISM'

Mounier asserted that the true community was a reality as fundamental as that of the person: communities which transcended mere material interests could become a 'person of persons'; 'spiritual' really meant the same as 'personal' ('spirituel = personnel'); for the Christian 'every community, including the total human community, is rooted in the Mystical Body of a divine incarnated Person.'[51] In order to grasp what Mounier meant one must juxtapose the notion of 'person' to that of the 'individual.' Individualism was 'completely devoted to well-being and security, and completely devoid ... of all madness, of all mystery, of the sense of being and the sense of love, of suffering and of joy....'[52] The person was 'animated' by the spiritual, 'revealed' in communities; it was not a 'personality,' but a 'presence' in someone: 'My person is the presence and the unity of an eternal vocation in me, which calls me to surpass myself indefinitely....'[53]

If some of this appeared Nietzschean, Mounier was adamant in distinguishing his personalism from that of his errant comrades:

One [way] would lead to the apotheosis of the personality, that is, to the values of tension, of 'aggressivity,' of mastery, of heroism. The hero would be the ideal. A Stoic branch. A Nietzschean branch. A Fascist branch....
   The other way would be open onto the depths of the authentic Person. ... That person only finds himself in forgetting, in giving himself – the Christian would go to the limit: in abandoning himself. ... The saint would be the result of that way as the hero is the result of the first.[54]

What was the difference between the 'person' and a 'spiritual man'? Since 'spirituel = personnel,' personalism appeared in many respects to be the Bergsonian spiritualism of Chevalier with a different vocabulary:

We feel that in any case one only finds the person ... through the effusion of a reality which transcends him. ... The believer says ... that man only finds himself in God – the Christian adds, by the incarnated Person of Christ. ... Many non-Christians ... are looking for a reality all-consuming enough to vanquish their avarice to the point where they forget the self.[55]

Clearly 'personhood' was not something peculiar to Catholics, for there were many people who transcended their individuality by contact with the 'burning reality' of strong beliefs. But Mounier added that the person could only be truly completed in community. While the pseudo-person of the fascists stood in pagan isolation beyond the crowd, the person-saint would be warmed by the flame of fraternal charity.

   This same fixation with community shaped Mounier's ambivalent evaluation of the rise of fascism and communism in Europe:

Fascism and communism ... are the first starts of the immense communitarian wave which is beginning to break over Europe. ... Men ... are going to try to rediscover the path of community. All their efforts will be spiritual to some degree. ... Most will also menace the spiritual at some point. ... But one does not condemn a vital initiative for the dangers in its path ... we want to take our responsibilities in the face of the second Renaissance.

Remake the Renaissance. ... It is to be remade doubly ... personalist and communitarian.[56]

Mounier, like Marx, tended to view the excesses of his time in a world-historical perspective, but in Mounier's case the birth pangs were those of a very different revolution. His revolution was joined by participation in a living, dynamic group and self-willed isolation was Mounier's definition of treason. Private life was only valuable in so far as it allowed a man 'to work at the elaboration of some communities to his size and to achieve himself in their heart.'[57] But Mounier thought that he was experiencing the very beginning of the second Renaissance, and that persons living in true communities were still few and far between: 'A great number of men pass their lives without knowing a single true communion. Most never realize more than one, two, three collective persons. A true-love, a true-family, a single true friendship, how many get that far? True communities ... reconcile a man to himself, exalt him, transfigure him.'[58] It was impossible to 'found the community on anything other than solidly constituted persons,' so the fact that they were few and far between implies that the fortunate were obliged to set an example, inspire, and lead as in a religious order.[59]

Did this notion of a spiritual élite smack of fascism? In 'Révolution personnaliste et communautaire' Mounier did, in fact, argue that fascism had carried certain societies 'to the highest form they can assume': 'The collective will is young, effervescent ... a bit drunk on hopes. ... Moreover, there we can grasp in a striking way the drama of what we might call the personal potential of the entire human universe.' Again, however, Mounier was speaking only in terms of the historical process, and he quickly pinpointed the dangers inherent in giving unlimited power to an individual. 'They give a strong man, the excitement of his glory, to a depersonalized mass. That would be perfect if the man were a saint, who would propose to everyone a doctrine and an example of personal regeneration and autonomy. But he only represents the state and himself....'[60] All Mounier's comments on fascism juxtaposed virtues and vices, but he clearly found fascism aberrant. The model for Mounier's 'personalist community' was probably to be found among Roman Catholic religious orders, not in the jack-booted camaraderie of the Brown Shirts.

A certain hierarchy unrelated to class, education, or occupation was central to Mounier's personalist and communitarian revolution. He took over Max Scheler's distinction between the ordinary *Lebensgemeinschaft*, or day-to-day community, in which a man finds himself, and what Scheler called the *Gesamtperson*, or 'person of persons.' Mounier, refusing to use the term 'community' to describe the various inferior sorts of human groupings, saw the only entity worthy of the name as the 'personalist community,' the 'person of persons.' The rest were mere 'societies.'[61]

Hitler vaunted the *Volksgemeinschaft* as the supreme reality. Mounier condemned this as 'a false mysticism,' but linked true mysticism to Christian charity:

In a perfect personal community ... Love alone would be the bond, and no constraint, no vital or economic interest, no extrinsic institution....

Such a community, dreamed of by the anarchists, rhapsodized over by Péguy in his *Cité harmonieuse*, is not of this world. The Christians believe it is living in the Communion of Saints. ... It realizes the perfect Person of Persons, grouping all humanity in the Mystical Body of Christ. ... Every personal community, however impure, is for the Christian an image and a participation in it.

Ever since his student days Mounier had perceived 'spirituality' in non-religious friends. Now he perceived all humanity striving towards what the new Catholic theologians were calling the 'Mystical Body of Christ': every personal community, every 'spiritual' community 'participated' in it. Mounier explained that 'at times, in a love, with a family, some friends, we touch that personal community. A country can approach it in the most beautiful moments of its history.' There was St Louis leading France into the Crusades, and, the 'creation of the collective Person-France, for a certain number of years, with Joan of Arc.'[62]

The main themes of *Esprit*'s personalism were set by these essays of late 1934 and early 1935 and despite vast changes in Europe have not varied to this day. Mounier's 'révolution personnaliste et communautaire' drew from the 'spiritualism' of Henri Bergson, the heroism of Nietzsche, and the anti-individualism and anti-liberalism of the Catholic tradition. He drew also from the sense of great changes in the offing which both fascism and communism promised Europe. To this sense he blended the apocalyptic metahistorical prophecies of Nicholas Berdyaev and the hierarchy of communities of Max Scheler. All this he sought to pull together by the new theology of the Mystical Body of Christ. Mounier proceeded from the Bergsonian study groups, to the 'spiritual friendship' of the Davidées, to the first meetings of *Esprit*, to the mystical notion of a 'person of persons,' with an ineluctable logic. From his student days Mounier relished the experience of communities nourished by the spiritual. They simply became larger and larger in scope, by a process of spiritual annexation.

If personalist revolution seemed understandable given Mounier's peculiar background, how did this idea fire the enthusiasm of so many others? Some of Mounier's friends had Bergsonian or German philosophical backgrounds which warmed easily to ideas such as person, *Gemeinschaft, Gesamtperson*, and so on. Still others, 'friends of *Esprit*' in backwater towns were cut off from the communist or socialist parties by their Christian beliefs. Isolated teachers, architects, engineers, doctors, artists, lawyers, and priests were delighted to find a philosophy which spoke to 'persons' in a despiritualized mass and which offered membership in a local cell and an international movement. Even if one found some of Mounier's rhetoric unrealistic it was stimulating to work with some of France's brightest intellectuals at elaborating something new. If one were a Christian, tied by tradition to inflexible old parties, it was exhilarating.[63] No longer need one feel oneself part of a rearguard for the retreating Christian Middle Ages; one was now in the vanguard of the second Renaissance.

What of Nizan's warning that *Esprit*'s communitarian personalism would constitute a distinctive and artful French national socialist doctrine? As the Communist party began calling for a Popular Front coalition, Nizan said he had been 'on the wrong track' about *Esprit* and was going to admit it publicly.[64]

It has long been acceptable to call oneself a Marxist and reject Stalinism. But what of one who can admire national socialism while anathematizing racism, Hitler, and anti-Semitism? Of the three currents – parliamentary democracy, Communism, national socialism – Mounier's communitarian personalism seemed to draw the most inspiration from the national socialist. The important point, however, is that the differences with national socialism were also great – and crucial to Mounier.

If dictatorship was the only way to reverse the tide of materialism in Europe, Mounier was ready to go along with it. But he did not have his own Joan of Arc waiting in the wings. Rather he insisted on creating a tiny élite of spiritual men and women: 'When Rome fell apart under the barbarian invasion, the Western community gathered around tiny little groups, islands lost in the flood.' For this reason he sought miniscule 'perfect communities' to affect the much larger society in which they existed.[65]

As similar as Mounier was to Marx in seeing events against a changing world historical perspective, Mounier's source of that historical change was the opposite of Marx's. Mounier considered ideas and spiritual forces decisive in history and mystics and saints its vanguard. While in Marx the triumphant proletariat purified the other classes, in Mounier it was the spiritual élites which did so. While Marxists looked back to the Paris Commune, Lenin, or Stalin as prime movers in history, Mounier looked back to the Crusades, Bernard of Clairvaux, Joan of Arc, and Ignatius of Loyola.

Mounier set about trying to form a network of 'persons of persons' to begin the spiritual revolution in Europe. But this required time, a 'pluralistic state,' and a 'decentralized economy.' For this reason he opposed the totalitarianisms with false mystiques which retarded the advancement of the spiritual: 'Only a perfect community has the right to be totalitarian.'[66] Mounier began to commute between Paris and Brussels, trying to work out the guidelines of perfect communities.

A PERFECT COMMUNITY IN BELGIUM

Belgium was one of the few predominantly Catholic countries which industrialized rapidly – and without a significant corresponding decline of traditional religion. This situation resulted, in part, because of the creative responses among Catholics to the problems of economically advanced nations. Mounier and his friends were particularly interested in the initiatives of a young leader of Catholic Action, Raymond de Becker, and, of course, the socialist theorist Henri de Man. Mounier called attention to de Becker's new review, L'Esprit Nouveau, saying he found it remarkably similar to his own.[67] Jean Lacroix hailed de Man's analysis of the relationship between religion and socialism. De Becker soon began to introduce de Man's ideas into the personalist movement. His success reflects de Becker's determined brand of spirituality.

Raymond de Becker had abandoned his studies before university to work for the Catholic Action movement, where he was particularly impressed with the effort of Léon Degrelle to start a youth movement, Christus Rex. But de Becker was less worldly than the brawny Degrelle and was captivated by Berdyaev's notion of a dedicated community of laymen transforming the world by purely spiritual means. With two friends he took up residence in a separate community in the austere Trappist monastery of Tamié, on a barren plateau in the mountains above the lake of Annecy. But after two years there was opposition to a proposed oath of perpetual fidelity and liturgical innovations – such as the mass in French – and de Becker was abandoned by his cohorts. Like a medieval mendicant he set off on foot for Sainte-Beaume in Provence, begging his food and shelter along the way. Like Zarathustra, after a period of solitude in a mountain cabin without water or electricity, he returned to Paris where Maritain, Berdyaev, and Mounier devoured his account of his experiences.[68]

Mounier praised de Becker's variety of 'personalist revolution,' but cautioned that its asceticism seemed only for the few.[69] Just after *Ordre Nouveau* published its 'Letters to Hitler,' Mounier informed Izard that he would no longer work with de Becker.[70] In the January 1934 *Esprit*, de Becker called for an 'army of saints' who were to be 'the dynamite of a Christian revolution.' At the same time, de Man sought to prove that 'a revolution is not made with programs but with strength of soul.'[71]

After the February riots and the *Ordre Nouveau* controversy, Mounier was increasingly receptive to de Becker's conception of saintliness as the cutting edge of social change. For the Belgian, fascism and communism were essentially totalitarian religions which inevitably clashed with Christianity, 'which is itself totalitarian.' While fascisms, according to de Becker, tended to tolerate racism as a subordinate factor in their synthesis, Christianity, too, could respect 'national values and racial values' – but only subordinated in Christianity's synthesis. De Becker outlined in *Esprit* the guidelines of a national Catholic revolution which secured the primacy of Christianity.[72]

Some of de Becker's ideas were suspect, such as his description of his 'Order' as '*national*, because it tends to develop national values, vital values of blood, of the race, of the fatherland against the dissolution of Marxist, Jewish, free-mason internationalism.' Mounier immediately noted in his friend a 'confusion of thought,' at times 'mystical disorder,' as exemplified by 'that premature and unhappy brochure on the national Catholic Order.' But he attributed such errors to de Becker's youth, and still thought that 'something very big' might come out of an order – 'large, situated outside of parties but at the heart of the action.'[73]

In early 1934 de Becker had become director of *L'Avant-Garde*, the Louvain student newspaper which Léon Degrelle had made influential among Belgian youth. Mounier was warned that the paper was receiving German funds, but saw only 'a young, vigorous milieu.' Twenty signed up with the *Esprit* group after his lecture, and *L'Avant Garde*'s editors promised to promote *Esprit*'s circulation.[74] Mounier thought that 'Friends of *Esprit* should become members of the order, and even create a communal residence headquarters with them.[75]

In Paris, Mounier and de Becker went so far as to attend a meeting of young Nazis which Mounier recorded in his diary: 'the German National Socialist students ... tried with remarkable politeness and a sustained and attentive enthusiasm to defend the spiritual values of obedience, total commitment to the leader....'[76] Another night they attended a meeting of the Association des Ecrivains et Artistes Révolutionnaires, after which Mounier concluded that the communists were harder to address than the Nazis: 'Decidedly, nothing can be done with these people. ... At the rear of the hall de Becker and I had our newly composed declaration in our hands. A bomb in that Communist lair? The future will say.'[77] Mounier was clearly infatuated with the idea of a joint project with de Becker, but awaiting him at home was a sobering letter from Maritain.[78] With characteristic clarity and insight, Maritain pointed out the hazards of Mounier's new ally:

My dear Emmanuel,
I have thought about our conversation with de Becker. ... [He has] a great deal of generosity, dynamism, and charisma – [but] an intellectual and spiritual structure which is still insufficient. One does not go into action with that, one does not risk drawing lives into a puerile experience which could turn tragic. ... I have much affection for de Becker, and I would want him to write articles, study, *prepare* to act. But the lack of proportion and of equilibrium in what he is taking on is very dangerous. You had to protect *Esprit* against the 'Third Force.' Be careful not to have an experience even more dangerous with de Becker, because this time the very values which you defend would be involved.[79]

This time, however, Mounier was not prepared to give in so quickly. He confided in his diary that he considered himself, in a sense, a 'feminine force, which wants to be fertilized by outside impulses: that was Izard's role. ... Perhaps de Becker's role is to take the place in my life for which Izard, in spite of everything, was not suited.'[80] After a discussion at Meudon in early June, Mounier, with a certain disingenuousness, thought he could get around Maritain:

There was a good deal of sympathy there, but from intellectuals. Men of action are needed to get off the ground in France, and we still do not have any. The whole range of reactions from Maritain that we have seen before regarding *Esprit*: after the adherence which seemed total, the fears, the slightly shocked letter, the reservations (that one can get a lot out of after the first irritation has passed), and then, when we have been good boys, he gets used to the things accomplished, beyond concepts. We know that he will string along.[81]

Mounier was to learn a lesson. Maritain did not go along, and Paul Vignaux also expressed reservations about de Becker's ideas.[82] One of the young Belgian mystic's quirks was a sympathy for certain aspects of German national socialism. In late June his friend Mèves, who had introduced the program of the early Nazi party in *Esprit*, brought dissident leader Otto Strasser to meet Mounier, and de Becker was even making oblique approving references to Hitler's achievements.[83] In the July *Esprit*, for example, he discussed the amount of time a spiritual revolution would take, in terms that are ominous in retrospect:

Surely it is slow and long when only average men are working at it. But then heroes, geniuses or saints come along: a Saint Paul, a Joan of Arc, a Catherine of Sienna, a Saint Bernard or a Lenin, a Hitler and a Mussolini, or a Gandhi and suddenly everything picks up speed ... human irrationality, the human will, or simply, for the Christian, the Holy Spirit suddenly provides elements which men lacking imagination could never have foreseen.[84]

By this equation Hitler must have been a genius, for presumably even de Becker would have balked at making him a hero or saint. Not surprisingly, this juxtaposition of St Paul, Gandhi, and Hitler troubled the Catholic hierarchy, but Mounier continued to work with de Becker on a movement ('Communauté') to embody their ideas.[85] De Becker was active in *Esprit* in Brussels and Mounier wanted him to move to Paris and try 'spiritualizing' Izard's Third Force.[86]

While Mounier's wing of *Esprit* was engaged with de Becker, Izard's was becoming involved in French politics. On 10 October 1934 Maurice Thorez, in the name of the French Communist party, launched the idea of a broad coalition – from the moderate Radical Socialists in power, through the socialists, and communists – against the threat of fascism. Gaston Bergery had been one of the first to formulate the idea of a broad Popular Front in France and so, despite socialist and communist doubts about his intentions, he seemed at the centre of French politics in these months.[87] Ambitious Georges Izard proposed that *Esprit*'s Third Force place itself at Bergery's disposition. Ninety per cent of the sixty members present at the decisive meeting voted to follow Izard, abandon *Esprit*, and merge with Bergery's Common Front to form the 'Front Social,' dedicated to finding a new third-way political solution for France.[88]

Mounier took a detached view of their departure and told Izard that 'it is not the masses who make history but the values which act on them through minorities unshakeable in their faith'; that only tiny élites could call forth the 'perfection, heroism, sanctity, total giving, sacrifice' from the masses which the spiritual revolution required. He privately regretted the Third Force's political preocupation. As he saw it, 'without ascetism, without reflection on itself, it could only lead to compromises.'[89]

In a series of articles in *Esprit* from November 1934 to February 1935, Mounier tried to define a technique for spiritual means – the difference between his personalism and ordinary politics. He began by insisting that only an individual examination of conscience on the extent of compromises with the sins of the modern world could 'cement a true revolutionary community together.' Revolutionaries fanned class hatred but, like the bourgeoisie, their ideal was a society in which one could 'fill his belly, and go to the movies every night.' He proposed a new, purer, ideal: that revolutionaries *'Centre action on witnessing and not on success,'* and *'treat each man like a person, not as a number.'*

spiritual action ... will guarantee our efficacy....

We can only guess at the first guidelines of properly organic or corporate action. We must ripen them over the coming months. We will not establish them without hesitations, trials and errors: it is contrary to our habits, and difficult, to invent these forms – our imaginations are so deformed....

First of all we must bear witness to our break with the established disorder.

Mounier suggested methods of 'non-participation': refusing to accept the Légion d'honneur, boycotting certain newspapers or books, 'groups of whistlers for insolent shows,' tax strikers, and various other strikes against the state. Loyal personalists should travel in third class, take inferior places in hotels and theatres, abstain from loaning money at interest, and surrender all superfluous income to the community.[90] This mixture of Gandhian non-violence and Péguyiste spirituality was designed to promote a sense of poverty and simplicity. These ideas fit the friends of Francis of Assisi better than they fit the angry young men who stormed the Republic's barricades in the streets of Paris.[91]

In the February 1935 *Esprit* Raymond de Becker thought he had the proper response to Mounier's desire in a new type of monastic lay community:

We need a new Order whose members would consecrate themselves to the re-christianization of the profane, of art, of culture, of political, social, and economic life ... founded on friendship and poverty ... with an intense community and liturgical life, with a profound ascetic and contemplative formation ... for the realization of the Christian revolution in all areas of life, the constitution of a new Christianity, the divinization of the human, of the created.[92]

In de Becker's Order, the interior life and the active charity of the Christian revolutionary would move the masses. The project assumed that an order could transform twentieth-century Europe just as those of Benedict, Francis, Bernard, and Ignatius had in the past. As much as this modern order might appear to be tender-minded, it had a tough-minded dimension. The thirty-three theses of Communauté published in *Esprit* were firmly authoritarian, hierarchical, élitist, and undemocratic. Both Mounier and de Becker recognized only Catholicism as legitimately totalitarian, and for members of Communauté, as in the Jesuit Order, 'true freedom' was in obedience and submission to the rule.

While Mounier lamented Izard's descent into 'mere' politics, he did not seem so sensitive to de Becker's political activities.[93] In 1933 de Man's Plan du Travail had been adopted by the Belgian socialists as the best way to fight the economic crisis. *Esprit* published it with sympathetic commentaries by Jean Lacroix and André Philip in February 1934. De Becker was fascinated by the 'spiritualist' socialism of de Man, and in *L'Avant Garde* called on Catholics to study the possibility of working with the socialists. In December 1934, de Man, now vice-president of the Parti Ouvrier Belge, went to Louvain to meet de Becker and forty Catholic students. The two then exchanged a series of letters in the socialist newspaper *Le Peuple*. Although de Becker's 'advanced' wing of Catholic youth and de Man's socialists were not immediately allied, the two agreed that a new alignment of Belgian political parties was necessary – de Becker criticized Degrelle's rexists as not 'new,' but merely a dissident section of the Catholic party. The de Becker-de Man conversations suggested a possible third way for Belgium – a joining of Catholics, nationalists, and socialists.

Esprit quoted de Man as describing his socialism as 'inspired as much by the morals of the Gospels and St Thomas as by the political economy of Marx,' and himself as 'a thirteenth-century Catholic.' *Esprit* also reported through de Becker on the new faces in the Belgian Workers' party around the deputy P.-H. Spaak.[94] De Man's ideas were studied in *Esprit*'s groups and with André Philip Mounier began giving joint conferences on de Man's ideas in France.[95] The Dominican fathers seemed particularly enthusiastic about these new initiatives.[96] Mounier described de Man as 'nourished by the German experience yet immune from its faults' and inspired by a 'spiritualism so close to being Christian.' De Man's *L'Idée Socialiste* was 'le livre culminant de l'après-guerre,' fundamental for each friend of *Esprit*.[97]

Religious orders for laymen date from the great medieval fraternities of Knights to the Opus Dei founded in Spain after World War I. But de Becker and Mounier's was unusual in so far as it was to be completely independent from the Catholic clergy and 'ecumenical' – attracting men and women of all confessions.[98] It would be the cutting edge of a spiritual 'revolution.'

Despite Mounier's association with de Becker, Maritain continued to join Gabriel Marcel, Landsberg, Le Senne, and Berdyaev in studying the 'person' in Paris. But he warned Mounier of the danger of compromising 'your movement, your mission, through poorly elaborated metaphysics which are not yours.'[99] He urged Mounier to reflect on what the Germans experienced with *Gemeinschaft*:

When religious assemble into a monastery, they do not want to be together, they want to attain perfection – and to be together for that purpose. The feeling of togetherness is a condition and an accompaniment on the material plane which is indispensable, certainly, but secondary.

I believe that the Germans, starved for an emotional unity which could offset many problems, and looking in the area of immanence and subjectivity, are demanding *much more* of the temporal community than it can possibly give: a mystical communion.[100]

When Maritain insisted that the 'feeling of togetherness' in a religious community was 'secondary,' he displayed an understanding of community different from that of de Becker and Mounier, who sought a religious experience in 'the feeling of togetherness.' Maritain reaffirmed the essence of the religious life as the pursuit of individual perfection and salvation.

Maritain was equally troubled by de Becker's suggestion in the February *Esprit* that, in the case of war, the 'revolutionary community' would take precedence over 'la patrie.' At a time when many were awakening to the need to rearm against Germany, de Becker seemed to imply that the international fraternity of spiritual revolutionaries took precedence over national defence. The Dominicans of Juvisy near Paris were excited to be questioned by the police about de Becker's suspiciously 'pro-German' activities.[101] Maritain insisted that de Becker not figure in the special issue on the army which *Esprit* planned for May.[102]

In early 1935 the archbishop's office in Paris issued a private warning linking *Esprit* with the modernism of the Bergsonian Catholic Father Laberthonnière, and Maritain again urged Mounier to screen major writings of Catholics at *Esprit* with theologians.[103] At the founding congress of Communauté in Paris on 14 and 15 April, Mounier found it 'touching to see Maritain and Berdyaev come to sit and listen like schoolboys among the forty young people there.' Mounier, however, was unsettled by a certain lack of solidity, a 'pliability,' in de Becker.[104] The May 1935 *Esprit* noted that 'friends of *Esprit*' and members of Communauté should join in common study sessions, and, if they were agreed, common action.[105]

Neither de Becker's community nor L.-E. Galey's effort to have the third force work with de Becker seemed to catch on quickly. Galey soon joined Bergery's Common Front after all, and de Becker soon seemed more interested in Belgian party politics than in a Franco-Belgian lay order. This second *Esprit* effort to translate the 'spiritual' into practical activity revealed that the more Mounier tried to lead the personalists into 'revolutionary' programs the more he irritated devout Christians. And the more he defended transcendence, the more he exasperated younger friends anxious to translate generous sentiments into practical programs.

Jacques Maritain had profound reservations about the 'impure' politics in both Bergery's opportunism and *Ordre Nouveau*'s rhetoric. Thus it was understandable that Mounier bridled at Maritain's reticence about the young Belgian who had demonstrated an almost heroic asceticism in the medieval mould. Mounier hailed de Becker's determination that the spiritual dimension of existence transform human beings beyond the Maritain salon in Meudon. The great failing of Izard, Déléage, Dandieu, and the rest had been their lack of spirituality, while de Becker, the former mendicant and hermit, seemed a veritable spiritual athlete. Since Mounier believed that God touched people in mysterious ways, his lack of caution about de Becker was understandable. Mounier displayed the same lack of 'discernment of spirits' about Raymond de Becker as de Becker had when he made spiritual comrades of Hitler, Gandhi, and Joan of Arc. However, in the Roman Catholic tradition there was a certain prudence in its response to mystics which Maritain displayed in his analysis of de Becker and his projects. Mounier, inspired by Bergson's adventurous evolutionary philosophy, had thrown much of that customary caution to the winds. This tendency to abandon the ancient discrimination between true and false mysticism left Mounier and his generation remarkably ecumenical, and relatively unprepared for a Europe more and more given to collective frenzies.

6

Controversies, Restructuring, Discipline 1935–7

The extreme ascetism and indifference to politics of the early *Esprit* personalism was soon challenged by a series of international crises. The review's first articles on French foreign policy appeared only after Hitler's reintroduction of obligatory military service in March 1935 occasioned a Franco-Soviet pact. Typically, however, the *Esprit* correspondent in Berlin called for a new St Louis who would respond to German rearmament with 'the only efficacious weapon': 'integral disarmament.'[1] This was an inauspicious beginning for a journal that would fit its post-war editions with trumpetings of its resistance credentials.

The refusal to countenance resistance to Hitler appeared naïve to that hero of World War I and leader of the Fédération Nationale Catholique General Edouard de Curières de Castelnau, who had lost three sons in the war. He championed a two-year conscription law and railed against its Catholic critics as 'defeatists,' if not 'foreign agents.'[2] In the March *Esprit*, Mounier, like his friend Maurice de Gandillac in Berlin, urged his readers to admit to France's faults and seek an inner purification which would foster peace. The big capitalists who would profit from the carnage 'will never have our silence in the face of their enterprise of public deception.'[3] And Mounier challenged General de Castelnau: 'General, three sons, isn't that enough?'[4] This cruel remark, which Mounier saw as 'a blow from God' through him provoked understandable outrage in the nationalist press.[5]

Christian pacifism waxed strong in the debate over the conscription law, and, at first *Esprit*'s anti-militarism could easily have been confused with simple pacifism.[6] But *Mounier* and *Esprit* repudiated most pacifism[7] – and endorsed Péguy's ideal of the Army: 'a powerful mixer of classes, a school of discipline and heroism.'[8] Maurice de Gandillac's on-the-spot observations, particularly when Mounier made a point of defending them, 'situated' *Esprit* in the debate over rearmament.[9] De Gandillac, a former member of the Action Française who had come to Mounier's circle via the Maritain gatherings in Meudon, defended Hitler's 'reasonableness' and displayed empathy for the German people despite the growing influence of Nazism. Since much of the French Left, haunted by memories of World War I, remained resolutely pacifist, the bitterest criticism of *Esprit*'s attitude came from the French political Right, which tried to work against Mounier's review and its sympathizers in the Vatican.[10] In May, Henri Massis read compromising passages from the review to Cardinal Pacelli, papal secretary of state.[11]

Then another young former member of the Action Française and regular at Meudon, Jacques Madaule, ran against Jean Chiappe, former prefect of police, for the Municipal Council of Paris. Madaule associated himself with de Gandillac's call for 'justice and charity for Germany' rather than an alliance against her.[12] His symbolic candidacy (Chiappe was re-elected without difficulty) in the very Catholic quarter of Notre-Dame-des-Champs underlined that another young Catholic intellectual had joined Mounier's circle with its 'revolutionary' rhetoric, questionable theology and marked tendency to accommodate the hereditary enemy across the Rhine.

Mounier encouraged further charges of naïveté when, in May, he and André Ulmann attended a three-day fascist youth congress. Mounier met 'a veritable congress of young French movements in the Rome-Express' on the way there, such as Robert Aron, organizer of the French delegation; Claude Chevalley and René Dupuis of *Ordre Nouveau*; Galey for Bergery's Front Social; Paul Marion of *L'homme nouveau*, Jean de Fabrègues for the Young Right.[13] While the French Catholic press had been generally favourable towards Mussolini's régime, *Esprit* had been more circumspect and Mounier scandalized some of his friends by attending.[14] For its part, the Congress had been partially organized by Professor Ugo Spirito, previously cited in *Esprit* as a creative and original theoretician of fascism, and attracted some important governmental figures.[15] Mounier reported that the majority in attendence were 'bold, radically anti-capitalist and daringly constructive'; their speeches a healthy contrast to the 'artificial ... rhetoric of our politicians.' Mounier cautioned, however, that the 'state' was supreme for the fascists, and the 'person' for the personalists. Therefore, he argued in *Esprit*, one could only wait to see if 'the authentic anti-capitalist spirit which animates at least an active fraction of the fascist world will have the importance and efficacy that we hope it will.'[16]

Privately, Mounier had hopes for a 'fascist Left' in Italy, analogous to the SA in Germany, with roots in the syndicalist tradition and a power base in the workers' organizations of Milan, with Ugo Spirito as the most important philosopher. These elements had organized the Congress and Mounier thought that they might win out in the internal power struggle. Although at the time Mounier disliked seeing Italian priests in fascist demonstrations, 'profaning their cassock,' and knew there were hidden tensions with the Church, he regretted the French ambassador's preventing him and the rest of the French delegation meeting the duce in the palace in Venice. After a fascist's militantly anti-capitalist closing speech Mounier had to admit that 'we were all swept up ... the Congress closed on a note of friendly enthusiasm.'[17]

Years later, *Esprit*'s distinctive early attitude towards the Nazis and fascists was forgotten, although it was one of the most noteworthy themes of the new review. French Syndicates and Christian Democrats sought to rationalize Hitler's activities out of hatred for war and a general internationalist sentiment, but *Esprit*'s line was rooted in neither. Mounier's perceptions were founded in a vision of the evolution of spiritual forces in the twentieth century. His analysis of the long-term meaning of Nazism and fascism, and the possibility of something positive coming from them in the long run, appealed to generous, imaginative young men dissatisfied with the knee-jerk reactions of the French Right and Left. It also brought *Esprit* into some down-to-earth political controversies.

NEW FRIENDS

By the summer of 1935 *Esprit*'s new 'communitarian personalism' was giving voice to an increasingly common aspiration, and a wave of new, talented collaborators began to seek out Mounier.[18] The quarrel over conscription with General de Castelnau caused Roger Leenhardt, who, like André Ulmann, was in the pay of the prefecture of police in Paris, to join other young members of the HSP (Haute Société Protestante) at *Esprit* – notably François Goguel, son of the Lutheran·dean of the Protestant theology faculty of Paris, and Goguel's militantly pacifist brother-in-law, Roger Labrousse.[19] Leenhardt, although originally charged with film reviewing, with Denis de Rougemont and André Philip soon became one of the most fecund Protestant theoreticians of personalism at the review.

Hereafter Aldo Dami, a veteran of *Plans* and partisan of de Gandillac's overtures towards Germany, elaborated a sophisticated and distinctive foreign policy line for *Esprit*. Pierre-Henri Simon, from the Catholic faculty of Lille, began to contribute essays on politics and philosophy, and a book on personalism in 1935.[20] March 1936 saw the first major contributions from a young Catholic political economist at the University of Lyon, François Perroux, who elaborated a 'personalist corporatism' in the review and soon became known as one of the most distinctive and original corporatist economists in inter-war Europe.[21] Perroux joined Lacroix, Denis de Rougemont, P-H. Simon, and Paul-Louis Landsberg as one of the major new theorists of the personalist movement. Perroux's work began to elaborate a social and economic theory for personalism, and soon the planist elements in the hierarchy of the CGT published in *Esprit*. Perroux, too, shared de Gandillac's attitude towards Germany.

Although Mounier's personalism drew people to the review, most contributors did not employ his special vocabulary and some new arrivals did not even take it very seriously. Henri-Irénée Marrou, for example, a young historian teaching in Naples, sent essays denouncing conditions under Mussolini and thought of personalism as a sort of 'handy label,' 'never technically elaborated,' well worth satirizing if taken too seriously.[22] For the Dominican fathers, as for the young philosopher Maurice Merleau-Ponty in bucolic Chartres, Jean Grenier in Algiers, the young law professor Jacques Ellul in Bordeaux, and Jean Daniélou in the Jesuit seminary of Fourvière (Lyon), *Esprit* was simply the most lively vehicle for Christian thought in France in 1935.

Conversely, the summer and fall of 1935 saw Jacques Maritain distance himself from *Esprit*, and neither he, Berdyaev, Marcel, Le Senne, nor any of the older study group in Paris played a central role in the personalist movement after that.[23] The elders (Maritain, Chevalier, Mauriac, Blondel) either openly disapproved of the direction the review had taken or maintained a discrete silence. Mounier's great friend of student days, Jean Guitton, followed Chevalier away from *Esprit* after the Gandillac-Castelnau affairs. Maritain became active at the new, large-circulation weekly of the Dominican fathers, *Sept*, which was critical of the de Gandillac soft-headedness on Germany.[24] Its informed and pluralistic Catholicism seemed closer to Maritain's original vision of *Esprit*.[25] He also joined the new anti-fascist weekly *Vendredi*.[26]

The withdrawal of Maritain as mentor and the last subsidy from Desclée de Brouwer coincided with *Esprit* falling totally under Emmanuel Mounier's sway.[27] What he later called 'a period of commitment' began for the review.[28] On 1 July 1935 there was the first general assembly of *Esprit*'s major theorists at Georges Zerapha's house: Lacroix came from Dijon, P-H. Simon from Lille, and Lefrancq from Brussels.[29] In September the first general meeting of the 'friends of *Esprit*' was held in a youth hostel in the Brie region, with representatives from Strasbourg, Beauvais, Bourges, Grenoble, Marseille, Lyon, Lille, Tours, Montpellier, Dijon, and Avignon, as well as from Brussels, Ghent, Bâle, Rome, Naples, and Madrid. The 'correspondents' for *Esprit* numbered thirty-six in France and thirty-two in other countries.[30] If its circulation figures were not impressive (c1,400 or 1,500 subscribers in 1936), the quality of its essays, the geographical range of its young representatives and their academic credentials – over forty of them *agrégés* – certainly were. Mounier saw *Esprit* as the doctrinal organ of an élite whose views would subsequently filter down to the masses.[31]

At the September meeting, representatives of the groups excommunicated under pressure from Maritain – the old Third Force, *Ordre Nouveau* – were reconciled with *Esprit* and Mounier exulted that they had 'created *Esprit* a second time.'[32] *Esprit* announced it was seeking a 'Third Force,' drawn from all parties, which would surmount the old differences.[33] *Esprit* began a 'Chronicle for a Third Force' and the young engineer Robert Loustau, who had just abandoned an effort to elaborate a social doctrine for Colonel de la Rocque's Croix de Feu, was so enthusiastic about Mounier's idea that, with his fellow veteran of X-Crise and *Ordre Nouveau* Robert Gibrat, he began to plan a central telephone switchboard for French youth movements.[34] Mounier saw the new third force, in contrast to the French Popular Front, as a movement which would ripen among 'a small group of men' and avoid taking 'electoral or partisan positions.'[35]

It was an upbeat moment for Mounier, and on 20 July 1935 he married Paulette Leclercq, an *Esprit* enthusiast despite her upper middle class, 'liberal' (ie, non-Catholic) Belgian family. They moved into the small pink house of Jacques Lefrancq, in a cauliflower garden on the outskirts of Brussels; she continued to work and took instruction in the Catholic faith. In many respects, as demonstrated by a special issue of *Esprit* in February 1936, the third force seemed more advanced in Belgium than in France. While most French intellectuals would have found Brussels dull after the vibrant debates in Paris, Mounier felt at the centre of the action there.

THE JANUS FACE OF COMMUNISM

One of the most unique aspects of the new *Esprit* for young intellectuals was its line on communism – a great challenge to personalists because it was professedly devoted to the liquidation of the spiritual heritage of the

West. Jacques Maritain maintained that atheism was the very linchpin of Marxism.[36] Berdyaev, in the first *Esprit*, praised communism's critique of capitalist society, its rejection of exploitation, its determination to plan the economy, and its evolution towards a theocratic culture analogous to that of the Middle Ages. Still, for Berdyaev, communism's great lie, even greater in magnitude than its partial truths, was its negation of God. The Russian régime had installed a new militant religion, exclusive of all others, 'the religion of the kingdom of this world.'[37]

This spiritualist critique of communism became solidly implanted in the *Esprit* movement and Mounier, much like Berdyaev's admirer Alexander Solzhenitsyn, always looked to the Soviet people as embarked on a great adventure. He saw a country of great human emotions, of suffering and misery which engendered the virtues of authenticity, asceticism, and heroism that he admired.

Esprit presented some sophisticated analyses of Marx by Marcel Moré, and what was intended to be objective information on conditions in the Soviet Union by Brice Parain and various Russian exiles in contrast to the violent anti-communist polemics of many other reviews. So, despite the violent attacks on the new *Esprit* by Nizan, Mounier was the target of some of the earliest communist overtures in the effort to head off fascism in France. In June 1935 Mounier was invited to the Association des Ecrivains et Artistes Révolutionnaires, where he was treated with great deference – Louis Aragon was 'fluttering around me like a little socialite,' he wrote; he noted the 'melting' of communist dogmatism and recognized that the Popular Front was going to be an important phenomenon.[38]

On the other hand, although Mounier had contact with French communist intellectuals – not with rank-and-file members – he still found the same sort of mindless activism that had troubled him in third force enthusiasts and Italian fascists. At the Marxist Congress for the Defence of Culture in June 1935, he noted 'conformity and platitudes: the Great Stalin and the infallible USSR! Same impression as at Rome: sequences of orators ... to draw a semblance of conviction from the masses.' After André Malraux lauded him for giving 'one of the most significant speeches of the Congress,' Mounier saw Malraux 'sign the programs of three or four trembling and respectful workers, acting like an almsgiver towards servants, without ... loosening his fixed smile, nor glancing at them.' In J.R. Bloch and André Gide he saw 'an absurd attempt to identify themselves with a working class from which their own protected backgrounds had isolated them since childhood.'[39] But of all the communist or 'fellow-traveler' intellectuals, Mounier seemed to prefer Malraux in his 'hard and solitary heroism.'[40] Malraux's revolutionaries, strong personalities with a vigorous sense of fraternal solidarity, were praised in *Esprit*, as were the heroes of Malraux's friend from the opposite end of the political spectrum, Pierre Drieu la Rochelle.[41] Mounier seemed more attracted to Malraux's 'Marxists' than to Marxism itself, and Malraux confided to Mounier his own sympathetic interest in some sort of Christian socialism.[42]

Drieu la Rochelle charged early in 1934 that a glaring example of the 'superficiality' of French intellectuals was the *Esprit* group's being 'one hundred per cent ignorant of Marxism.'[43] And, in fact, while French Catholics have looked back to Mounier as a daring pioneer in dialogue with Marxism, he knew very little about Marxism at this time.[44] A Marxist study group was formed only after the riots of 6 February and a promise to Berdyaev to bring some genuinely 'revolutionary' Christians into *Esprit*. Marcel Moré, its director, promised that the group would approach the study of Marx's thought in a neutral, objective way – 'as St Thomas Aquinas had approached the thought of Aristotle.'[45]

Moré, then in his early fifties, was a graduate of the Ecole Polytechnique, a stockbroker managing his own large portfolio, a disciple of Léon Bloy, and a great admirer of the bizarre Catholic 'decadent' J.K. Huysmans. Poorly shaven, with blackened teeth and dark, anxious eyes, Moré published important articles on Marx in *Esprit* before the war, and his own extremely influential ecumenical theological review, *Dieu vivant*, afterwards. Obsessed with metaphysical and religious concerns, his elegant apartment on the quai de la Mégisserie became a salon for his young friends from *Esprit*.[46]

This was a generation of 'conspicuously immature Marxists' in France, as the academic establishment refused to sanction the study of a doctrine considered at best ridiculous, at worst pernicious.[47] Moré soon became, with the great Jesuit expert on Hegel, Gaston Fessard, the only prominent French Catholic intellectual to have studied Marx seriously at the time.[48] His long, sophisticated articles in *Esprit*, from April 1935, underlined the importance of the work of the German scholar Auguste Cornu, who was pioneering in the study of the writings of the young Marx, the humanistic roots of Marx's political thought, and the need for a new definition of historical materialism.[49] Moré rejected the common naïve equation of Stalinism and Marxism, and common Christian critiques of Marx contradicted by the writings of the young Marx. Moré challenged both anti-communists and rigid Stalinists, juxtaposing the riches of Marx's thought to the aberrations of contemporary communism, and thought the *Esprit* movement could help save Marxism: 'it is useless to oppose oneself to an ineluctable revolution that Marxism, with its profound analysis of the conditions in which capitalism was developing, was able to predict more than fifty years ago. Our sole task is to prevent that revolution from stifling man's aspiration toward the infinite.'[50] He argued that Marxism could be radically humanistic: 'If you think that the human personality is something sacred, you shall begin by destroying what oppresses that personality. Marxism can be summarized this way.'[51]

In the first of a series of monthly *Esprit* meetings which began in November, Moré, to an audience of 180 at the Palais de la Mutualité, challenged the Maritain thesis that Marxism was 'pure materialism' and argued that 'spiritualists' ought to complete the work of Marx by reintroducing a personalism for which Marx did not make a place, but for which he left a place.[52] He urged the personalists to study the role of the superstructure in history: 'to complete, assimilate, enlarge Marxism; and for that, utilize, to the great scandal of the Communist parties, all the developments of bourgeois thought since Marx (philosophy, economy, sociology, ethnography, etc....).'[53]

Moré's analyses of Marx, despite similarity to *Esprit*'s after World War II, did not seem to interest many followers of the review at the time.[54] The series stopped in January 1936, just after Mounier learned of a new danger of ecclesiastical condemnation of *Esprit*, with Moré attacking Stalin for having undermined all Marx's aspirations.[55] Enemies of Stalinism could find plenty of ammunition in Moré's essays – and they ran concurrently with a continuing series in *Esprit* reflecting horrendous living conditions in the Soviet Union.

It was Emmanuel Mounier, 'head of a school more than thinker,' who set the personalist 'line' on Marx.[56] In the same April *Esprit* that contained Moré's first article, he enthusiastically praised Henri de Man's *The Socialist Idea*, which also proposed to 'get beyond Marxism' by using the latest bourgeois intellectual advances.[57] As Mounier later observed, the *Esprit* group could never be revolutionary proletarians, 'feeling generations of oppression on their backs,' but were rather revolutionaries through a rebellion 'of intelligence, of sensibility, of spirituality.'[58]

Mounier's own early attitude towards Marxism, more influenced by Berdyaev than by Moré, deferred to social criticism and was sceptical of the metaphysical premises. Marx's thought was faulty, one-sided, rather than 'incomplete.' It was 'a remarkable method of investigation into the human condition,' in which certain analyses 'correspond to the more profound insights of Pascal and of Christianity,' but also a 'totalitarian philosophy' which made 'all spiritual activity a reflection of economic circumstance ... denying the mysteries of man ... menacing the person by the very mechanisms with which it intends to free him.'[59] Unlike Moré, Mounier often blamed Marxism itself for Stalin's despotism. His central concern was with the human person so he saw Marx, the constructor of a conception of man, responsible for the faults of the communists. (Much the same objections greeted Marx's early work. His use of the concept *Gattungswesen* [species-being], an idea derived from Feuerbach, was attacked with particular effect by Max Stirner in *Der Einzige und sein Eigenthum* [*The Ego and His Own*] in 1844.)

Mounier condemned Marxism for denying the spiritual side of man and 'his proper values, freedom and love.'[60] He was less interested in Marx's economics than in his deficient anthropology: 'Four years after his first writings, you did not find Marx, like *Esprit*, involved in concrete issues. ... If he had continued ... not his Hegelian tangent, but studying man and civilization as he had studied economics, Marxism would not, perhaps, be the inhuman thing that it is.'[61] So Mounier blamed Marx for a 'misconception of the interior reality of man' that fostered oppression in the communist state.[62] Like Henri de Man, Mounier urged study of a superstructure to create an equilibrated revolutionary ideology.

On the eve of the April 1936 elections in France the new *Journal of the 'Friends of Esprit'* recommended that Henri de Man's *Au-delà du marxisme* and *L'idée socialiste* be used as basic documents in 'discussions on Marxism.'[63] When Mounier codified his position in the *Personalist Manifesto* a few months later he attacked Marxism for '*a fundamental negation of the spiritual as a primary, creative and autonomous reality.*'[64]

Esprit's position on Marxism was challenged by the 'Marxist' *Terre Nouvelle*, a monthly review founded in 1935 by Maurice Laudrain, a journalist and former secretary to an auxiliary bishop of Paris, with some fiery young Christians impatient with *Esprit* – André Philip, Paul Ricœur, and the mercurial André Déléage. *Terre Nouvelle* perceived social catholicism in need of the scientific base which Marxist economics and sociology could provide, and criticized the relevance of the movements which attracted young Christians of the period.[65] As 'a Catholic student' put it in the second issue (June 1935): 'The revolution, for us, is not a vague and distant dream absolving us from acting in the world of men. ... Social revolution will not be made without some degree of violence. Many

Christians draw back from that idea.'[66] A young Protestant student of philosophy with an important future, Paul Ricœur, expressed *Terre Nouvelle*'s reservations about the esoteric verbalisms of their contemporaries:

Do you truly think something is behind each of those words? Aren't you dupes of linguistic habits? Be careful that socialism does not become mere verbalism. Be certain that there are always ideas behind the words.

...It is with the mass of workers and proletariat, non-capitalist middle classes, intellectuals and artists ... that the socialist order will be made. And this we will repeat again and again to all the constructors of new worlds, who would build without materials, and speak of the new city in select circles: 'You will do nothing without the masses.'[67]

Another contributor emphasized that *Terre Nouvelle* was '*not a doctrinal movement like Esprit* ... but rather a movement of *liaison*, of *solidarity*.'[68] *Terre Nouvelle* ridiculed the idea of transforming the world through 'spiritual means,' and the personalists' 'purely sentimental' fear of 'blood on the pavement.'[69] Even the review's cover symbol – a white hammer and sickle with a cross of red in the background – represented a challenge to Mounier and the *Esprit* group.[70]

The presence of some of Mounier's early associates on this review was compromising for an *Esprit* constantly threatened with ecclesiastical condemnation. *Terre Nouvelle* joined Christianity and revolutionary politics in a way which Mounier knew could never pass the scrutiny of Rome. He attacked them for being 'Catholic communists' and 'Christian revolutionaries,' guilty of the error of his right-wing nemesis General de Castelnau.[71] In Mounier's words: 'to place *on* the cross ... the hammer and sickle, symbols of a temporal régime, is to foster the same confusion as those who put their patriotism and religious faith on the same level.'[72] The Christian Marxist's political hope had to be distinct from his Christian hope or one would deny the autonomy of the spiritual order.[73]

In sum, *Esprit*, on the eve of the crucial spring 1936 elections, had little sympathy for the 'dialogue' proposed by the French Communist party. Brice Parain's horror stories of the Soviet Union were reinforced by the observations of a group of friends of *Esprit* led by P-A. Touchard, who had visited there in the fall of 1935. Few took Maurice Thorez's pretense of independence from Moscow very seriously. While a handful of contributors to *Esprit* – Marcel Moré, Georges Izard, and Paul Vignaux –

found valuable insights in Marx, Mounier led an effort to articulate an original philosophy whose very starting point was antithetical to that of Marx.

NEW COALITIONS FOR A NEW ORDER: BELGIUM

The friends of *Esprit* in Brussels had become so numerous by May 1934 that they had to be divided into three sections. Young Catholic intellectuals in Belgium had been shocked by the condemnation of the Action Française and were drawn to alternatives such as *Esprit*'s Third Force.[74] Raymond de Becker had secured the collaboration of like-minded young Belgians, such as the corporatist theorist Emile Hambresin, whose essays were studied by the *Esprit* groups, and his conversations with Henri de Man during the winter of 1934–5 brought the prospect of an alliance with the new-style Belgian socialism. Since de Man was named minister of public works in March 1935 and had the support of the Parti Ouvrier Belge, the possibility of a 'personalist socialism' of some kind seemed far less remote in Belgium than in France.

In November 1936 Léon Degrelle disrupted a meeting of Belgium's Catholic party and denounced the delegates as corrupt. He launched his own Rexist movement – with violent denunciations of Belgian political parties, capitalism, and parliamentary democracy – and championed rural traditions as the only hope for national regeneration.

The Rexist rallies soon became exalted affairs, with searchlights playing on the speakers, and massed red and black banners. Robert Brasillach helped introduce Degrelle's ideas in France and saw the movement as closer to the Action Française than to national socialism or fascism.[75] Degrelle's lieutenants José Streele and Pierre Daye became frequent contributors to Brasillach's *Je suis partout*.[76] The Rexists, like the early Falange, repudiated racism in their effort to recruit among both Flemings and the French-speaking Walloons. As devout Catholics, the Rexists chanted the Magnificat in the streets of Rome and found Italian fascism more attractive than Nazism. Raymond de Becker, however, dismissed 'Rex' as a right-wing clerical party in early 1936, and called for a true third force in Belgium – closer to the de Manian positions in *Esprit*.

In February 1936, *Esprit* published a special issue setting out the possibilities of a 'new order' in Belgium. In the lead article, Elie Baussart, director of the review *Terre Wallonne*, explained that all young Belgians were united by anticapitalism.[77] The issue went on to explain how acceptance by the Belgian Worker's party of the de Man 'Plan,' of his 'ethical and personalist' socialism, had inspired enthusiasm among the young. The two movements drawing their direct inspiration from *Esprit* – Communauté and Avant-Garde – were singled out as a particularly efficacious catalyst of the third force, for under their auspices Belgian Catholics and Belgian socialists were 'beginning to be conscious of their common orientation.'

For *Esprit*'s friends, Degrelle's movement was 'an unhappy, misdirected manifestation of the noble hopes of youth formed in Catholic Action,' going 'in a direction opposite to our efforts.'[78] Rex's muscled anti-intellectualism had little attraction for the highly educated, spiritually oriented young men around *Esprit*.

In Germany, Otto Abetz, now 'unofficial' representative of Ribbentrop, seemed to share *Esprit*'s view of Belgium.[79] The bilingual, lavishly illustrated *Deutsch-Französische monatshefte/Cahiers Franco-Allemands*, successor to *Sohlbergkreis*, published by Abetz in his native Karlsruhe 'to encourage Franco-German understanding,' devoted a special issue to Belgium which all but ignored the pro-Italian Rexists and saw other phenomena in Belgium as distinctly positive: the 'Arbeitsplan' of de Man and 'the Walloon groups' – Terre Wallonne, Communauté, and the Belgian *Esprit* circle, which were struggling 'against Versailles and for a policy of understanding with Germany.' The review noted that Communauté and *Esprit* tried to bring socialists and even communists together with Catholics to discuss the isuses of the day in a 'pluralist and communitarian' spirit.[80] Indeed by this time Abetz needed all the partisans of an open-minded attitude towards Germany he could find, for in the first week in March, in direct contradiction to the Treaty of Versailles, Hitler had reoccupied the Rhineland.

Although *Esprit* remained primarily a French-based review, by early 1936 the *Esprit* group in Belgium had a broad spectrum of third force allies and the possibility, with Henri de Man, of broadly based Catholic-socialist co-operation. In the May 1936 elections, Rex achieved spectacular success for a new party, but an analysis of the results demonstrated the justice in *Esprit*'s scepticism. Rex won some support from all classes in the countryside, but its urban base was predominantly among the Catholic petite bourgeoisie, with practically no backing among the urban proletariat. *Esprit*'s Catholic-socialist initiative was encouraged when premier Paul van Zeeland named Henri de Man minister of finance in his second cabinet in June. De Man had served as minister of public works despite van Zeeland's refusal to implement the Plan du Travail. Now in June 1936 van Zeeland sought a broad liberal-Catholic-socialist coalition, inspired by the 'Plan,' to respond to the Depression, and to meet the spectacular rise of Rex.

The initiatives of the dynamic Henri de Man, the interest in de Becker of young socialists like P.-H. Spaak, the strong religious sentiments among the Belgian masses, and the shortcomings of Rexist fascism, all suddenly made *Esprit*'s position crucial in Brussels. While in France Mounier's doctrine remained a marginal curiosity, in Belgium it began to catch the attention of individuals with important political futures. The personalists held to an idea whose time seemed to be coming in Belgium.

The fierce debate over the remilitarization of the Rhineland revealed that *Esprit*'s efforts to create a 'new order' in Belgium, its attitude towards Nazi Germany, and its interest in a third force in France, were all interrelated. After the Gandillac-Castelnau quarrel, Aldo Dami, *Esprit*'s most prolific foreign affairs analyst, had generally defended the reasonableness of Hitler's politics, but Mounier had always presented a contrasting view, and insisted, when *Esprit* received a violent reproach from one of its Czech readers, that 'we profess no dogmatism in these complex matters of foreign policy.'[81]

Mounier did become involved in the controversy over the Italian invasion of Ethiopia. After his old enemy Henri Massis and others published a 'Manifesto for the Defence of the West and Peace in Europe' in October 1935, opposing League of Nations' sanctions against Italy, Mounier signed a counter-manifesto with Mauriac, Maritain, Paul Claudel, and other prominent Catholic intellectuals. Although the Manifesto explicitly denied either sympathy or antipathy for Italian fascism, it was taken as an important turning point in the attitude of French Catholics towards Mussolini's régime.[82] Indeed, from this time, *Esprit*, like other Catholic publications, presented several essays sharply critical of conditions in Italy.[83]

Mounier's attitude towards Hitler did not immediately parallel his reservations about Mussolini. When, in March 1936, Hitler used the pretext of the Franco-Soviet treaty to send troops into the demilitarized zone of the Rhineland, French opinion was divided: *Esprit*'s old nationalist nemesis, the *Echo de Paris*, favoured French mobilization but both Léon Blum on the Left and Charles Maurras on the Right opposed a military reaction. In *Esprit* Aldo Dami, a consistent critic of French diplomacy, had been predicting the remilitarization of the Rhineland for some months, and Mounier described the crisis as a consequence of the alliance that *Esprit* had consistently opposed.[84] Mounier juxtaposed Hitler's arguments, which he cited at length – hard, self-evident, forceful – to the 'mediocre,' 'corwardly,' weak protestations of President Sarraut that

France never wanted to attack the honour of Germany. Sarraut, Mounier lamented, governed with regard for the next election; Hitler was beginning a reign of one thousand years. 'It's in those sorts of figures one should count,' wrote Mounier, 'when one makes a policy, shapes or reshapes a nation physically and spiritually, founds or restores a religion.' He condemned Hitler's unilateral repudiation of Locarno, called for league sanctions, and blamed Hitler for the massacre of the 'opposition-ists' and for what was becoming an intolerable totalitarian régime. But Mounier held France responsible for Hitler: 'all the post-war history of Germany is clear if one considers it the revolt of a people against its humiliations.'[85]

Mounier joined the French Committee for an International Plebiscite for Peace, an idea launched by Gaston Bergery so that the threat of war could be revealed as an artificial creation of politicians, and governments would be forced to engage in peaceful negotiations of their differences.[86]

Mounier's injunctions to the French to cure their faults first of all, then the world's (Physician, heal thyself), his solidarity with the people against bellicose rulers, had a Péguyiste, populist Christian orientation. But these 1936 essays also described Hitler, albeit critically, as in some respects offering, an attractive contrast to the flabby politicians of the Third Republic. The führer took the broad view, and was vigorous, decisive, and tough. He certainly was not bourgeois.

The main thrust of *Esprit*'s response to the Rhineland crisis did not entail condemnation of Hitler's bold initiative – in fact, Aldo Dami, Maurice de Gandillac, and Georges Duveau justified it. Rather, Mounier described the situation as making the personalist revolution all the more urgent. What the French needed was also crucial to Swiss, Belgians, and English:

another revolution, which will not only be for or against national socialism but which will be profoundly *other*. Only a personalist and communitarian revolu-tion can assure the dynamic equilibrium of Europe. ... We should not hide the fact that the forces are not yet crystallized on the path of salvation in France. Let this be an occasion to make an appeal to French youth ... that the time makes pathetic.[87]

While the forces for 'personalist communitarian revolution' may not have crystallized in France in 1936, the great coalition of the Left against fascism had. But Aldo Dami claimed that the popular Front could never bring important changes to France.[88] Mounier, for his part, seemed contemptuous of the possibility that the impending French elections could help cure France's malaise. In the middle of the election campaign he ridiculed electoral politics:

A grotesque three-week carnival has just opened....
We have judged it necessary to awaken Frenchmen, who are still complacent, to that scandal: that is why we have given all its grandeur to the German awakening. But beware! That grandeur is a carnal grandeur. It is so to the extent that it annihilates the person while exalting vague enthusiasms and collective deliria. It exposes the mediocrity of our politicians, it is useful to shake small investors from their stupor, but it has nothing to seduce our new forces. ... *The true struggle begins for us there where their grandeur stops.*[89]

Esprit was vehement about the dangers in communist participation in the French anti-fascist coalition.[90] When *Esprit* representatives participated in leftist meetings or publications, they steadfastly promoted a 'personalist and communitarian revolution' as the only hope for France, and it could not be effected through liberal and democratic political structures.[91] The *Esprit* of 1936, Mounier insisted in January, was to continue to work out 'a political philosophy "beyond marxism".'[92] On the eve of the elections, economist François Perroux ignored the French parties and drew attention to the Third Reich. The National Socialist state, he insisted, was constructed on pseudo-absolutes (*'Volk, Rasse,'* etc.) which led to a general disrespect for human persons. But certain structures of the régime, analysed in greater detail in his recent book *Les Mythes hitlériens*, should be studied at *Esprit* because they were 'personalist.'[93]

For *Esprit*, there was something in Nazism that had to be incorporated by Belgium and France. This was not to excuse Nazi barbarism. It was simply that one could not react with complete negativity to a world historical movement of Nazism's scale, as the French Popular Front seemed to propose.

THE POPULAR FRONT: POWER TO THE PEOPLE

An episode in what Mounier called the French 'election-carnival' of April 1936 was Maurice Thorez's radio speech proposing Catholic-communist co-operation

We offer our hand to you Catholic, worker, employee, artisan, peasant, we who are 'laiques' because you are our brother and are weighed down with the same cares as we.
We are the great Communist party, of poor and devoted militants, whose

names have never been mixed with any scandals and whom corruption cannot touch. We are the supporters of the purest and most noble ideal that men can propose.[94]

For some months the French right-wing press had been warning of Bolshevik terror, while left-wing journals had cartoons of Adolf, Benito, and Casimir (De la Rocque) dividing up the map of Europe.[95] Many French Catholics feared a brutal Bolshevik persecution of Catholics, as in Spain and Mexico.[96] Thorez's 'outstretched hand' was thought to have been proferred on orders from Moscow to encourage an anti-Nazi coalition government for war with Hitler – to gain time for the Soviet Union.[97] Christian Democrat candidates, accused of being soft on the 'Reds,' were defeated in Catholic regions.[98]

Favourable reactions among French Catholics to the overtures of the Popular Front were largely confined to the small parliamentary group called the Jeune République, heirs to the Sillon and Marc Sangnier. This marginal political grouping, with only four deputies, offered a sharp contrast to the anti-republican militant right-wing Catholics in this period.[99] But even the Jeune République hardly took Maurice Thorez's offer seriously, and only a few Catholics did – notably an obscure young novelist, Robert Honnert, editor of *Vendredi*, Louis Martin-Chauffier, and the 'Catholic-Marxists' of *Terre Nouvelle*. Martin-Chauffier, a friend of André Gide, had a singular long-range vision in which 'communism would complete Christianity, and Christianity complete communism.'[100] Maurice Laudrain's *Terre Nouvelle* mixed some hot-headed rhetoric with a precocious conception of a classless society purifying Christian spirituality: 'For the reign of Christ, Vote Red' was its election advice.[101] *L'Humanité* gave some prominence to the gestures of Honnert and Martin-Chauffier, which were ridiculed by the Catholic press. *Terre Nouvelle*, however, was violently attacked as heretical by both communists and Catholics.[102]

This minor sidelight to the 1936 electoral battle became of major concern to Emmanuel Mounier. At the end of 1935 Maritain had warned of new rumblings in Rome over *Esprit*'s religious 'syncretism,' and his friend, the Abbé Journet, advised *Esprit* to publish a position paper on its notion of the relationship between believers and non-believers as soon as possible.[103] Mounier quickly complied.[104]

Now a few contributors to *Esprit* seemed to envisage the possibility of a guarded, critical support of the French Popular Front, but in general the review kept its gaze fixed firmly on a distant horizon.[105] The April and May issues contained long expositions of conditions in the Soviet Union by the well-known anti-Stalinist old Bolshevik, Victor Serge.[106] After the election on 3 May, however, much of the bitterness over the rise of the socialists and communists was directed against those who had divided the Catholic bloc, notably the Christian Democrats and *Esprit*'s intellectuals. General de Castelnau violently attacked P.-H. Simon for a controversial book which appeared on the eve of the election and had, for the general, undermined Catholic sensitivity to the dangers in the Blum experience, and in the German threat. Mounier had supported Simon, and so was also implicated.[107]

In May, too, Maritain learned that condemnation of *Esprit* by Rome was imminent: someone had been regularly sending *Terre Nouvelle* to all the cardinals in Rome and now even *Sept* was considered 'red' there.[108] Mounier then learned that the old Gandillac-Castelnau incident figured in the background: inquiries had come from the secretary of state, after an initiative of the ambassador; there had been a 'Castelnau-Pironneau initiative' against *Esprit* in the Vatican. Mounier imagined the Castelnau circle exploiting the Vatican's fear of communism to attack a review for its 'pacifism' towards Germany. Maritain was angry over such ignorant meddling in French Catholic affairs and tried to help clarify *Esprit* positions. Monsignor Courbe, general secretary of Catholic Action in France, asked Mounier for a defence of *Esprit* for Cardinal Verdier; theologian Marie-Dominique Chenu sent a strong letter of support to P.-H. Simon in Lille, which embarrassed Cardinal Liénart.[109] While this threat of condemnation was extremely serious, this time the theological bases for it were not. The papal nuncio had been far more concerned about *Esprit*'s 'syncretism' in 1934 than the Vatican seemed to be in 1936.[110] Then too, Mounier could more easily defend *Esprit* against vague charges of communism than against the quarrels of theologians with his definitions of the spiritual.

After the victory of the Popular Front there was a certain disparity between Mounier's public and his private reactions. Publicly, in the June *Esprit*, Mounier greeted the coalition of the Left with 'a fraternal salute to the victor' and described his feeling of 'profound joy' at a popular triumph which made him recall his own humble origins. He argued that the socialists could perform necessary surgical operations, 'clearly prescribed in the papal encyclicals,' like 'dismantling of the financial fortress of capitalism, the abolition of the trusts and financial oligarchies ... the nationalization of public services ... the abolition of the proletarian condition ... the collective organization of production, the substitution of a contract of association for the salary contract.' Mounier urged support for the Front's initiatives promoting social justice but also re-emphasized the ever present danger of a 'materialistic dictatorship.'[111]

Privately, in the *Journal intérieur des groupes d'amis d'Esprit*, Mounier stressed the fact that Georges Izard had been elected, in the first ballot, as deputy for Bergery's Parti Frontiste from Longwy. Izard and other comrades of the Third Force had given a 'new style' to Bergery's movement; now, Mounier hoped, Izard would prove himself capable of resisting 'the virus of parliamentarianism.'[112] For Mounier, in the circle of his friends, the election of Bergery and Izard was a major event. Despite the left's victory he tried to keep attention focused on the 'movements' which could foster the 'Révolution Personnaliste et Communautaire' and not the 'parties' in power.

Mounier's private defence of *Esprit*'s positions for Cardinal Verdier also stressed the originality of *Esprit*'s efforts. Young French and Belgian Catholics used *Esprit* to 'work out non-communist alternatives on the institutional, social, and economic plane.' The communists, he boasted, could no longer 'accuse the spiritual of evading problems of technical efficacity.' The *Esprit* movement, he claimed, was '*almost alone among the ... movements of the young to oppose communism on the metaphysical plane at the same time as competing with it* (in so far as four years of effort can struggle against fifty), *even on the plane of technical research.*' Mounier also argued that the time had come for Catholics to penetrate all non-communist, political groupings. And already 'the contacts that *Esprit* has been able to establish ... can be put to the service of the spiritual interests of the Church ... to normalize and spiritualize impetuous forces.'[113]

Although Maritain and Mounier consciously wrote this report to harmonize with the 'reflexes, habits, and clichés' of the ecclesiastical administration, it was a fair reflection of the *Esprit* group's attitudes at the time.[114]

It was soon clear that Rome was less concerned with the theological ideas of *Esprit* than with the political situation in France. But the victory of the Popular Front did not spark an offensive against Catholics. Léon Blum's moderation and scrupulous respect for legality and the communists' refusal to participate in the government allayed conservative fears.[115] Finally, by the end of May, France experienced an unprecedented wave of strikes despite the efforts of Blum and the communists to head them off. Several prominent French Catholics were moved by this great popular demand for a more fraternal and just society.[116]

What finally provoked the pope was the suggestion that pragmatic co-operation between Catholics and communists might be possible. On 10 June Mounier learned that the Christian Democratic daily *L'Aube* had been the object of suspicion, not *Esprit*.[117] A subsequent decree condemning *Terre Nouvelle* warned the faithful 'to distrust ... (even under the pretext of friendly teamwork to promote charitable works), collaborations of Catholics with the partisans of Communism.'[118] Indeed certain Christian Democrats had seemed far more interested in working with communists than had Mounier and his friends, and *Esprit*, in this case, was left undisturbed.

During the night of 7–8 June 1936, Léon Blum, the CGT, and representatives of the French factory management association (CGPF) worked out the 'Matignon agreements,' which helped provide some of the most important benefits gained by French workers to that time – the forty-hour week, paid vacations, the right to collective work contracts. Nevertheless, for the next week, the mass strikes continued regardless of the appeals of the Left leadership.

During these tumultuous days Mounier, despite the excitement of the French political scene, left with his wife for a two-week visit to Denis de Rougemont in Frankfurt am Main, where the latter had been an exchange professor since December. De Rougemont took his visitors to a night-time Nazi rally, which he later described in his diary:

The choir spoke: 'We were wallowing in the mud, held to the ground and humiliated....' Some mournful and muted rolls of drums. 'The people were divided, led astray....' We heard the sounds of civil war, cries, a machine gun, fragments from a disorderly, quarreling choir of voices. Gloomy silence. Then a clear voice shouted: 'But the old Germanic legend told us that the Liberator would descend from the snowy mountains....' Popular singing, then fanfares: 'The old legend has become reality! *He* has come to reawaken his people!'....

The drama is visibly inspired by the Protestant liturgy; it copies the general format: Decalogue, confession of sins, promise of grace, credo.[119]

Returning to Paris at the end of June, Mounier was invited to a debate on Christianity and communism with Paul Nizan and André Malraux. Nizan insisted that the party wanted to encourage collaboration in the spirit of the Popular Front, but without a terrible doctrinal 'confusion' like *Terre Nouvelle*'s. Mounier was interested in André Malraux's claim that Marxism held to the same moral values as Catholicism but simply wanted to humanize them. Marxism, said Malraux, wanted man to enjoy his faculty for creating gods, 'to divinize himself': 'the revolution is thus his divine element.' The three talked on into the night on these themes.[120]

After the well-publicized Christianity and Communism debate Mounier returned to Belgium for a longer private dialogue organized by

Edouard Didier on an estate near the seacoast village of Zoute. The 'Didier salon' in Brussels was frequented by Otto Abetz, who sometimes spoke under the auspices of Didier's bulletin *Jeune Europe*, which favoured rapprochement with Germany.[121] Its program for European federalism, in turn, had been reported in Abetz's *Sohlbergkreis* – and *Esprit* – as offering hope for a new order in Belgium.[122] Mounier had, in *Jeune Europe*, called for the revsion of the Treaty of Versailles in Germany's favour and a European federalism, and was invited to the 'Jeune Europe international camp' organized by Didier for dialogue with the Hitler Jugend from 11–19 July.[123]

In May, Henri Nicaise had presented the conclusions of 'the sub-group on international questions' of the Brussels *Esprit* group: French foreign policy was 'dangerous for European reconciliation,' and Germany's peace propositions were 'very healthy,' although some details should be provided regarding Hitler's intentions in eastern Europe.[124] In the Zoute camp in July, Mounier proferred these themes with the German delegation led by M. Schultze, führer of the Hitler Jugend. Mounier, according to the Brussels personalist newspaper, also 'remarked how he understood the historical reason for the German national movement ... but also how most of us had the impression that the national aspect of Hitlerism had suffocated its socialist tendency.' Mounier and his friends criticized the Nazi identification of the state with the *Volk* and also 'the underlying attitude of Nazism regarding life':

we think that the popular community has no other raison d'être than to permit each person to accomplish himself, while the Hitlerites think community to be an end in itself. Schulze [sic] honestly recognized that there one touched ... the essential divergence between the personalist and the National Socialist conception of life.[125]

But there were still also broad grounds for agreement in 1936: 'On international affairs, on the contrary, everyone remarked an almost complete agreement and real possibilities of collaboration....'[126]

The remilitarization of the Rhineland in March 1936 marked a turning point as the French Right then joined the Briandists in opposing armed intervention against Hitler, so *Esprit*'s position was less isolated than before.[127] There was also pacifist sentiment among the leadership of the French CGT – men like Léon Jouhaux's heir apparent, René Belin, and Belin's chief 'theoretician,' Georges Lefranc, in the French Socialist party (SFIO), and among writers such as Alain, Céline, Jean Giono, Magdeleine Paz, and Simone Weil, who were militantly anti-Soviet.

After the confrontation at Zoute, Mounier settled in an isolated Belgian farmhouse and put together in five weeks a synthesis of the positions elaborated over the previous months.[128] This 'common testimony of *Esprit*' attempted to prove personalism to be a 'third way' between capitalism and communism, a distinctive alternative to the Popular Front if that faltered.[129] The *Personalist Manifesto*, shorter and less philosophical than *Révolution Personnaliste et Communautaire*, articulated the basic doctrine of the personalist movement. The *Manifesto* was also verbose, abstract, and difficult to read. But Mounier came down more strongly against Italian fascism and Marxism and presented a more subtle analysis of national socialism than he had earlier. Borrowing from François Perroux, he also sketched the 'structures of a personalist régime.'

The *Personalist Manifesto*'s Third Way did little to encourage co-operation with Blum's coalition, or with Marxism.[130] Since the Spanish Civil War had begun, the French communists had created tensions within the Left by calling for aid for the republic. The *Manifesto*'s suggestion that nothing could be done with Marxists unless they abandoned several basic tenets of their ideology did not encourage co-operation.

The July 1936 *Esprit*, devoted to syndicalism, did not promote co-operation with communists either since it contained an essay by Georges Lefranc, the young ex-normalien influential in the CGT's Bureau d'études, which was modelled after that of the Belgian Workers' party. The Plan of Economic Renovation created by Lefranc and his friends had been presented to the National Committee of the Popular Front but since 1934 the socialists and communists had attacked the 'fascist plan of the CGT.' When Lefranc's chief, René Belin, proposed the nationalization of banks, credit, insurance, railroads, electricity, and mines, the communists, promoting the broadest possible coalition, and a delicate rapprochement between France and the Soviet Union, accused the planists of demagoguery. After the CGT congress in March 1936, which saw the fusion of the communist CGTU with the dominant CGT, Belin and his lieutenant Lefranc emerged as key figures in the planist, pacifist, and anti-communist wing of the CGT. When, after the Matignon meeting, Léon Jouhaux, had to admit to Lefranc 'that no structural reform inspired by the Plan of the CGT had been accepted by the government,' Lefranc and other young 'planists' such as André Philip began to contribute to *Esprit*, and Lefranc began asking *Esprit*'s help for his worker education projects.[131] The inclusion of these young Turks in the journal did much to radicalize the journal politically.

Esprit at this time also published Victor Serge's detailed information on concentration camps, prisons, deportations, and surveillance in the Soviet Union.[132] Serge, a Bolshevik who had participated in the revolution, had been persecuted by Stalin. *Esprit*, along with *La Révolution prolétarienne*, the review of 'revolutionary syndicalism' to which the *agrégée* factory worker Simone Weil contributed, had followed the Serge affair; and when he was liberated he brought his horror stories to *Esprit*.[133]

Despite attacks on *Esprit* by Soviet propagandists as late as August 1935, the French communists of *Commune* had, in the spirit of the Popular Front, engaged in a series of 'dialogues' with Mounier.[134] But after the Serge revelations Georges Sadoul warned of the new role of 'Trotskyists' at *Esprit* and noted *Esprit*'s silence on the Civil War in Spain despite 'the clear pro-Republicanism of at least a fraction of its friends there.' Although *Commune* soon declared itself reassured about *Esprit* 'at least as far as the events in Spain are concerned,' the personalist review had not responded to the 'outstretched hand' in the manner of a review which the *Action Française* continually denounced as left-wing.[135]

Those in the *Esprit* group are often remembered as among the few French Catholics who were in the French Popular Front. But in fact this whole episode illustrated *Esprit*'s unwavering determination to create a 'new politics' on its own. Mounier's *Manifesto* clearly reaffirmed *Esprit*'s determination to follow its own path. Victor Serge's revelations about the Soviet Union, and Blum's spurning of the 'planists' of the CGT, complicated *Esprit*'s relationship with the Popular Front. Mounier, for his part, seemed to operate on a different wavelength.

ANARCHISM IN SPAIN

After the events of 18 and 19 July 1936 it was clear that the rebellion against the Spanish Republic, prepared for some time by Francisco Franco and three other generals, had the support of the financial establishment, most of the Church, the Carlists of Navarre, the 'fascist' Falange, the army and the police – and, it was known afer a few months, Germany and Italy. On 19 July the president of the Republic, Manuel Azana, tried to form a new government uniting all the forces of the Left, and to that end he sent a telegram to Léon Blum requesting arms and planes. Blum's first thought was to aid the sister Popular Front across the Pyrénées. But given the violent anticlericalism in the Spanish Left and the firm support of the Spanish hierarchy for Franco, most prominent French Catholic spokesmen opposed French intervention in Spain. In a widely circulated article in *Le Figaro* on 25 July, François Mauriac warned of civil war in France, and Blum had to take this threat seriously.[136] Devout French Catholics seemed almost united en bloc against him on this issue. *Esprit* reinforced its reputation for unorthodox opinion on foreign affairs at this point. Mounier, the Catholic, appeared to endorse the pro-Republican positions of its most prominent Spanish correspondents José Bergamin and J.-M. Semprun y Gurrea. They had, according to Mounier, found themselves between 'two walls of hate' and opted for the Republic, where they found the most sympathy for *Esprit*'s ideals.[137]

Mounier drew accolades from *Commune* and strong criticism from the confessional press, and especially Chevalier and Maritain. He had, however, not necessarily fixed the review's position: each national contingent of the 'friends of *Esprit*' was autonomous and the Spanish group had been one of the most liberal, along with the American, where C.G. Paulding cited *Esprit* as a viable liberal Catholic journal to Eleanor Roosevelt.[138] Mounier tended, on principle, to support the initiatives of the national groups; in Belgium this meant supporting P.-H. Spaak's effort to create a Belgian national socialism, in Switzerland it meant working with Dr Oprecht's tiny Swiss Socialist party, and in Spain within a 'Popular Front' government. The spirit sometimes moved in strange ways.

Many on the French Left supported the Partido Obrero de Unifación Marxiste (POUM), the party of dissident ex-communists founded by Joaquín Maurin. It also had the sympathy of anti-Stalinist Russian exiles at *Esprit*. Mounier reported in his private *Journal Intérieur* that *Esprit*'s influence in the republican government, besides Semprun and José Bergamin whom André Malraux portrayed as Garcia in his novel *L'Espoir*, included two ambassadors.[139] Semprun's vague hierarchical personalist political model for Spain was dutifully printed in *Esprit*.[140] But while *Esprit* blamed the nationalists for the war and had great sympathy for its friends within the Azana government, it did not declare its unqualified support for the republic.

In October *Esprit* published two essays on Spain: in the first Semprun denounced the Christian crusade myth of the nationalist forces while in the second 'AMV' opted for a double rejection, a position of neutrality in the conflict.[141] Mounier's introduction seemed to favour the Semprun position, but he privately assured Jacques Chevalier that *Esprit* was 'leaning towards a double refusal' in Spain, a position which Maritain also supported.[142] Nonetheless the mere refusal of Franco's Christian crusade was already a daring stance for the handful of French Catholics who adopted it.[143] Mounier's reasons for refusing to endorse the 'Catholic cause' in Spain were similar to those of Maritain and the Christian

Democrats: freemason generals, Moorish mercenaries, and 'the old feudal establishment, and the new feudalism, the bank' had unleashed an unjustifiable war.[144]

The republican forces, for Mounier, contained interesting elements – the POUM and anarchists – who might well turn the Spanish Popular Front into a new Third Force. Thus in early 1937 *Esprit* devoted considerable attention to syndicalism and to anarchist theories, presenting the views of René Belin, deputy secretary of the CGT, and Paul Vignaux for the CFTC. Vignaux, disquieted over the authoritarianism of his fellow *Esprit* contributors, stressed the dangers to syndicalist independence and liberty in André Philip's or de Man's 'planism.'[145] Jean Lacroix suggested that a pluralistic CGT might absorb the Christian union – one-third its size – and thereby counterbalance its recently incorporated communist minority (ex-CGTU).[146] The brilliant social critic, mystic, and CGT militant Simone Weil, inspired by her visit to the POUM and shocked by the CGTU effort to dominate the congress of the Union of Syndicats in Paris, also urged that the CFTC join the CGT to offset the growing influence of the Communists.[147] Mounier asserted, in March 1937, that after Victor Serge 'it was no longer possible to confuse the workers' movement and communism.'[148] *Esprit* described 'Stalinocracy' 'besieged by the hatred of an oppressed people.'[149]

For the April 1937 *Esprit* special issue on anarchy and personalism Mounier produced a long and extremely abstruse essay, with citations from Bakunin, Kropotkin, and Proudhon, to demonstrate the compatibility of Personalism with anarchism.[150] Then Jean Lacroix's short, equally opaque, book articulated 'the Proudhonian and democratic line of Personalism.'[151] Since Lacroix had introduced the authoritarian socialism of Henri de Man into the personalist movement, his effort to incorporate Proudhon into 'the great personalist tradition' required a gymnastic manipulation of abstractions.[152] An historian sympathethic to *Esprit* has argued that economic ideas of the review had 'their source in the Proudhonian tradition tempered by the planist ideas of Henri de Man.'[153] It is perhaps more accurate to describe them as rooted in Henri de Man, and corrected by the Proudhonian tradition, when the personalists were making overtures towards the French syndicalist movement or the Spanish Popular Front.

In the early months of 1937 the communists established discipline and efficiency in the loyalist war effort and determined to make the Spanish Popular Front thoroughly communist. In the spring the tension between the Communists and the POUM erupted into three days of bloody street fighting in Barcelona. Mounier's warnings about Communist intolerance of Third Way solutions seemed justified.

In June, after the bombardment of Guernica by German planes, Mounier joined Maritain, Bourdet, Mauriac, Marcel, Merleau-Ponty, Vignaux, Borne, and other French Catholic intellectuals in 'an appeal in defence of the Basque people.'[154] At the same time Mounier presented conflicting interpretations of the Barcelona fighting, by José Bergamin, who defended the communist position, and Victor Serge, who described a Stalinist grab for power in the loyalist forces.[155] An accompanying editor's note seemed to favour Serge's position – and thereby strongly qualified *Esprit*'s support for its Spanish correspondents.[156]

Privately, in response to Jacques Chevalier, who condemned *Esprit*'s complacency towards Spanish communists despite the new encyclical *Divini Redemptoris*, Mounier explained *Esprit*'s line on Spain:[157]

[in] that Encyclical ... I find only encouragement to persevere in our Third Way....

Note that *Esprit* will always be the first, in Spain and elsewhere, to struggle against the Communist menace. Our friends were convinced that their attitude was the only one which could free the Republic from Marxism, without delivering it to totalitarianism ... *Esprit* ... defended a republican legality against perjuring generals and the threat of a fascist state under Germano-Italian influence – that is against those who will be dressed tomorrow against your sons and your country. It defended the possibility of evolving in a non-Marxist direction....[158]

But *Esprit*'s hope for a Third Way in Spain troubled Jacques Maritain. He protested to Mounier in July about the Spanish anarchists: 'There are certainly some very noble personalities among them, but also some scoundrels. ... The present fashion in France among young revolutionary intellectuals for anarchists and anarchism is a stupidity. I know that you agree with me on that, but I think you give too much space to a Victor Serge.'[159] In reply Mounier assured Maritain that he was breaking from Serge.[160] *Esprit*'s flirtation with anarchism was over.

In the summer of 1937 *Esprit* was silent on Spain because of the 'Stalinist tendencies' in the republic.[161] Its final comments on Spain in April 1938 were denunciations of communist tyranny by Victor Serge and Simone Weil.[162] When Semprun complained of *Esprit*'s posture towards the anti-fascist cause, Mounier replied that the review could support neither side.[163] Mounier then denounced anarchism as a puerile and irresponsible ideology that had much to do with the failure of the third way in Spain.[164]

Esprit's refusal to support Franco added to the review's maverick reputation among Catholics, and it was, given the threat of troubles with the Church, highly courageous. However, it was no more a simple left-wing position than was *Esprit*'s line on the French Popular Front. In both cases Mounier held to a vision of a third way.

TOWARDS A BELGIAN NATIONAL SOCIALISM

In the summer of 1936, while Spain was sliding into civil war, there was a great struggle between the Belgian political factions under behind Prime Minister Van Zeeland, and Rex. After the May elections, Degrelle planned a March on Brussels in October at which he expected to draw 250,000 militant rexistes and push the king towards granting him the total political control he coveted. *Esprit* was involved in the contest through its commitment to a third way Catholic-socialist coalition. Raymond de Becker was proposing concrete political initiatives in his Catholic student newspaper at Louvain, *L'Avant-Garde*, whose circulation under its previous editor, Degrelle, had climbed to 10,000.[165] De Becker's Communauté movement had attracted young men from a variety of backgrounds: a former secretary of the Communist party, a libertarian, the socialist Léo Moulin, militant Catholic Henri Bauchau, co-founder of *L'Esprit Nouveau*, and Louis Carette and Albert Lohest, friends of *Esprit*.[166]

In Belgium *Esprit* was thought of as 'young socialist' like the French reviews *L'Homme Nouveau* of 'neo-socialist youth,' edited by E. Roditi and Paul Marion, *L'Homme Réel* of 'syndicalism,' edited by Pierre Ganivet, and *Ordre Nouveau*.[167] French neo-socialists, particularly Marcel Déat and Pierre Ganivet, an architect of the Plan of the CGT, had, like *Esprit*, been diffusing de Man's ideas among the French intellectual élite.[168] The several young De Manians at *Esprit*, critical of the Catholic party but hostile to Rex, put it in the de Man-Van Zeeland camp.

But the great inspiration of *Esprit*-Belgium was the mercurial Raymond de Becker. In July 1936, he went to Hamburg for the International Congress on Workers' Vacations, then to Berlin and Bavaria. He was particularly impressed by an evening he spent as the guest of Joachim von Ribbentrop, where he noted the 'democratic origins' of the young men around Ribbentrop. On his return he organized the first visit of the National Socialist press to Belgium, and explained to the readership of the *Cahiers Franco-Allemands* the differences between the Rexist and

Communauté currents of 'Belgian nationalism.'[169] Around Christmas, personalists Emile Hambresin and Marcel Vercruysse, representing Belgian youth, joined Max Liebe and the Hitler Jugend in a ten-day ski camp at Winkelmoos.[170] Early *Esprit* supporter Henri Nicaise found the Hitler Jugend's 'Communitarian idea ... really fundamental,' 'transcending all barriers of class and religion.'[171]

De Becker met the young socialist Paul-Henri Spaak, who shared an admiration for 'some of Hitler's magnificent achievements,' but Spaak 'thought the price of importing them into Belgium too high.' In the fall of 1936 both men were interested in a 'personalist socialism' but in succeeding months, in de Becker's words, it was progressively more rooted in the nation and national traditions, 'becoming for us, more and more, a national socialism.'[172]

In October 1936, one of *Esprit*'s Belgian correspondents, Guy Malengrau, imperiously informed Mounier that the 'spiritual decline' of three centuries would be reversed within four years and that *Esprit* had better engage itself politically or it would be outdistanced by history. In response Mounier reaffirmed a lofty notion of *Esprit*:

Do you know where souls [craving the spiritual] were, around 450, after four centuries of patrology, and preaching, and the supernatural influence of Christ on top of it? At a vague sauce of Gospels and of Seneca, of Cicero, of Plato, Epicurus, Plotinus, some Persians, some Alexandrians, etc.; still obliged to sweat through years of meditation before they could even conceive of an immaterial God.

...Because those who husband the eternal have lost the sense of the temporal, let us not lose, in the rediscovered temporal, the sense of the eternal.[173]

He did not shrink from applying this perspective to Raymond de Becker's news:

The leaders of *Communauté* have, in practice, deserted *Esprit*. I believe this was a grave error, and harmful – and for *them*! By that decision they consolidated that divorce between intelligence and action that we were fighting together....

P.S.: It goes without saying that the offer of liaison that I have ten times proposed to de Becker remains one-sided.[174]

De Becker, for his part, reviewing Mounier's *Personalist Manifesto* in Spaak's *Indépendance Belge* on 21 January 1937, cited 'the enormous possibilities for personalism in Belgium.'[175] But he shared all Malengrau's disdain for *Esprit*'s hesitancy and thought *Esprit*'s collaboration seemed more and more 'purely intellectual.' He found Mounier 'the very archetype of the pure intellectual, impervious to reality, for whom everything terminated in abstractions.'[176]

While de Becker, in a November 1936 conference at the University of Berlin, saw the concrete internal political situation in Belgium leading her to 'a new position in international politics,' Mounier published an abstract of his philosophy in Abetz's review.[177] The *Cahiers Franco-Allemands/Deutsch-Französische Monatshefte* rarely discussed ideologies in France and Belgium, outside the 'Planism' of de Man, Marcel Déat, and Paul Marion, and the 'fascist socialism' of Drieu la Rochelle, but it returned to a critique of the personalism of Mounier and Denis de Rougemont.[178] Again the person was set against the *Gemeinschaft*. De Rougemont considered the differences in the philosophy less important than the bases of agreement.[179] Mounier, in *Esprit*, insisted that German socialism was incomplete.[180] For him a proper definition of the 'person' was more important than raw political power.

When Degrelle's March on Brussels in October 1936 drew only a few thousand supporters he precipitated an election for the following April. In March 1937, however, Pius XI's encyclical *Mit Brennender Sorge* unequivocally condemned certain Nazi doctrines. In April, two days before the elections, Cardinal Van Roey formally condemned Rex. With the Catholics divided, Degrelle's subsequent electoral defeat marked the beginning of Rex's gradual decline.[181]

Degrelle's lack of urban support seemed to confirm the analyses of Raymond de Becker and *Esprit* that Rex was not the vehicle to transcend Catholic conservatism, and both relished the opportunity to spark a new political coalition.[182] In the summer, members of *Communauté* discussed the prospects for a 'new socialism' with the Brussels *Esprit* group, and in November Mounier intensified his contacts with 'young de Manian socialists ... the living element of the party.'[183] Soon the Belgian *Esprit* group was promoting a new coalition of Catholics, socialists, and liberals; the *Journal intérieur belge des groupes Esprit* stressed the new political void: 'the first coalitions which were conceived four or five years ago, outside of parties, notably between young Catholics, liberals and socialists were submerged by 'rexism'. ... It seems urgent to us to take up their formation once again...' It was decided 'to meet with M. Henri de Man to study the directions in which an activity inspired by the works of the author could be undertaken.'[184]

The decline of Rex also inspired hope in Otto Abetz's Belgian expert,

Max Liebe, who identified a watershed in Belgian politics with the declaration of P.-H. Spaak, in February 1937, that the hour of Belgian national socialism had come. He envisaged a Spaak-de-Man-Rexist alliance.[185]

In January 1938 an *Esprit*-Brussels spokesman complained of the Belgian government's inability to institute a strong anti-capitalist program: 'The 'Plan du Travail' aroused legitimate hopes. Hasn't Henri de Man forgotten it today in his budget preoccupations? ... and P.-H. Spaak ... his 'authoritarian democracy?' Belgium was described as divided and waiting for the crystallization of a new political force.[186]

In January 1938 Raymond de Becker announced to the Brussels *Esprit* group publication of a new review backed by Spaak, *Les Cahiers Politiques*, which was going to try 'to disengage a new political line outside of systems' and would be inspired by 'a politics of the person.'[187] Albert Lohest, of *Communauté*, the Didier salon, and the special study group on 'social renovation' of *Esprit* at Liège, and *Esprit* economist François Perroux would participate.[188] Still, despite the central role of its friends, the Belgian *Esprit* group was 'disquieted by certain patronages and certain possibilities of deviation,' and 'some doctrinal exaggerations' in the project.[189]

Indeed by February 1938 the Spaak-de Becker initiative became controversial. After violent denunciations of de Becker's presentation to them appeared in the press, the Belgian *Esprit* group limited its meetings to members only.[190] Henri de Man, frustrated at the parliamentary régime's inaction, resigned his ministerial post that same month, and, like Spaak, began urging Belgian neutrality after the anschluss in March.[191]

Despite his own anti-Nazi position on the anschluss, Mounier supported the original Spaak-de Becker position, in the summer of 1938, as a model for France: 'our Belgian comrades ... watched over, ripened, and joined an interior transformation of the Socialist party germinated under the influence of Spaak.' The socialist parties in Switzerland and Belgium, transcending 'bourgeois' social democracy, had produced 'socialist surgeons ... under the intellectual influence of Henri de Man, who are pursuing vigorous paths, often close to ours.'[192]

The Munich Agreement in October caused deep divisions in the French and Belgian intellectual communities. When Raymond de Becker explained Spaak's national socialism to the Belgian *Esprit* group in October, communist spies infiltrated the meeting and more controversy resulted, including dissension among the personalists.[193] An essay in the November *Esprit* described Spaak as working with pro-Nazi groups and recommended that France take steps before Belgium was irretrievably pro-Nazi. But in December *Esprit* ran a defence of Spaak, and Mounier concluded that the question was 'still open.'[194] Some of *Esprit*'s best-known Belgians – Elie Baussart of *Terre Wallonne* and the novelist Charles Plisnier – were demanding reaffirmation of Belgium's alliances with France and England, while Raymond de Becker drew ever closer to Nazism, and felt 'liberated' in leaving the Catholic Church at the end of 1938.[195]

In May 1939 Henri de Man, with the support of Spaak, was elected president of the Parti Ouvrier Belge. His authoritarian socialism promised the reform of the state through a reinforcement of executive power. It was a 'national socialism' drawing both the proletariat and the middle classes into the struggle against capitalism, and a 'neutrality' which would preserve Belgian national independence. The following summer Otto Abetz was denied entry to France, where he was said to direct a spy ring and furnish lavish publication subsidies, but he was able to visit Belgium. There he joined Max Liebe, attaché to the German embassy, in encouraging the Didier salon's core of 'young intellectuals of the Spaak-de Man-Van Zeeland school' to prevent Belgium from entering the war on the side of the allies.[196] The French government was forced to set up a counter-espionage unit to counter the influence of the 'Ribbentrop stable' in Brussels.[197]

In September 1939, with the declaration of war, Belgium was resolutely neutral. Henri de Man was made a minister without portfolio but, feeling isolated, resigned after a few months.[198] In October, Raymond de Becker, discretely supported by Spaak and aided by the writers Robert Poulet and Pierre Daye of Rex, founded a weekly newspaper, *Ouest*, to reinforce neutralist sentiment. In the spring of 1940 it received a substantial contribution from Liebe.[199]

Throughout 1939, and until the German occupation in June 1940, *Esprit* kept complete silence on the political situation in Belgium. In early 1939 Mounier, his wife, and Jacques Lefrancq were searching for a large property to house the *Esprit* community near Paris. Mounier had decided to help a movement of national renovation in France.

When de Becker opted for a Belgian national socialism in early 1938, the worst fears of Paul Nizan and Jacques Maritain were realized: Mounier's doctrine seemed transmuted into a crypto-Nazism. Personalism had transcended the world of small-circulation reviews and become, in the imaginations of de Becker and Spaak, the future orientation of the whole of Belgian society.

By the fall of 1939, a few Belgian *Esprit* figures had come out for all-or-nothing resistance against the Nazis but the review had also encouraged 'neutralism' and nourished speculation about how a 'revolutionized' Belgium might find a place in a Europe dominated by Germany. De Becker, enthralled by the vision of a dawning European golden age which came to him at the Ordensburg in Bavaria, soon called for a Europe dominated by Adolf Hitler.

In view of the disquieting evolution of some Belgian personalists, *Esprit*'s silence in this area is surprising. Mounier simply pulled up his stakes and returned to France, where he determined to run his own movement in his own way. It is difficult to say what he had learned – or failed to learn – from the evolution of his erratic former partner.

DISSIDENCE, EXCOMMUNICATIONS, NEW ALLIES

The faltering of the French Popular Front, particularly after Blum announced a 'pause' in its program on 21 February 1937, did not discourage the *Esprit* group. Although the Front had brought a quadrupling of subscriptions and influence among intellectuals as far away as Latin America and Canada, Mounier was dissatisfied with *Esprit*'s situation in France, where it recruited only in a limited 'intellectual and bourgeois milieux.'[200] To help create a political alternative in France, Mounier backed fusion with *Ordre Nouveau* at the *Esprit* Congress of 26–7 September 1936 and then, a few months later, helped form Clubs de Presse, in which *Ordre Nouveau*, Gaston Bergery's *La Flèche*, and *Esprit* joined to publish objective news unsullied by capitalism.[201] There was serious resistance to fusion with *Ordre Nouveau*, but Mounier was determined to form a more broadly based, and more disciplined, movement.[202]

Mounier tightened up the movement by making more stringent requirements for membership in the Friends of *Esprit* and by defining a more explicit ideological formation. Jacques Perret, director of the *Journal Intérieur*, wanted to distinguish 'friends' from mere 'sympathizers.' He suggested that each local group require of its members a common agreement on 'our fundamental positions,' that is, as contained in the *Personalist Manifesto*. He also insisted on a regular material contribution – either money or service, and regular attendance at meetings – despite the fact that these proposals had already met with much resistance from the local groups.[203]

In the spring of 1937 Perroux, Lacroix, Madaule, and de Rougemont began to visit Friends of *Esprit* in an orderly fashion in French cities as well as Brussels. While local 'friends' might number only ten or twenty, a public lecture such as by Perroux at Montpellier could draw as many as 500–600 auditors.[204] These talks contributed to the movement's ideological coherence, as did a recommended reading list for the Friends of *Esprit* with books by Henri Davenson [Marrou], Lacroix, Maritain, Robert Aron, Dandieu, de Man, Ramon Fernandez, de Rougemont, and P.-H. Simon. For good measure the list added Conrad Heiden's *History of National Socialism* and the studies of Serge and Souvarine on the USSR. More than half these authors were not Catholics and several did not even employ personalist vocabulary. *Esprit* was firmly rooted in 'personalism' but it was also in search of new allies for the spiritual revolution.

By the early summer of 1937 *Esprit* was also involved with certain key intellectuals of the syndicalist movement. Pierre-Henri Simon and other were working on a theory for transforming French education according to 'personalist and communitarian values'; the young producer Pierre Barbier was laying plans for companies of actors to leave the big cities and tour from village to village across the country.[205] There was a group of involved novelists and artists as well, including Marc Chagall, and François Perroux was using Henri de Man's theories to rethink the French state along corporatist lines.[206] Mounier was co-ordinating the whole, with the *Personalist Manifesto* as the point of departure.[207]

In the July 1937 *Esprit*, Roger Labrousse hailed the accomplishments of the Blum government – on its resignation.[208] Only a few months earlier, Roger Leenhardt had raised questions about the 'curiously nuanced reception' which Esprit had given to the Popular Front.[209] Unlike Leenhart and Labrousse, most at *Esprit* had all but ignored Blum's initiatives and followed Mounier in working towards something new. In his *Journal Intérieur*, Mounier described the *Esprit* Congress at the end of that month as decisive for the review, marking 'the end of our youthful years, and a great growth in size of the movement.'[210]

The congress held at the Ecole du Montcel in the countryside at Jouy-en-Josas drew 154 representatives from twenty different French cities as well as from Tunis, Casablanca, The Hague, London, Cracow, Naples, Madrid, Zurich, and elsewhere. The two-day program included the reports on education (Simon *et al.*), the state (Perroux), and the personalist doctrine (Mounier), and marked the fruition of Mounier's effort to rebuild *Esprit*.[211]

The organization of the personalist movement became tangibly tighter: the *Journal Intérieur* was 'strictly private' and no extract from it could be reproduced without Mounier's permission; the Friends of *Esprit*, which became 'Esprit groups,' were subjected to disciplinary standards.[212] Finally, Mounier expected members to drop what they were doing and meet him in a city he was visiting.[213] All this was challenged at Jouy, but there was as yet no question of purging recalcitrants.[214]

At Jouy study groups were directed by Landsberg (anthropology), Merleau-Ponty and Lefrancq (psychology), and Perroux (the problems of 'authority' and 'the function of the leader').[215] The Esprit doctrinal group met twice each month in Marcel Moré's apartment and attracted Berdyaev and Maritain as well as younger lights – Merleau-Ponty, Vignaux, Landsberg, Borne, Ellul, Jean Grenier, Abbé Journet, Lacroix, et al.[216] At this time Mounier discovered the essay Energie humaine by the Jesuit paleontologist and theorist of evolution Teilhard de Chardin; since Teilhard was forbidden to publish by his ecclesiastical superiors, his work was in mimeographed form. Teilhard, although living in China through most of the nineteen-thirties, was close to the Jesuit novice master at Fourvière, Henri de Lubac, an early backer of Esprit, and his essay was replete with personalist vocabulary. The December 1937 Esprit heralded Teilhard's work as of 'an exceptional importance': 'how reassuring ... that idea of the "human convergence" of movements at present violently opposed to one another: "May the democrat, may the Communist, may the fascist push the positive aspirations which inspire their enthusiasm to the limit, and plenitude".'[217] Mounier's belief that there was an element of truth in all strong beliefs coincided with Teilhard's vision of the inevitable spiritualization of humanity. In turn, such men who saw an inevitable convergence between all vital human commitments, could hardly see the Europe of 1937 locked in a life-or-death struggle between civilization and barbarism. Mounier and Teilhard seemed to envisage the reversal of the process of 'despiritualization' so troubling to Catholics – not a terrible war.

In the confidential Journal Intérieur, in October 1937, Mounier lamented Esprit's past sympathy for the Left: 'we have not yet begun to disassociate ... from the ideologies and politics of the Left with the same vigour that we applied to disassociating the spiritual from the reactionary.' Now, with the faltering of the Blum coalition, much had changed:

The Republic is dying comrades, as are peace, the laicisards, democracy, democrats, the representative régime, the parliamentarians, liberty, liberals, and the popular cause of the politicians, the madmen and the materialists, just as surely as the Christianity of the Pharisees, and the spiritual of the works of spirituality.

Because we have already marked the history of ideas and the play of forces with our disassociation of the spiritual (notably Christian) from the established disorder; we have not yet marked as momentous ... a disassociation of justice, civilization, and the people from the meagre, lamentable ideologies of the Left. ... I am calling on all of our friends ... to undertake that task.

He called on *Esprit*'s collaborators to undertake 'a general revision of the values of the Third Republic' and of 'the democratic idea.'

Mounier's call for a critique of the Left was anticipated at the Jouy congress by Perroux's announced intention to have his study group discover 'a new philosophy of democracy.'[218] Although this sort of *volte face* for *Esprit* elicited little reaction from most of the regional *Esprit* groups, Mounier went ahead to assign individuals to analyse the industrial proletariat (Simone Weil), the agricultural proletariat (Braibant), artisans and small businessmen (Izard), functionaries (the provincial groups), employees (Tessier), industrial and commercial cadres (Robin), middle-sized and large employers (Serampuy [Goguel]), doctors (Dr Vincent).[219] Various French political parties were also assigned to various individuals. François Perroux, according to Mounier, had already formulated plans for a 'personalist economy' that took a 'radically new direction.' Once they were completed, the *Esprit* groups would spread it among economists, technicians, industrialists, and syndicalists.[220]

Perroux's new prominence at *Esprit* reinforced its anti-democratic orientation, as did the influence of Henri de Man's ideas, much in evidence at *Esprit* when Mounier was already working with 'De Manian socialists' in Brussels and in Zurich.

Transformation of the review from a free and open laboratory of ideas into the organ of a disciplined, ideologically coherent movement soon brought the dissent of several important young intellectuals. The director of *Esprit*'s research group on psychology, Maurice Merleau-Ponty, *Esprit*'s correspondent in Chartres and signatory of several 'Left Catholic Manifestos,' bailed out after the Jouy congress despite Mounier's appeals, and in so doing abandoned both the personalist movement and Catholicism to become a prominent phenomenologist and Marxist political theorist.[221]

For Mounier, however, the disaffection of 'Merleau' was less important than the apostasy of Jacques Ellul and Bernard Charbonneau. Both were Protestants – Ellul a convert from Judaism – and their Bordeaux group was one of the most active. Ellul had already begun the critique of the technological society which would make him famous. He had been involved with both *Esprit* and *Ordre Nouveau* from the beginning and among the Bordeaux group's imaginative projects were experiments with communal living in the Pyrénées and its own bulletin, *Le Journal Intérieur des groupes personnalistes du Sud-Ouest*.[222] At the Jouy meeting Mounier had criticized 'secessionists' who had refused to meld into the 'new force' launched at the Congress, and, in January, openly ridiculed the Bordeaux group – 'camping, above all camping; outside of camping no salvation.'[223] For Ellul, Mounier had become 'extremely authoritarian' and would no longer tolerate opposition within the movement.[224] Ellul and Charbonneau and the 'Personalist groups of the South West' severed their ties with *Esprit*.[225]

Another revelatory quarrel involved Christian Syndicalist leader Paul Vignaux, an ardent proponent of trade union liberty, who attacked the authoritarian and corporatist theories of François Perroux. Silence, reservations, or outright opposition on the part of important thinkers such as Berdyaev, Gabriel Marcel, Maritain, Merleau-Ponty, and Vignaux was the price that Mounier had to pay for the movement's attachment to Perroux.

After the 1937 congress, *Esprit* made overtures towards *Ordre Nouveau*, the *Nouvel Age* of George Valois, the Jeunes Groupes Duboin, and 'revolutionary' elements in the CFTC.[226] In January 1938 Mounier directed his colleagues' efforts to the reviews *Nouveaux Cahiers* and *Jeunes*, the technocrats involved in the projects of Jean Coutrot, *La Flèche*, and the young syndicalists at *L'Homme Réel*. Followers of *Esprit* were to fight for personalist ideas in these circles.[227]

In 1938, several *Esprit* people – Moré, Landsberg, de Rougemont, Reinach, Vignaux, Gosset, Chatreix – began working at the review *Nouveaux Cahiers* with young technocrats such as Dautry, head of the French railways system, his lieutenant Jean Jardin, of *Ordre Nouveau*, and the militant syndicalist become Christian mystic, Simone Weil.[228] This extension of *Esprit* influence among 'men of action' conformed very well to Mounier's desire.

Another *Esprit* lien was with the small Swiss Socialist party, directed by the Zurich bookseller, Dr Oprecht. Oprecht published an essay on Switzerland and quietly attended the Jouy congress.[229] The *Personalist Manifesto* inspired the study program of the Swiss Socialists' Centres of Worker Education and Federation of Co-operatives.[230] Oprecht's admiration for Henri de Man and André Philip helps explain his interest in *Esprit*: Mounier spoke there and, as cryptically noted in the *Journal Intérieur*, 'his anti-Marxism was expected, and welcomed.[231] The Swiss Socialist party was very small and Switzerland's political situation far less dramatic than Belgium's. But an international network of de Manian socialist theorists seemed to be forming with *Esprit* as a hub.

Esprit efforts to penetrate French political groupings were mostly directed towards the socialists and the CGT. At the end of 1937 Georges Izard left Bergery's *Parti Frontiste*, notorious for its 'pacifist' line on Germany and authoritarian socialism, to join Edmond Humeau, L.-E. Galey, André Déléage, and Georges Duveau in working for 'the personalist tendency' within the divided SFIO.[232] *Esprit* also worked with the CGT's Collèges du Travail – similar to Oprecht's Workers' Education Centres – at Georges Lefranc's urging.[233] *Esprit* loyalists helped oppose the communists' efforts to draw syndicalism into an 'anti-fascist crusade,' but any personalist 'conversion' to the SFIO was tenuous.[234] With the bitter divisions over Munich at Christmas 1938, and the victory of socialists demanding a firm anti-Nazi line, Izard, Déléage, Duveau, and Galey, joined by Jules Romains, declared their independence from the SFIO with a polemical book calling for the dismantling of parliamentary institutions and the 'radical interior rebuilding' of the country.[235] In retrospect we know that these efforts to influence the SFIO and CGT were co-ordinated, secret, and intended to help promote total national renovation.[236]

In February 1938, the *Esprit* study projects formed a Comité directeur of Madaule, Touchard, Landsberg, and Perroux, to meet bi-weekly in Marcel Moré's apartment and report on their respective groups.[237] The new spirit of *Esprit* group meetings was now proudly antithetical to 'liberalism.'[238] At the next *Esprit* congress, Mounier announced, only recommended individuals would be admitted.[239]

Mounier's obituary for the Popular Front in March 1938 noted that it had lacked 'a strong spirituality which could have inspired men, articulated doctrines, and formed characters.'[240] That same *Esprit* demanded 'a plan,' 'a disciplined revolutionary politics,' and 'leaders with the required authority' strong enough 'to break with the routines' of the old, to 'create new values for France.'[241]. Mounier's passionate essay called for a new doctrine for the Left inspired by Nietzsche and Dostoevsky, André Malraux, and Henri de Man.[242]

Esprit's call for a new politics in France was accompanied by an endorsement of the Spaak-de Becker cabal in Belgium. But a few days after this issue the anschluss with Austria was consummated. French domestic politics were pushed into the background as Hitler began pressuring Czechoslovakia. Nevertheless *Esprit* did not abandon the search for total renovation in France as Mounier pushed, with ever more urgency, for discipline, a concrete program, new alliances, and a broadened base. He remained convinced that Personalism was the last, best hope of France.

Why did Mounier, after 1937, suddenly try to make the personalist movement so ideologically coherent and tightly disciplined? Even old *Esprit* hands Ellul and Vignaux, who objected most strongly to the new direction, were relatively silent on the matter. Maritain did not publicly comment, nor did Merleau-Ponty even after he left the Catholic Church. Perhaps most thought it only logical that Mounier react to the spectre of war by gathering his loyal friends into tightly organized formations. What other method could one anticipate from the personalist leader? If personalism was the key to France's salvation Mounier could be expected to use it. If Mounier was 'going fascist' neither the anti-fascist *Esprit* dissidents nor his old communist critics reproached him at the time. His concentration on his ideas and his élites seems to have been generally respected and understood. This says a great deal about the ideological desperation in French intellectual circles at the time.

7

Esprit and the Onslaught of Hitler

Esprit was unique among French reviews in the number of its collaborators who had German philosophical roots. Many *Esprit* partisans betrayed admiration for the German National Socialists' spirit of *Gemeinshaft*. The early French personalists' sympathy for the 'revolutionary' wing of the National Socialist movement helped explain their shock at the consolidation of power by Hitler. Perhaps the very ties with the 'Voelkisch' or 'Europeanist' national socialism of Strasser and the 'social democratic' national socialism of Otto Abetz encouraged *Esprit*'s disdain for the militarism of the Wehrmacht and the imperialist Nazism of Rosenberg and Himmler. The kind of national socialism favoured by the personalist movement was revolutionary, spearheaded by youth, and involved European federalism. In the young Otto Abetz's words, 'the meeting of nationalisms, sure of themselves ... will reinvigorate our Occident....'[1] The future of Europe depended on the Nordic and Latin peoples, conscious of their common Greek cultural heritage, uniting against the materialistic barbarians threatening from the east.[2] The romantic vision of the francophile Abetz attracted 'spiritual revolutionaries' repelled by Stalinist tyranny and sensitive to the injustices inflicted on Germany after World War I. But Abetz was only a counselor to von Ribbentrop, himself a counselor. Nor did Europeanist national socialism often correspond to the immediate strategic interests of the Wehrmacht. Furthermore, Rosenberg and Himmler were convinced that only Germanic élites should dominate Europe and that 'nationalisms sure of themselves' were enemies of the Reich. This internal conflict became evident during the german occupation of several European countries.[3]

In 1936, Emmanuel Mounier thought 'communitarian feeling' 'one of the most exciting psychological aspects of the Nazi vision of the world.' He found the essays of a group of young Nazi theoreticians of community suffused with 'freshness' and 'health,' and agreed with their analysis of 'the solitude of modern man.' Only when Nazi community was one 'of blood and race' was Mounier 'radically opposed' to such 'biological dogmatism,' this 'new form of rationalism and materialism.'[4] Mounier's seized an opportunity in Abetz's review to clarify the basic philosophical differences between his sense of the person and that of the Germans:

is the person the *primacy* of man over matter, or indeed only a lien which would attach the individual to the collective spirit? All of our opposition to fascism and to national socialism resides ... in that definition of the person. And we consider ... that German socialism, like Russian socialism moreover, could only be one stage – perhaps necessary *in that country* – towards integral personalism, the natural and spiritual end of the civilization of the West.[5]

On the German side, too, there was a flirtation, on grounds equally hard to follow from a modern perspective. Hitler Jugend were interested in the French personalists because of their strength in the provinces, especially in Grenoble and Lyon. German National Socialist youth tended to think *montagnard* peoples superior to plains dwellers and had a special interest in the young Frenchmen who had grown up near the highest mountains in Europe. French youth visiting Abetz in Karlsruhe were taken on a ritual hike up the Sohlberg, from whose summit they could glimpse the magnificent spires of the Cathedral of Strasbourg.[6] From 1934, the Hitler Jugend organized ski vacations with young Lyonnais and Grenoblois, and Abetz's circle maintained a special interest in French Alpine regions and peoples.[7]

In the same February 1937 issue in which personalism was analysed, the *Deutsch-Französische Monatshefte* suggested that a Germanic people existed in the high mountain valleys southeast of Grenoble. According to legend, the 'Alleman' family, holding all their possessions in common, from time to time descended from their mountain fortress 'bearing the banners of Uriage or Valbonais' to reassert their dominance over the people of the Grenoble plain.[8] Four months later in the *Monatshefte* François Berge, who the next month became director of *Esprit*'s 'ethnology study group,' described the populations of Savoy and Dauphiné, with their blue eyes and pink skin, as a sort of 'Nordic' race in France.[9]

Mounier was proud of his Dauphiné ancestry, but for the values he inherited, not the racial characteristics. Nevertheless, Raymond Millet of

Ordre Nouveau published a pamphlet analysing 'alternatives to communism,' wherein Mounier is described in 'ethnographic' terms: 'that idealist seems more of Nordic origin, tall and blond like the Scandinavians, at once gentle and rough like them, he knows how to show in his eyes – pale but changing like the water of the cold seas – friendship, will, and irony in turn.'[10] Millet's profile of a Nordic Mounier was repeated by the German author Paul Distelbarth in his survey of new movements in France which were interesting from the National Socialist point of view.[11] Distelbarth, who had met Mounier in Paris, situated the ideas of *Esprit* between those of *Ordre Nouveau* and Marcel Déat, and also praised the thought of Catholics Teilhard de Chardin, Gustave Thibon, and even the strong anti-Nazis Cardinal Verdier and Maritain.[12] He warmly dedicated a copy of his book to Mounier just after the latter's denunciation of France's compromises with Nazism at Munich.[13]

Esprit's personalists were not – unlike Jean Luchaire, Bertrand de Jouvenel, and the Comité France-Allemagne – singled out by the Hitler Jugend for their efforts to promote Franco-German understanding, nor, unlike Alphonse de Chateaubriant, for their attitude towards Hitler. Rather, like the 'neo-socialism' of Déat and Marion, the 'fascist socialism' of Drieu la Rochelle, and the *Plan* of Henri de Man, Mounier's personalism was seen as an initiative towards a 'new order' in France. Philosophical differences were obvious to both sides and Abetz's review covered all bases by hailing the French Scouts, the Jeunesses Patriotes, the Croix de Feu, and above all, the Action Catholique de la Jeunesse Française as other movements which contributed to the 'new consciousness' (*neues Bewusstsein*) required for a new French socialism.[14]

GERMAN EXPANSIONISM: THE END OF DIALOGUE 1937–9

In February 1937, the *Ordre Nouveau* circle published a periodical to promote a 'revolutionary consciousness' among syndicalists in France. Edited by Millet, it was notably sympathetic towards several Nazi domestic programs.[15] This was one of the last personalist efforts to promote Franco-German understanding. In March, Pope Pius xi's letter *Mit brennender Sorge* defended basic Christian principles against the myths of blood and race and infuriated the Nazis.[16] While *Ordre Nouveau* continued to publish articles favourable to a 'pure,' 'anti-statist' national socialism – 'the contrary of "fascism"' – *Esprit* seemed awakened by the papal admonition.[17] In the summer, Mounier both documented the persecution of Catholics in the Reich and underlined his differences with the pro-Nazi

French Catholic Alphonse de Chateaubriant.[18] Mounier granted that Hitlerism had 'reawakened the old sources of German poetry,' but castigated the bearded poet for ignoring the 'night of the long knives,' the concentration camps, the ss, the situations of the Jews, and all the aberrations cited in *Mit brennender Sorge*.[19]

In November 1937 *Esprit* published further evidence of disquieting developments in the Reich. An anonymous author explained that until 1935 the Nazi party had tried to use the 'German Christians' – a liberal, anti-Barthian, left wing of Protestantism – against orthodox German Protestantism. The failure of this tactic now led the government to support 'neo-pagan, germano-deist' movements inspired by individuals like Rosenberg. Such tendencies were alien to the Christian faith, but intended to achieve some sort of a synthesis with Christianity. The Hitler Jugend began to avoid religious services. The Nazis wanted a more Voelkisch education in which the Old Testament, the Jews, and the teachings of St Paul would be de-emphasized in favour of a Nordic Christ.

Mounier was particularly concerned with the new ideological orientation of German youth movements and requested a report on this matter from the German Catholic thinker, Romano Guardini.[20] *Esprit* was not averse to ecumenism, but its definition of the 'spiritual' was within the Judeo-Christian tradition; Mounier found Chateaubriant's notion that Hitler was 'hand-in-hand with God' absurd.[21] Finally, notwithstanding *Esprit*'s sympathy for German territorial grievances and its disdain for conservative Catholics, the personalist savants were incensed when the Nazis harassed Catholics, as in Austria.

In 1935 a young historian active at *Esprit*, Philippe Wolf, visited the heartland of Habsburg glory and found the high Alpine redoubts above Innsbruck and Salsburg crawling with young national socialists. Symbolically, 'Heil Hitler' was replacing 'Grüsse Gott' as the common greeting on the mountain paths. Towards the end of 1937, militant national socialists, encouraged by Berlin, were active in the cities of Austria. By the following March, Hitler had succeeded in forcing the assassinated Dollfuss's successor, Kurt von Schuschnigg, from the Austrian chancellorship and his Nazi replacement, Seyss-Inquart, called in German troops.

Esprit, in contrast to most French Catholic publications, had never been particularly sympathetic to the conservative, clerical régimes of Dollfuss or Schussnigg. But in the April 1938 issue, under the title 'Some Men Resist ...' Mounier warned that 'with the Nazi anschluss it is not ... only Germany which is extending its shadow over Europe: it is fear, and soon the hatred of spiritual liberty and of any style of civilization that could be founded on it.' After noting that the 'Christian state' of Dollfuss had shamefully massacred workers and that now Cardinal Innitzer welcomed Nazi troops in Vienna, Mounier drew a parallel with Spain: 'a Christendom which gives such signs of weakness, at Vienna and Madrid ... is a dying Christendom. ... Defeats, blood, and despair ... will be necessary before a new Christendom can regain its heritage from the ruins of nineteen centuries of effort.'[22]

Esprit still stopped far short of a call to arms against German expansion. In fact Aldo Dami, while regretting the violence of the anschluss, justified the fait accompli.[23] Mounier and Jacques Madaule tried to focus attention on the internal situation in France.[24] 'Never,' Mounier wrote, 'have the terms French revolution, national renovation ... taken on a more precise and more urgent meaning. France is, in this month of March, like a rich man who has suddenly been ruined. ... Strengthened by our new poverty, and the courage which a certain despair provides, we may more easily ... undertake enterprises with some scope.'[25] This 'French renovation' had nothing to do with the efforts of Léon Blum or Paul Reynaud to form a national union government to face the threat. Rather than worry about ministries, supply lines, or armies, Mounier's France would purify herself through a national revolution led by her youth. But how were the young to face the Wehrmacht? Place flowers in the Panzers' gun muzzles? Mounier simply decreed that a long and bloody purgation was coming.

In the May 1938 *Esprit*, Perroux called for a new sort of national anti-Marxist socialism, and Mounier privately urged *Esprit* groups to broaden the base by integrating divergent philosophers into doctrinal discussions.[26] In July, Lacroix, suggesting an imminent 'dismantling of socialist and communist élites,' called for the rediscovery of 'the authentic French revolutionary tradition' represented by men such as André Philip, Gaston Bergery, and Georges Izard.[27]

Esprit's search for an authentic French revolutionary tradition became centred largely on trade unions and education. Paul Vignaux and Charles Blondel stated their fears about corporatism, but Mounier also published essays by Georges Lefranc and Perroux and came out in favour of their 'communitarian' corporatist views.[28] Along with Henri de Man, Perroux had become a leading expert on German labour policies and favoured a disciplined, orchestrated economy for France.[29] The August 1938 *Esprit* pushed for revamping French educational institutions along personalist lines.

The second Jouy Congress of the *Esprit* groups, held 26–31 July 1938, found two-thirds of the editors of the review already in uniform. It was announced that the failures of Georges Izard and André Philip in the French Socialist party confirmed the difficulties personalists had in working effectively within a social democratic context.[30] On the other hand, François Goguel saw hope for Bergery's 'Frontisme' now that personalists like Robert Aron were elaborating its program.[31] There was hope, too, for personalism within the CGT following a repetition of Georges Lefranc's request for the *Esprit* group's 'discrete' collaboration in the workers' Colleges.[32]

Mounier dismissed the old 'non-conformism' of the youth groups between 1930 and 1935. In an ecumenical spirit he cited André Malraux and called for a new, virile union of the young, a 'third force' free from the 'prejudices' of the Left and the Right. He hailed the Belgian personalists and Belgian and Swiss 'de Manians' as models. Despite a glimmer of hope for 'an entirely new tendency' in the French socialist party through the efforts of Izard, Duveau, Galey, and Philip, he admitted that *Esprit*'s influence was still limited – one city's Jeunesses Socialistes had adopted *Esprit*'s ideas, the federal secretary of the SFIO in a department of the west belonged to an *Esprit* group, and so on. Progress was being thwarted by groups such as the Christian Democrats of the PDP, and the Jeune République with its 'frenetic' attachment to parliamentarianism and electoralism.[33]

Mounier proposed that the *Esprit* political line be articulated more precisely. For this purpose he initiated 'Voltigeurs,' a small cell of political analysts within each *Esprit* group. A new weekly journal, *Le Voltigeur français*, directed by P.-A. Touchard, who had directed the old *Front Social* sheet for Bergery, began with essays from Mounier, Lacroix, and Madaule.[34]

In September, on the eve of the Munich capitulation, Mounier denied that *Esprit* was either essentially Catholic or leftist.[35] In the midst of the Munich crisis he confided to a friend that he foresaw the possbility of a French 'semi-fascism,' and, in *Esprit* he called for 'the revision of democratic values and structures.'[36] He did, however, violently denounce the weaknesses France and Great Britain were displaying in negotiations with Hitler.

By the summer of 1938 the anschluss had made it difficult to maintain a 'balanced' approach towards Hitler and German National Socialism. Yet the formation of the Voltigeurs showed that the *Esprit* group held to the notion that France needed a radical, authoritarian internal transformation to survive, and that some positive elements in National Socialism had to be incorporated into France. At the same time Mounier's opposition to Nazism kept hardening. Such confusion in directions was slow to surface in the journal itself. While *Esprit*'s Aldo Dami, regretting Hitler's methods, justified Austria's absorption into the Reich, Roger Labrousse saw little hope for France resisting Hitler's pressure on the Czechs, and urged a great effort to avoid war over the Sudetenland.[37] Jacques Madaule, speaking for a majority at *Esprit*, argued that Germany was experiencing 'the greatest revolution of its history since Lutheranism,' and urged the Czechs to undertake the 'necessary reforms' which would avoid war.[38] *Esprit*'s position on the Sudetenland was clear: Hitler's demands were reasonable; war was to be avoided at all costs.

In the late summer Mounier condemned the effort by German Catholics to adapt their programs to those of the Nazis and stressed the incompatibilities as never before.[39] But despite such anti-Nazism, the September *Esprit* reaffirmed the majority line on Czechoslovakia. François Goguel reiterated Simone Weil's insistence that German demands be met, arguing that compromises over Czechoslovakia would give France a freer hand to resist totalitarianism in Spain and the Mediterranean region.[40]

Even the October *Esprit*, put together after the Berchtesgaden meeting but before the Munich Agreement, reflected receptivity to any massive French and English concessions. Most seemed to want peace, above all, as in Jacques Lefrancq's emotional call for disarmament.[41] But Daniel Villey violently denounced the 'dishonour' of the Franco-British position and Jean Lacroix endorsed Maurice Schumann's call for uncompromising resistance against the Hitlerite threat.[42] While there was, as Roger Labrousse remarked, unanimous agreement at *Esprit* that Versailles had to be revised, the group had come to see the 'Hitlerite problem' from different angles.[43]

Mounier passionately denounced the French and British negotiators:

For six years we have been waiting for France to receive some salutary wound. ... We thought that France was too rich, and the vital shock would some-day foster a certain poverty. ... On 20 September 1938 the collapse uncovered the disease. ... When the men of a government, of a country, which made itself the champions of the given word and of the rights of small nations for twenty years, renounce their signature with premeditation, and in twenty-four hours, with a sort of impatient haste which smacks of the foul crime, lead their 'protégé' to suicide, how can one not speak of dishonour? ... It condensed in one historic day the jitters of four generations of petit bourgeois, their indifference to the misfortunes of others, their morose perfidy, their deference to force, their generalized I-don't-give-a-damnism, to make it the Great Day of their history....[44]

Only a few French editorialists, such as Christian Democrat Georges Bidault and Communist Gabriel Péri, demanded total firmness against Hitler's demands at this point.[45] Mounier's position, at first glance similar, was in fact significantly different. While some thought the Nazis the antithesis of the values France should defend, Mounier suggested that the Nazi 'style' should command 'the style of our defence.' He argued that France should not give in to

a negative form of anti-fascism. We can abominate the inspiration of the Nazi revolution, but while it entails an absolute evil, it is not in all its aspects an absolute evil. ... It violently purifies the Church of its temptations to clericalism, the spirit from its wandering, the body of its softness, the individual from his narcissism. One can only hope that the operation will ... not introduce a new perversity along with the cure. The humiliation of France may also mark France's rebirth: on the condition that by the wound of error a radically new grace penetrates....[46]

In sum, Mounier violently denounced the Franco-British attitude at Munich, but claimed that this humiliation could foster rebirth, resurrection, and renewal. He concluded by insisting that disarmament was the key to the new Europe.[47]

Ironically, Mounier's essay was noticed more for its combative opening language that for its substance. Jacques Maritain urged Mounier not to become identified with the war party in France.[48] Maurice de Gandillac accused him of reversing *Esprit*'s position on the need to rectify the Treaty of Versailles, and joined Labrousse, Marcel Moré, and François Goguel in publishing a dissent from *Esprit*'s 'bellicose' position.[49] They argued that fascism should be confronted by an effort to encourage its 'evolution towards more human forms,' not with violence. Mounier responded that *Esprit* had never opposed negotiations and never come out for war.[50] In the November *Esprit*, Mounier accused his friends of condemning his position too quickly. He explicitly rejected the idea of resisting German expansionism by violence, while another essay in that same issue called for France's 'spiritual renaissance,' and Jacques Madaule's for 'rebuilding democracy.'[51]

In the days after Munich, Bergery called for a recasting of Europe even more drastic than that Hitler demanded, and his lieutenant, Jean Maze, wrote to Mounier that the Frontists' position was very similar to *Esprit*'s.[52] Mounier agreed.[53] The crisis had filled young men with the ambition to reconstruct France radically in the face of the threat and to forget their differences.

In fact, the November *Esprit* represented a withdrawal from the 'anti-Munichois' issue of the previous month. In contrast to some of *Esprit*'s friends, such as Maurice Schumann and J.-M. Semprun y Gurrea, who insisted that the time had come to reject any further compromises with Hitler, Mounier typically tried to focus personalist attentions and energies on a third way.[54]

Esprit's post-Munich rhetoric elicited Labrousse's protest that the review's 'revolution' would lead France 'to adapt our régime to the structures of the German regime while separating us to the equal degree from British-type structures.'[55] Acceptance of a progressively more authoritarian Europe did not sit well with several others in the review's circle. As an *Esprit* faithful recorded: 'We held a special congress to discuss these questions: its atmosphere was exceptionally troubled and confused.... Everyone looked worried and unsettled. Mounier tried to bring the dissenting parties to an understanding, but even his skill at conducting a debate failed to appease them.'[56] Finally it was agreed at that November meeting that 'any truly constructive foreign policy is subordinated to the revolutionary reconstruction of the country,' and all 'systematic' hostility to Germany was to be rejected.[57]

Mounier then called for a 'personalist democracy,' one which recognized that the parties no longer represented France. The new order would 'RESTORE IN DEMOCRACY, THREATENED WITH DEATH, THE FUNCTION OF LEADER,' which would 'draw the power élites FROM ALL SOCIAL CLASSES.' A 'personalist democracy,' Mounier claimed, could be instituted by 'a small number of determined men, centrally located in the vital cadres of the nation.'[58] Mounier's arguments were supported by Jacques Madaule, François Perroux, P.-H. Simon, and Jean Lacroix.[59] Mounier, arguing that fascism was 'a movement of the Left in the true sense of the word, more than reactionary,' endorsed the 'anti-fascist fascism' which P.-A. Touchard was outlining in *Le Voltigeur Français*.[60] Like Drieu la Rochelle, the *Esprit* group began to condemn both German expansionism and the weaknesses of democratic structures in the face of it. The personalists redoubled their efforts to make the alternative they offered more precise. Meanwhile, across the Rhine, a few German National Socialists continued to take the personalist effort seriously almost until the outbreak of armed conflict.[61]

Even after the dismemberment of Czechoslovakia, brutality against Jews, the invasion of Poland, and the war itself Mounier refused to recognize an absolute Christian imperative to fight the Nazis. On the contrary, even as he was mobilized as a chasseur alpine near Grenoble, he was preoccupied with the otherworldly. He lamented that the 'cosmic sense has scandalously atrophied in Christian thought' aside from certain works of Claudel, Teilhard de Chardin, and Edouard Le Roy which addressed larger concerns: 'When I reflect that spirit and person is the transcendent crown of the vital evolution, I note that the latter does not go frittering itself away, but is concentrated on more and more autonomous centres of unification....'[62] Mounier, nurtured on Bergsonism, was captivated by a metahistorical vision in which the historical process revealed man's supernatural destiny. For Mounier, 'the world has been abandoned by modern man; he has accepted being only a thing, space and movement, a disengaged and indifferent spectator of a meaningless procession.'[63] He could not accept the directionlessness of human history or the meaninglessness of the apocalyptic drama facing Europe. Mounier was one of the few Christians of his generation who was profoundly 'evolutionist' and, like Teilhard, thought that humanity was inevitably becoming more 'spiritualized' or 'personalized,' albeit in 'more and more autonomous centres of unification.' He was encouraged by what he called the 'Christian rediscovery of history' influencing the intellectual avant-garde, and he cited the extremely influential book *Catholicisme* (Paris 1938), in which Henri de Lubac explained that 'there is a genesis, an effective growth, a maturation of the universe,' 'a creation not only sustained, but continued.'[64]

An evolutionary theology of history, after Hegel, was not surprising, but such optimism on the eve of terrible slaughter in 1938 and 1939, certainly was. Thus, though Mounier and his friends were shocked by the Nazis' barbarism, they still insisted in Teilhard's words that 'everything that rises must converge.'[65] Mounier could not believe that any major historical movement was completely evil. Also it was undeniable that Nazism expressed the aspirations of multitudes of men, and was definitely on the rise.

Mounier's metahistorical interpretation of the modern world left him open to charges of complacency towards Nazism – although after the war, when he applied it to Stalinist expansion, he became a visionary apostle of Christian-communist dialogue.[66] Was the personalists' insistence on

French internal weakness a self-fulfilling prophecy? Young men convinced of the rottenness of their country could hardly be expected to challenge a Spartan Germany, especially when several of her grievances were justified. Finally, if a new European order was needed, why fight to the death to defend the old?

Could one blame Mounier in 1938 for not foreseeing the bombardment of Rotterdam and the horrors of Auschwitz, any more than Hiroshima or the fire-bombing of Dresden? Still, he did warn that Hitlerism might precipitate some cataclysmic disaster. However, while a Maurice Schumann was ready to fight the Nazis, Mounier judged that his country could not resist the Nazis in its present state. Hubert Beuve-Méry, another foreign correspondent, had seen what Schumann had seen, and come to Mounier's conclusion: France would have to transform herself to withstand Nazi aggression. *Esprit* had had contacts with the vigorous, disciplined legions of the Hitler Jugend and so knew the success of the Nazis in mobilizing young people. Mounier and his friends thought that France and Belgium held little hope for revitalization. When their armies disintegrated in May and June 1940 the *Esprit* faithful saw their prophecies vindicated.

What most set *Esprit* apart from other reviews may have been its analysis of the long-term meaning of Nazism. Mounier thought there was something universally human in German National Socialism, that his fellow Catholics across the Rhine were no more barbarous than the Belgians, French, Spanish, or Swiss, and that Nazism was neither rooted exclusively in German nationalism or in the personality of Adolf Hitler, nor was it evil incarnate. He knew that aspects of National Socialism could appeal to Belgians, French, and Swiss as well as to Germans, and thought that Hitler's rival Otto Strasser was living evidence that National Socialism was not just an outgrowth of Hitler's personality. Mounier knew decent and idealistic human beings who were National Socialists and found it difficult to believe the movement was bad to the core.

Behind such an attitude towards Nazism was a religious perspective which assumed that the Spirit of God moved history with a long-term wisdom. Thus it was difficult to believe the 'religious' fervour of the German people was any more absurd than the selfless ardour of the French communists. The dilemma had been posed years earlier in Mounier's disagreements with Jacques Maritain: Mounier could not believe that the extraordinary ascetic drive and spiritual force of the young Raymond de Becker could be misdirected or pathological. In an age best described as a spiritual desert, would God allow the few humans deeply concerned with Him to be perverted or unbalanced? Within the *Esprit* circle there were great strides in mutual understanding among representatives of religious traditions which, in the previous generation, had considered one another's beliefs false or even demonic. Thus the *Esprit* circle searched for the hidden good behind the apparent evil in Hitlerism and in Stalinism.

The young people of *Esprit* were far more tolerant of a wider circle of rival ideologies than most of their contemporaries. This is not unprecedented, for Christians have always had difficulty in establishing clear criteria to distinguish true from false prophecy and authentic from inauthentic divine inspiration when faced with inspired sects and charismatic movements.

RETHINKING EUROPE

Esprit's political ambivalence in this period is best described as a grudging admiration for particular achievements of the Nazis in transforming Germany, and a horrified fascination for Hitler's toughness and decisiveness in the conduct of foreign policy.[67] *Esprit* also published gruesome reports of pogroms and concentration camps in the Reich.[68] After Munich, *Esprit* regulars such as Denis de Rougemont finally came to see the struggle in black and white terms.[69] Thus they joined individuals such as Paul Vignaux, who had done so from the beginning.[70] But Mounier, always looking for a third way, was determined to avoid the Scylla of 'warmongering' on the one hand and the Charybdis of 'pacifism' on the other, which would only encourage violence.[71] He thought it less important to be 'munichois' or 'anti-munichois' than to be deeply committed to peace.[72] This was mirrored in the review's analyses of Germany's 'push towards the east' after Munich by 'P. Borrel' (Philippe Wolf), Aldo Dami, Nicholas Spoulber, and Roger Labrousse.[73] Mounier argued that the German 'expansive push' probably would have occurred even without Nazism and was an understandable characteristic of a nation at Germany's stage of historical evolution.[74]

The Prague coup in March 1939 caused Mounier to eschew future dialogues with Hitler.[75] But he still thought a war over Czechoslovakia unjustified, and France's interests largely Mediterranean, with a line of resistance which should be Spain and her own frontiers.[76] In the summer of 1939, on the eve of the invasion of Poland, Mounier called for another effort to 'rethink Europe' because 'the "resistance spirit" is turning to a purely negative *poincarisme* that we cannot accept.'[77] The reports to the review's annual meeting in July reflected a pacifist orientation which Mounier found only among a few of his countrymen, notably Gaston Bergery in *La Flèche* and Léon Emery in *Feuilles Libres*, leading spokesmen in what one historian has described as 'the pacifist-defeatist coalition.'[78] *Esprit* tried to be both firmly 'anti-fascist' and 'pacifist.' It was still focusing on the need for France's internal renovation, what Mounier called an 'offensive on all the fronts which do not depend on an accord with the totalitarians.'[79] The August *Esprit*'s position papers written by Mounier, Duveau, and Spoulber were not so different in spirit from the sort of 'fascism of the Left' which Bergery began to propose as the sole path of salvation for France.[80]

Izard had left a position on *La Flèche* at the end of 1937 to work within the Socialist party. When Blum's 'warmongering' faction won out in late 1938, Izard's resignation from the Socialists helped convince Mounier that the party was bankrupt. Just as Bergery and *La Flèche* evolved towards the Right in the last months before the war, so did Mounier and *Esprit*. Bergery's was hardly a mass movement, but its organ was far more widely distributed than *Esprit* and its well-dressed, self-consciously élitist young men had a well-known politician at their head.[81] Bergery's group was ferociously anti-communist while *Esprit* was not – at least not before the Hitler-Stalin Pact in August 1939 – but the similarity of attitudes towards war drew them together. After Munich, Jean Maze, a former member of *Esprit*'s Third Force who had passed to the Frontists, called for a revival of the Third Force élan.[82] At the *Esprit* meeting the following July, Mounier's endorsement of Bergery's views was part of a pattern of renewing ties with 'revolutionary' friends whom he had dropped, often to mollify Maritain.[83]

Mounier took the initiative in *Esprit*'s contacts with the *Ordre Nouveau*.[84] In Lyon, where François Perroux and André Philip were active, *Esprit* groups began to work together with *Ordre Nouveau*, Les amis de Feuilles Libres, the Nouvelles Equipes Françaises, the Centre des Fédérateurs and others in an effort to 'recast democratic doctrines.'

Esprit found several new allies among individuals not necessarily interested in abstract personalist doctrines. One of them was Hubert Beuve-Méry who, although uninterested in philosophy, came to play an important role in spreading personalist ideas in France. This young journalist had resigned as correspondent in Prague for France's most prestigious newspaper *Le Temps*, over its 'Munichois' stance, which he violently denounced.[85] Having observed the Nazis and becoming convinced of France's inability to offer effective resistance, he turned his attention to internal renewal in his homeland. After the Prague coup, he argued that France could only be saved by new teams (nouvelles équipes) of young men from thirty to forty-five years of age immune to Hitlerite propaganda. If the French could not accomplish their own revolution, 'they would, like the Czechs, submit to a revolution which would be imposed from the outside....' Beuve-Méry's belief in the inevitability of some kind of authoritarian revolution in France and his call to resist Nazism through a movement of youthful élites received favourable attention at *Esprit* as another summons to a 'personalist revolution.'[86]

Beuve-Méry was well known as an anti-munichois journalist.[87] And Mounier, in the summer of 1939, joined a variety of personalities – including Beuve-Méry, Izard, well-known anti-Hitlerites, and the notorious fascist sympathizers Drieu la Rochelle and Thierry Maulnier – in calling for a Third Force in France.[88] Mounier drew a parallel between the disappointing Popular Front, *'parlementaire et politicien,'* having hamstrung the new forces 'which might have broken hereditary inertia,' and similar developments in Belgium: 'In the same way, in Belgium, Rex, Van Zeeland and Spaak ... blocked the front which was taking shape five years ago, above and beyond the old parties ... of young Catholics formed by *Avant-Garde* and young socialists formed by de Man.'[89] Mounier implied that Hitlerite aggression proved the necessity of a juncture of 'spiritualized socialists' and 'socialized Christians' in France. He called for an unprecedented dialogue between young right-wing 'revolutionaries' and socialists because, as Mounier put it to a friend just days before the outbreak of World War II: 'It is a question of employing the values which many socialists judge "reactionary". ... And finally freeing oneself of the automatic labels of "reactionary" and "advanced" to see directly what conforms to man and what does not....'[90]

Thus, during the terrible months from the Munich agreements to the declaration of war, Mounier's review clung to the vision of a sweeping personalist revolution in France – while other publications by young French intellectuals simply resigned themselves to a disastrous war. The review steadfastly rejected 'warmongering.' Internal revolution first with no compromises with the totalitarians – these were the two central *Esprit* themes. It was as if no war were possible. Mounier's friends in the provinces continued to work with Georges Lefranc's Workers' Colleges in the CGT and Lefranc wrote in *Esprit* of restructuring French syndicalism.[91] François Perroux remained a key figure in the elaboration of *Esprit*'s 'new politics,' while criticism of corporatism received less attention. Mounier's own ongoing 'criticism of the Left' led to more and more guidelines and structures for a 'new democracy.'

The abandonment of Czechoslovakia by the allies prompted Mounier to call for 'a rallying to a personalist democracy' because the old political parties 'no longer represent France.' He proposed a 'Statute of the Person' as the basis for a completely new set of political principles avoiding the errors of both 'an individualist Constitution' and 'a totalitarian Constitution.' Mounier's ambition was considerable: all the 'problems with democracy' were going to be rethought at *Esprit*.[92]

In early 1939 *Esprit* sent out 600 questionnaires to French deputies inviting them to make a sort of examination of conscience regarding the parliamentary régime. There were only twenty-four responses, which prompted Mounier to conclude that there was no choice but to condemn 'liberal democracy' out of hand.[93] Perroux, faithful to the principles of his important blueprint for a French corporatism, sketched a new system of representation – family suffrage, representation of cultural and scientific bodies and economic and professional groups, and so on – which would favour a 'selection of leaders,' the 'new men' France needed.[94] His outline of new hierarchical, political structures, Mounier admitted, 'evoked certain mechanisms of totalitarian régimes'; but he saw the 'Statute of the Person' as a guarantee of the most important liberties.[95]

The May 1939 *Esprit* contained analyses by anonymous contributors, *Esprit* regulars, and sympathizers such as Jean Maze and Raymond Millet, of all the French political parties. The plan to analyse all the parties, first formulated by Mounier at the end of 1937, was reiterated after Munich when Mounier called for '*a recasting of the doctrines and fundamental structures of democracy.*'[96] *Esprit*'s 'stop fascism' orientation had become centred upon France's national *redressement*.[97] With the possible exception of the neo-socialists around Marcel Déat and the small Parti Démocrate Populaire, political formations were described as completely inadequate for the task.[98] Indeed, the last prewar *Esprit* dismissed the entire French democratic tradition since 1789 as full of ambiguities.[99]

Mounier came to work more closely with Perroux, Lacroix, Touchard, and Madaule, and other authoritarian syndicalist theorists and anti-democratic revolutionaries. At the same time he drew away from defenders of democracy like Maritain, Villey, and Vignaux. Except for Touchard, the core of *Esprit* was Catholic and convinced of the need for élites with a completely new outlook to direct French affairs. The review remained a great source of ideas and encouragement for a totally new approach, while the movement itself had new élites and plans waiting if France slid into disaster and the old structures disintegrated.

CHATENAY-MALABRY

After Mounier lost his teaching position in Brussels in the fall of 1938, and lost his followers to Spaak's effort to create a Belgian national socialism, he moved back to France. In relocating in Paris he received help from a new recruit from Lyon, a young psychologist named Paul Fraisse. A former Jesuit seminarian and student of Jacques Chevalier, Fraisse was also a leader of the French Christian Student movement and newly dedicated to Mounier's ideas. In December 1938, he took the initiative to create formal Paris *Esprit* groups over and beyond the different study groups.[100] The result, the Fédération de la région parisienne, became an archetype for the different regional federations which Mounier began to set up throughout France.[101] Adherence to the basic principles of the *Personalist Manifesto* was the prerequisite for membership and their purpose was 'to form the pure and the strong,' the new men needed to transform France.[102] But aside from *Le Voltigeur* there was still no effort to translate the *Esprit* message for the masses.[103] Mounier would draw 100–200 people to his lectures in the provinces but the main effort remained the elucidation of a personalist doctrine, the organization of a small number of talented and well-placed people.

Mounier spent January 1939 searching for a large property in the outskirts of Paris for a headquarters.[104] This 'Maison Esprit' was to be the residence of five families and site for an experimental school in which Fraisse, Jacques Lefrancq, Paulette Mounier, and Emile-Albert Niklaus were to educate six to eight boarders between the ages of fourteen and eighteen.[105] In spring 1939 the *Esprit* house was purchased with the private funds of some 'comrades.'[106] It was a lovely old estate, with several acres of park, surrounded by high, white walls, down a cobbled street from the Romanesque village church of Châtenay-Malabry. Châtenay was still a country village, not yet a fashionable bedroom suburb for the great metropolis to the north, and the giant cedars were said to have been planted by Chateaubriand when he had owned the property. A cream-coloured old convent lay across the dirt road, which ran in front of the towering main gates. It was a fine womb for the yet-to-be-born personalist élite.

Setting up a new school when war was just weeks away was entirely consistent with *Esprit*'s singleminded pursuit of interior rearmament. *Esprit* had consistently attacked the Third Republic's school system, and Mounier's educational program dovetailed with *Esprit*'s search for new élites. The practicality of such a preoccupation was being rudely demonstrated across the Rhine:

'The essential of a revolution is not the conquest of power, but the education of men.' A man wrote that in 1922. Another one of your dreamers? Some theoretician of the spiritual revolution? That dreamer, in effect, spends three billion a year on vacations for workers and, for six years already, has been forming eight million young men with an iron education. Month by month he leads them into God knows what hurricane of historic madness whose first symptoms are ... the occupation of the left bank of the Rhine, the anschluss, Munich, Prague.

Mounier clearly still found much to admire in fascist method, if not its German result:

Forty million Frenchmen display a regression or a discordance in all their forms of behaviour: instincts, emotions, character, intelligence are affected one after the other ... a régime 'of the masses': 80 per cent of adult males, of all classes, in all walks of life, with all sorts of educations, are mediocre either in intelligence or in their ability to make decisions. ... Decidedly our dreamer was right. ... The statesman who would have consecrated since 1933 the sums poured into the sinkhole of armaments in France onto the formation of young Frenchmen from fifteen to twenty years old ... would have been our saviour. And neither Munich, nor Prague, would have happened. Too bad that the dreamer's name is Adolf Hitler.

Mounier went on to say that the personalist psychologists knew that there was no longer 'any firm conception of man' in France. And from this came the *Esprit* alternative: 'Our strength, in common with the totalitarians, is that we know what we want to do with the child, or rather what we want to awaken in him ... an authentically free, that is consciously committed, person....' Mounier told his readers they could trust their children to the personalists 'so that we might organize ... a first nursery of men of our spirit,' and he concluded: 'Save our children ... a duty of hope, the only, perhaps, which might be capable of exorcising the fear.'[107]

In 1935, de Becker's idea of a lay order committed to personalist ideals had been a tender-minded enterprise: a whimsical mixture of Gandhian non-violence, Franciscan poverty, and Péguyiste socialism. Now Mounier's call for élites after the Munich crisis was accompanied by new political aggressiveness, new alliances, Perroux's corporatist projects, and the blueprint for an élitist youth-training centre. Lest this entirely contradicts Mounier's opposition to 'totalitarianism' one must, perhaps, try to distinguish between authoritarianism and totalitarianism the way some Catholic supporters of Salazar did in this period.[108] Though Mounier took no notice of the Salazar régime, François Perroux actually admired Portugal's 'peaceful revolution.'[109] The personalist movement may have consistently opposed 'totalitarianism' but it was becoming progressively more authoritarian.

On 23 August 1939 Joachim von Ribbentrop flew to Moscow to conclude the Nazi-Soviet non-agression pact. The day before, the French communists had demanded that France ally herself with Russia to stop Hitler. Now their press welcomed the pact as 'saving the peace.' On the 26th, Premier Daladier, furious at this about-face, suppressed communist daily newspapers. On 1 September German, and then Soviet, troops moved into Poland. On 2 September, France and Great Britain declared war on Germany.

Mounier's effort to create a personalist community at Châtenay-Malabry was interrupted by the mobilization. But there was no actual fighting for several months, and among his fellow conscripts in Grenoble he found neither bellicose oratory nor hatred for Germans, only a common feeling that Hitler was 'a sort of bothersome insect.'[110] Mounier, because of his impaired hearing and blind eye, was assigned to the secretarial service in a Chasseurs alpins camp. Pierre-Aimé Touchard installed *Esprit* in his wife's country home at Dreux and took in Paulette Mounier and the Mouniers' infant daughter, Françoise, already tragically ill from the effects of a smallpox injection.

Hitler's invasion of Poland meant the mobilization of most of *Esprit's* contributors but the internal transformation of France remained the review's first concern. At the outbreak of war Edouard Daladier appointed as French minister of information someone else dedicated to the rejuvenation of French society – Jean Giraudoux, playwright and high functionary in the Quai d'Orsay. Giraudoux had been a leading apostle of Franco-German understanding until Hitler came to power and his book

Pleins pouvoirs sharply criticized French politicians, hygiene, and athletic programs and proposed measures to improve the birth rate and control immigration.[111] Some thought at the time that Giraudoux was promoting a 'pacifist fascism' without being conscious of it.[112]

Despite the fact that Giraudoux's national regeneration project seemed racialist and included some thinly veiled anti-semitism, it was warmly reviewed in *Esprit*, where Julien Reinach lauded the dramatist's appointment to the new national propaganda post.[113] Mounier wrote to Giraudoux to explain the role *Esprit* could play, among 'the two thousand individuals in France whose "morale" will only hold up if they try to introduce the maximum amount of non-war into the war.'[114] He allowed his name to be submitted for a post in the Ministry and forwarded his curriculum vitae there.[115]

It was quite a change for Mounier to envisage service in Giraudoux's office since, until then, an individual automatically resigned from his personalist group if he so much as joined a political party. Mounier evidently felt that the disruptions of war would change old ideas and old habits in his country. He confided to his wife: 'one ought to break with everything in one's life from time to time to start all over again. This new start from the beginning ... would be exciting if it were not for the horrible side....'[116] In free moments Mounier wandered off from his camp to read Max Scheler in a nearby woods and reflect on the differences between him and his fellow conscripts:[117] 'I think of everything which adapts these people to one another ... the same capacity for banal manual tasks, the same amusements (belote, etc.), the same vocabulary, the same spontaneous attitude towards work, women.... What alienation, on the other hand, in an intellectual of mixed Christian and bourgeois background set against all of them!'[118] Their faith in élite cadres notwithstanding, personalists had been troubled by communication barriers between intellectuals and the masses and found the military camps mirroring this problem in the daily contacts which broke down the old class lines.[119]

Reflections on class and flirtations with government service could not, however, wholly distract Mounier from events. The Nazi-Soviet pact and the subsequent joint invasion of Poland could be seen as representing the bankruptcy of *Esprit*'s analysis of the national socialist revolution. In the first wartime *Esprit & Le Voltigeur français*, P.-A. Touchard tried to justify mistakes in judgment that were becoming embarrassingly visible: 'There subsisted, under all the false values of national socialist Germany often denounced here, an authentic élan, a German unity, a German truth whose grandeur and nobility had to be recognized by even the most ferocious adversaries of Nazism. ...' But the Hitler-Stalin pact had stunned everyone and shattered illusions.[120] Mounier's bitterness was framed in a metahistorical perspective that took care of fascism and Marxism in one blow:

The strange brutality which wells up from the depths of the Germanic soul ... is not in the Soviet alliance by accident. For a long time we have known the superhuman cruelty which subverted the Russian soul when it abandoned the vast mystical riches natural to it, to graft the inexorable Reason of the age of positivism directly onto the last seedlings of mongol barbarism. ...

This harsh and bizarre language was curiously balanced by a courageous restatement of France's culpability. Mounier claimed that *Esprit*'s insistence on French responsibility for the bellicosity of Germany had been and still was correct: 'All of Europe, and each of us, bears the sin of this war which is beginning.... Money, parties, state politicians, adventurers, through your self-satisfied, greedy petit bourgeois hearts – the infection has spread everywhere through the flesh of the modern world. No nation can ignore this....' But after each individual *mea culpa* what attitude should one take towards shouldering a rifle? Mounier advised that one 'preserve as best we can that "right intention" ... which the old Christian jurists made an essential condition of the just war.'[121]

This was hardly a call to arms in the spirit of Péguy, nor was it that 'integral pacifism' that some at *Esprit* had supported. The November-December *Esprit* was lifeless, printing letters which were dreamy, ethereal, and devoid of hostile feelings for the enemy.[122] Even Paul-Louis Landsberg, who had fled from the Nazis a few years earlier, favoured a mood 'absolutely independent of the bellicosity of the adversary,' while Touchard mused 'who could say in advance alongside whom, and against whom, we will be in conflict when hostilities will cease ... before what kind of Europe we will find ourselves....?'[123] 'We are, perhaps, at the beginning of the "New Middle Ages",' Mounier confided to Berdyaev, and he asked: 'What could, and ought Russia bring to the federal Europe of tomorrow?'[124] He assured Jacques Lefrancq that *Esprit* would never participate in the 'immense dehumanization' which war literature represented and Paul Fraisse that he no longer considered himself a combatant, and was 'going to turn all my forces towards the post-war.'[125]

Several of Mounier's friends urged that he continue *Esprit*.[126] Others in the Quai d'Orsay pulled strings to have him offered a foreign post; and then the chief of staff of Yvan Delbos, who was minister of foreign affairs, asked him to teach philosophy as a form of service in the reserves.[127] Yet another friend proposed his services to Giraudoux.[128] While Mounier insisted that *Esprit*'s activities multiply despite wartime conditions, as late as March 1940 he was still hoping to join Giraudoux.[129] In the interim he kept three or four hours to himself each evening after his desk work and so still had *Esprit* firmly in hand.[130]

The *Esprit* group's *Journal intérieur* was absolutely free of militaristic sentiments, and full of lighthearted anecdotes of life in the camps during the 'phony war.'[131] Though the January *Esprit* accepted strong anti-Nazi pieces by Berdyaev and Landsberg, Mounier set the tone with a vibrant summons to rebuild France. French youth, he argued, particularly 'those mobilized for the preparation of the après-guerre,' could do it.[132] Meanwhile François Perroux, at Mounier's request, was working on plans to create 'shock troops' who could create an internal renaissance in France.[133] A new, virile education system, with a course in alpinism, was an important part of his program.[134] *Esprit* was still more interested in changing France than in chastising Germany.

As *Esprit* began to take a clearly anti-democratic line, democrats like Borne, Maritain, and Paul Vignaux redirected their essays to *Les Nouveaux Cahiers* or *Temps présent*. There was an attempt to bring all Catholic youth into the Nouvelles équipes françaises, but the militant anti-Nazism of Christian Democrats Maurice Schumann and Georges Bidault was so different from that of Mounier and his friends that a common program proved elusive. In January 1940 the prominent Christian Democrat journalist Francisque Gay charged that *Esprit* had adopted an untenable attitude towards the war and that P.-A. Touchard's formula for rebuilding France was at best peculiar.[135] Mounier, in his camp near Grenoble, expressed shock at Gay's attack and reaffirmed responsibility for the review.[136] When Etienne Borne then announced that he would no longer write for *Esprit*, Mounier told him that Gay's tone had been 'unacceptable' and his paper, *L'Aube*, 'trumpeting jacobinism' against Germany since the previous September.[137] Mounier, in a long letter to Gay, explained that *Esprit* was not a left wing of Christian Democracy and that its general criticism of democratic parties applied to the Christian Democrats as well.[138]

In the January 1940 *Esprit*, Mounier did call for a Europe in which both

Russia and Germany would be 'freed of their tyrants,' but with a peace treaty 'which a German loving his nation ... could accept with honour in the framework of the European order.'[139] He denounced the excesses of anti-Hitlerite propaganda in France, and was happy to find himself and Maurice de Gandillac – now that the quarrel over Munich had been healed – in complete agreement.[140] Mounier envisioned a special issue on Germany with a post-war focus, Denis de Rougemont and Albert Béguin contributing the Swiss view, playwright Eugène Ionesco analyzing the new Rumania, and so on.[141] He also asked Berdyaev to direct a special issue showing Russia transcending communism in a new sort of synthesis, 'a Russia which would have integrated the best of the recent experience with the past.'[142]

Esprit's 'rethinking Europe' ignored the possibility of a return to the pre-Hitler situation.[143] Although *Esprit* did contain militantly anti-Nazi missives such as theologian Karl Barth's in April, Mounier set the more general tone with his concern for the 'cosmic perspectives of Catholicism' as elaborated by Teilhard de Chardin.[144] On this lofty plane it was not even essential who won or lost the war.

In January 1940 *Esprit* privately announced a 'Cahier tribune libre de la jeunesse française' for which contributions would be solicited from right-wingers like Thierry Maulnier as well as from the young syndicalists on the Left and from the Spanish correspondent of *Esprit* who had become a falangist.[145] By this time Maulnier had 'seized a leading position among fascist intellectuals' with his prolific pro-Munich writings, and was bitterly resented by anti-fascist French Catholics since he made a point of his Catholic loyalties.[146]

Mounier's overture to Maulnier was not an isolated gesture. He also courted Drieu la Rochelle, who had condemned the unwillingness of the French Left to admit the possibility of a strong authoritarian régime on the Left.[147] Drieu, hostile to the Nazis yet advocate of a 'spiritualized fascism' for France, complained in *Je suis partout* in January 1940 that his views made him feel isolated.[148] In March he contributed an essay to *Esprit*, and in April Mounier wrote a favourable review of the novel *Gilles* in which he thought Drieu 'perceived that mixture of socialism, Christianity, and virile virtue' which was 'the very scent of tomorrow's Europe.'[149]

If Mounier could co-operate with prominent 'fascist' writers it was because *Esprit* had redefined its purposes. The February 1940 issue had a new principle function: 'the preparation of the post-war, and of the spiritual reawakening which is the immediate condition for it; our projects of special issues on the *problems of the leader*, on the problem of the *birthrate*, on the methods of an *education of the person*.'[150] Mounier told Paul Fraisse that the first phase of the personalist movement in France had provided a formation for a few individuals; now he felt 'as free as the air' to start new initiatives.[151] He was 'rethinking' *Esprit*, and had already received an interesting article on 'scout leaders' in keeping with the review's new function.[152]

During the heyday of the Popular Front, Mounier's review had been considered one of the most progressive organs for Catholics interested in Marxism. Now all of that was set aside as Mounier praised the expulsion of the seventy communist deputies from the Chamber after the Hitler-Stalin pact. This act was a surgical operation against a 'cancer' in the French body politic, 'the first phase of French renewal.' Mounier thought that 'the organisms and rebel chiefs on all levels should be hit hard and quickly.' He did, however, again maintain that party militants had some worthwhile qualities – 'a certain sense of community, of order, of discipline' – and so should be given 'a new faith to which to consecrate themselves,' a sort of 'blood transfusion.'[153]

The last letters from *Esprit* people at the front reflected a sense of ambiguity towards the coming conflict.[154] Between the lines, Jacques Madaule suggested that in an essential way France had already been defeated and that each Frenchman should begin a personal examination of conscience.[155] Amid rumours of imminent attack, just five days before the German onslaught, Mounier confided to a friend that although he rejected most forms of pacifism and saw 'the necessity of carrying on war in the present historical conditions,' he still thought that war was 'the daughter of Cain ... tears up the Mystical Body, and is *in itself* the anti-Christ.'[156] He obviously had little enthusiasm for military war against the enemy.

Esprit's efforts to 'rebuild France' continued during the German blitzkrieg. Georges Valois' suggestion that France 'change régime ... to win the war' was endorsed by Mounier.[157] Valois thought that France and England should exchange their outworn democracy and Italy its fascism for a Euro-African federalism.[158] Mounier was also still flirting with Drieu la Rochelle's idea of a French fascism: '"To turn fascism against Italy and Germany," the formula is still ambiguous, poorly balanced. But to turn the virtues of fascism against the monstrosities of fascism ... yes, there will be no durable victory ... without that integration.' Drieu, Mounier noted, envisaged the revival of a heretical 'virile Christianity of the Third Century' similar to that of Bloy, Péguy, Claudel, and Bernanos.[159] All Frenchmen, Mounier insisted in the last pre-invasion *Esprit*, should think 'spiritual revolution, first of all.'[160] He had not faced up to the magnitude of the German threat.

The German invasion found the May *Esprit* at the printer's in Lille, but somehow there was a June issue to summon readers to 'turn towards that ray of light ... to catch a glimpse of the after-war years.' The 'free tribune of French youth' had contributions from Jean Maze, editor of *La Flèche*, Jean-Pierre Maxence of *Gringoire* and the 'Young Right,' Pierre Prévost of *Ordre Nouveau*, and syndicalist Georges Lefranc.[161] The ray of light which Mounier saw on the horizon must have been small consolation to the French. Mounier was still seeing Nazism in a world-historical context, as a purging, if unduly violent, agent: 'The whiplash that Hitlerism gave to Germany in six years, the strength, the vitality, the aggressiveness, the imagination that he, in the face of a massive despiritualization, blew into the flabby Weimar republic....' Mounier foresaw 'entirely new conditions and realities' of a novelty 'which may be frightful, but which will at least bring us out of the blind alleys of the past.'[162]

All *Esprit*'s essayists trusted in the emergence of 'new élites' in France – 'the post-war militia' (Mounier), 'the élite of efficacy with the sense of grandeur' (Prévost), or trade-union élites (Lefrancq).[163] In turn, these would 'form men of character' (Prévost) and thus spark 'the French interior renaissance' (Maze).[164] The Swiss Albert Béguin envisaged new élites curing Germany of her terrible barbarism.[165] Poet Pierre Emmanuel offered 'prayers for our enemies.'[166] Although Jacques Madaule was alarmed over one of *Esprit*'s friend's 'disquieting speech on foreign affairs' in conquered Belgium, the general tone of *Esprit* was hopeful.[167] At the time of the Munich crisis Mounier even admitted that he had been hoping for a 'salutary wound' for France for some time. In June 1940, his 'wish' was coming true.

On the eve of the collapse, few groups in France were better prepared for such an eventuality than Mounier's circle. Ever since the early nineteen-thirties, personalists had been arguing that France could never stand up to Germany unless her youth and political structure were transformed. Neither had been. Personalists were, however, in a position to take advantage of the resulting disaster.

Esprit had discovered a network of like-minded individuals throughout France and Belgium, with a common set of ideals and contacts with similar Third Way revolutionaries. Personalists were bound together by friendship, and, often, a common faith; they had a philosophy, some plans to radically reorganize labour, a body of educational theory, and an outline for the transformation of Europe beyond the weaknesses of the liberal democracies. They were able to make a certain sense out of the triumph of Nazism in Europe and to make the best of it. In a few weeks, following the collapse of their countries, several French and Belgian personalists were catapulted from obscurity into positions of influence and importance. At long last the high-sounding phrases of personalism would be applied practically and the children of the new Renaissance would face the new dark ages.

8

Personalism in Power

I believe that we have won the war; that is a less 'mystical' perspective than one might think. *Mounier to Touchard, 6 July 1940*

On 29 May, the day after King Leopold's surrender had been announced, and then again on the 31st, Pierre-Aimé Touchard wrote to Mounier for advice on how to bury *Esprit* until better days.[1] Mounier responded that, come what may, *Esprit* would continue. In spite of Touchard's surprise and strong objections Mounier insisted on 4 June that he knew exactly what he was doing in deciding to continue the journal:

You think I am beside myself, losing my head, my old Pierre; you cannot believe how one of your letters, the temperature of which rises from day to day, seems very 'Parisian' here and Paulette could tell you the calm with which I have deliberated over, and resolved, that question. ... I received a mandate from our comrades to continue *Esprit*, I am in agreement with it. ... If, after a consultation of some breadth, that mandate changes, you will see me first to give it up.[2]

The next day Mounier wrote his old mentor Jacques Chevalier, dean at Grenoble, who, a few weeks later, was unexpectedly named to head the French educational system, to ask for a position as examiner for the *baccalauréat* – and to complain that *Esprit*, 'despite our resistance against Nazism from September 1938 to September 1939,' had been under suspicion. He wanted to renew ties with the older man and place himself at Chevalier's 'disposition.'[3] Thus as Panzer units were rolling over the allied armies in Flanders, as Dunkerque fell and the remnants of the French First Army surrendered, Mounier was working to continue

Esprit's project for French national rebirth. He was one of those few Frenchmen who expected the Wehrmacht to smash the French army with remarkable ease, but less because of an ineffective use of potential than because of France's weakness as part of that entire civilization he had been denouncing since 1932.

On 25 June, in announcing the armistice, Pétain charged that 'our defeat came from our decadence; the spirit of pleasure destroyed everything that the spirit of sacrifice had built.'[4] The next day, from Radio London, the young General de Gaulle offered a less metaphysical perspective: the military defeat had a technical as well as moral explanation; the French high command had failed to grasp the new strategic use of aircraft, tank columns, and motorized armies.[5] Pétain's responsibility for the disastrous 'Maginot Line mentality' and for the refusal to let the government retreat to North Africa seems to have been far from the minds of the deputies who straggled to Vichy on 1 June ahead of the advancing Germans. The old marshal seemed to have struck a responsive chord when he insisted that France had been sick, that her politicians had failed, that authoritarian régimes were the wave of the future, and that France had best create a 'new order' in harmony with them.[6] Some, like Mounier, had been calling for an authoritarian revolution in France until the very oubreak of hostilities.

THE COLLAPSE OF ROME AND THE SHADOW OF ODOVACER

Mounier observed the collapse of his country with relative serenity. On 17 June he was on a train bound for the Bordeaux region, with the possibility, he thought, of disembarking for North Africa. But after some confusion, Mounier's company found itself in the village of Saint-Savinien in the Charente river valley, surrounded by refugees and receiving confused and contradictory orders while the Panzer divisions continued their drive south. On 19 June, the day after General de Gaulle's appeal to continue the struggle, Mounier shared his thoughts on his country with his wife: 'Is she dead? We will see. In any case France must experience the ordeal, have it touch each one of her petits bourgeois, of her little gardeners. "He" will go down to Marseille and Bordeaux, out of a need to rape the whole country. But that will be salubrious for everyone. There will be no one left who has not been forced to see.'[7]

Mounier remained in the camp near Saint-Savinien – Panzer divisions, rushing south, had surprised him washing his socks and had taken pictures of the disheveled French soldiers as they roared past – reading

Duruy's *Histoire romaine*. The story of the Roman Empire was, Mounier confided to Touchard, 'very timely, hardly encouraging at all for England....' 'I bless the poverty which is coming,' he wrote. 'We thought that France would remake herself in the trials of the war. She will remake herself in those of the defeat and that will perhaps be better, because everyone will be touched....' Mounier then confessed his astonishing belief that France had 'won the war.'[8] In the first issue of *Esprit* published under Vichy, Mounier called on his readers to 'aid in the birth of that new world which little by little ought to be born on the ruins of the old.'[9] Would the child of this 'rape' be a better France? Mounier seemed to believe that it would.

Not surprisingly, Touchard thought *Esprit*'s editor 'excité' and not completely lucid in his analysis of France's disaster. But in the first chaotic days of the defeat Mounier's 'collapse of the Roman Empire' perspective was also shared by a number of his colleagues. As is so often true, the world-historical perspective had the alchemist's touch, turning apparent defeat to long-term victory.

BLUEPRINT FOR THE NATIONAL SOCIALIST REVOLUTION
IN BELGIUM AND FRANCE

Nazi 'French expert' Otto Abetz and his entourage seemed to envisage the possibility of transforming Belgian and French youth within a new social and economic order – hierarchical, disciplined, authoritarian, with deference for the Führerprinzip at each level of society. Both Belgium and France after the military collapse had a symbolic national authority figure – Leopold III, Marshal Pétain – with sophisticated social engineers in his immediate entourage – Henri de Man in Belgium, François Perroux and the non-communist leaders of the CGT in France. Both countries had youth movements interested in transforming the young through 'spiritual revolution' – the 'neo-socialists,' *Esprit*, Communauté, *Jeune Europe*, and Rexist groups in Belgium; the *Ordre Nouveau*, neo-socialists, *Esprit*, and *Temps Nouveau* in France. Both Belgium and France, however, were honeycombed with intense political, ethnic, and ideological rivalries. These, together with the inconsistent policies of the conquerors, made the path to the Belgian and French 'national socialist revolutions' fraught with difficulties.

In May 1940, after Belgium was invaded, prominent Belgian 'fascists' Joris van Severen and Léon Degrelle were passed across the border to the

French police. The former was shot dead, the latter passed from prison camp to prison camp, beaten, and released with the formal Belgian surrender on 22 July. The leader of the Flemish fascist party (the Vlaamsch Nationaal Verbond), Staf de Clercq, was freed by the Belgians on 9 June and put his '30,000 members at the disposition of the Reich.'[10]

With Degrelle under guard in France, Abetz's old contacts were influential in Brussels. Mounier's former model, Henri de Man, president of the Belgian Socialist party, was given a special mission in the entourage of the royal family and, it is alleged, persuaded the king not to flee into exile with his ministers. De Man thought the 'desertion' of the old élites afforded the opportunity for a revolution: at the end of June his famous 'Manifesto to Militant Socialists' called on his party faithful to 'Prepare to enter into the cadres of a movement of national resurrection which will absorb the living forces of the nation, youth, the veterans, into a single party, that of the Belgian people – united in fidelity to their King and in the will to realize the sovereignty of labour.'[11]

This manifesto received wide support in the belgian press, where habitués of the Didier salon soon became prominent. On 13 June the leading Brussels daily Le Soir reappeared, this time directed by Mounier's firebrand comrade Raymond de Becker and funded secretly by Abetz. De Becker, aided by the talented Rexist Pierre Daye, was soon publishing 25,000 copies. Other newspapers were also directed by 'neutralists': the Nouveau Journal by de Becker's old collaborator at Ouest, Robert Poulet, and Paul Colin; Pays réel by the Rexist movement's chief Didier contact, José Streel; and Le Travail by Henri de Man himself.[12] Didier established Editions de la Toison d'Or, which began publishing visionary proponents of the new order such as de Becker and de Man. Von Ribbentrop provided secret funds for this venture.[13]

During the first months of the German occupation Henri de Man united all of the syndicats into one formation, the UTMI, to help open the way for the kind of reforms envisaged in the 'Plan du Travail.' An effort to form 'Volontaires du Travail,' youth élites according to Henri de Man's ideas, was made. Its director on the Walloon side, Henri Bauchau, came from de Becker's old Esprit Nouveau group and he drew from it (Jean de Villers, Marcel Vercruysse) and Esprit (Guy Malengrau) for his key aides. By November there were 134 francophone VT units, and by July 1941, 1,342 volunteers had passed their six months in the camps.[14] Like that of de Becker's old Communauté movement, the aim was to form an élite of Belgian youth who could in turn form larger circles of élites and eventually reshape society.

After Degrelle was released from his French internment, he was summoned to Abetz's headquarters in Paris with de Man to discuss the creation of a new belgian government around a de Man-Degrelle team.[15] Abetz's Deutsch-Französische Monatshefte had urged a reconciliation between the Rexists and de Manian socialists and Abetz seemed one of the few Nazi leaders to believe in the real possibility of a national socialist Belgium and France. He sought the reconciliation of 'nationalists' and 'socialists' in both countries, the reorientation of youth, and co-operation between individuals of fervent religious sentiments with individuals of strong, authoritarian, social convictions. Abetz had fused his strong Catholic upbringing and youthful social democratic leanings into his own brand of Nazism and seemed to want to project his personal synthesis onto the whole of Belgium. From its inception that plan intended to make extensive use of *Esprit* regulars, or contributors linked to the journal in the past.

The prospect for a 'national socialist revolution' in France was rendered doubly difficult by the initial division of the country into occupied and unoccupied sections, with the latter maintaining a semblance of independence under Pétain. Thus Abetz had to deal not only with contending factions in the legally constituted government at Vichy but also with rival 'national socialist' figures in occupied Paris, notably Marcel Déat and Jacques Doriot. The rival sympathizers of some sort of new order in France seemed less capable of smoothing over their old differences than were the habitués of the Didier salon in Brussels.

In Paris, Abetz's old Sohlbergkreis friends Luchaire and de Brinon became press czar and ambassador of France, respectively. Another Sohlberg regular, Drieu la Rochelle, took over the directorship of the NRF, in which he was aided by Jacques Madaule of *Esprit*. Thus old contacts of Abetz influenced journalism in Paris as did de Becker and de Man in Brussels. If Vichy faltered, Abetz had fresh ideas and important personalities in Paris: Déat, former minister of air, *normalien*, and *agrégé* in philosophy, was an expert on Henri de Man; Doriot had been head of the Young Communists and deputy for Saint-Denis, and commanded the loyalty of the militantly anti-bolshevik Parti Populaire Français. Abetz could directly aid national socialism in the occupied zone, but his position relative to Vichy was far more delicate.

France, although more than half occupied, was the only country able to negotiate an armistice with the Reich, state to state – Spaak and other Belgian ministers had sought an armistice but the Germans had refused.[16]

For the first hundred days the Vichy government seemed largely free, as it took time for Germany to establish organs of direct political control. At first Abetz simply represented the Auswärtiges Amt to the real German power in France, the Militärbefehlshaber in Frankreich. He was named ambassador on 8 August and, bit by bit, an independent political service was constituted in the capital.[17]

Since a number of individuals who had connections with the old Solhbergkreis appeared in Pétain's entourage, anti-Nazi Frenchmen were soon denouncing the Vichy 'National Revolution' as the result of a concerted, long-term plot against the Republic. When one recalls the evolution of a few reviews like *Esprit* in the last months before the collapse this attitude is understandable. At the beginning of 1940, *Esprit* was an obscure, 'outsiders' review with a readership of left-wing Catholics, spiritualist socialists, authoritarian educational reformers, unemployed intellectuals, adventurous priests, and schoolteachers in the provinces. By the end of that year the review had become a key publication in an effort to transform all French youth; some of its contributors were advisers to Marshal Pétain, aides to his chief ministers, leaders of the youth movement or, in the new Ecole Nationale Supérieure des Cadres, intellectual architects of the metamorphosis of France.

The *Esprit* group was, however, decimated by the war: some had been killed in the fighting, others were in German prison camps (Maxime Chastaing, Paul Fraisse, François Goguel, Adrien Miatlev, Marius Richard, Pierre-Henri Simon, Daniel Villey), a few were with de Gaulle in London (Zerapha, Wolf), others were, or soon would be, in self-exile in the United States (Denis de Rougemont, Jacques Maritain, Paul Vignaux). Roger Labrousse, unreconciled to bellicose elements in *Esprit* after Munich, had gone to live in a commune of intellectuals in Patagonia. Mounier wanted to continue *Esprit*, but it was soon evident that the available 'friends of *Esprit*' were divided in their attitudes towards the new rhetoric and initiatives which began to come out of Vichy.

However, Mounier and his friends were united in considering themselves relatively untainted by the defeat. The Third Republic had often been united by the struggle against 'clericalism' and, for over half a century, Catholics had been attacking the parliamentary system, laissez-faire capitalism, socialism, communism, and laicism. Could they be blamed for the collapse of a régime which they had despised? Personalists were similar to many devout Catholics in this regard.

In the summer of 1940, Catholics represented a tradition of discipline and authority within the confusion of defeat. They had varied in their assessments of the Nazis, but most had seen good points in authoritarian values and so appeared suited to finding a place for their country in the new Europe that was emerging. The Catholic youth movements boasted both youthful innocence and the ancient, durable values of traditional France – the only values, some thought, which could heal her.

Six hundred senators and deputies gathered at Vichy on 10 July. Pierre Laval, who had entered the cabinet as vice-premier, fought hard for a new constitution. France was beaten and helpless, he insisted, but still capable of taking her place in the new order. The two houses met together on 10 July and by a vote of 569 to 80 mandated Pétain to promulgate a new Constitution of the French State. Thus the Third Republic was killed by most socialists and radicals. The French episcopacy unanimously summoned French Catholics to join in the reconstruction of France.[18] For François Mauriac, 'the words of Marshal Pétain, the evening of June 25, had an almost atemporal quality'; 'it was not a man who was speaking to us but ... a great humiliated nation.'[19]

One of the first initiatives of the Vichy régime was an effort towards moral reconstruction, a 'national revolution.' The new government stressed France's culpability for the defeat, her internal decadence and need for authority, la patrie, and tradition. Orators condemned the individualism and capitalism that had undermined the Third Republic, and called for a youth movement transcending old political divisions. Some of the general principles of Vichy's political philosophy seemed close to the Action Française, but Esprit's early appeal for a spiritual revolution among youth, a revolution that was neither 'Left' nor 'Right,' did not seem far from the rhetoric of the National Revolution.[20]

To make up his mind about the realities behind the language of the new régime, Mounier decided to visit Vichy himself. He felt isolated in Grenoble, devoid of information, but knew that several old friends of Esprit – notably Gaston Bergery, the maverick radical, René Belin, the syndicalist, and Action Française dissident Georges Valois – were there. Thus Mounier was at Vichy at the end of July and beginning of August 1940 when the new government established the youth movements Chantiers de la Jeunesse and Compagnons de France.

Although Belgian personalists seemed to be one of the only groups with clear ideas on how to deal with Belgian young people after the terrible shock of defeat, this did not seem to be the case in France. Mounier's advice and his influence on some younger intellectuals seem to have been of little interest, at least initially, to Vichy. While his old partner de Becker seemed at the centre of initiatives to precipitate a 'national resurrection' from Brussels, Mounier wandered curiously through the rococco corridors of Vichy, greeting old friends in the new governmental apparatus and trying to evaluate the directives coming out of the venerable marshal's court. Many an odd project seemed the brainchild of a young man Mounier had known before the war; others seemed to emanate from circles with a long history of enmity towards *Esprit*.[21]

Vichy's youth movements almost doubled in size in the first year following the armistice; one had the impression that all young Frenchmen were in uniform – except in the occupied zone, where Vichy's youth movements were forbidden by the Germans.[22] The Chantiers de la Jeunesse, which soon 'profoundly marked a whole generation of young Frenchmen,' was founded by Vichy law on 30 July 1940 to restore the morale of the young French soldiers who had been inducted the previous June just in time to surrender.[23] The Vichy government, rather than swell the ranks of the unemployed, decided to divide these soldiers into forty groups of 2,500 each, with a leader for each group. In January 1941, the Chantiers became obligatory as each Frenchman had to spend eight months in their rugged, outdoor camps during his twentieth year. The Chantiers' day was spent working – reconstructing abandoned mountain villages, repairing roads or bridges, bringing abandoned fields back into cultivation – and in sports or 'moral education.'[24] This latter activity was important for the Chantiers and Mounier's personalism soon found a place there.

The Chantiers were led largely by the leaders of the French Boy Scout movement, under the orders of the secretary general for youth at Vichy, the dynamic young Catholic engineer Georges Lamirand. Scout encampments, rustic and Spartan, far from the grime of the industrial cities and the cafés of the Latin Quarter, were considered ideal settings for nurturing healthy qualities in the young. The general named to head the Chantiers, Joseph de La Porte du Theil of the army's Seventh Corps, had been the Scout leader in the Paris region and recruited fellow Scout leaders as assistants, such as Père Forestier, national chaplain of the Scouts, who became general chaplain of the Chantiers. In the fall of 1940 there were seventy chaplains for the first thirty-five groups of the movement, and religious symbols and devotion to the marshal were among its most notable characteristics. For Père Forestier 'the structures of the new order, built upon authority, hierarchy, and the disappearance of class struggle,' were extraordinarily harmonious with the scout ideals. La Porte du Theil frequently made religious references in his speeches and there were Chantiers masses and Chantiers pilgrimages to various shrines of the Blessed Virgin. Fathers Doncœur and Sertillanges, Jacques Chevalier, Henri Marrou, and Jacques Madaule of *Esprit*, as well as Mounier's old lycée colleague, Robert Garric, whose Equipes Sociales inspired Chantiers theorists, wrote for its publications.

Despite the Catholic inspiration of moral education, La Porte du Theil insisted that the individual beliefs of the uniformed young men in the camps were to be respected, but a correction camp for delinquents, the undisciplined, and communists was established near Murat. Vichy seemed tempted to use authoritarian structures to Christianize the younger generation.[25]

Soon 90,000 boys were passing through the camps of the Chantiers every eight months. On their second anniversary Pétain saw in them 'the realization of that community of souls without which it would be impossible for me to reconstruct France.'[26] Even Christian Democrat Etienne Borne later described the Chantiers favourably, as 'practising a sort of primacy of the spiritual ... in the form of a simple, humbly natural life.'[27] The Chantiers seemed to be Vichy's most effective vehicle for the 'struggle against individualism,' the effort to 'transcend class struggle,' the national 'moral renovation' which the marshal had proclaimed.

The youth movement Compagnons de France, for boys between the ages of sixteen and twenty, was organized by Henry Dhavernas, a pre-war Scout leader, with the aid of Père Forestier; André Cruziat, leader of La Route, an organization for older Scouts; *Esprit* co-founder Louis-Emile Galey; and some Protestant Scout movement leaders. The forty-six French youth leaders, from the ACJF, the Jeunesses socialistes, the Eclaireurs unionistes (independent Scouts) who camped out from the 1–4 August 1940 in the forest of Randan, near Vichy, were visited by Pétain. The 'Charter of Randan,' to which all agreed, requested government support for extant youth movements but also approved creation of the independent Compagnons de France to 'form the personality of youth while respecting, and deepening, the convictions of each one.'[28] This organization promoted a political and religious 'ecumenism' not unlike the personalists'.

The Compagnons sought 'a moral climate totally different from that of the pre-war period.' Under the 'Maitre Compagnon' were 'Provinces,' 'Pays,' 'Triades,' and 'Compagnies,' each of which had a leader. 'Compagnies' with more than fifty 'Compagnons' were divided into 'Equipes' of ten boys, each commanded by a young 'chef d'équipe' who was to be 'an example and a guide for each Compagnon.' There were Compagnies where the young unemployed did farm work and Compagnies in the city where all social classes were mixed. The Compagnons followed strict rules and wore blue shirts with a tie, short pants, and berets.[29] Director Colonel Guillaume de Tournemire, who had served under Marshal Lyautey in Morocco, said: 'Our conception of the world seeks to introduce the primacy of the interests of the community over the interests of private individuals ... to give community reflexes to the new generation.'[30] The Compagnons, Pétain told them, were to be 'the avant-garde of the National Revolution.'[31]

The Compagnons was not official but Vichy did fund it and choose its leadership. Thus the Catholic clergy feared there would be an effort to create a single youth movement with a 'Pétainist religion' which would absorb the JOC, JAC, and all the rest – there were precedents in other countries for such a development.[32] Nevertheless, some well-known Catholics played key roles in the Compagnons, with veterans of *Esprit*'s Third Force such as Galey, 'chef des provinces,' and Jean Maze, director of the weekly, *Compagnons*, and the movement soon adopted Mounier's 'personnalisme communautaire,' fostering a distinctive form of left-wing Catholicism.[33] Young radical Catholic writers such as Maurice Clavel became leaders in the Compagnons and joined Mounier in late 1940 in working with Père Maurice Montuclard's Jeunesse de l'Eglise towards reforming the Catholic Church by promoting a greater sense of community among believers.[34] Many of these projects continued during Montuclard's post-war Chrétien progressiste movement.[35]

The Chantiers de la Jeunesse and Compagnons de France were attached to Pétain and not to Laval, who seemed to have reservations about them. The Compagnons did not mobilize nearly as many young people as did the Chantiers, but they did reveal the distinctive style of Pétain's National Revolution.[36] Mounier returned to Lyon from Vichy on 4 August and told a friend that the ministry of youth and the Compagnons de France were 'certainly what is best there, a little lacking in ideas, but with clear and healthy intentions.'[37]

In the 15 August 1940 *Revue des deux mondes*, Pétain, like Mounier, ascribed France's defeat to spiritual and moral causes which the school system should remedy:

individualism ... is ... what almost killed us.

Individualism has nothing in common with respect for the human
person....
The French school of tomorrow will teach respect of the human person, the
family, society, the fatherland. It will no longer make a pretense at neutrality....
There is no neutrality possible between the true and the false, between good
and evil, between health and sickness, between order and disorder, between
France and anti-France.[38]

In September, Pétain outlined the principles of his social policy, and again
the rhetoric recalled some of the 'neither Right nor Left' manifestos of the
personalists: the new social organization would not be 'liberalism' nor
'socialism' or 'capitalism,' since it would 'put an end to the reign of
economics.' It would 'subordinate the money factor to the human factor.'
Pétain argued that Christianity had conferred 'a spiritual value on
the most humble labour,' and declared 'we aspire with all our soul to
restore that value, which ultimately reposes on respect for the human
person.'[39]

In an October speech, the Marshal groped towards a new order for
France: 'The new order must not be a slavish imitation of other people's
experiments. Some of these experiments are not without meaning or
beauty. But every people should conceive a régime adapted to its climate
and national spirit.' He lamented that the French had to 'bring about in
defeat the revolution that in victory ... we were unable to achieve....' But
now the revolution would create a 'French hierarchy' solely on the bases of
'work and talent.' Again Pétain echoed the old personalist call for good
men in key places: 'So will arise the true élites, which the former régime
spent years destroying ... the cadres needed for the well-being and dignity
of all....'

Thus the economy had to be 'organized and controlled' to 'break the
influence of the trusts': the working classes and the bourgeoisie were to
'make an immense effort to escape from idle routine,' recognize 'their
common interest as citizens in a nation henceforth united....' The address
closed with a father figure's veiled threat to errant children: 'Soon I shall
ask you to come together, so that assembled round me ... you may lead this
Revolution to its conclusion, by rallying those who hesitate, breaking up
hostile forces and combined interests, so that in this new France true
national fraternity may reign supreme.'[40]

Mounier had consistently maintained that France was 'sick' from
'individualism' and that her only hope lay in the creation of a 'revolutionary New Order' – anti-liberal, with a general 'anti-capitalism' theme

like that of Pétain. Mounier, too, had granted the 'beauty' of the 'experiments of other peoples' but called for an initiative from France's 'true élites' – men sensitive to the 'human person.' Now Pétain summoned 'the true élites, which the former régime spent years destroying,' to positions of leadership. Was this, in fact, the *Esprit* vision come to life?

There was an undeniable similarity between *Esprit*'s pre-war aspirations and some of the rhetoric of the new government, if only because Pétain's initial statements of the National Revolution were written by the Catholic intellectual René Gillouin and Gaston Bergery.[41] René Gillouin had hosted the first meetings of *Ordre Nouveau* and was a great admirer of Péguy, Bergson, and Berdyaev. He intervened for Mounier on several occasions with Vichy's censors. Gillouin, with François Perroux, has been described as one of the Marshal's key ideologists.[42] Gaston Bergery's Parti Frontiste had been built largely around old *Esprit* members: Galey, secretary of *La Flèche*; Izard, deputy of the Parti Frontiste in 1936 and political editor of *La Flèche* until 1937; and Jean Maze, assistant editor of *La Flèche*.

The marshal's subsequent formulations of the National Revolution were also worked out by men with some affinities for *Esprit*'s personalism. His discourse at St Etienne on 1 March 1941 on labour and social policy was composed by the engineer Robert Loustau, a former member of *Ordre Nouveau* who in late 1935 had told Mounier that like his fellow member of the X-Crise group, Robert Gibrat, he owed his ideological formation to *Esprit*.[43] Vichy's Labour Charter, promulgated on 26 October 1941, was elaborated over several months by Mounier's friend René Belin of the CGT, the Jesuits of L'Action Populaire, and Loustau. It embodied several concepts of *Esprit*'s Perroux.[44]

Some of the key early ministers of Pétain, such as Paul Baudoin, a devout Catholic and the minister of foreign affairs, Yves Bouthillier, minister of finance, and Marcel Peyrouton, minister of the interior, may also have been spokesmen for certain personalist ideas.[45] Robert Loustau was head of Beaudoin's staff. Jean Jardin of *Ordre Nouveau* was on Bouthillier's staff before he became head of Pierre Laval's staff. One of the ministers closest to Pétain was his godson, Jacques Chevalier, minister of education in 1940, then minister of health.[46] In short, personalists as well as pious Catholics were strong at Vichy in 1940 and 1941.[47]

Could personalism flourish from the Friends of *Esprit* and, with the right patronage, transform French youth? In the fall of 1940, Mounier seemed to believe that this was a distinct possibility. But France then, he soon discovered, was not the Christian Roman empire overrun by rude but innocent Visigoths.

If Mounier had had any contact with Belgium in the confused months following defeat, he might have been able to place the prospect for creating a new order under the Nazis in a more balanced perspective. As it was there was an hallucinatory aspect to the grandiose speculations of the ardent creators of new worlds who trailed down to Vichy after the humiliation of their country. These were often based on a naïve estimate of Nazi intentions for France or an inaccurate assessment of the elements in the Reich which would influence the policies of the occupying forces.

A DOUBLE GAME

After he had visited several acquaintances at Vichy, Mounier returned to Lyon in full agreement with his friends Jean Lacroix and Charles Blondel. With a Hegelian fatalism worthy of Karl Popper's worst fears, they concluded that 'what is dying is dead; a new face is imposed on the history which is coming, an authoritarian face; we cannot avoid these oscillations in ... history, we cannot work at cross-purposes to elementary themes.'[48] The three agreed to defend their old values and ideals 'with new gestures and formulas, in the new material.' Blondel suggested that they 'fabricate secret spiritual weaponry,' that is, 'profit from the similarity of names between our values and those publicly proclaimed to introduce, through that coincidence, the desired content.' This implied that the three men, despite their reservations, could work with the new régime, and several of Blondel's Christian Democrat friends were flabbergasted by an idea which they considered to border on treason. Their need for secret weaponry, however, also implied a guarded attitude towards the Vichy régime despite all the high hopes of the Randan meeting.[49]

In mid-August, after visiting the Marrous, the Mouniers spent ten days in the mountains at Montverdun with the avant-garde Dominican fathers Paul and Maurice Montuclard, discussing the 'reform of Christianity' through the reintroduction of the Church's traditional communitarianism and worker priests. The Montuclards' radical, sociologically based critique of a Church dominated by the bourgeoisie fueled their desire to build a new, manly Christianity among the working classes. All this transformation was envisaged by Mounier in the context of the triumph of the barbarians over Rome; his essay in *Marianne* at this time recommended the substitution of resistance by an effort to Christianize the occupying forces.[50] He was, he confided, 'at the same time pessimistic, because I believe that the trials are only beginning and we will see worse – and optimistic, because we are entering into a vigorous epoque.'[51]

Mounier tried to explain his view of the situation to friends in neutral Switzerland and the United States.[52] In the American liberal Catholic magazine *Commonweal*, Mounier predicted a new illiberal Europe:

the Europe of the next few years ... will be an authoritarian Europe because it was too long a libertarian Europe. Whoever has not made a serious revision of his philosophy of freedom and of the political forms that it implies is a conservative, even if he lists himself among the 'advanced' spirits. We are obliged now to find a place for freedom in authoritarian régimes....[53]

In sum, Mounier seemed convinced that Germany would win the war and that it was the duty of Christians to Christianize the new Europe as their predecessors had been obliged to leave aside their beloved Roman customs and, from within, transform the society of the savage people who had swept down from the north.

Mounier knew that Bergery was preparing Pétain's speeches and might have been pleased that ideas which he and a handful of his young friends had pioneered were to be guiding principles of the new France. But as early as July 1940 he wondered if Pétain might not turn out to be a Kerensky or a Bruening.[54] At the end of August, he decided to keep his diary again because he thought himself 'entering into a clandestine period, where all thoughts cannot be flaunted, all facts published, all intentions affirmed.' He wanted to keep a record to show later to prisoners such as Paul Fraisse, the Belgians, and residents of the occupied zone.[55]

Mounier and Lacroix decided to embark upon a curious – and soon, controversial – 'double game' within a régime with theorists who were their old comrades but whom they could not completely trust. Behind Mounier's reservations about Vichy was his scepticism over the conservative nationalists of Action Française in the Vichy hierarchy. On 11 September, François Perroux, new doctrinal adviser to Pétain in his position at the Ministry of Family and Youth wrote that Mounier's request to give courses to the youth groups on the French radio system, in which Roger Leenhardt of *Esprit* was director of the *Radio Jeunesse* section, would almost certainly be refused. At Vichy, the young economist complained, 'not only does one not think in a new way, but one is rigorously forbidden to do so'; 'having been suspected of fascism in the *Esprit* group, here I find myself considered a dangerous, distrusted innovator....' A major part of the problem, he thought, was that *curés* were afraid of losing their influence over youth. 'If things continue like this,'

Perroux warned his friend, 'the young will be enrolled in Hitlerite platoons which will solicit the opinions of neither the fine *curés* nor the sublime *bien-pensants*.' Despite Mounier's influence on several of the new government's younger *cadres*, Perroux saw little possibility for Mounier's finding a place at Vichy and suggested he seek a teaching position.[56] Perroux's premonition was confirmed a few weeks later when Jean Maze ran into difficulty about publishing a Mounier article in the first issue of his weekly *Compagnons*.[57]

Following Perroux's discouraging advice, and refusing an offer to teach in an American university, Mounier wrote to Jacques Chevalier about his desire to have his review included among those approved for publication by the new government: 'To start *Esprit* again! I want this with all my heart; a review on a smaller scale, certainly, freed from all the past, completely devoted to promoting the spiritual, to the rebirth of the West....' He was asking his old mentor for the opportunity to explain his intentions to the authorities.[58]

At the end of September, Mounier returned to Vichy to plead his case for resurrecting *Esprit*, and gained more insight into the new régime. On 25 September René Gillouin, personal secretary to Pétain, denounced Pierre Laval to Mounier as 'scum of the earth, a bandit – and, I fear to have to say, traitor.'[59] Mounier reflected, soon after, that there were some who were supporting the themes of German propaganda that France should return to her true vocation as an agricultural country and become 'the peaceful garden of the totalitarian Europe ... charged with supplying fresh vegetables to the workers in the gigantic German factories.'[60] Mounier saw Laval as the leader of a sinister Pro-Nazi element in Vichy versus the young personalists around Pétain. Chevalier was measured in his encouragement about publishing a new *Esprit*, and warned that supporting England would retain 'all the old gang' to power in France. Nevertheless, a month later Mounier received approval for *Esprit*.

He decided to ignore all warnings and adopt an active role in the 'new order' in France. In publishing *Esprit* in these circumstances, Mounier lent an air of respectability to a régime about which he was privately extremely reticent. He joined the effort for the National Revolution with a complex of motives which varied with his interlocuteurs. His reborn journal, however, began on a positive note. Jean Lacroix described Hitlerism as a revolution on the march, part of the 'revolution of the twentieth century,' while Mounier described the National Revolution as the culmination of a decade of personalist effort: 'that necessity of a total revolution, we were almost alone in affirming in 1932. ... It was not an opinion among others but the very meaning and vocation of our twenty-fifth year. ... All of the formulas thrown as stimuli of hope to the youth of France today, in embryonic form in this program, we have been deepening and spreading for years.'[61]

Mounier's sanguine rhetoric was in marked contrast to his private misgivings. On the day his first *Compagnons* essay appeared, he noted the 'shameful statute on the Jews' promulgated by the government.[62] On 24 October Pétain met Hitler at Montoire and Mounier had serious questions about the independence of the French régime. He registered his disgust over Nazi policies towards Jews in occupied Alsace. P.-A. Touchard, from the occupied zone, reiterated his misgivings about starting up again under Vichy and was joined by Paul Fraisse from prison camp, Paul-Louis Landsberg, who was shocked by Mounier's article in *Marianne*, Victor Serge, who found Mounier's tactic 'risky,' and Robert Delavignette, who joined his firm protest to that of Touchard.[63] After *Esprit* reappeared in November the protests mounted: Christian Democrat Marcel Prélot and syndicalist Paul Vignaux firmly told Lacroix: 'One can only hope for the victory of England, all other hypotheses are meaningless.'[64] François Goguel, writing from a German prison camp, also objected, along with Jean Gosset, who later died heroically in the Resistance. In succeeding months Etienne Borne, Jacques Perret, Daniel Villey, and Marcel Moré all opposed publishing their old review.

In the end, few of *Esprit*'s major pre-war essayists supported Mounier in this venture and he had to rely on a few unknown young men and a few major pre-war sympathizers of the review such as philosopher Gabriel Marcel, Jean Daniélou, and the journalist Hubert Beuve-Méry. Poet Pierre Emmanuel also offered his services. On 30 November Mounier organized an 'intergroup reunion' in his apartment in Lyon for some twenty people to evaluate the information they had on current events. Besides Lacroix, Beuve-Méry, and Marcel there was Maze of *Compagnons*; the militantly anti-fascist Jesuit Gaston Fessard, who soon helped found the Resistance tract *Témoignage Chrétien*; Christian socialist André Philip; and Catholic journalist Stanislas Fumet, whose weekly *Temps nouveaux* was another attempt to publish progressive Catholic opinion within Vichy's guidelines and censorship.[65] Although Mounier pointedly invited 'Lavaliens' to this meeting, he tended to blame Pierre Laval for the humiliating concessions made to the conqueror.[66] At this time even several future Resistance leaders seemed to believe that French national independence would assert itself behind Pétain.[67] Those who thought that France would have to find a place for herself in a new authoritarian Europe could still converse with those who insisted upon uncompromising resistance against the enemy and non-cooperation with Vichy. Mounier, however, considered the latter attitude 'dangerously abstentionist.'

On 13 December 1940 marshal Pétain suddenly asked for the resignation of Pierre Laval, who was taken to his estate at Châteldon and kept under guard. This began a period of great tension between the Pétain government and the occupation authorities. On the 16th, Otto Abetz, accompanied by armed soldiers, rushed down into the free zone and, after demanding the constitution of a new government acceptable to the German ambassador, took Laval back to Paris with him. The crisis resulted in the closing of the line of demarcation between the two zones and a near rupture in diplomatic relations.

On the very day Laval was arrested, Mounier had an essay on Laval censored as too disrespectful. When Mounier tried again the Lyon censor did not know what to do under the fluctuating circumstances. Mounier then wrote to René Gillouin asking his aid, and soon the censor withdrew his objections.[68] This brief period between the temporary fall of Laval and the rise of Admiral Darlan was the high point of Mounier's influence in the National Revolution. He suddenly emerged from his relative obscurity to notoriety as the chief theorist of several ambitious projects to transform the youth of his country.

URIAGE

Youth movements were to be the schools of the National Revolution and the Ecole Nationale des Cadres d'Uriage was to be its Ecole Normale Supérieure.[69] In August 1940 Marshal Pétain had said that 'each profession, each métier, will have its élite, and we will encourage the formation of these élites on the local and regional level with all our strength.'[70] Youth movements were to be the nurseries of the natural élites. The Ecole Nationale des Cadres was to train the special élites needed to direct youth movements.

Captain Pierre Dunoyer de Segonzac, a dashing thirty-four-year-old graduate of Saint-Cyr and Action Française sympathizer, had gone to Vichy after the defeat with the conviction that 'we had collided with an army animated by an ideal, a mystique or a faith, something very powerful ... we did not have a similar élan on our side to oppose it.'[71] The Ecole Nationale des Cadres, established by Vichy in August 1940 with Dunoyer de Segonzac at its head, was to provide young Frenchmen with a new mystique. It was first installed in a Louis XIII château not far from Vichy, lent by Philippe Lamour, the former director of the review *Plans*, with a staff of about a dozen army, airforce, and navy officers. It also had a chaplain, the abbé de Naurois, a professor at the Institut Catholique of Toulouse who had been interested in *Esprit* for several years. In November, the ENSC moved to the medieval chateau de Murinet, said to have belonged to the family of the heroic knight Bayard and romantically perched at St Martin d'Uriage, on a high plateau near Grenoble.[72]

The Uriage School was to complete the education of the personnel of the Secrétariat général de la Jeunesse at Vichy as a 'Grande Ecole spécialisée' for the youth movements of Vichy, like Saint-Cyr for the army or 'Centrale' for engineers before the war.[73] But in a larger context, Uriage's staff, as Dunoyer de Segonzac later wrote, was 'preoccupied with defining the conditions for the birth of the new man and of the crystallization of new élites, because Uriage believed in élites and in their decisive importance.' They planned to create subsidiary institutions to form the 'élites populaires,' 'élites d'encadrement social,' 'élites de gouvernement,' and 'élites de civilisation.'[74] Uriage was, according to one of its directors, modelled after a German Ordensburg, one of the four order castles modelled on the fourteenth- and fifteenth-century castles of the order of the teutonic knights, where the 'golden pheasants,' the élite of the Nazi élite, were trained in romantic settings.[75] The officers at Uriage made a personal oath of fidelity to Marshal Pétain, and a student swore fidelity to 'the rule of the Order' while 'merging himself into the evolution of the world towards forms of collective life, and adopting for a goal the liberation of man on the economic, social and spiritual levels.'[76] Its members came to consider it a 'secular order.'[77]

A Uriage day began with a salute to the flag and ten to fifteen minutes of callisthenics and closed with songs around a bonfire and another salute to the colours. The students ran a half-hour obstacle course on the athletic field on the Uriage plateau; and their vigorous outdoor life included alpinism, skiing, and various labouring projects in neighbouring mountain valleys. The students came from all social, educational, and occupational backgrounds and, like their instructors, wore grey uniforms. They marched in step from one activity to the other and were prompt to execute orders. The ideal young man at Uriage had 'a firm jaw, an energetic and confident manner, bulging muscles, short hair, and sang folk songs in rhythm.' From the outset, they combined spiritual and moral education with physical training, studying Péguy, Proudhon, Maurras, as well as 'personnalisme.'[78]

Uriage's earliest staff included Eric d'Alançon, 'soldier-monk' and father of sixteen children, Roger Wuillemin, well-known expert in physical education, Paul-Henry Chombart de Lauwe, sociologist and fighter pilot, Paul Reuter, professor of international law, Joffre Dumazdier, a self-styled 'orthodox Marxist,' Bertrand d'Astorg of *Esprit*, Gilles Ferry, Gilbert Gadoffre, *agrégé* in English, and 'a number of future generals and admirals.' The dynamic director of studies was the foreign correspondent Hubert Beuve-Méry.[79] It looked as if the third force was to become a reality.

In succeeding months, distinguished Catholic intellectuals such as Père Maydieu, director of *La Vie Intellectuelle* ('For us, in search of a new élite,' Dunoyer de Segonzac wrote later, Père Maydieu seemed 'a captivating prototype'), and Professor Jean-Jacques Chevalier, 'chantre de l'ordre viril,' began to give courses. Among participating theologians were Father Dominique Dubarle, specialist in the philosophy of science, Father Dillard, economics expert of the Jesuits' Action Populaire movement and regular preacher at Vichy, M.-D. Chenu, medieval historian and expert on the 'theology of labour,' Henri de Lubac, interpreter of Teilhard de Chardin and expert on Proudhon, as well as Msgr Bruno de Solages, professor in the Institut Catholique at Toulouse.[80] In December 1940 three former students of Jacques Chevalier were invited to join the work at the Ecole Nationale Supérieure des Cadres: Mounier's old friend Jean Guitton, then giving philosophy courses in a German prison camp, Jean Lacroix, professor in the 'Khâgne' of his lycée at Lyon, and Mounier. Guitton preferred to continue working with his fellow prisoners; Mounier, and Lacroix on Mounier's urging, joined the Uriage team.[81]

Among the prominent figures who came from the outside to give regular conferences at Uriage were the Catholic poet and diplomat Paul Claudel; the diplomat François-Poncet; Péguy's son, Pierre; Jean-Marcel Jeanneney, who lectured on economics; Henri Marrou, historian and folk musicologist; Alfred Fabre-Luce, Henri Daniel-Rops, and Claude Roy. Regular visitors from Vichy included René Gillouin and Admiral Fernet, who, according to Dunoyer de Segonzac, 'thereby showed their opposition to Pierre Laval,' and Pétain's unofficial representative at Uriage, the Catholic writer René Benjamin. Marshal Pétain himself quietly visited the Ecole Nationale des Cadres, and Dunoyer de Segonzac, who had ready access to the marshal, also travelled several times to Vichy.[82] Among those who came to Uriage later and stayed were Captain Henri Frenay, an old Saint-Cyr friend of Dunoyer de Segonzac, and Jean-Marie Domenach, a former student of Jean Lacroix at Lyon, and his friend Gilbert Dru.[83]

At the end of 1940, the 'Vieux Chef,' Dunoyer de Segonzac, invited

Henri Massis, then a prominent Action Française representative at Vichy, Robert Bothereau, a 'Proudhonian' syndicalist, and Mounier to a symposium at the chateau. They were leaders of the opposing sides within the school, but Dunoyer de Segonzac was disappointed by the failure of this attempt at 'ecumenism.'[84] In March 1941 he was summoned before the youth commission of the Conseil National at Vichy, which included General de La Porte du Theil, General Lafont, Msgr Beaussart, François-Poncet, Henri Massis, Pastor Boegner, and Gaston Bergery.[85] Generals Lafont and La Porte du Theil attacked the 'personalism' of Uriage and insisted that Mounier and the Abbé de Naurois be eliminated from the institution. However, Bergery's defence saved the day and the 'Vieux Chef' was allowed to continue.[86] In fact Esprit's personalism became the unofficial doctrine of Uriage, largely through the efforts of Mounier and Lacroix.[87] In part, this success reflected the fact that Dunoyer de Segonzac shared Mounier's distaste for 'bourgeois Christianity' and searched for a new relationship between action and contemplation, a more manly and aggressive Christianity.[88] A hostile General de La Porte du Theil was forced to found his own Ecoles des Cadres to form the Chantiers de la Jeunesse leaders, but this merely encouraged the visionaries of Uriage, who continued to search for what they called the 'style of the twentieth century.'

The Uriage school alumni later maintained that it was a peculiar 'island of freedom' in a more and more authoritarian regime. In 1940–1, however, Uriage sometimes seemed to be fulfilling Paul Nizan's prophecy: Mounier was distilling the thick foreign currents into the spiritualized national socialism of a French Ordensburg above Grenoble. Precisely where, according to German ethnologists, the Nordic Alleman family had maintained their aerie centuries earlier, personalists in grey anoraks formed earnest young men according to the doctrine worked out previously in Esprit. The 'individualism' of these new élites was broken so that their 'persons' might develop. Group singing, sports, and personnalisme communautaire promoted an effective day-to-day fraternal socialism inspired by devotion to the nation and its leader. There was a balance between reflective thought and vigorous outdoor activity, physical courage and medieval chivalry. Besides devotion to Pétain there was also the cult of the handsome young officer, neither liberal nor democrat, who instilled in his young men discipline and devotion to the leader. They in turn were to create mini-Uriages from one end of France to the other.

Many Catholics were enthusiastic about Uriage because it was to be the keystone of a vast effort to 'spiritualize' French youth. When one considers how remote the prospects of 'spiritualizing' them were before, one can grasp why Uriage seemed charged with heady possibilities. Only Christianity, according to Raymond de Becker, had the right to be totalitarian. Many at Uriage seemed to agree with this and so tried with a perfectly clear conscience to create a totalitarian society. The 'individualism' of the new generation would be crushed but their 'persons' would flourish.

The Ecole Nationale Supérieure des Cadres was, in certain respects, the culmination of Mounier's career. After years of fidelity to an esoteric and marginal set of ideas, he was suddenly *the* philosopher of an institution which, in theory, was going to educate the entire youth of France. Uriage was, in a sense, a noble, romantic enterprise which played a role in freeing France from Nazi domination. It was also an imprudent and dangerous venture under the circumstances. Some miles to the north, at the Ecole des Cadres in the occupied zone, young Frenchmen were walking on broken glass, bloodletting, and engaging in a whole set of pagan rites that recalled Heinrich Himmler's black order. The young Uriage idealists considered the Ecole des Cadres in the Nazi zone to be 'the enemy,' but Uriage's philosophy sometimes seemed a Christianized version of the same thing: élitist, totalitarian, gnostic, and arrogant. 'What is this operetta for the enemy?' an angry Daniel Villey demanded of Mounier when he returned from German prison camp to see personalism ornamenting the National Revolution.[89]

The instructors at the Chateau de Murinet worked hard to create new élites for a régime they mistrusted. Mounier's place in Uriage and Uriage's place in the National Revolution became progressively more difficult, particularly after Hitler's invasion of the Soviet Union slowed and the war began to turn against the Axis.

The *Esprits* of late 1940 and early 1941 described Vichy's cultural projects in detail, especially those of Jacques Chevalier. Mounier wrote that he hoped 'to remake *Esprit* into one of the principal creative centres of a true France and of a true revolution.'[90] During the winter of 1940–1 he elaborated an innocuous 'program for the French Youth Movement' which declared 'war on the world of money,' formed an alliance 'with the simple life,' and sought to 'restore the sense of authority and of collective discipline' and to 'substitute for indifference, scepticism and dilettantism a love of the committed life.' He cited as exemplary 'the force with which the German revolution ... rallied the entire country, especially the socialist current, and spread the sentiment of working for the service of the

German people.' The final note was characteristic: 'Twelfth Theme: we are happy boys. We will rediscover French song, the community holiday, the theatre of the professions and of the village, the joy of building, gaiety in general. Because a healthy people, a people busy at work, is also a people crowned with festivals, with liturgies, and games.'[91] This same *Esprit* included articles by authors of the 'former' Left and Right and Mounier rejoiced that all 'revolutionaries' were reunited in a common effort to form French youth.[92]

In early 1941, in order to counter Marcel Déat, who was organizing a pro-Nazi movement against the 'reactionaries' at Vichy, a committee for the national revolution was created in the free zone. Among others, Thierry Maulnier, Antoine de Saint-Exupéry, and Robert Garric joined, but Mounier declined, although invited.[93] At the end of January 1941, however, he was called by telegram to Vichy where he received a more attractive proposal. The Secrétariat Général à la Jeunesse created Jeune France to 'renovate all forms of French artistic life.'[94] Its directors, Pierre Schaeffer and Pierre Barbier, wanted Mounier to help shape the movement.

Mounier preferred to contribute 'tangentially,' as at Uriage, without accepting an official post, but Jeune France's principal figures came from the *Esprit* group, where the idea of a travelling popular theatre had been developed by Barbier. They came from both the 'old' Left and Right, and thus it was in harmony with the new spirit sought since the spring of 1940. In *Esprit* Mounier called Jeune France 'one of the richest promises of the France of tomorrow,' and urged his readers to join.

Jeune France was a high point of unrestrained fantasy. Here within the larger dreamworld of the National Revolution young Catholics and 'spirituals' tried to create, in microcosm, the 'new middle ages' which Berdyaev had predicted a decade earlier. At the beautiful, sand-coloured medieval chateau of Lourmarin, set on a hillock above a bucolic village in the Vaucluse celebrated by the poet Henri Bosco, Jeune France first met 'par de blondes journées de fin de janvier' in 1941. The organization was going to 'reconstruct the cultural components of the country, beginning with its young people.' Its first project was to rebuild one of the Roman fortified towns (*Oppidum*) in the foothills of the mountains of Provence, as old workers were turning young people into master masons, master carpenters, and master stone-cutters. These new master workmen and artisans were to inspire a whole network of similar centres all over France until, Mounier predicted, one would be able to make an entire 'Tour de France ouvrier.'

Mounier and *Esprit* colleague Roger Leenhardt, director of Radio-Jeunesse at Vichy, persuaded many poets, artists, musicians, and writers to work with the organization. Mounier poetically recalled the memorable September 1941 meeting in the Lourmarin chateau:

Pierre Emmanuel, allant de la douce gentillesse à la grande éloquence lyrique; et le petit Loys Masson, menu et chantant comme un oiseau des iles ... Lanza del Vasto, le barde sicilien, immense, sa longue tête maigre au haut front étroit sortant du chandail blanc ceinturé de cuir, les pieds nus dans les sandales, en bandoulière le sac de poil de chèvre, portant sa boîte à poèmes, gravée par lui....[95]

Mounier in early 1941 seemed most concerned with Jeune France and the Uriage school. Reporting progress in the April 1941 *Esprit*, he claimed that: 'the school of Uriage is already a school of culture and of character ... the sense of French dignity and civic courage are helping to eradicate political and social prejudice ... and making it ... a school for young hearts, souls, and minds ... in a true national community where parties and classes are not masked, but positively eliminated.'[96] Despite public enthusiasm, Mounier continued to debate *Esprit*'s role in Vichy. He did reject the 'all or nothing' anti-fascist position of Etienne Borne and Jacques Maritain: responding to Borne's reproaches in February, he defended 'the genuine little islands of health, the corners of France truly free, the Uriage school, Jeune France.' Mounier did not think that 'between asphyxiation and health there is no worthy compromise'; *Esprit* was giving off 'a little bad air' but was also 'slowly introducing more and more oxygen.' He rejected an uncompromising defence of democracy and 'inflexible anti-fascism' because 'in France, where it was necessary to create something new at any price, it was obstructing the very spirit of creation.' Certainly one had to resist 'all infiltration of the conqueror's spirit,' but 'in these, as in military matters, defensive positions, however heroic, are bad and kill the spirit of creation.'[97]

In the privacy of his diary Mounier often reflected about the fifth-century Roman Empire, in which Christian culture was confronted with barbarians' 'evil' and nihilism. A few Christians of that period had refused to defend the Church in a 'decadent form' and recognized 'the strength that the barbarian hearts were bringing to them.' Mounier mused that it would perhaps be only by fire and iron that 'we will pass from the bourgeois man and from the bourgeois church.'[98]

For Mounier, one impetus for the new order was anti-capitalism:

'Whatever one may say in favour of England and of Anglo-Saxon capitalism, we are now paying for "working-houses" [sic] and for a hundred years of hardness of heart.' He thought that 'the Western world ought to submit to a profound revolution' and that certain Nazi values, though presently 'excessive or warped,' had their role in it. The triumph of the Nazis came from 'an impressive expansionist force ... from below ... The Revolution of the 20th century, which we support with all our strength, is also coming from that direction.'[99]

In May 1941, Mounier spoke of 'the terrible ambiguity of all historical forces' which was 'perhaps making us ignore the magnificent adventure that a Franco-German collaboration would have been, merely because Nazism is pushing it.' Of Charles de Gaulle and his followers he privately noted: 'Tomorrow ... we will have to fight them ... if they return to their petty nationalist protectionisms.' He did envision the possibility of an allied victory, though without great enthusiasm and was aware of the possibility that his historical perspective had been wrong.[100]

In March 1941, Mounier noted in his diary some reasons behind his reluctance to join the resistance:

I am completely unequal to engaging in an offensive political action, clandestine (too much cunning is required) or public (too much eloquence is necessary). I am too sensitive to all that which deforms men in action, too relativist in the matter of political regimes, too unenthusiastic for that which concerns them.

He felt that he could not work within a 'sub-Nazi or communist' régime, but 'in a pro-communist régime or under Vichy, yes, to the degree ... to which one could still push ... in a humanist direction.'[101] His colleague Beuve-Méry described this as 'a period when, after [the Pétain-Hitler meeting at] Montoire, but also after the arrest of Laval, the attitude of the Vichy government did not seem definitively fixed.'[102] Mounier admitted that his own position bordered on 'the apolitical attitude that I have denounced many times due to feeling myself too close to it.' His influence, he concluded, had 'a point of insertion that was other than political.'[103]

Whatever Mounier's intentions, his influence on the National Revolution grew through the spring and summer of 1941. The youth movements needed something more than the exhortations of Marshal Pétain if they were to reconstruct their country along new lines, and, in 1941, there seemed to be two ideologies to which youth leaders could turn – Esprit's and that of the Action Française. Mounier remained enthusiastic about

Jeune France, especially the Uriage school, providing an alternative to unhealthy tendencies at Vichy.

Esprit seemed to prosper in its first year under Pétain. In December 1940, the ministry for foreign affairs took 250 subscriptions for its embassies and consulates throughout the world. In February, Mounier received congratulations from the minister of youth for his youth program, which was partially adopted by the new 'Jeunesse de France et d'Outre-Mer.'[104] In August, Mounier's diary noted 'growing success of the review and of our influence. The "Chantiers" subscribe now by packets of ten and fifteen for all their groups. I met leaders at Jeune France meetings who have not derived their doctrine from any other source.'[105] *Esprit* was recommended to the Chantiers by their national bulletin and so popular that in one year it almost doubled its general circulation within the unoccupied zone.[106] Curiously, *Esprit* published Mounier's ringing appeals to French youth along with more and more notorious resistance material such as Marc Beigbeder's satire, 'Suite aux mémoires d'un âne.'[107]

In July 1941, Admiral Darlan, then second to Marshal Pétain in the Vichy hierarchy, was impressed by what he saw at Uriage and decided to make three weeks there obligatory for all young men successful in the examinations for foreign affairs, finance, the Cour des Comptes, and the Conseil d'Etat. Since all the administrative personnel of Vichy were to pass through this 'Ecole Normale,' Darlan increased its financing in line with its new importance. This obligatory feature was new to Uriage, whose volunteers had undertaken far longer stages of training. At this juncture, when Mounier seemed at the height of his influence, his elimination from Vichy's hierarchy began. After Darlan's visit, another major change in the Ecole Nationale Supérieure des Cadres was the elimination of Emmanuel Mounier from the staff.[108]

ELIMINATION AND PRISON

Mounier's difficulties with the régime, which became more serious after early 1941, were rooted both in his own growing doubts about the government and the hostility to the success of his personalism.[109] Then, too, the military situation changed after the German invasion of the Soviet Union in June 1941, and Vichy evolved towards overt collaboration with Germany while instigating more and more coercive legislation in France. In January 1941 Mounier broke with Jacques Chevalier, then minister of education and confidante of Pétain, over legislation against Jews. At

Henri Bergson's death, Mounier learned of his request that Chevalier not be informed; Mounier considered it a rebuke of 'the executor of the anti-Semitic laws.'[110] Mounier himself had been reg ilarly interceding with his friends at Vichy – René Gillouin, and Pierre Dominique, head of Vichy's press services – to aid individual Jews.[111] Earlier, Chevalier's program to 'restore God in the schools' had been denounced by Gabriel Marcel in *Esprit* as ineffective, imprudent, and a violation of teachers' consciences.[112] Chevalier had become a 'public scourge,' Mounier thought, and when he was moved to the position of Secrétaire d'Etat for the family, and the God in the schools project was scuttled, Mounier was greatly relieved.[113]

'Merde!' was Mounier's reaction when he heard that Pierre Laval might be brought back into the government.[114] He worried whether or not Pétain prevailed at Vichy over the sinister influences of Darlan and Laval.[115] Each month Mounier received more criticism from his friends for his 'spiritual arms' tactic and received no help in it from *Esprit* associates. As Nazi pressure on Vichy mounted, he and Jean Daniélou decided to make more distinctions between personalist notions of 'community, the sense of mystery, dynamism, youth, etc....' and those of the Nazis. But the more Mounier set off his personalism from the 'false personalism' in France, the more he seemed a resister and created enemies.

His growing influence among the young irritated his old adversaries of the Catholic Right and Action Française. In March 1941, as we have seen, there had been an attempt to eliminate him from Uriage, but Dunoyer de Segonzac had successfully resisted it.[116] In the summer of 1941, when he was finally eliminated from the school, he blamed his old adversary Henri Massis.[117] Indeed, that summer Massis, Vichy minister of youth, and Gustave Thibon, sometimes called 'the philosopher' of the National Revolution of Vichy, discussed Mounier's 'nefarious' influence on the Christian philosophical milieu.[118] A month after Mounier's elimination from Uriage, *Esprit* was ordered to cease publication by Admiral Darlan because of 'the general tendencies it manifests.' In September, Mounier was removed from Jeune France, and soon imprisoned. The Third Force had turned on him too.

Mounier soon learned that his interdiction had resulted from a campaign by Massis, the Action Française, and 'the new Pucheu-Marion group,' who had recently come to power and who were resolved to promote 'a totalitarian state accepting a minimum of Christian human- ism.'[119] Mounier considered his silencing part of a struggle for the soul of

Vichy's national revolution.[120] He was very bitter when rightist Jean de Fabrègues founded the weekly *Demain* to rally French Catholics to the Vichy régime with a circulation built upon address lists taken by the police from the *Esprit* offices.[121] In three months Mounier had been eliminated as a major intellectual figure in Vichy France, and, from the fall of 1941, he withdrew into silence for the duration of the occupation period. Vichy continued to vaunt a certain 'personalism' as its doctrine; Beuve-Méry and Lacroix continued to be involved in Uriage and François Perroux in important Vichy study groups, but the heyday of *Esprit*'s personalism as the official ideology of France seemed to pass with the elimination of Mounier from the youth movements.

METAMORPHOSIS OF THE NATIONAL REVOLUTION
IN BELGIUM AND FRANCE

After the invasion of the Soviet Union in June 1941, the pressure on Belgium and France greatly increased. Henri de Man's efforts to achieve advantages for Belgian workers had run up against German authorities who wanted Belgian salaries low so as to attract workers to Reich factories. De Man's protestations led to the disappearance of his newspaper *Le Travail* and, in November, he exiled himself to La Clusaz, high in the French Alps, where, however, he kept up his contacts with Otto Abetz and Edouard Didier's publishing house[122] until he fled to Switzerland under Dr Oprecht's protection at the end of the war.[123] When Léon Degrelle rallied to the cause of a greater Germany at the beginning of 1943, that was the last straw for de Becker and several of his Belgiciste friends. He resigned from *Le Soir* and published a lively attack on the annexationist and anti-Christian tendencies of the ss and the general failure of collaboration. He was sent to a German concentration camp in September 1943, only to be transferred to one of the allies' at the time of the liberation. His friend Henri Bauchau abandoned his leadership of the Service du Travail to join the Resistance.[124] Thus many of the idealistic young Belgian personalists and national socialists cultivated by Abetz throughout the nineteen-thirties were soon in exile, prison, or the Resistance.

When, on 22 June 1941, the Nazis invaded the Soviet Union the clandestine French Communist party, whose newspaper had welcomed the conquerors to Paris just one year earlier, joined the Resistance.[125] Terrorist acts against the occupant multiplied and the Germans responded with large-scale executions of Communists and other hostages.[126] Vichy passed severe laws against terrorists and, on 12

August, Marshal Pétain explained the reason for the new measures: 'I have serious things to tell you. I have sensed an ill wind in several parts of France for some weeks. ... The authority of my government is questioned, orders are often poorly followed ... a true sickness is affecting the French people.'[127]

If almost all the French were for Pétain in June 1940 and for de Gaulle in August 1944, the intersection point of those two curves would probably be after the occupation of the free zone by German troops in November 1942.[128] Despite the nationalistic rhetoric of the National Revolution, well over fifty per cent of the French national product between 1940 and 1944 was drained into the Nazi war machine.[129] Even before the Nazis occupied all France, the National Revolution was no more than the naïve and romantic dream of men with considerable faith in spiritual forces but little grasp of economic, political, and military realities.

The elimination of Mounier from Vichy's youth organizations seems part of a process in which Catholics were forced out of the National Revolution by hard-line partisans of collaboration with the Nazis. The tensions in the youth movements were increased by the appointment in the fall of 1941 of atheists like Pierre Pucheu as minister of the interior and Paul Marion as minister of information. The influence of devout Catholics in higher governmental circles steadily declined, as Pucheu purged the youth ministry in early 1942.[130] The following summer Abel Bonnard, the new minister of education, opted for rigid, authoritarian, and collaborationist youth movements. G. Pélorson, who became director of youth in June, wanted a large authoritarian Vichy youth movement to supercede all the independent ones.[131] In October 1942 Pélorson and Georges Lamirand were locked in violent debate over youth programs which seemed to clash with the original guiding principles of the National Revolution. In December 1942, after the occupation of the 'free' zone, the Ecole Nationale des Cadres d'Uriage was disbanded; in February Lamirand resigned; and in April, two publications of the ACJF were silenced.[132]

On 28 May 1943, the Chantiers were 'demobilized' and asked to volunteer for labour service in Germany. General de La Porte du Theil, like the leaders of the Compagnons de France, told his young men to respond and many did. But, like Henry Bauchau in Belgium, he resisted many pressures. After refusing the German consul's demand for 100,000 more Chantiers youth, La Porte du Theil was arrested in January 1944 and imprisoned in Germany, as the Chantiers and Compagnons were disbanded by Laval and Bonnard. The youth movements came to be simultaneously distrusted by Laval and his circle at Vichy and among the allies; they were seen as encouraging rebelliousness by the former, the nazification of France by the latter.[133] Attachment to the original ideals of the National Revolution and to Pétain, as distinguished from Laval and Darlan, had become anachronistic. But, wrote René Rémond, 'in 1944 public opinion joined together in a common proscription of all who had ... participated in the experiment of the National Revolution. One cannot expect the public to have drawn at that time the distinctions that the historian can establish twenty years later.'[134] Mounier and his collegues later wisely identified with the Resistance and, like many communists and socialists, simply rewrote the early history of Vichy to suit the temper of a later time. But Vichy's National Revolution was perhaps the most important episode in the history of Mounier's personalism, the only time when he actively participated in French political life. For a brief period *Esprit* seemed to have become a vital organ in the shaping of French youth.

The success of the Action Française in killing *Esprit* and Uriage was fleeting. By the end of 1941, after the silencing of Mounier, Dunoyer de Segonzac's Ecole des Cadres became more and more wary about Vichy. After the Germans occupied all France and Laval dissolved the institution in December 1942, the 'vieux chef' and most of his *cadres* went into hiding and created a group to 'provide ideological formation for the *maquis* of the Resistance.' Among the 'graduates' of Uriage was Henri Frenay, leader of the Resistance movement, Combat, who transformed many of the ideals of Beuve-Méry's Uriage into an ideology for resistance against the Nazis and requested Mounier's aid in that effort. Gilbert Dru, whose ideas had influence on post-war Christian democracy, was also a graduate of the Uriage school.[135] The post-war impact of the National Revolution, for example on 'theological renewal' in the French Catholic Church, has yet to be sufficiently appreciated. Among the over four thousand alumni of the Uriage 'school of élites' are many of the present ambassadors, generals, presidents in the public and private sector, bishops, and union leaders of France.[136]

At the liberation in 1944, there was an effort to reconstruct and unify France according to the new 'spirit of the Resistance.' The Resistance rejected all that Vichy had represented and, at times cruelly and unjustly, took its revenge upon 'collaborators.' The Resistance and Vichy came to be considered the antithesis of modern French political history. But the Resistance and some post-war political movements, including Gaullism, had certain ideals in common with the National Revolution.[137] Mounier saw good and bad elements in both 'revolutions' and fought for personalism, with some success, in each one.

There is probably no historical issue more sensitive for French people than the occupation. Mounier's activities during this period remain a subject of passionate controversy decades later. One reason is that Mounier seemed divided in his attitude towards both the Nazi domination of Europe and the Vichy régime: he was a firm *résistant* with some friends, and far more complacent towards the new order with others. In this he was not alone and the subsequent refusal of much of his generation to admit that they had had qualified hopes for a new order in Europe has contributed to the confusion. Mounier and several key personalists thought that there was high tragedy in the abortion of the National Revolution and the dissipation of its energies. They consistently placed the interests of Christianity ahead of a concern for liberty.

9

War and Transition 1941–4

After *Esprit* was squelched, Mounier resigned himself to public silence and, with his severance pay from Jeune France, made good use of the opportunity for study and reflection.[1] He wanted to continue to study the relationship between action and contemplation that had concerned the staff at Uriage, to isolate characteristics of the man who 'tried to live in the eternal' (ie, for whom religious experiences were important) and contrast him to the man 'who lives only in the moment, or in the past, or in dreaming of the future.'[2] Although he joined Jean Lacroix, who stayed on at Uriage, the philosopher Jean Wahl, and others in drafting a new Déclaration des droits de la personne, he seemed reconciled to refraining from political involvement, clandestine or otherwise, for the duration of the war.[3]

But on 15 January 1942, Mounier was unexpectedly arrested by the Lyon police. His name had been found among the papers of leaders of the movement Combat, who had been arrested earlier that month. The immediate charges were unclear but the Déclaration des droits de la personne was later introduced as evidence in his case. He knew that a number of his colleagues at Uriage, such as Henri Frenay, were plotting against the Nazis and 'Lavalians,' but, since he had not been involved, he was indignant at his imprisonment.

Mounier was kept in confinement until the summer of 1942 without being brought to trial. He protested to Vichy of his innocence and 'commonly acknowledged total incapacity for political action' and the authorities were unable to produce anything incriminating. After five months of judicial inertia regarding his case, Mounier, with a few fellow prisoners including Mme Bertie Albrecht, the secretary of Frenay, staged a hunger strike to draw attention to their plight. Mounier reiterated his innocence of involvement in the Resistance and demanded the legal processing of the charges against him. Soon after the fast began on 19 June, the Free French radio in London made a *cause célèbre* of it. Only when it appeared at the end of June that the prisoners were starving did the government move them to a hospital.[4]

Mounier's case was finally processed in October 1942, and since there was no evidence against him, he was soon freed. His gesture did not go unnoticed. In 1942, loyalty to the Pétain government was considered a duty by French ecclesiastics, and the disobedience of a well-known Catholic intellectual was scandalous. His own prison chaplain, with the concurrence of religious superiors, refused to give him communion while he persisted in his rebellion against 'legitimate authority.'[5] Amazing as this seems in retrospect, Mounier's act was one of the first indications that Vichy could not simply assume the support of all devout French Catholics.[6]

On his release Mounier moved to the little mountain village of Dieulefit in the Drôme, where he remained, under a pseudonym, with the poet Pierre Emmanuel and a few others for the duration of the war. He clung to a dogged belief in the legitimacy of the Vichy government and, just after his release, pictured North Africa as under 'attack' by the Americans and called General Giraud a 'traitor' for joining them. Similarly, in 1944, he spoke of the 'blunders or arrogance' of the Allied aviators, risking their lives to liberate France, and of the 'growing tension between de Gaulle and Anglo-Saxon imperialism' dissipating the 'myth of liberation.'[7]

Mounier was more reconciled to his forced exile from the 'double game' at Vichy that his disciples may have imagined. His health had nearly been broken by his hunger strike (was it a penitential exercise, or a protest?), which friends later considered responsible for his early death. The calamities of war had also been accompanied by personal tragedy for him: no progress could be made in treating his daughter Françoise, whose mental development had been seriously affected by encephalitis and who had to be institutionalized for the rest of her life.

In looking back at a decade of the history of *Esprit* Mounier seemed to wonder if it had created anything more than heaven-storming rhetoric and grandiose schemes. A few months of influence in Vichy's 'national revolution' had been followed by equal time in its prisons, and more and more personalist language was being distorted to suit evil purposes. It had been a slow but nonetheless rude awakening.

Mounier had watched Pétain, like Franco, restore the trappings of religion to the centre of national life. Pétainiste Catholicism preached obedience, authority, stability, order, and compromise with the enemy. The Church itself, while courting favours from Vichy, pretended to be apolitical. Yet when Mounier had lodged a simple protest, a priest had been ordered to shut a cell door in his face. Mounier, who suffocated in the Third Republic, soon found Vichy even worse. The Third Republic had been as anticlerical as Vichy was 'clerical,' but both perpetuated the 'established disorder' and he found that he could not live, as a Christian, in either one.

Thus, in the war years, a troubled Mounier turned inward, in search of the reasons for the prostitution of personalist ideals and the source of the failure and ineffectiveness of his movement. To get at the heart of his personalism he had to examine his own religiosity. This he undertook with harsh, lucid self criticism.

His impulse, as in his twentieth year, was to recreate Christian spirituality in its radiant purity and simplicity. As the battle raged throughout Europe, Mounier found, in the calm of Dieulefit, that he was not overly concerned about its outcome. He was more determined than ever to seek the true 'revolution.' He came to think that Roman Catholicism was an integral part of almost all he hated. Then, when he searched his soul, he discovered that the aspects of himself which he appreciated least were his 'Catholic' traits. He found that many of his failures and inadequacies were cultural and he was determined to root out these 'illnesses,' even if this forced him to attack Christianity.

NIETZSCHE AND THE RADICALIZATION OF THE CRITIQUE

While western Christian civilization was being torn apart by war, Mounier examined the Christian personality. He urgently wanted to free the authentic spiritual man from its caricatures and imitations; he wanted to distinguish true religiosity from self-deception and self-interested hypocrisy. Accordingly, he plunged into characterology, the science of human character types, and produced a vast synthesis of character readings.[8] Inevitably, he was drawn to the writing of that most corrosive critic of the 'spiritual man,' the master dissector of the Christian psyche, Friedrich Nietzsche.

Nietzsche and Mounier had similar intellectual methodologies: both had 'man' at the focus of their reflections, not social class or economic structures. Both were obsessed with Christianity and both evaluated everything from the point of view of its value, for the Übermensch or the 'person.' Mounier was fascinated by Nietzsche's diagnosis and through it discovered where Christianity had gone wrong. Nietzsche pinpointed what he detested about his co-religionists and what he was struggling against in himself. Mounier published his most autobiographical essay, begun in the ethereal atmosphere of Uriage, in the form of a dialogue with Nietszche.[9] Its colourful Nietzschean style and imagery indicated a new direction in Mounier's thought. After a brush with the Antichrist himself, Mounier's personalism would never be the same.

Mounier now flatly denounced old-fashioned Christianity and Christians. Christianity, he wrote, was 'conservative, defensive, sulky, afraid of the future.' Whether it 'collapses in a struggle or sinks slowly in a coma of self-complacency' it was doomed. 'Christians,' he castigated in even stronger terms in a rhapsodic style worthy of his new master: 'These crooked beings who go forward in life only sidelong with downcast eyes, these ungainly souls, these weighers-up of virtues, these dominical victims, these pious cowards, these lymphatic heroes, these colourless virgins, these vessels of ennui, these bags of syllogisms, these shadows of shadows....'[10] Mounier was nauseated by 'that dreary and somewhat stupid sadness that one too often sees on the faces of those entering and leaving churches and chapels.' After describing various foibles of French Christianity, more and more 'a religion of women, old men and small tradesmen,' he described the contemporary Christian 'type': 'The timorous believer ... vaguely aware of the divorce between the Church and life, does not dare to cast himself either into the deep waters of the Church ... or into the flowing currents of life. He remains poised between God and Mammon, a sad and sickly creature, forever bent over in a cramp of anxiety.'[11]

In his fury, he even turned against that foundation stone of Western culture, the Christian family. He deplored a situation in which Catholic children were being raised to extirpate the passions, when such an emphasis becomes 'the main emotional draining force of the Christian upbringing.' Catholic parents were extinguishing the very fire which should be the root of spiritual growth. The young Christian, having spent his youth restraining, repressing, and repelling, could respond to life only with gesture of negation and withdrawal.[12]

Mounier held puritanical sex education responsible for 'that awkwardness before life, that puerile timidity and sense of constraint' that characterized many Christians. One indication of this kind of moral training was an inverted obsession with sex. To Mounier, the principal aim of an adolescent's education too often seemed to be to protect him from sexual transgressions, 'even if the means employed permanently castrate all his energies ... steep him in spiritual cowardice.' Mounier blamed Christian mothers, their 'little heads cozily furnished with pious literature and sentimental illusions,' for this situation. 'When one sees these mothers so extremely anxious to protect their sons from the spirit of the times, one wonders if they are not rather protecting themselves against a revelation of their own emptiness.'[13] Not a line of this could not have been taken from *Beyond Good and Evil*.

For generations the French Church had been extolling the 'family' as the cradle of Christian piety and values. It was those very virtues usually associated with the 'Christian family' in France that Mounier challenged in this diatribe on world-wide Christianity. Typically, he projected his own provincial middle class French Catholic milieu – the divorce of the Christian from 'real life,' – onto Christians the world over.

Again like Nietzsche, who distinguished between the Church and Jesus Christ, the 'only true Christian,' Mounier's use of the term 'Christianity' was ambiguous. Sometimes he attacked Christianity as modern Western civilization in the name of Christianity, an ideal of what Christian life could be. Often he did not seem to include Protantism or Orthodoxy in the term since his remarks were applicable only to Catholics. Sometimes Christianity referred to an individual's orientation, at other times to a mass cultural phenomenon. Under Nietzsche's influence Mounier's thought was evolving from the Thomist notion of an ideal medieval Christianity to an avant-garde view that Christianity had not yet been attained. Of course, he differed from Nietzsche in thinking that such Christian goals were desirable and possible.

Mounier's provincialism was particularly noticeable in his attacks upon the vices of Christian intellectualism – not exactly the sort of problem to concern a Bible Belt Baptist in North America, a Bolivian tin miner, or the average farmer in the Garonne valley – and his language was especially brutal in the discussion of France's prestigious Christian philosophers. Metaphysical speculation, Mounier declared, was a characteristic of lifeless schizoid personalities. If this schizoid trait was dominant, intellectuals fell 'into a vague, obscure exaltation on mystical or metaphysical themes, with a tendency to systematization or schematization.' He cited Jung to prove that most intellectual systematizations were 'instruments fabricated by a fear of living, to protect us from living experience.' Such schizoid intellectualism was particularly prevalent in *modern* Western culture: 'the men who cut the clearings in the Celtic forests were not inclined to complications of feeling any more than workers struggling to make a living.' It was wealthy, comfortable, epochs which encouraged a disequilibrium in favour of reflection, when there was no vital contact with reality. Catholic philosophers, Mounier thought, shared the responsibility for an educational system which tried to 'dilute the combative instinct' as well as the sexual instinct 'by not talking to children of the fire in the veins.'[14] Mounier even referred to intelligence and spirituality as 'bodily diseases' and attributed the indecisiveness of many Christians to their ignorance of 'how to jump a ditch or strike a blow.'[15]

Mounier's new passion for a manly purity also drove him to re-examine what he saw as the core of the Christian personality, the religious sentiment. Nietzsche inspired his psychological analysis of a phenomenon traditionally reserved for theologians and mystical writers: prayer. He found validity in Nietzsche's view that the 'stunting of the life of the Christians' was often masked under 'an illusion of interior aspirations and spiritual consolations.' Modern psychiatry, Mounier wrote, had shed light on 'the morbid taste for the "spiritual," for " higher things," for the ideal, and for effusions of soul.' Psychiatry, in short, revealed much about the way in which 'the undisciplined imaginings of feeble souls' had invaded Christian spirituality. He cited modern psychiatrists on the '"feelings of elevation" characteristic of certain psychoses, the spiritual intoxication, the bliss, accompanied ... by an affected contempt for everyday reality and precise tasks.' He cited an analysis of psychosis as a 'weakening of vitality accompanied by a "hyper-spiritualization" ... the subject affected ... paints his nudity in order to deceive himself; he persuades himself that he is favoured with some flattering particularity.' Mounier emphasized the similarity between this psychosis and 'the life-sickness of the deformed and anaemic participants in the spiritual struggle.'

Like Nietzsche, for the feeling of 'holiness' he offered a simple explanation: 'vanity makes a virtue of Christian exaltation and of the attention it brings. It confuses the desire to exploit interior emotion, and exhibition of the idea of perfection, with the true desire for perfection.'[16] Thus many forms of religious devotion were the result of psychosis, self-deception, or vanity. Prayer was often a sign of psychological illness and weakness. Mounier agreed substantially with Nietzsche – and Marx – on this point. Debilitating religious practices coupled with cloying family life and a repressive education produced 'the modern Christian' – inhibited, emotionally emasculated, and ridiculously self-deluded.

Only after some analysis of the character of 'the modern Christian,' according to Mounier, could the progressive desertion of French Catholicism by the working classes be understood. He thought that the process of secularization in his country was rooted less in the rejection of a system of beliefs than in repugnance for an unattractive way of life. He cited the book *La France, pays de mission?* (1943) by Abbés Henri Godin and Yvan Daniel on the loss of the French proletariat to the Church:

The modern worker is not prevented from entering some sphere of Christian life so much by the necessary spiritual leap from unbelief to faith, as by the social uprooting demanded of him if he is to accept the average way of life of pious Christians. 'It seems to them that in order to love Christ, they would have to accept a sort of degradation, a sort of dimunition of their own rough working-class personality,' and they hold back from what seems to them a loss in humanity.[17]

For Mounier, the urban worker refused to become Christian because in the modern context it meant to become an inferior type of human being.[18] Like Nietzsche, the workers saw and rejected the Jesus who chose to be silent and spat upon before Pilate. But in becoming 'inferior' human types did Christians follow the true example of Jesus? That was Mounier's dilemma.

He thought that his rigorous scrutiny of Christianity did not cut him off from Christ but from modern Christianity, not from religion but from religious impurities. As he saw it, neither modern Christians nor contemporary Christianity were truly Christian. He thought that Nietzsche had unmasked religious decadence but not religion itself. When one penetrated the mystification, hypocrisy, and lies, one found that the modern Christian was not a Christian at all: he was bourgeois.

In Mounier's Uriage and Dieulefit essays, the contrast between 'true Christians' and 'bourgeois Christians' became more and more pronounced. Time and again he railed against how the bourgeoisie had come to dominate his religion. Faith, hope, and charity had been displaced in the heart of the churchgoer-businessperson by a concern for 'security, economy, measured ambitions and social immobility.' There had been a twofold process by which Christianity became a shadow of itself:

The more greedily the bourgeoisie took possession of Christianity, the more widely were the Christian masses attacked by corruption – and the most lively parts of the social body detached themselves from Christianity ... abandoning it

more completely to the evil parasite upon it: the more Christianity became
conservative, defensive, sulky, afraid by the future, the less it received that in-
vigorating sap which comes to a society from its aggressive elements, its youth
and its vanguard.[19]

Thus the transformations in Christianity caused by middle class culture
effected the expatriation of true Christians from the sociological body of
Christianity. If a time came when it would be necessary to abjure faith in
order to have something to eat and drink, Mounier prophesied that the
religious edifice would crumble away in enormous sections, to the point
that it would be possible to ask whether there was a single Christian left in
the civilized world. It might then be necessary, he concluded, 'to search in
the byways and thickets for that heroic Christianity which shall remake, in
boldness of life, a new vision of the eternal tradition.'[20] Christianity no
longer was Christian because, for Mounier, a bourgeois Christian had
become a contradiction in terms.

By differentiating between Christians in this way, Mounier was able to
create a workable synthesis incorporating Nietzsche's anti-religious analysis into the broad outlines of Christian renewal. However, this new, ever
more anti-bourgeois direction, had an importance beyond Mounier's
personal spiritual development. The anti-bourgeois impetus spread after
World War II and posed a great challenge to the accepted forms of
spirituality Mounier had known in his youth.

Léon Bloy, Maritain, and other important Catholics of the earlier
generation had been aggressively 'anti-Catholic' in their concern for
religious authenticity and their violent condemnations of the Catholic
'bien-pensants.' But pre-war Catholicism sought 'repristination': Christian reform was to come from a purifying return to sources, to scripture,
to the intellectual harmony of the high Middle Ages, to the best in an
ancient tradition.[21] This effort was habitually indifferent to social thought
or contemporary social or political forms, as much to the monarchism of
the Action Française as to the Christian social thought of the papal
encyclicals. Catholic monarchists and democrats, aristocrats, bourgeoisie
and peasantry, were concerned with a religious quest rooted in both the
metaphysical and the mystical traditions of the Church, which conceived
of the Christian life in a transcendental, vertical rather than horizontal or
communal perspective.

The young Emmanuel Mounier's 'repristination' effort had involved
mining the interior life with Jacques Chevalier, scripture with Father
Pouget, philosophy with the Maritains and Berdyaev, and patristics and

the mystical doctors of the Church on his own. In Mounier's pre-war writings, Catholicism was the source of the energy for moral reform and certainly not part of the 'established disorder' which he attacked. In his criticism of the influence of the Action Française on the Church, Mounier had reproached the Right for mixing the spiritual with the temporal. Whatever antibourgeois and anti-capitalist critique had been inspired by his personalism, he often insisted, was neither essentially Catholic nor necessarily Christian.

Mounier's new indictment of twentieth-century Western culture, however, was no longer preoccupied with fervent versus indifferent Catholics as were Maritain, Claudel, Bloy, and Bernanos. Mounier now described Christians, even when serious believers, as the victims rather than potential saviours of the corrupted bourgeois culture. Liberation required the adoption of radically different social and intellectual structures. Mounier, breaking with the preceding generation of Catholic intellectuals, hailed totally new kinds of Christians and declared that religious renewal presupposed social and spiritual revolution.

The effect of the war years was particularly evident in Mounier's analysis of philosophy and the intellectual life. At Dieulefit he seconded Nietzsche's attacks on Christian intellectuals, and demanded a revolution in Christian thought to accompany the necessary social revolution. His call for the reconstruction of the Christian intelligentsia was a radical departure from French Catholic tradition. Since the nineteenth century, French Catholic intellectual leaders had been convinced that the progressive apostasy of the masses was philosophically inspired, that the Church had been undermined in much the same way as had the monarchy. Maritain for example, had depicted in *Trois Réformateurs* a process through which the underlying premises of the faith had been undermined by the scepticism of the philosophes, and later, the positivist philosophers. The whole magnificent ecclesiastical structure had appeared anachronistic to the people, like the pre-revolutionary monarchy.

Jacques and Raïssa Maritain had been more concerned with defending the faith on the philosophical battlegrounds of Paris than in renewing it in the worker suburbs. Like many intellectuals, especially those of French training, they believed in the efficacy of ideas and that the Church would flourish if its intellectual underpinnings were solid. Christian faith would displace scepticism when the people recognized that it was more rational than the alternatives and answered their deepest needs.

Before Mounier, Catholic intellectuals tended to view the Church with a 'fixiste' rigidity founded in their Thomistic vision of the contingent world kept in existence by an all-powerful God.[22] The Church, mediating between eternity and time, was neither completely in one realm nor in the other; its structure and sociological base were of little consequence in comparison with its cosmological role as the sole vehicle of transcendence in a world of change. These intellectuals had only a secondary interest in the effects of changes and time upon the Church, in the evolving quality of spirituality among the mass of believers.

In his mountain retreat, Mounier decided that Thomist Catholic cosmology needed radical reconstruction. Even before the war, as we have seen, he had little sympathy for it, and his Vichy experience and study of characterology and Nietzsche renewed his suspicions about the value of abstract philosophy. A Christianity dominated by the bourgeoisie, even if it was a bourgeoisie with a solid metaphysical background, could not be true Christianity. The latter would be less a culture with a common ontological perspective than a community of virtue and commitment. In Mounier's view, ideas were less important than their consequences; a lucid intellectual élite was less important than the moral and religious vitality of the mass of believers.

Thus, in *L'affrontement chrétien* Mounier announced that the vigorous intellectualism of the metaphysicians had outlived its value for his generation. The fixiste view of the universe co-existed with bourgeois Christianity as it had harmonized with the feudalistic Middle Ages. But a Church corrupted by the bourgeoisie could not afford such a historical religiosity. The traditional ontological thrust of Christianity, juxtaposing being and eternity, ignored historical context and its religious requirements. Christian belief must instead be a vital, living thing: 'Nothing ... bears less resemblance to a system of explanation than does Christianity'; it was 'a principle of life, and if it is also a principle of truth, it is so in the life it communicates.'[23] In an age spiritually strangled by the bourgeoisie, faith remained the great, untapped source of spiritual vitality. The times demanded that it be dynamic and forward-looking, facing the challenges of its historical environment, and rooted in deeds rather than in formulas.

To meet this challenge, Mounier proposed guidelines for the revitalization of Christianity. He demanded, first of all, a new recognition of 'agnosticism's share in the composition of faith.' He claimed that a sense of paradox was a more viable foundation for the modern religious intelligence than elaborate logical buttressing. This was so because faith required the believer to maintain

positions the most contradictory to good sense; to die for the world while we committed ourselves to it ... to sorrow over our sins while rejoicing in the new man; to value only what is inward, but to ... conquer the whole of life for inwardness; to see in ourselves the dependence of a nothing and the liberty of a king and, above all, never to regard any of these divided situations as substantially contradictory, nor as finally resolvable in human experience.[24]

Thus the modern Christian, in Mounier's view, rejected not 'every Christian philosophy ... but every Christian philosophical system; not every Christian temporal order ... but every Christian temporal utopia; not joy ... but happiness; not peace ... but tranquility; not plenitude ... but satisfaction.' The 'Christian agnostic' was less interested in the ontological insights of the Thomistic tradition than in the gropings of Pascal. 'To the eyes of the abandoned reason,' Mounier wrote, 'faith is a wager, and ... in the interminably repeated instant which maintains us in faith there is a hazard more desperate than turning upside down in the absurd – the leap ... from non-Being to Being.'[25]

In Mounier's view, this element of decision was lacking in modern Christianity. 'Christian agnosticism,' he believed, was not only an intellectual attitude which accurately reflected modern Christian experience, it was also a revolutionary, dynamic, committed, active possession of the faith. It contradicted the fixiste, passive acquiescence in the eternal orders of things, and implied that it was more important to live than to understand the faith. The Christian faith could be *understood* in a culture permeated with bourgeois values, but Mounier insisted that it could not be *lived* in such a culture. In abandoning the metaphysical tradition of Catholicism for a 'Christian agnosticism,' Mounier was entering uncharted waters.

This intellectual break with the Thomists was a significant moment in the history of modern French Catholicism. For Maritain and other metaphysical Catholics, modern man's confusion was a result of his arrogant refusal to view the eternal world as created and sustained by an omnipotent God. There was less and less attention to the questions of the origin of the universe, the immortality of the soul, and the ultimate bases of morality or intellectual coherence. The fact that such major questions were simply dismissed outside the Catholic intellectual ghetto as unanswerable was the great frustration in Maritain's school. Accordingly, Maritain's group lionized cultures that had displayed the spiritual seriousness to raise the question of the final meaning of the universe and man's place in it. One could only hope for a 'new middle ages.' Mounier, however, now rejected such idle longings.

When Mounier turned upon metaphysicians, he reflected a developing tension in much of the French Catholic Left. His pre-war position had been to attack contemporary Western culture while maintaining an uncritical fidelity to the institutional Catholic Church. He had distinguished that Roman Catholicism from bourgeois culture, old social hierarchies, and the positivist mentality. But in the face of the events of the Spanish Civil War and Vichy, it was difficult for Mounier to continue to distinguish his Church from the age he loathed. He was forced to oppose the cultural forces which represented the majority of his Church; increasingly the most 'Catholic' cultures and groups were the most morally reprehensible to him. He had tried to purge the Church of 'alien elements,' but found himself turning more and more against Catholicism itself. Mounier's harsh indictment of bourgeois Christianity was no longer based upon longing for the Middle Ages; the Christian order seemed, more and more, something to be worked towards. On the plateau of Uriage the hope for a new, manly, purified Christianity was born in Emmanuel Mounier, a Christianity that was unrecorded in the chronicles of the past simply because it had yet to be realized.

The true Christian, as he emerges in Mounier's wartime writings, was really anti-Christian in the best Nietzschean sense. The authentic Christian personality would emerge only 'beyond' bourgeois culture and beyond metaphysics. Nietzsche had pictured his élite 'living in the trees of the future nourished from the beaks of eagles.' Here was a new, Christian 'superman,' building his life outside a corrupted modern Christianity, with none of the vices of the sickly moderns and all the strengths and virtues of the Nietzschean hero. Mounier prophesied the birth of a new kind of Christian, who, instead of rejecting modern life and forming his spirituality on a timeless ahistorical model, would throw himself into the uncompromising battle against all that had corrupted Christianity, inspired by a burning faith in future possibilities. Mounier courted the masculinity, self-reliance, and scorn for spiritual consolations of the Nietzschean 'superman.' The goal was no longer imitation of the past. 'Who are the first Christians?', Mounier asked. 'Perhaps ourselves.'

How were these 'first Christians' to be created? Mounier's vision of a post-war Christian renaissance was essentialy linked to revolution and destruction of the bourgeoisie. But the means by which the revolution might be initiated are vague in *L'affrontement chrétien*. The last paragraph refers ominously to a possible alliance with the 'new forces which claim to reconcile ardour and realism, militant youth and the control of society, action of a revolutionary scale and individual adventure.'[26] Mounier was perhaps thinking of the new élites formed on the plateau at Uriage or the young Left Catholics then active in the Resistance.

Notwithstanding, or precisely because of, its vague political dimension, this denunciation of bourgeois Christianity has inspired serious Christians in North America.[27] More concretely, it demonstrated inherent possibilities in a combination of Christian spirituality and Nietzschean criticism in an effort to reform Christianity. Nietzschean Christianity was a very radical derivation of the personalism of the thirties but by no means the only one. Mounier also had to come to terms with his past views in their many applications as exhibited in the different wartime paths chosen by *Esprit*'s followers. At the time of his incarceration by Vichy, a majority of the prewar contributors to *Esprit* seemed to have objected to his involvement in the National Revolution. The fact that Mounier's slogans were profitably used by a corrupt and dishonourable régime should have underlined the weakness of a personalist movement that could lead a Jacques Maritain or a Paul Vignaux to uncompromising resistance at the same time that François Perroux, Jean Lacroix, Raymond de Becker, or René Gillouin trumpeted personalism as the philosophy of a new France in an authoritarian Europe. One would assume that Mounier would admit, however ruefully, that personalism had been used in an effort to infect Belgium and France with certain fascist values. He made no such admission.

He never seemed to accept any responsibility for the personalist movement's promoting complacency towards Nazism. On the contrary, as we shall see, he later insisted that personalism had been an important force in the Resistance in Europe. In an even greater display of logical agility, Mounier blamed the fascist direction of Raymond de Becker, not on personalism, but on bourgeois Christianity:

In the aftermath of 1940, a young Belgian upon whom, ten years earlier, the vital Catholic forces of his own country set a certain hope, published some *Souvenirs* which have a warning value. Let us forget for a moment their pretentious tastelessness and the conceits which are mixed up with a certain will to greatness. This boy who for a time pursued the lost fragrance of an adventurous Christianity in the wandering life of a pilgrim and in the silence of the cloister, is no mediocrity. No doubt he is a little too inclined to mistake the fervour of the senses for greatness; but if, in the end, he thinks he has found this greatness at the antipodes of Christianity, must we wholly absolve from blame for his renunciation that somnolent Christianity which, by arousing his disgust, first stimulated him to revolt?[28]

Thus, the 'warning' which this personalist-turned-Nazi represented for Mounier was not that there was something warped in Raymond de Becker or his ideas but rather that there was something wrong with a Christianity which could not satisfy de Becker's instincts. Maritain and Vignaux had warned Mounier that de Becker's mysticism was unbalanced, that he made extravagant demands on the sense of community; and, soon, de Becker was rhapsodizing over the golden pheasants in the Ordensburgen and the coming Nazification of Europe. But Mounier, rather than isolate the perversions in the 'Christian personalism' of de Becker which spun off into a crypto-Nazism, attacked traditional Christian philosophy and spirituality, the very traditions behind the refusal of Maritain, Vignaux, Denis de Rougemont, and Yves Simon to traffic with Vichy's National Revolution.

The most important theorists of the personalist movement on the eve of the war were Mounier, Berdyaev, Lacroix, Denis de Rougemont, Maritain, and Perroux. The three who chose to work within the National Revolution – Mounier, Lacroix, and Perroux – were self-consciously Catholic and personalist. The two who chose the Resistance, Maritain and de Rougemont, had differences with the 'Catholic personalists' by the time the war came. That Mounier still would attack the 'sterile' philosophy of a Maritain or the 'gloomy Barthianism' of a de Rougemont after the experience of the National Revolution persuasively suggests that he was critical of some basic impulses of the Resistance. Mounier did not see the National Revolution as a threat tied to the wave of fascism in Europe but rather as a tragedy: a movement full of promise for the spiritualization of France which failed due to external circumstances.

Remote as this appears from present popular interpretations, Mounier's perspective was probably that of many, if not most, devout French Catholics of his generation. They had been raised to fear that progressive secularization of Europe, that decline of hierarchy and authority which seemed a death threat to their most cherished values and to the Roman Catholic Church. It is understandable that for a time Catholics should have been seduced by forces or ideologies which promised to reverse the tide of history.

10

A Marxist Reformation of Christianity 1944–8

Emmanuel Mounier and *Esprit* flourished in post-war France. The personalist movement, however, as a vigorous, disciplined, hierarchically organized effort to create a new kind of Europe had found embarrassing expression in the 'national revolutions' of Belgium and France and faded away with the severities of the occupation in those countries. Personalist ideals, however, endured and inspired several post-war proposals for European reconstruction.

After World War II, *Esprit* became popular, well known, and although of the 'radical Catholic Left,' relatively respectable. To Mounier's chagrin, it was also no longer a review of the young. Nor, understandably, was it eagerly spearheading a Europe-wide effort to find a new path between capitalism and communism. Worse still, despite the talent of new, younger men such as Jean-Marie Domenach and Paul Ricœur, it was no longer the voice of an intellectual generation to the degree it had been when it was much smaller. The Friends of Esprit were no longer tightly organized, coherent, and bound to the principles of the *Personalist Manifesto*. Mounier and his closest collaborators did establish certain *Esprit* 'lines' on the important events of the day but opposing views were aired and there was no longer a whole network of intense young people across Europe eagerly awaiting the journal. The review became progressively more pluralistic, Mounier more philosophical, and, after a brief Stalinist period, an easy liberalism, good humour, and tolerance came to characterize the whole enterprise. Personalism was defined in relation to Marxism more than as a new and exciting approach to life.

After the war, the *Esprit* group no longer consisted of obscure, often unemployed, intellectuals. Many had risen to important positions in French literary and academic life. In addition, the social and political circumstances in which *Esprit* was published were very different from what they were when France seemed split in two and fascism was on the march.

RESISTANCE SOLIDARITY

Returning to Paris in the fall of 1944, after an absence of four years, Mounier found the city joyful and full of hope for the future. Resistance unity seemed to have transcended most of the old ideological quarrels. General de Gaulle, provisional president of France, was, by general consent, a temporary dictator. The mass of the French seemed to want change: in the referendum of 1945 more than ninety-six per cent of the voters rejected the constitution of the Third Republic and demanded a new set of political institutions. A French legislative body had never been so strongly weighted to the Left as in the fall of 1945. The communists, socialists, and Christian Democrats drew almost seventy-four per cent of the nation's votes, ostensibly reflecting widespread support for the common 'resistance' ideals of the Left. It was hard to predict what this meant for the Church.

The very symbol of the Resistance, General de Gaulle, the president of its national council, Georges Bidault, and the voice of the free French from London, Maurice Schumann, were all professed Catholics. The triumphant march down the Champs-Elysées on the liberation of Paris concluded with a service in the cathedral of Notre-Dame. But the cardinal-archbishop of Paris was not present at that ceremony: Cardinal Suhard, as well as the papal nuncio Valeri, received open rebukes from Resistance leaders in this period. Bidault requested at Rome that the papacy replace several 'collaborationist' French archbishops and bishops. Marshal Pétain and Charles Maurras, symbols of the Right, were soon in prison, as was Mounier's old mentor, Jacques Chevalier.

World War II transformed much in French Catholicism. The hope for a French Catholic 'alternative,' so strong before the war, waned with the rise of Admiral Darlan and Pierre Laval at Vichy and the decline of the pro-clerical elements around the old marshal. Vichy's National Revolution had divided the Catholic youth movements, trade unions, hierarchy, and intellectuals. The great wave of Catholic extraparliamentary movements abated as Vichy simultaneously raised and dashed pre-war hopes for the re-creation of a Catholic France. The prominent Christians of the Resistance, often Christian Democrats, tried to sustain the old religious disputes of the thirties in the Vichy period; right-wing French Catholics had excluded the 'heretical' Christian Democrat minority from their régime.[1] The Right engineered the exclusion of Mounier and pushed him, like his Christian Democrat friends, towards the Resistance. When the Resistance triumphed, the Christian Democrats shared in the victory, while Catholic traditionalists often bore the brunt of the defeat.

The French Catholic hierarchy had supported the Pétain régime's fleeting effort to govern France according to principles approximating the official social teachings of the Church. Catholics who joined the Resistance did so in defiance of their pronouncements. Many Catholic resisters – critics of the Action Française, the Croix de Feu, and the Fédération Nationale Catholique, before the war – simply persisted in their pre-war anti-fascism or anti-authoritarianism. Many younger Catholic *résistants* had, like Mounier, broken out of the ghetto of the Catholic Right and, as a self-conscious avant-garde, been of marginal influence within the Church. At the Liberation, however, with the wholesale discrediting of older Catholic leadership, this situation changed.

The integration of Catholics into all levels of the Resistance and into the cadres of the Vichy régime not purged at the Liberation meant that professed Catholics were participating in French political life to a much larger extent than before.[2] Devout Catholics were scattered from one extreme of the political spectrum to the other, even involved in executing or imprisoning one another. Thus, Catholics of the Resistance, in their fight against the Nazis and Vichy, learned to co-operate with non-believers, also a goal of Vichy's National Revolution. The *Esprit* group had experimented along these lines in the thirties; Vichy, and then the Resistance, had offered this experience to the nation as a whole. Since communists were often the nucleus of the underground opposition, Resistance Catholics and communists came to know one another. The desperate political situation had forced many clergy from their parish houses, and laymen from their middle class suburbs, and into contact with the rude, irreligious working classes. Mounier often remarked in these years that ancient animosities seemed to be giving way to fellow feeling and hopes for national reconciliation.

Ultimately it was the war itself that forced the French Church to accept political pluralism. The bitterness left by Pétain's chimeric effort to create a clerical, Salazarian France, did much to end the idea of a Catholic politics. And once Catholics came to recognize the French Church, and French society, as pluralistic, Catholics could themselves be accepted simply as another spiritual family within the nation. The national prominence of some self-conscious Catholics at the liberation was due to their wartime records and also to the fact that French Catholics were deeply divided, without a common 'Catholic alternative' for France, and thus no longer dangerous. The French Church was abandoning its ancient pretense of representing the majority of the French, so Catholics could be included in a Republican régime because, in the ruins of Pétainisme, the prospects for a 'Catholic France' were not bright, to say the least.

The Christian Democrats' political party, the Mouvement Républicain Populaire (MRP), quickly became a major political force in France. The stars of the MRP, such as its first president, Maurice Schumann, often combined the reformist spirit of the Resistance with the spiritual vitality of a new style of Catholicism, which, ironically, had been partially fostered by the Vichy youth movements. Catholics now seemed to represent much of the spirit of national renewal and reform that inspired liberated France.

The Christian Democrats' call to national renovation echoed a variety of clandestine journals which had appealed for opposition against the Nazis and Vichy. This involved transcendence of the old spiritual and class cleavages in order to achieve social and economic progress. For influential movements such as Henri Frenay's Combat, a spirit of community and respect for human personality were to replace bourgeois competition and material goals. The Christian Democrats tried to turn some of this idealism into policy.

Fraternal ideals, like those of the Resistance, had been proclaimed in the early days of Vichy. The Ecole Nationale des Cadres of Uriage, whose ideology was shaped by Mounier and his friends, had influenced individuals such as Gilbert Dru and Henri Frenay, who later helped create a distinctive ideology for the Resistance and then for Christian Democracy. Practical co-operation between socialist and 'spiritual' men of the Left was bridged by the pre-war personalist movement. Several post-war slogans recalled Mounier's pre-war rhetoric.

The rise of the Christian Democrats was helped by the fact that, in the spirit of Resistance unity, the communists were willing to join in the effort at post-war reconstruction. Furthermore, there were many who had supported Vichy who now much preferred the Christian Democrats to the rest of the post-war coalition.[3] In the elections of October 1945, the MRP captured a surprising one-fourth of the nation's votes – their total vote was more than the socialists' and second only to the communists'. Eight months later, in the second Constituent Assembly, the MRP replaced the communists as the largest political party in the government.

The communists, like the Christian Democrats, came from the fringes in 1940 to prominence in 1945. After the Hitler-Stalin pact the party had seemed finished as a major force in French political life, but the Soviet Union had subsequently borne much of the battle against Hitler, and French communists much of the Resistance in France. In 1944 the French Communist party was the only major pre-war French political party relatively unsullied by connections to Vichy. Also there was a new openness towards Stalinist Russia among members of the Resistance who, like General de Gaulle and Mounier, feared American domination of post-war Europe. De Gaulle allowed Maurice Thorez, leader of the French Communist party, to return from Moscow, despite his desertion from the French army in 1939. In December 1944 de Gaulle visited the Soviet Union and signed a twenty-year alliance with Stalin's government. Communism was at last respectable.

The French communists in 1944, like the French Catholics, had a different orientation than they had had four years earlier. The communists had also been forced into close contact with other persuasions during Vichy's National revolution and then in clandestine struggle: a new mutual trust, respect, and confidence had emerged. The French Communist party, with Soviet encouragement, displayed a new openness, something akin to that of 1936, and, for the first time since the Popular Front, the party drew significant support at the polls. In October 1945 the communists were France's most popular political party with 26.6 per cent of the votes cast, twice that of 1936.

It was a transformed Emmanuel Mounier, too, who emerged from the seclusion of Dieulefit, determined to combat the ineffectual idealism that he had denounced in his wartime essays. Again, as in the early days of the Popular Front and Vichy, Mounier discovered an exalted atmosphere with interest in far-reaching cultural and political changes. In contrast to the period before the war, when a large Catholic block seemed set off against the parliamentary régime in France, in the post-war period there were large parliamentary political groupings in which Catholics were well represented. Among the attractive political groups were the Christian Democrats, who divorced Catholicism from the old Right, had a progressive political program, and numbered among their leaders various old friends of *Esprit*. Beside them were the communists, with what was undeniably the most revolutionary rhetoric. *Esprit* had always been firmly anti-communist but it seemed as if the communists must have an essential role if post-war France was to have a new kind of politics.

On his return to Paris in the fall of 1944, Mounier made known his solidarity with the most radical forces for change. At Marcel Moré's, on 23 December 1944, he announced: 'We are not, as before, in a phase of remote preparation. ... The revolutionaries are ready. Since they are ready, it is necessary to work with them. We cannot permit ourselves a project demanding fifty or a hundred years. We have a revolution in process.'[4] And at a time when Resistance credentials were of supreme importance, Mounier boldly claimed an impeccable record for *Esprit*. Perhaps in response to the ambiguities in *Esprit*'s wartime image, he rushed to Paris as soon as it was possible and recommenced *Esprit* in December 1944, the first review to appear in liberated France. In this issue *Esprit* was described as not merely taking up where it had left off but embarking on a 'new series.'[5]

In resurrecting *Esprit* Mounier was joined by pre-war contributors of the journal who had shared in the Uriage experience: Jean Lacroix, Bertrand d'Astorg, and Henri Marrou. But for every former contributor who resumed his collaboration with *Esprit*, such as François Goguel, there were several new men: notably Jean-Marie Domenach, a student of Lacroix who had been an instructor at Uriage, Marc Beigbeder, who had joined *Esprit* in the Vichy period, Chris Marker, Jean Cayrol, and the philosopher Paul Ricœur. Most of those who had opposed publication of the review under Vichy were no longer around. But like the new daily newspaper *Le Monde*, directed by Hubert Beuve-Méry, and for which old *Esprit* hands Jean Lacroix and Pierre-Henri Simon directed the philosophy and literature sections, the new *Esprit* was an immediate success. From a pre-war circulation of between 3,000 and 4,000 its post-war circulation jumped to four or five times that, and grew steadily throughout the nineteen-fifties and sixties.[6]

In launching the new series Mounier deftly rewrote its history, retouching its intellectual tradition, its Vichy experiences, and its post-war prospects with an obvious eye to the new political climate. Abandoning the pre-war 'neither Right nor Left emphasis,' he described personalism as a movement deriving from 'the tradition of humanist socialism peculiar to France since 1830.' The juncture of socialists with the clergy in 1848, he said, had been the first major approximation of the personalist position; the diverse forms of Christian socialism, and the Sillon, were more immediate precursors.

Under Vichy, Mounier explained, *Esprit* had chosen to fight in 'open clandestinity' rather than flee the danger. 'The stupidity of the censor of Lyon' had enabled him to pursue this tactic. The *Esprit* of 1940–1 he described as a subtle series of Resistance documents in which 'each phrase hid a dart, each synopsis an ambush.' The youth program supported by the personalists had become 'a rallying point of the opposition,' and when Vichy had finally discovered Mounier's true motives, *Esprit* had been quickly suppressed.[7]

In the post-liberation issues Mounier sidestepped his early enthusiasm for Vichy's national rejuvenation projects, and downplayed personalist influence at Vichy – and with the Lyon censor. Instead he depicted the personalist movement as always having been in the socialist tradition and therefore inevitably in the Resistance. Again, as in 1936 and the winter of 1940, Mounier thought France was on the threshold of revolution and was anxious to cement his solidarity with the forces of change.

Mounier also decided to reshape personalist theory along the lines of his artful revision of the history of *Esprit*. He seemed to want to extirpate the weaknesses of pre-war personalism, at the very time he was demonstrating that personalism had remained essentially unaltered since *Esprit*'s founding in 1932. Not surprisingly, he was forced to concede that there were difficulties in understanding personalism's consistency as a system, but that was because it was 'perspective, method, exigency' and had to be understood as such.[8] Mounier, much like everyone else in post-war France, was quick to jockey for position.

He seemed to want to downplay the pre-war militant anti-communism of *Esprit* and its search for a Third Force between capitalism and communism. Despite the mental gymnastics and historical editing which this entailed, the basic positions of personalism perhaps did allow for such a transition more than its critics imagined. In any case, the 'spirit of the Resistance' was a banner that rallied an even larger ideological contingent than had Vichy's National Revolution in its early days. Mounier was not alone.

One of *Esprit*'s first 'left-wing' positions was opposition to the new influence of the United States in Europe. The personalist group had long been hostile to the United States, which Mounier had depicted, before the war, as the capitalist analogue to Soviet communism.[9] He had little gratitude for the liberating United States troops that passed through Dieulefit in 1944, describing them in his diary as 'very American, childishly playing with dice, like they play with life and war,' and remarking sarcastically that 'they do not like Italy: that dirty country ... where they do not even find the women beautiful because they are not neat and hygienic.' He foresaw a bitterness towards 'that luxurious army, those luxurious victories which had snatched the brilliant glories' from the Free French.[10] Mounier's anti-Americanism was common among French left-wing intellectuals, and the men of Uriage.[11]

The United States' new rivalry with the Soviet Union forced Mounier to admit that he considered the Americans the greater threat to the West. In the fall of 1946 he warned of 'American fascism' with its 'universal pretensions' and the danger that 'America could enter into a great crisis, when the attempt to check its course before the abyss would only rigidify that whole enormous machine, running at full speed, eyes closed.' He feared a day when America's 'enormous technical apparatus' would descend upon the whole world 'with all the weight of its desire for domination and the perfect good conscience which is mixed with it.'[12] In effect, the United States, symbol of the laissez-faire economic system, represented an imperialistic, 'fascist' challenge to Europe. Similar to a few years earlier, when Mounier had described the 'person' as threatened by the violence of the Stalinists and the Hitlerites, he now saw the greatest peril to post-war peace in the righteousness of a capitalist superpower which impeded imaginative revolutionary initiatives in France.

Mounier's post-war anti-Americanism was his first disagreement with the attitudes of Christian Democrats and other devout French Catholics, who saw the United States as a bastion of Christendom against the atheistic barbarians of the East. The barbarians that Mounier now feared most were the GI's.

Mounier's anti-Americanism was unusual for a French Catholic, and his position vis-à-vis Christian Democracy even more so. Ironically, the Christian Democrats tried to offer an alternative to the communists, and to American domination, with Third Way appeals not unlike those of the pre-war *Esprit*: their party seconded the Charter of the Resistance's call for radical economic, social, and political reforms.[13] In one of its early platforms the MRP called for the end of old pre-war parliamentarianism through a new constitution, as well as for economic changes which would give more influence to workers while nationalizing industry. The MRP wanted an upper chamber representing local, professional, and family interests; proportional representation; liberty of trade unionism to protect the Confédération Française des Travailleurs Chrétiens and of education to protect the Catholic schools; and a special place within the new structures of France for the 'natural communities' – so precious to the pre-war *Esprit* and the social Catholic tradition. There was much to make Mounier forget the party's aberrant Americanism.

Along with these noble ambitions, however, the early MRP programs leaned towards the empirical and pragmatic, confronting political problems as they arose. As long as the Resistance mystique was strong the MRP did well. In spite of the innovative language of its major documents the party came to sit in the centre of the Chamber. Its policies sometimes seemed imprecise, eclectic, and self-contradictory, but these latter qualities were hardly absent from the personalist movement and Mounier might have been expected to support the MRP.

Recalling Mounier's pre-war stance, however, his reticence is no surprise. Since the nineteen-thirties he had disdained the idea of an explicitly Christian political party as a poor fusion of religion and politics. Before the war it was the Catholic Right which had made this mistake and now, he argued, it was the 'Christian' Democrats.

Mounier's main criticism of Christian Democracy was that it identified Christianity with stodgy parties of the centre throughout Europe. The Christian religion, he thundered, 'is not a brake, it is a madness, an irrational force for upheaval and progress.'[14] Christ's legacy could never be confounded with 'social timidity, the spirit of balancing ... a fear of the people.' That 'Christianity' possesses 'the only words of life' he accepted, but whether or not 'the Christian milieu' was 'the sole or principal bearer of them today' or 'the will of God was necessarily represented by its practical majority judgments,' he saw as a different problem.[15] Mounier was opposed to Christian Democracy because its Christianity did not exemplify what he saw as a truly Christian spirit.

Mounier had described authentic Christianity in his wartime essays as fostering 'upheaval and progress,' not prudence or moderation. Thus in March 1945, while the spirit of Resistance unity was still strong, Mounier scandalized many Catholics by dismissing the MRP as petit bourgeois 'with a nervous reaction to all authentically popular movements.' *Esprit* was opposed to the 'narrowing of the revolution' that the Christian Democrats sought.[16] Mounier, refusing even to consider the positive aspects of concrete MRP programs, soon became one of the most prominent left-wing Catholic critics of that party.[17]

In the first half of 1946 the struggle over a new constitution for France strengthened Mounier's reservations about the MRP. The communists and socialists proposed a single, commanding legislative assembly. The communists hoped that under this constitution a new Popular Front majority could install an all-powerful, one-house legislature which could govern France through an executive committee free of checks and balances. They campaigned for ratification in May 1947 with the cry

'Thorez au pouvoir!' The MRP fought this constitutional draft, warning of the dangers to liberty and the French empire. To Mounier, this simply proved their conservatism.

He declined to offer concrete personalist alternatives to the Christian Democrats' 'non-revolutionary' policies. As in the 1930s, he stood aloof from day-to-day politics yet remained adamant in his commitment to total change. And once again, a set of concrete proposals began to emerge outside of the personalist movement which he could support.

Mounier's new orientation soon became obvious in a striking change in the post-war *Esprit* attitude towards the Soviet Union. In late 1945, as the French communists were enjoying great electoral successes, Mounier opposed the idea of a buffer zone between the Soviets and the United States, insisting, rather, that Europe should favour the mutual contact and cross-fertilization of the two great powers.[18] He did not seem to distrust Soviet intentions in Eastern Europe at all. In the spring of 1946, after a visit to Poland, he noted Russian unpopularity there but thought that elections would have the 'catastrophic' result of reintroducing a reactionary régime. He opposed the anti-communist machinations of the Americans and English, and was enthusiastic about the future of Catholic Poland (without elections) becaue he saw the possibility of a socialist revolution that was not anticlerical. His great regret was that Polish Catholics did not perceive the historic importance of this opportunity to reconcile the Church and socialism.[19] Thus Stalinist Russia, which Mounier had earlier denounced as tyrannical, was now the only willing agent of an historic attempt to reconcile the Church and socialism. As before, Mounier seemed rather short on memory and long on rationalization.

Along with Mounier's about face towards the Soviet Union came a revised analysis of Marxism. Before the war he saw Marxism as a materialistic threat to the 'person,' though 'an error with a great deal of truth in it,' and his personalism was to be a *via media* between the capitalists and the communists. But soon after the greatest post-war election victories of the communists, in the January and March 1946 issues of *Esprit*, Mounier's long theoretical essays on personalism revealed a new sympathy for Marxism. He declared that personalism and Marxism both saw twentieth-century man as profoundly alienated, that personalism linked up with 'Marx's own early inspiration, which focused ... on the alienation of the person and aimed, beyond the restructuring of society, at the liberation of man.'[20] Where Mounier had found sharp contradictions, he now found harmony and resonance.

He reiterated personalism's ability to shed a broader light than Marxism on *intériorité* and transcendence, but he found Marxist thought superior to personalism in its social and economic analysis of the contemporary world and in its understanding of practical action. Therefore Mounier envisaged the future relationship of personalism to Marxism as a 'mutual surpassing of each other' and he thought they could 'undertake together the great and total exploration of the new man, in which all the lasting values of eternal man could be saved and transfigured.'[21]

In early 1946 Mounier still maintained that personalism contributed *intériorité* to Marxism, but he was far more modest in his claims for this personalist contribution than he had been before the war. Modern man, he wrote, suffered from both exterior and interior alienation. The latter amounted to 'a devitalized spirituality' pretending to be inner life, 'a decadent self-complacency, the fruit of usury and idleness.' Thus what was called spiritual life was often simply a product of bourgeois leisure. Mounier, after his reading of Nietzsche, had become a severe critic of false spirituality. Now he declared that Marxism had been 'the most vigorous modern reaction against this decadence.'[22] He had wandered far from his pre-war call for 'the primacy of the spiritual in all of life.'

Nevertheless, he continued to warn that Marxism threatened modern man with another kind of alienation: the 'materialistic alienation' arising from the exaggerations of the materialists' attacks upon idealism. He surmised that it was the task of his generation to take up materialistic criticism, free it from an outmoded positivism and from 'the simplifications which were imposed in the first flush of combat.'[23] Personalism, again, would lend *intériorité* to the critical process.

It was against two dominant ideologies that Mounier was forced to define personalism after the war. Bur rather than juxtaposing the capitalist and communist cultures, he described personalism as seeking a remedy for idealistic and materialistic alienations.[24] Marxism was the most vigorous modern reaction against idealistic alienation; its curative value was apparent. As for materialistic alienation, the personalists seemed to see it as a recurrent, but remediable, characteristic of immature Marxist societies. Marxism seemed to have won an important role in personalist hopes.

If Marxism was so important to the 'personalist revolution' after the war, why had *Esprit* been so critical of it in the thirties? A number of

Mounier's post-war comments seemed a *mea culpa* for the past, such as when he condemned his or anyone else's efforts 'to "get beyond" a position before one has acquired even an elementary understanding of what it is.' He also rejected the 'Proudhonian anti-statism' of the early days of *Esprit*, as bound up with the spirit of individualism: it served 'mainly to make barren revolutionaries out of the refractory groups in all parties.' Neo-anarchists, he wrote, tried to carve out a third way when all they had to contribute was bitterness, negation, and impotence. Thus Mounier seemed to abandon much of personalism's past efforts to get beyond Marxism, to create a third force. The new personalist objective was not to get beyond Marxism by blunting the edge of its historical analysis, its revolutionary vigour. The new 'personalist realism,' Mounier wrote, 'aims at the edification not of socialists but of the socialist city.'[25] Marxists were to build that city, persons were to inhabit it. The masters of dialectic had met their master.

The personalist movement, so independent, original, and ambitious before the war, now appeared more and more to be a sophisticated 'school' of theoreticians complementing the Marxists. Rather than forge an independent Third Force revolutionary movement in France, Mounier travelled a good deal: to Belgium in 1944; to Switzerland and Poland in 1945; to Austria and Belgium in 1946; to Germany, French Equatorial Africa, Geneva, and Italy in 1948; and to England and Scandinavia in 1949.[26] Despite his post-war intention to make *Esprit* more committed, he seemed even less involved in day-to-day political issues than he had been before the war. The Marxists were handling many mundane matters for him.

PROGRESSIVE CHRISTIANS

If support for Marxism could be justified in a personalist perspective after the war, was the same justification possible from a strictly Christian point of view? For most French Christians, the closer one advanced towards communism the further one separated oneself from Christianity. Yet as demonstrated in his war-time esays, Mounier entered the postwar period with a determination to be a purer Christian. How could he reconcile his new sympathy for Marxism with his Christian beliefs? He would not be the last to face this abiding riddle.

For Mounier, at least publicly, there was a happy dovetailing of aspirations. His post-war essays developed previously unremarked parallels between Marxism and personalism, and between Marxisn and

Christianity. Marx's attack on idealistic alienation, for Mounier, was neither anti-religious or atheistic, nor even an attack on Christian spirituality. (Many scholars continue to argue that Marx, particularly the young 'humanistic' Marx, can be reconciled with religion. Shelves full of argument support both sides, and no solution to the controversy is attempted here.) He found that Modern materialism, in its anti-idealism, was 'not aware that it is here strangely at one with Christian tradition.' 'All the spiritual writers of Christendom,' Mounier wrote, 'denounced subjective self-love and complacency as the greatest deviation of the spiritual life.' It was Romanticism and philosophical idealism, he insisted, that had caused religion to develop that subjectivity which allowed Feuerbach and his followers to identify religion with alienation.

Thus Mounier could second Marx's criticism of idealistic alienation in so far as it was directed against a false religiosity, not against true Christianity. Mounier's radical distinction between bourgeois Christianity and authentic Christianity allowed him first to assimilate the anti-Christian vitriol of Nietzsche, then the anti-idealist lucidity of Marx. Even the brutally anti-religious character of communist movements was not a sign of advancing atheism: 'The violently negative barbarism in the working classes' attitude towards religion,' he wrote, masked 'a powerful drive towards civilization and spirituality.'[27]

Before the war Mounier had considered communist totalitarianism incompatible with the Christian conception of human dignity. After the war, however, he put more emphasis on his criticism of Western liberty as 'too careless, too lighthearted, too introverted ... only an abstraction, a refusal or a defiance.' The essence of true liberty was 'to give oneself to something greater than oneself.'[28] Mounier had always argued that liberalism had little in common with personalism or with Christianity. Now he stressed the differences between the individualistic and Christian ideas of the free man. He hailed the fact that it was 'beginning to be understood that Christian tradition, at least up to the Reformation, was essentially communal and hostile to individualism.'[29] He interpreted this rediscovery of the true Christian attitude towards liberty as in agreement with Marx's conclusions because: 'Marx definitely proved that the liberty of liberalism ... is an historical corruption, tied to particular economic and social structures. ... A Christian ought to be the last to reject that analysis. That rootless liberty, cut off from all foundation in the human condition, has always been repugnant to the Christian conscience.' In contrast to the early days of *Esprit* when he had called his group Proudhonians, Mounier now declared that the bent of the Christian, at least of the Catholic Christian, ought to lead him to Marx rather than to Proudhon.[30] He imagined not only Maritain and Berdyaev, but also Marx, joining in the rebuilding of the Renaissance.

At Uriage Mounier had worked towards training a Christian revolutionary élite, but his program there had been Nietzschean rather than Marxist: the intellectual and psychological renovation of individuals took precedence over the reconstruction of social and economic structures. Mounier's Christian revolutionary posture had been justified primarily as an individual commitment, in existential terms; he had not provided a broader historical and theological background. Thus, after the war, he spent a good deal of time trying to justify personalism's new posture by elaborating a new philosophy of history and a theology of history. In 1944 he began to describe the historical context in which Christian revolutionaries would inevitably triumph.[31]

An optimistic celebration of intellectual progress ran through Mounier's immediate post-war essays. He saw man

in the dawn of modern times lying in the womb of a universe closed around him like an egg, and in the heart of a Church that kept control over his first steps. Christianity alone, introducing ... the idea of creation and irreversible time, had made a breakthrough into the infinite from the foreclosed world. ... At last ... under this inspiration ... Galileo launched the earth into space. ... On all sides immobility, equilibrium, form, limits, circular perfection ... gave place to linear movement ... unfolding, indefinite expansion and the idea of series. ... Man introduced the theme of a destiny which is open, ahead of him, directed towards the unforeseeable and the infinite, to replace the concept of a destiny already fixed....[32]

Like Auguste Comte, Mounier unified history with the theme of the intellectual growth of man from childhood to adolescence and then, in modern times, to early maturity. (Hegel, of course, might have been a model through the medium of Marx, his pupil.) Mounier simply argued that this was the true Christian view: not to believe in progress was an aberration.

The Marxists had called for the liberation of all men through the labour of the proletariat and the technological mastery of the environment. Mounier admitted that the West had many Christians who did not share this hope, but their pessimism, he asserted, was caused by a perverted Christianity. He pointed repeatedly to the proletarian status of Christ and the apostles and cited early passages of Genesis as support for the dictum of Ecclesiasticus that the godly man should 'hate not laborious work, nor husbandry, which the most High has ordained.' He underlined the distinction in scripture between *operare* and *laborare*, between labour as creative work and labour as pain or punishment. He claimed that 'in direct opposition to the philosophies and spiritualist religions which flourished in the decline of antiquity, Christianity ... plants its God in the solid earth.' In his perspective, the determination to transform the earth into a realm of peace, freedom, and joy through creative labour was closer to the authentic Christian tradition than was the gloomy, world-hating resignation of many contemporary Christians.[33] Again, in his endorsements he mirrored Marx and in his castigations, Nietzsche.

Christian alienation from the industrial age, the Luddite sentiment of such questioners of progress as Ruskin, Duhamel, and Bernanos was a particular object of Mounier's scorn. He rejected this widespread attitude among Christians as contrary to genuine Christianity. Mankind according to him was closer to its historical womb than it imagined. It was still reluctant to leave its mother's arms and was still at the age when the fetters of instinct were confused with the ties of religion. 'By clearing the ground of animism, monotheism made room for ... the technical analysis of a world directed by reason, not governed by ... genies, but left by God to run its own adventures.' Thus hatred of the machine, rather than mirroring a healthy Christian respect for nature, was a superstitious vestige quite opposed to the true religious attitude.[34]

Mounier blamed Charles Maurras for the historical myopia of modern French Catholics, as reflected in Maritain's early works *Antimoderne* and *Trois réformateurs*, which presented reformation, rationalism, and romanticism as causes of the decadence of modern times.[35] According to Mounier, this gloomy perspective misled a large proportion of Christians who, hostile to progress, committed themselves to traditional politics and an outmoded biology hostile to the theories of evolution. In philosophy, these Christians had a conceptual conservatism at the expense of 'a more flexible handling of the relationship between eternal truth and the conceptual and representational system by which each epoch tries to express it.' (Here, as elsewhere, there is a new Hegelian ring.) Mounier charged that the result of this long battle was to establish the totally false belief that Christianity was synonymous with fixity and atemporality.[36]

In sum, Mounier described true Christianity as a cultural force which had superseded the idealistic alienation prevalent in other religions. Genuine Christianity fostered not only a new notion of the goodness of the world and the dignity of labour, but also broke through the older 'immature' conceptions of circular time and of a static closed universe. As in his Dieulefit essays and like Péguy before him, he selected scriptural passages and quotations from saints which supported this view and simply ignored the rest, while implying that his critics were heretics.

This culling of the Christian tradition enabled Mounier to perceive in post-war France only two groups in which 'faith in the destiny of man' still burned – Marxists and Christians. Both these 'churches,' according to Mounier, opposed the literature of despair, that feeling of 'complete meaninglessness,' which threatened to paralyze the West.[37] His effort to demonstrate parallels between Marxism and Christianity was obviously directed to *Esprit*'s Roman Catholic readers' typical objections to Marxism. Before the war he had confined himself to philosophy and politics and had exhibited an uncritical acceptance of Catholic theology. Now he turned more and more to speculation on religious matters, theological conjecture, and a theology of history for Catholic left-wing activists.

One major stumbling block to Christian and Marxist rapprochement was the biblical notion of sin. Communists could imagine the historical emancipation of mankind because men were formed by historical forces, and thus revolutionized social and economic structures could liberate man's potential for self-perfection. Christians, in contrast, believed in the free man's choice between eternal salvation or damnation; the dialectic between virtue and vice in individual human souls. The gospels' insistence upon the inevitability of sin and suffering until the second coming of Jesus seemed to contradict the Marxists' hope to abolish the suffering, injustice, and human vices traditionally linked with sin.

The very idea of sin ran counter to Mounier's thesis that disdain for machines, hatred for labour, and atemporal concerns were distortions of Christian tradition. Mounier, like Péguy, simply presented his own Christian conception of sin. Citing Jesuit theologian Henri de Lubac, he asserted that sin was less a degradation of the individual than a breach of human unit; it was 'in the depreciatory sense of the world, an individualization.' The image of an individual ascent of the soul from sphere to sphere, escaping the prison of this world, was characteristic of cowardly 'spiritualized evasion.' Christianity, he insisted, had transcended this image with one of all humanity, moving collectively from age to age, redeeming the physical world with itself. The authentic biblical perspective had 'a deeper affinity with ... Marx than with the Platonist, idealistic type of inspiration ... usually associated with "spiritualism".' Mounier concluded that there was no worse enemy of 'spiritualism' than Christianity.[38]

Mounier had come a long way from his 1932 calls for the primacy of the spiritual. How did historical events such as Jesus' life, death, resurrection from the dead, and second coming fit redemption? Here again Mounier was imaginative: the incarnation of Christ 'was only delayed – that man, having ... the experience of misery, should feel the need of a Redeemer; that ... he should become, in the audacious formula of St Irenaeus ... "accustomed to Divinity" through the teaching of the Prophets and the Sages.' The second coming was also delayed since man must learn progressively 'to assimilate and, as it were, to develop Christ.' He envisaged levels of spiritual achievement attached to each stage of spiritual progress, just as there were economic and social conditions. Mounier admitted that whenever man approached the 'divine dimensions of his vocation,' he was 'liable to the pride and self-sufficiency of Lucifer.' However, in a style again reminiscent of Péguy, Mounier proclaimed that 'man is made to do violence to God ... God manifests his joy in struggling with his creation.'[39]

Why was there progress in history? Why did God not create both man and nature in a state of instantaneous perfection? Mounier replied: 'God is the Father, but He is not paternalistic. He wishes man's liberation to be the fruit of toil, of genius, and of suffering ... that man should savour one day the full fruit of his labour, these toils and His loving, and not receive it as an overpowering gift from Heaven.'[40] Like Péguy, Mounier personified God as an actual father and confidently described His personality and intentions.

Where did Mounier get this distinctive view of history? According to Mounier, Henri de Lubac's exiled friend, the Jesuit paleontologist Teilhard de Chardin, established 'the cosmic perspective of the Christian message' while reintroducing an ancient tradition in Christian spirituality earlier exemplified by Church fathers such as Eusebius and St Gregory of Nyssa.[41] Mounier's larger vision of the relationship between Christianity and Marxism reflected both the style and imagery of Teilhard: 'Man does not only humanize nature, as in Marx; he renders it divine through his own participation in divinity.' Man was established as master of nature by the creator, and received both the promise of divinization and the burden of achieving it from Jesus. Therefore, man was both 'Son of Christ' and 'Christ of the cosmos.'[42] Mounier applied – and vulgarized – Teilhard's vast perspective in ascribing a particular role to Marxism in the twentieth century.

This exalted cosmological construct influenced Mounier's ethical emphasis and the character of his spirituality. He downplayed the struggle between virtue and vice in the individual soul and the dramatic salvation of sinners from hellfire through the sacrifice of Jesus. Professing an optimistic view of world history and faith in progress, he, like Péguy, stressed boy scout virtues – simplicity and confidence – as the proper attitude for the individual Christian. Behind the banalities of everyday life Mounier saw a drama which was 'more transparent in silence than in shouting' and more noticeable 'in the simple words of everyday – father, bread, joy, death, sin – than in all the dramatic nervous tension.' 'The whole of Christian teaching,' Mounier concluded, was 'contained in the two words: work and good-will.'[43] Thus, from the complexities of a cosmic perspective, one quickly descended to the simplicities of monastic virtues.

It is well to recall that this 'theology' was formulated in the dramatic political context of post-liberation France. Mounier made no pretense of dispassionate analysis or circumspect weighing of evidence in his effort to offer a corrective to the dominant historical and spiritual attitudes. He wrote for the broad readership of *Esprit*, not for professional theologians and metaphysicians. If he exaggerated and oversimplified, it was with concrete, historical change as his goal. Still reflecting the influence of Nietzsche, Mounier's citations from scripture, the Church fathers, and lives of the saints, selected the more worldly, life-affirming elements of Christian history. Always a synthesizer and balancer, he thought that his contemporaries were glutted by a life-hating 'spiritualism,' so he engaged in propagandizing.

The faith in historical progress Mounier exhibited in his post-war essays contradicted his private sense of the issues' complexity. The dichotomy between Mounier's public confidence and secret misgivings continued into his mature life. The sufferings of the war years had been compounded by the incurable illness of his infant daughter, the poor health of his wife, and his own severe imprisonment, yet his essays were suffused with a 'Teilhardian' optimism.[44] Mounier thought that one reason why post-war Catholics were not supporting the Marxist revolution was because they saw human progress as illusory. He responded with ringing praise for modern human accomplishments. There is little evidence of private optimism in Mounier's post-war attitudes but when, as leader of the personalists, he felt obliged to reaffirm his faith in man, he did so eloquently. He was a soldier of the personalist revolution performing his intellectual duties.

When Mounier presented his positive, progress-oriented doctrine as the central tradition of his religion, and implied that other religious tendencies were spiritual vices, he gave further evidence of the influence of Nietzsche's criticism of emotional self-indulgence and spiritual escapism. Since authentic Übermensch Christianity had been practised only by élite minorities like the Order at Uriage, most Christians and most contemporary Christian spiritual positions were inferior. Therefore, just as one had to pick and choose a few saints and mystics among Christians to isolate authentic Christianity, one had also to pick and choose in the tradition and, even in scripture, to isolate true Christian spirituality.

Mounier's acceptance of much of Marx's criticism of Christianity – after accepting much of Nietzsche's – made the personalist criticism of Christianity even more harsh. Not only should Christians possess the lucid self-reliance and spiritual vigour of the Nietzschean superman, they should also possess the faith in economics, class struggle, and technological progress of the Marxist. Turning this theme in the Church's tradition into a central current of Christian religious vitality was not easy.

The doctrine of sin muddled Mounier's synthesis and led him to flirt with Pelagianism. His definition of sin as an 'individualization' and his declaration of man's duty to 'develop Christ' suggested that sin was a social condition which could be removed through the adjustment of societal machinery. He may have been pointing the way to a reconciliation between Marx's (and Nietzsche's) belief in human perfectibility and the speculations of contemporary theologians, but it was difficult to see his analysis as growing out of the mainsream of Church tradition. The Christian doctrines of man's fall from grace, his redemption through Jesus' blood sacrifice, and the necessity for penance and sorrow for sin as preparation for a final judgment were always aspects of the Christian drama played down by Mounier.

In contrast to the dominant Roman Catholic theology of history, derived from Thomas Aquinas, which considered the progress of moral good in history to be accompanied by an equal and attendant progress of evil, Mounier implied that there was not only material but spiritual advancement as men 'developed Christ' and increasingly fulfilled their collective destiny as 'Christ of the cosmos.' Mounier simply transmitted this progressive formula into the 'central' spiritual tradition of the Church.

His important early post-war essay *La petite peur du XXe siècle* was a sort of dialogue, not unlike his confrontation with Nietzsche in *L'affrontement chrétien*, with the ideas of Marx and Teilhard. It demonstrated how eclectic Mounier was becoming towards Christian history and spirituality; and how he was filtering more and more of his religion through the Marxist prism.

THE NEW PERSONALISM

Mounier's fascination for Marxism brought a new focus to his personalism. Even in 1944 he had described the setting for the post-war *Esprit* as one of a 'revolution in process.' In 1932, he had argued, prospects for a revolution were remote and *Esprit* had sought to make spiritual men revolutionary; but now, in the post-war period, revolution was imminent and the personalists should devote themselves 'to making the revolutionaries spiritual.'[45] In the May 1945 *Esprit*, Mounier explained the new deference of personalism toward Marxism. Personalists hoped to produce a body of theory that would give personalism an 'authority' comparable to that of Marxism but it was not 'only in the first stages.' For the present, he thought that *Esprit* should stop 'decreeing an abstract historical destiny *a priori*, from formal principles' and maintain a more modest conception of both personalism's theoretical ambitions and influence.[46]

Again, as in the early days of the Popular Front and Vichy's National Revolution, Mounier's timetable was sharply altered: the apocalypse seemed on the horizon. With his ambiguous Resistance record and his sense of opportunities lost in the past through lack of commitment, he was determined to be in the new revolutionary vanguard in liberated Paris. He considered the proximity of revolution to present only two alternatives: support or opposition.

The French communists, at this time, were flirting with the idea of acquiring political power by democratic processes and found co-operation with the rest of the Left advantageous. The party also identified itself with the spirit of the Resistance, and Mounier was anxious to identify himself with that. Then, too, the party was making specific overtures to Catholics as it had in 1936: Louis Aragon professed the compatibility of communism with family life and Roger Garaudy praised the Christian masses, although he contrasted them with the reactionary hierarchy.[47] Not long afterward, Maurice Thorez publicly lauded Mounier and asked him to join the Communist party.[48] In that atmosphere it was not unusual for an independent review of the Left like *Esprit* to co-operate with the communists, and in the case of *Esprit* there was more than the usual inducement to do so.

Mounier had had doubts about the personalist movement well before the Liberation. In three of the great crises faced by *Esprit* – the Popular Front, the Spanish Civil War, and Vichy – the personalists had committed themselves to revolutionary initiatives and then withdrawn out of concern for the purity of their principles, while history had been made by others. By 1945, Mounier's pronouncements implied that he was ready to sacrifice purity of principle to efficacity; his conception of revolutionary change had become more determinedly hardminded. An older, somewhat disillusioned Mounier had realized that the revolution would be primarily the work of others. He had accepted a secondary, though presumably no less essential, role for personalism in the future.

There had been much implicit self-criticism in Mounier's dialogue with Nietzsche; and the outcome was a new conception of Christian ethics. Religious men, he had concluded, 'were too often absent on grounds of conscience when battle was at its height.' *L'affrontement chrétien* had been Mounier's supreme intellectual effort to exorcise his personal demon. Since he was a man of spiritual temperament who had forced himself into a life of action, Nietzsche's moral stoicism seemed to offer some help in transcending a perennial agony. The vigorous Christian 'superman' was an archetype compatible with both the stance of a Marxist revolutionary and the new man who would emerge in the post-revolutionary society. This positive and optimistic temperament, this faith in progress, that Mounier required of his new Christian was rooted in both Nietzsche and Marx. The olympian perspective of Teilhard de Chardin also provided much-needed support for the vision of the flowering of the human person that had taken hold of the young men of the plateau of Uriage.

Although some of Marx's analyses attracted Mounier, they were not the chief stimuli for his interest in the French Communist party. Rather, like many French intellectuals, he was led to Marx by the party; he now found the personal characteristics of communist revolutionaries attractive. Mounier never had the serious intellectual confrontation with Marx that he had had with Nietzsche, nor did he appreciate the Social Democrats' sense of the disparity between Marxist theory and party practice. Before the war he had usually attributed Stalinism to Marxist theory, not to a perversion of its principles. Mounier, relatively unfamiliar with Marx's writings, often seemed to have assumed that Soviet communism was Marxism in action. After the war his attraction for the communists was basically pragmatic; he thought that they were the most authentic revolutionary types, the most likely agents of radical change.

In so far as Mounier grappled with Marx intellectually, he was most taken with the young Marx's attack on alienation – a position which Marcel Moré had outlined in *Esprit* before the war. Although professing solidarity with Marxism, Mounier seldom wrote with the vocabulary, or in the framework, of Marxist analysis. He ignored Engels and Lenin, avoided mentioning Stalin after the war, and seemed indifferent to the mature direction of Marx's thought or the different Marxisms of different people. He centred his attention on 'Marx's view of man.' The mature Marx had condemned speculation about 'man,' as if man had a fixed, eternal nature, as metaphysical obscurantism. Mounier identified himself with what he saw as the spirit of the young Marx, and in this way tried to get beyond the tension between Marxism's devotion to man in general and personalism's focus on the person.

Mounier's post-war Marxism was sometimes as simplistic as much of the anti-Marxism on the opposite end of the political spectrum.[49] In his approach to Marxist theory, Mounier was similar to the 'conspicuously immature Marxists' of the first generation of French communism. When he was a student, French schools and universities resisted a philosophy which the academic establishment regarded as both ridiculous and pernicious.[50] Mounier had few colleagues who could be considered serious students of Marx, and, like other intellectuals of the French non-communist Left, he was influenced by Jaurès, Péguy, Proudhon, Berdyaev, Teilhard de Chardin, and others. His sympathy for the Marxist mystique was more developed than his grasp of its theories. It is also worth noting that the sympathetic young Marx, though perhaps more speculative, was already an inveterate foe of any role for religion. Witness his attack on Wilhelm Weitling's synthesis of religion and socialism and his friendship with the 'Messiah of Atheism,' Bruno Bauer, with whom he once planned to produce an Archives of Atheism.

Mounier's period of greatest sympathy for the communists coincided with the brief era (c1944–7) of good feeling on the Left that grew out of the Resistance and thus was part of a broader phenomenon. But an evolution in Mounier's thought also caused him to support the French Communist party while rejecting the Christian Democratic alternative. He came to renounce the 'too pure' personalism of the past and traditional Catholic, fixiste spirituality. This critique of his Catholic past was significant because his religious faith, more than his personalist philosophy, had always been behind his most important reservations about Marxism.

Mounier's reappraisal of Christian spirituality led him to question the assumption that Christian faith and communist militancy were essentially incompatible. It seemed to Mounier that either Christians or communists would have to change to promote co-operation between the two groups which, according to him, were almost alone in the post-war epoch in 'sharing faith in man and history.' Mounier, who always thought himself a serious and loyal son of the Church, would not consciously change his religion to conform to political and social exigencies. But in his exacting fidelity to his 'voices' he became obsessed with the incongruity between principle and practice, belief and action. His hatred for comfortable Christianity impelled him to seek a demanding 'authentic Christianity' wherever he could find it. The aggressively reformist element in his religious conscience led him to sympathize with the fiercest opponents of the bourgeoisie. If true Christianity was, in fact, practised by only a small élite rejecting middle class spirituality, then the dominant value system was in need of radical revision. In the eyes of his critics Mounier was simply rewriting the gospels; in his own view he was husbanding the flame that had always been present at the heart of Christianity. In any case, Mounier's new Christians thought they had more in common with the Marxists than with most Christians. Both Christian 'supermen' and Marxist revolutionaries had contempt for the self-indulgence and alienating escapism of mainstream Christian spirituality. Both considered social revolution the prelude to moral revolution; and both were inspired by faith in man and historical progress while viewing constructive, selfless, communal activity as the key to the regeneration of mankind.

Mounier's growing sympathy for Marxism was logical given his spiritual evolution. He did not think that his religous concerns gave place more and more to worldly occupations; in fact, Mounier's most sophisticated spiritual reflections were produced during the war and after it. He did not consider himself more and more 'tempted' by the Marxist view of the world at the expense of the Christian cosmology. A religious concern remained at the centre of his efforts: Marxism was a tool to produce a personalist and Christian revival. Mounier's greatest sympathy for French communism came from his deepened criticism of Christian spirituality and his continuing search for Christian renewal. The Marxists seemed in the vanguard of a national revolution, as Pétainists had been in 1940, and Mounier had joined them in yet another effort to rejuvenate Christianity.

There were several attempts to reconcile Marxism and Christianity in France immediately after the war. Mounier's was neither the most original nor the most daring, and soon he was, as we shall see, outdistanced on the Left by his friend Father Montuclard and the Chrétiens progressistes. Still, Mounier's effort was significant in so far as it proposed a distinctive orientation to the Left of Christian Democracy for young French Christians marked by personalism before or during the war. Here Mounier and Jean Lacroix followed their own path; several of the earliest personalists – Alexandre Marc, Robert Aron, Thierry Maulnier, and Denis de Rougemont – remained militantly anti-communist and turned their concerted energies to building European federalism. Although Mounier's quasi-Marxism created some differences between several of the older personalists and himself, he seems to have won over a number of the younger generation to his own views.

Bringing oneself, and others 'over' was the order of the day. Both the fascist Drieu la Rochelle and Drieu's close friend André Malraux had confided their sympathy for a Christian socialism to Mounier in the nineteen-thirties. Drieu went from authoritarian socialism, denunciation of the Munich agreements and the Nazis, to collaboration during the war and suicide rather than face execution afterwards. Malraux passed from heroic marxism, to fame in the Resistance, and to leadership in Charles de Gaulle's RPF. Mounier passed from Third Way efforts in the nineteen-thirties, through Vichy's National Revolution, to become one of France's leading proponents of Christian co-operation with communism. How does one explain the apparent radical swing of these three men from one end of the political spectrum to the other?

All had literary interests and were fascinated by the prospects for the full flowering of the human personality. They began from very different starting points – fascism, Marxism, Christian spirituality – but discovered a remarkable concurrence of aspirations when exposed to one another. One reason was that all three were 'personalists' in the large sense of the term. That is, each was above all concerned with the greatest possible fulfilment of each human being, not the mere 'individual' but man in his full spiritual and communal potential. If, in our day, human beings seek self-fulfilment through sex and drugs, in Mounier's time many men were moved by deep and exalting commitments to movements inspired by Nietzsche and Marx. Mounier began with an intense Christian commitment but learned, through exposure to men like Drieu and Malraux, that some Nietzscheanism and Marxism could contribute new dimensions to the human experience.

Did Mounier think that Christianity needed strong outside transfusions of ideology to survive? It seems rather that the central truths of Christianity always held the keys to life for him. But as a student he had undergone a 'spiritual revolution' with Jacques Chevalier's group which changed the course of his life, and he kept looking for ways to diffuse this experience to his countrymen. In France, just after World War II, he seemed to believe that a Christian-communist alliance held secret promise. Christianity needed a transfusion, not to survive – which Mounier believed it would do in any case – but to prosper.

A New Disorder 1948–50

After 1947, reports drifted westward of the more heavy-handed dimensions of Stalinism. The persecution of the agrarian political leader Petkov in Bulgaria in September 1947 and the 1948 coup in Czechoslovakia were followed by the brutal Comintern campaign against Tito and new revelations about Soviet slave labour camps. Mounier, like other critics of American influence in Europe, had to reappraise his glib political dismissal of the West. By the fall of 1947, with the creation of the Cominform, the dark side of post-war Stalinist imperialism was more clearly defined. Mounier followed the trial of Petkov with special interest as symbolic of the plight of someone in the Soviet sphere who sought to reconcile East and West. At its conclusion, he empathized with Petkov, 'crucified between the socialist world and the liberal world.' Mounier identified with 'that man who wished to reconcile the two worlds and was rejected by both' and sadly concluded that communism 'by its reviving exclusivism' was 'for the second time in the process of forcing the masses into fascism.'[1]

The coup d'état in Prague in early 1948 convinced Mounier that Stalinist communism would co-operate with non-communist groups in the pre-revolutionary stages of political action but not afterwards. He concluded that communism repudiated its allies, whatever their 'creative diversity,' and tolerated only 'subordinates.'[2] Therefore the prospect of personalist input after a communist takeover, or of personalists having an opportunity to 'spiritualize' the revolutionaries, seemed less and less likely.

Developments in France also swayed Mounier's attitude towards the communists. After the disruptive strikes of May 1947, the socialist premier Ramadier dismissed the communist ministers from his government, endorsed the Marshall Plan, and adopted a distinctly pro-American position. This was the end of tripartism and the beginning of the open war by the Communist party against the socialists and the MRP. With this ebbing of the Resistance spirit the possibility of a revolutionary coalition in France seemed remote – even to someone with Mounier's resilient optimism. The communists, echoing Moscow's new rigidity, moved towards a narrowly sectarian position.

Mounier sided with the communists on most issues which divided the old Resistance coalition. But by 1949 Gide, Nizan, Malraux, Sartre, and Koestler were all targets of vicious attacks from the party's 'intellectual hatchet-men,' and soon Esprit regulars such as Louis Martin-Chauffier, Vercors, and Mounier himself were denounced.[3] Mounier was also troubled by the excesses of the 'Catholic communist' Chrétiens Progressistes. His own intellectual base for participating in 'Christian-Marxist dialogue' included a solid grounding in theology and philosophy which he considered co-equal in importance to humanistic communist ideals. Thus, when a number of young Chrétiens Progressistes progressed from 'dialogue' to unreserved support for the communists, beyond that of the old Terre Nouvelle group before the war, he recoiled. He had drawn some young Christians to the new Esprit series, but too many of them were very different from the old guard who had had 'spiritual training,' who were well read in scripture, metaphysics, and Catholic doctrine. The younger personalists had grown up in the chaos of Vichy's National Revolution and the Resistance, when there had been little time for metaphysical or theological studies.

Jean-Marie Domenach's generation had become politicized without passing through a 'spiritualist' stage and their revolutionary commitments were often much less guarded than Mounier's. The Chrétien Progressiste movement had a strong concern for community which grew directly out of Father Maurice Montuclard's wartime Jeunesse de l'Eglise, with which Dunoyer de Segonzac, Mounier, some worker priests, and theoreticians of the Compagnons de France had worked during the early days of the National Revolution.[4] Like the Uriage school, the Jeunesse de l'Eglise and its successor, the Chrétiens Progressistes, sought a more community oriented Christianity, a new, more masculine type of Christian, in an effort to foster a 'Christian restoration.' But Montuclard's attention had shifted from the élite at Uriage to the French working class, whose Marxist ideology, he decided, had become the only means of reviving a sterile and moribund Christianity.[5] Intellectual weight was provided to the movement by another Dominican, Henri Desroches, who wanted 'to Christianize the Marxist synthesis' with the aid of the social and economic research of Economie et Humanisme, a movement founded in the Vichy period by a Dominican enthusiast of corporatist forms of social organization, Louis-Joseph Lebret, and which came to include major theorists of the National Revolution such as Gustave Thibon and François Perroux.[6] Despite their Vichy origins, however, the Chrétiens Progressistes were now as close to the communists as the most daring left-wing worker priests.[7] Mounier and *Esprit* were certainly a step in this pilgrimage of young Catholics from Pétainism to Stalinism, and some of the most prominent older personalists blamed him for this great embarrassment to the Church.[8]

Since the war, Mounier had seized a position at the avant-garde of Roman Catholicism, sniping at the Christian Democrats from the Left. Now he found himself outflanked by young Christian revolutionaries, some of whom professed to be his disciples. Such Christian communists forced Mounier to reasses his influence on young Catholics. He also took a second look at the long-term implications of the Christian-communist 'dialogue' and collaboration he had encouraged.[9]

Thus by the end of 1947 the excesses of the Soviet Union, the newly intolerant French Communist party, and the upstart Chrétiens Progressistes all pushed Mounier into a corner. The new secondary role for the personalists vis-à-vis the communist revolution compromised some of the basic aspirations of *Esprit*. It seemed that one commitment or the other, to the person or to the communist revolution, would have to be made.

Mounier was again suspended between political commitment and the claims of the spirit. Before the war he had drawn back in dismay as several of his zealous companions slid towards fascism. Now, after the war, he was troubled to find that some of his young disciples had been seduced into a thoroughgoing materialism. Distaste for this new false direction, when added to Mounier's abiding interest in *intériorité*, was to turn *Esprit* towards a new, more scholarly ally.

EXISTENTIALISM

In his post-war pronouncements Mounier vigorously disavowed the excessive 'subjectivism' or 'idealism' of the pre-war *Esprit*, which he blamed for his pre-war ineffectiveness. But at the same time he admitted this, he also became involved in a literary and philosophical movement which was the very symbol of subjectivism. Mounier praised existentialism, a *bête noire* of many Marxists, as a trend in French thought which would aid the personalists in preserving the dimension of 'interiority' against the Marxists. Marx had not taken away his taste for Nietzsche.

Mounier considered existentialism not a passing trend but a mutation in modern thought: 'a reaction of the philosophy of man against the excesses of the philosophy of ideas and of the philosophy of things.' He depicted it as descending from an impressive intellectual heritage with Socrates and the Stoics as great forerunners, and Tertullian, Bernard, Augustine, and Pascal as outstanding representatives of its Christian variant. In more modern times, he cited Nietzsche of course, but also Kierkegaard, Maine de Biran, and Bergson as immediate forebears.[10]

Despite his earlier apologies for pre-war subjectivity, Mounier lauded the existentialists for 'revising the objective point of view,' for rejecting 'the prejudice that the desire to detach oneself from the object automatically facilitates the acquisition of knowledge.' He argued that all non-scientific knowledge involved 'an intimate participation ... of the knower ... in the life of the known,' and he seconded the existentialists' call for decision and engagement. He saw the act of decision as 'a movement of the whole person ... focused upon some act of difficulty but of promise, which integrates the person and his experience in a fresh experience.' Mounier joined personalism to the existentialist spirit, as when he wrote:

> To live intensely is to be exposed, in the double sense in which the words indicate detachability from outward influences as well as the characteristic daring of the person. It represents courage to expose oneself. To live personally is to assume an everchanging situation, and responsibilities, and to reach out ceaselessly beyond the situation which has been attained.[11]

Mounier valued existentialism in his abiding struggle against intellectualism and 'uncommitted' liberalism. He rejoiced that existentialism did away with 'the last refuge of spiritual immobility, subjective certitude or assurance'; and that existentialist reflection could lead one 'almost to the point of maintaining that the important thing is, not so much truth, but the attitude towards the truth of the man who has gained knowledge.'[12] Mounier's own oscillating political commitments were evidence enough that the élan of revolutionaries was sometimes more important to him than the 'truth' of their positions. Existentialism's stress on the virtues of commitment – any commitment – merely redefined a theme which ran through Mounier's writings since the early days of *Esprit* when he became determined to redirect the spiritual in order to transform the world.

Consistent with this effort, Mounier also elaborated yet another vast historical scheme wherein he presented Karl Marx and St Thomas Aquinas as intellectual bedfellows. 'Although their thinking has often taken the form of crude objectivism,' he declared, 'medieval philosophy and contemporary Marxism are the two types of philosophy which have best demonstrated the irreducible solidity of the world of things.'[13] He called for an exploratory dialogue to isolate 'attitudes which are still opposed to each other' in the two philosophies, as well as hitherto unsuspected areas of agreement.[14] This was part of his effort to demonstrate Marxism's similarity to Thomism, and existentialism's to personalism. He saw a subjectivist personalist attempt to balance objectivist Thomism, and a similarly subjectivist, existentialist reaction to objectivist Marxism. Jean-Paul Sartre sought to counterbalance Maurice Thorez as Mounier had sought to equilibrate the influence of Jacques Maritain.

Mounier regretted that Marxists condemned existentialism for renouncing 'the objective world.' He argued that existentialist commitment had an importance analogous to the notion of inwardness, and that Marxism and existentialism were closer to one another than most people realized. While 'Marx's Marxism was much more a form of humanism than a form of naturalism,' contemporary existentialism showed a humanistic concern 'to integrate objective existence.' He thought that the most active forms of contemporary thinking were following paths which would ultimately converge. The great task for the coming years was to reconcile the philosophies of Kierkegaard and Marx.[15]

Mounier also argued that when Marxism and existentialism 'ultimately joined together,' it would profit the Marxist revolutionary movement. Existentialism helped correct the Marxist notion of historical determinism, an urgent task because 'if there is nothing in man superior to history ... then he may be given over to history without any further comment ... history was the creator of Dachau.' Mounier concluded that the defence against future Nazism had to be a conception of man which acknowledged the superiority of man over history. Thus existentialism had the important double task of upholding subjectivity in opposition to an objective world, and of preserving that 'inwardness' (*intériorité*) which was so rare and precious in 'the technological brave new world.'[16]

Mounier noted a similarity between the preoccupations of existentialists and personalists, particularly in the works of Gabriel Marcel and Berdyaev. In existentialism: 'the existent is described as colliding with the inertia or impersonality of the thing. Existentialists are unanimous on this point. They have called for a revival of personalism in contemporary thought.'[17] Mounier thought the existentialists heralded a reawakening of religious concern as well as personalist themes. The recent 'death of God' had left an instability in the modern soul: 'Forces ... powerful emotions, which supported man ... in the supernatural world, suddenly found themselves with nothing to support.' Sometimes these emotions threw themselves into the 'mysticisms' of nationalism, racism, or communism; or they encouraged a sense of weariness with life and philosophies of absurdity and despair. Existentialism, Christian or atheist, marked a revival of religiousness. Mounier considered Christian existentialism 'an obvious defence against the various types of secularization of the faith, a form of prophetic revival'; atheist existentialism was a research into 'dark mysticisms' suggesting a genuine revival of atheism. He welcomed both as allies in the struggle to create a communal society in which the person could achieve his natural and supernatural potential.[18] Thus, for Mounier, all religions, even if 'atheist,' contributed to the progress of personalism. Again we see how broadly Mounier defined 'religious' and 'personal' phenomena.

Since he saw existentialism as vital to the future communist society, he seemed to drift back into a subjectivism at the same time that he was attacking excessive concern for the interior life. But he was always conscious of his audience: when addressing personalists and religious men he defended a hard-line, 'objectivist' stance; when he confronted communists he championed existentialist subjectivity. Mounier personally seemed suspended once again between his two polemical positions. As an opportunist, pragmatist, and propagandist for transcendence, he formulated a Christian existentialism when he thought that the Communist party might have great influence in France, and tried to promote Marxism among Christians by criticizing Christian *intériorité*. Similarly he found existentialist analyses useful for promoting *intériorité* among Marxists. Mounier's response to existentialism suggests that his fundamental reservations about Marxism had changed less than his political essays seemed to indicate. He seemed to embrace almost any new 'religion,' from whatever direction, as an ally against 'materialism.'

Mounier's empathy for existentialism was another symptom of the broad wartime shift in his thought. While Christian existentialists such as Gabriel Marcel encouraged the antimetaphysical disposition of post-war personalism, they disagreed with its progressive, optimistic themes. In fact, there was a fixiste tendency in existentialist thought, particularly in that of Marcel. Mounier's sanguine synthesis of all post-war intellectual developments led him to transcend existentialism and to stress similarities among such divergent minds as Marcel and Berdyaev, Teilhard and Maritain. But the inevitability of their paths all 'ultimately connecting' was not as evident to them as it was to him. All religions, all spiritualism, did not and do not fuse as easily as Mounier seemed to think. Later stresses and strains in Roman Catholicism indicated that deep differences remained among them.

YES, PERSONALISM IS DISTINCT

The Chrétiens Progressistes scandal forced Mounier to articulate his basic disagreements with the 'Catholic communists' in 1947. He thought that 'the militant communist often displays a more authentic sense of God ... than that of the bien-pensant property owner.' But he insisted that 'The rapport of communism and Christianity is not that of two doctrines which ... neatly share heaven and earth, as certain Christian communists would have it. Communism and Christianity are tied together as Jacob with the angel, in the rigour and fraternity of combat.' Yet communism was 'still to contemporary Christianity what the gentile world was to Israel, denier and persecutor of the one God, but heir apparent to the gospel.'[19]

Mounier maintained that Christians who joined the Communist party and viewed the supernatural as a mere superstructure, who became too taken with 'imminence in order to escape the trap of idealism,' were only nominal Christians. 'The more audaciously the Christian commits himself,' Mounier argued, 'the more he has the duty to closely observe, and maintain the rigour of, his Christianity.' He should constantly oppose his religion to his political faith in an interior dialogue so that both became more precise and stronger in this struggle.[20] That was his strong advice for the Chrétiens Progressistes. But was Mounier following his own counsel? Some of his critics thought his Christian faith was becoming less and less clear.[21]

Throughout 1947 Mounier was in the awkward position of supporting the communists while urging the young Left Christians to keep their distance from the party. Finally the daring January 1948 *Manifeste des Chrétiens Progressistes* provoked Mounier. He criticized its silence on the persecutions of Christians in Russia, arguing that Christian revolutionaries had a special obligation 'to reveal to Christians and to communists the total perspective of a situation in which each side sees only one aspect.' He also challenged the Chrétiens Progressistes position that the Communist party offered the sole means of defending the working classes, the only hope of a popular democracy. Mounier said that to consider the party as the *only* way to those ends was an unacceptable position for a Christian.[22]

Thus, once again, determined Christian revolutionaries pushed Mounier to reaffirm the political agnosticism that always helped keep him back from complete commitment.

The Chrétiens Progressistes not only forced Mounier to articulate Christian reservations about communism but also some strictly personalist ones. Pulling back from his postwar solidarity with the communists, Mounier began to suggest the need for a new force which could gather all revolutionary forces 'in an atmosphere of liberty and mutual respect.' For a true national regeneration, the communists would have to stop denouncing every attempt to find 'another crystallization, another political atmosphere.'[23] In sum, the young Christian communists forced Mounier into a position resembling his older call for a movement which would co-operate with the communists, and not only after their construction of a socialist France.

After the Prague coup d'état in early 1948, Mounier called for a new 'proletarian socialism' between 'the massive Soviet state, where it risks asphyxiation, and the infirmities of social democracy.' He now sought 'a living and rigorous socialism growing out of the European peoples, but with new men and an open spirit,' inspired of course, by the personalists.[24]

By February 1948, Mounier and the communists, though apparently sharing some of the same goals, seemed to have taken quite different paths. Once again Mounier had been excited by a 'revolutionary' movement, only to draw back in the face of its aberrations. Once again he had been frustrated as an altruistic revolutionary mystique had degenerated into a vulgar, and disappointing politique.

Mounier tried to reaffirm the basic personalist position after his disillusionment with the communists. His final major theoretical work, *Le personnalisme* (1949), was another ambitious effort to reconcile his sympathy for the communists and existentialism and his new progressive conception of Christian experience. Since he maintained that personalists were always faithful to their central intuitions, he again sought to harmonize these new currents at *Esprit* with the 'neither Right nor Left' independence of its early days.

To rise above the complexities of *Esprit*'s recent political commitments, Mounier tried to define personalism's place in the vastness of intellectual history. But rather than go back to fifth-century Athens, as did existentialism, he found the chief precursor of personalism in Pascal, 'the father of the dialectic and of the modern existential consciousness.' The nineteenth-century spiritualist philosopher Maine de Biran was 'the latest of the forerunners of French personalism,' along with Bergson. Laberthonnière and Maurice Blondel were important for having defined 'a dialectic of spirit and action that badly upset ... all the abstractionists.' Jacques Maritain had usefully applied 'the clarifying reason of St Thomas to the most immediate contemporary problems.' Max Scheler, Martin Buber, and Berdyaev were valuable to personalism because they had simultaneously maintained the value of technological progress and spiritual freedom. Beyond these, Charles Péguy had a special place in the history of personalism: at the beginning of the century he gave 'lyrical expression' to all its themes. More recently, Gabriel Marcel, Karl Jaspers, and P.-L. Landsberg had made significant contributions to the structural description of the personal universe. In contemporary personalism, Mounier discerned 'an existentialist tangent ... (comprising Berdyaev, Landsberg, Ricœur, Maurice Nédoncelle), a Marxist tangent often concurrent with this one, and another tangent more classical, in the French philosophical tradition (Lachièze-Rey, Nabert, Le Senne, Madinier and Jean Lacroix).'[25] Marx and Nietzsche were, of course, not personalists but useful, purging influences.

If, as Mounier implied, so many disparate thinkers were 'personalists' to one degree or another, we might agree with Henri Marrou that post-war personalism, at least, 'was never more than a handy label or rallying cry,' which was 'philosophically never technically elaborated.'[26] In fact, personalism meant quite different things to different people by the time of Mounier's death. Perhaps it was elaborated too often.

Once his prestigious intellectual credentials were established, Mounier directed the major part of *Le personnalisme* to a further analysis of the relationship of personalism to Marxism, implicitly reconsidering the extreme deference shown to Marxism in his book *What is Personalism?* published three years earlier. He conceded that Marxist economic analysis was a valid approach to all human phenomena, and granted that most spiritual and moralist doctrines were incomplete because they tended to neglect biological and economic facts. But now he insisted on regaining ground for the spiritual: 'The spiritual, too, is a substructure. Psychological and spiritual factors ... may undermine any solution achieved on the economic plan alone. And the most rational of economic systems, if established in disregard to the fundamental requirements of personality, bears within it the germs of its own decay.'[27] Mounier called for recognition of the importance of 'the spiritual' as he had in 1932, and for re-establishment of the importance of personalism by insisting that the study of the 'spiritual substructure' was as significant as the analysis of the economic substructure. He implied, in contrast to his position a few years earlier, that it would be self-defeating to construct the socialist city on a purely materialistic basis, even allowing for a later infusion of 'personalization.' Where he had earlier found the communist revolution practicable but insufficient, he now found it impracticable as well as insufficient. A full consciousness of the Marxist and of the personalist views of man were again, as before the war, equally essential to the revolution from its earliest stages.

A new element in Mounier's analysis of the futility of a Marxist revolution was its ignorance of human freedom which came from disregard of the spiritual substructure. It had to be remedied before viable revolutionary action was possible. Personalism, Mounier claimed, was the enemy of totalitarianism: 'In questions of the collective life personalism always gives education and persuasion priority over discipline.' Although this had not always been true of personalism, many of Mounier's other comments recalled the spirit of the early *Esprit*. The timetable for the personalist revolution was put back once again: the achievement of a true personalist community was at the end of 'a long and difficult road' and not after a 'brutal acquisition of power.'[28] Some in Mounier's generation, such as Henri de Man and Roger Garaudy, moved from Marxist materialism to Christian spiritualism; others, like Paul Nizan and Maurice Merleau-Ponty, moved from Christian spiritualism to materialism. Mounier's itinerary was probably the most convoluted and sinuous of all.

Was there a firm personalist philosophy behind the transformations and fluctuating political engagements of *Esprit*? Was Mounier's personalism an autonomous, self-sufficient set of analyses? A philosophy? Even Mounier's philosopher-collaborator, Jean Lacroix, has conceded that Mounier was not a great philosopher, but 'a great educator,' who 'even inherited, to a large extent, his conception of the person.'[29] Paul Ricœur, sometimes described as Mounier's philosophical heir, simply dismissed the issue as of marginal relevance:

One plays a sterile game in comparing piece by piece the 'philosophy' of Mounier to the existentialist 'philosophy' and to the Marxist 'philosophy.' The game is sterile because the three 'philosophies' are not different solutions for the same set of problems, they are not even different problématiques situated on the same theoretical plane; they are divergent ways of projecting the rapports of theory and practice, of reflection and action.[30]

Mounier's 'philosophy' found its most influential expression in that effort at uniting theory and practice, reflection and action, the spiritual and the material, that was his day-to-day struggle. Some have found this effort extraordinarily successful, others have seen it as vacillating or escapist.[31]

THE FINAL POSITIONS

Mounier's philosophical reservations about communism by early 1948 did not directly effect a major revision of *Esprit*'s politics. Despite his doubts, Mounier often stood with the Stalinists on controversial issues during the last years of his life, as he had stood with the anti-Stalinists before and during the war.

Esprit never returned to its former anti-communism. The December 1947 *Esprit*, for example, was devoted to the danger of fascism, not communism, in France; and Mounier insisted that the Left, including a reformed Communist party, was the best hope for the future. He found the Left infinitely preferable to Gaullism and a number of veterans of the National Revolution agreed.[32] Even in the March 1948 *Esprit*, in which he recorded his disillusionment with the Czech situation, Mounier insisted that as long as French communists had the confidence of the working class – and as long as socialism was so inconsistent and untrustworthy and the MRP conservative – it was absurd to speak of an effective resistance to fascism without the co-operation of the communists.[33] In fact, for Mounier, de Gaulle represented 'fascism' in a way Vichy never did. The personalists supported the communists in opposing the Atlantic Pact, the Indo-Chinese war, and domestic anti-communist policies – the major political quarrels of the period. Maurice Thorez pointed, to these personalist stands in a speech to a party congress on 10 April 1949, when he invited Mounier to join the French Communist party.[34]

Mounier also defended the Soviet Union in some of the causes célèbres which stimulated the cold war anti-communist crusade. Most remarkable was his position on an issue which infuriated many Catholics: the persecution of Cardinal Mindszenty in Hungary. Mounier, refusing to share the outrage of his coreligionists, emphasized Mindszenty's aristo-cratic and reactionary ties, the distinction between the churchman and the political symbol. Mounier's rather severe conclusion was that the true history of the Church was one of poverty and suffering; it was illegitimate to use Mindszenty as a symbol for an anti-communist religious war.[35]

Conversely, while Mounier was unwilling to defend Cardinal Mind-szenty, he did support Marshall Tito of Yugoslavia against the Comin-form, in so far as Titoism represented a counterforce to excessive Soviet rigidity.[36] Communist Roger Garaudy acidly charged that 'after Pétain, there is Tito. The bourgeoisie [again] summons: *Esprit*, are you there? and twice *Esprit* responds: Maréchal, nous voilà!'[37]

Mounier did, however, strongly second the communists during the early post-war period in their denunciation of the United States' imperialistic ambitions. At the time of the Atlantic Pact he considered the United States to be in a vast process of economic expansion: both the Marshall Plan and Truman's 'Fair Deal' were attempts to ensure the health of the United States' potential markets and influence European politics.[38] He saw this 'economic conquest' as signalling a drift towards war that could end in the exploitation of Europe by American military strategists.[39]

After 1947, Mounier's anti-Americanism was balanced by a growing disenchantment with the Stalinists. He was willing to concede that 'neither America, despite the egoism of its wealthy classes and the ambitions of its manufacturers, nor the USSR, despite the excesses of its police and the rigidities of its socialism, represents a fundamental anti-humanism comparable to Nazism.' Nevertheless, Europe's prospects were gloomy, as it was 'faced with a democracy ruined by money and a socialism ruined by statism.'[40] In international affairs, too, Mounier's disillusionment with Stalinism was leading him to a neither Right nor Left position.

In the winter of 1949-50 the French Communist party 'froze' towards many of its allies. Roger Garaudy attacked Mounier for collaboration in the Vichy period. He marshalled the most florid passages from the *Esprit* of 1940-1 and ignored Mounier's 'double game.' As we have seen, Mounier could be described as 'objectively collaborationist,' but a fair critic would also be obliged to describe him as having been subjectively 'anti-collaborationist,' and an object of Vichy's punitive measures.[41] A comparison of Garaudy's selections with the originals indicates that he quoted some sections out of context and, in a few cases, apparently reversed their meaning. Garaudy could have built up a case for a form of 'collaboration' with aspects of Vichy but he misrepresented facts in his effort to discredit Mounier at a time when 'collaboration' with the Nazis was a terrible charge.

Garaudy also scorned Mounier's post-war effort to promote understanding between Christians and communists. Another young party intellectual with an important future, Jean Kanapa, in August 1948 had charged in *Cahiers du communisme* that Mounier attracted young intellectuals by 'his pretense of independence from the Church,' but in order to maintain his influence on them was obliged 'to play the Marxist game.'

Mounier, he said, risked playing that game too seductively. As a result he had 'to "leave" Marxism, coldly rejecting Leninism and Stalinism as impure and unfaithful to "original" Marxism, to finally be able to turn discreetly towards Christian spiritualism.'[42]

Garaudy added that Mounier created a straw man called 'Marxism' for his clientele, because many of these young men had a vague sympathy for Marxism. The essence of Mounier's effort, he said, was to hold them aloof from militant action. And when Marxism was no longer world-spinning but 'a living and constructive reality, that of Lenin and of Stalin,' Mounier called it too narrow, 'scholastic.' Mounier wanted his Marxism so pure, continued Garaudy, that he preferred 'to castrate it' rather than have it become part of 'the soul of the party's battles and of the Soviet structure.' According to Garaudy, young Christian intellectuals had followed Mounier as a means of access to communism; some of them, after they became tired of Mounier's 'Byzantinism,' decided to maintain consistent positions and had joined the party.[43]

Summarizing his arguments, Garaudy directly addressed Mounier: 'Against living Marxism, you found the metaphysical alibi of the "scholastic." Against the socialist countries you found the political alibi of Tito. You have exhausted all diversions, furnished all the alibis ... followed the forces marching boldly towards the future, only to be able to stop and divert their march at the decisive moment.' Garaudy concluded that despite his rhetoric Mounier had always wanted to turn promising young men from the party. He asked finally: 'How, Mounier, will you dare to face them when they angrily say to you: "You want us to turn our backs on the joy of a new life".'[44]

Not surprisingly, Mounier spent the first months of 1950 agonizing over the relationship of the personalists to the communist movement. This effort ended with his sudden death from heart failure in April 1950. In answer to Garaudy's charge of collaboration he had described the resistance side of *Esprit*'s efforts under Vichy much as he had formulated it immediately after the war. As for Garaudy's methodology, Mounier replied: 'Honesty, that metaphysical whore, should have required you to provide a continuous series to the reader, not stumps of phrases, but pages, articles ... special issues.'[45]

The communists' charge that Mounier consciously played an anti-communist game by holding young potential communists 'in suspense' is of course contradicted by Mounier's diary and private correspondence. He seems to have sincerely desired a 'personalization' of communism that would have allowed him and his entourage to join the party. This hope was never realized. But if Mounier honestly awaited a reformed – not diluted – communist movement, he never completely explained the fact that he found the 'revolutionary forces' in 1940 relatively pure and worth joining, but not the post-war communists.

In his last major articles Mounier seemed somewhat defensive about the long labour of the personalists to encourage co-operation with communist revolutionaries. In the end, *Esprit*'s editor downplayed his own 'progressivism' and insisted that he had never been 'directly connected to the Communist party, like Cassou and Vercors.' His personalism, 'which owes part of its health to Marxist waters, was yet never baptized in them.' If the personalists had paid special attention to communism in France after 1944, it was because of the particular conditions in France – and Italy – at the time: 'the Resistance left the promise of a communism reintegrated into the French tradition ... capable of rebuilding, in a new experience ... a French socialism.'[46] That the promise had not been realized was not the fault of personalism.

In 1950, Mounier lamented that attempts at intellectual exchange with the communists now produced 'an iron curtain of ideas, of feelings ... a dialogue of the deaf.' He thought that the enemies of communism had done much to create obstacles but that communist thought, too, had played the game of its adversaries when 'on its side, it hardened and installed itself ... in an airtight system.' *Esprit*, for its part continued to refuse both 'scholastic anti-communism' and 'scholastic communism.'[47]

The personalists, Mounier continued, would continue to defend their basic values 'at the side of whoever, in each case, defends them without equivocation, and against whoever, in each case, would compromise them.' But he thought that three lessons could be drawn from the history of France since 1944. First, 'any attempt to reconstruct socialism on the plane of literary clubs, without the ballast and vigour of the proletariat, is headed for a morass – the failure of the post-Resistance demonstrates that.' Second, 'any union of heretics and schismatics of the Left, without a forceful doctrine and a popular base, ends in impotence – the failure of the RDR demonstrates that.' Third, 'all groups which through their ideological weakness, their mimicry of communist theses and absence of autonomy, only appear to be instruments of the Communist party are at present incapable of widening their activity – the failure of the Front Nationale, the PSU and many other para-communist groups demonstrates that.'[48] In short, Mounier came close to saying that in post-war circumstances one could act neither with the communists nor without them. The rigidity of the Stalinists forced the personalists to renew their search for a new politics.

Marxism-Leninism, Mounier claimed, while destroying pre-Marxist socialisms, had at least promised short-term historical efficacy. But, looking at the price, he could no longer accept a socialism which destroyed three generations in order to save the following ones.[49] What was needed, he concluded, was a movement in 'the great French revolutionary tradition' – and 'also that of Rosa Luxembourg and Gramsci' – which could provide 'a forceful, imaginative doctrine with the living impetus of the proletariat.'[50] Mounier did not want 'the heretical reformation which dismembers a Church' for communism but rather 'the interior reform which saves and revivifies it': not a Tito but rather 'a Saint Theresa or a Saint Ignatius and, to finish the job, a Paul II.'[51] Esprit would try to aid in extricating the 'poisons' from the communist party and Mounier hoped to 'co-operate one day with a communism that had emerged from its blind alley.'[52]

In Mounier's final essays on communism there was no hint of giving up the fight: 'the Christian does not leave the poor, the socialist does not abandon the proletariat, or they perjure their names.'[53] The personalists 'remain on the terrain that we have occupied, difficult as it is to hold it today. History rewards those who persist, and a well-placed rock corrects the course of a stream.'[54] Despite these brave words Mounier's more private writings again reflected some bitterness and disillusionment at the fading of prospects for revolutionary change in France.

CHRISTIAN TO THE END

According to his friend P.-A. Touchard, Mounier's religious faith was always 'lodged firmly, like a block of granite, at the centre of his life.'[55] No one has suggested that his religious zeal ever wavered or flagged; it seems to have been his most consistent and unalterable trait. Mounier's understanding of his religion, however, did evolve. In some important ways his spirituality was profoundly altered after his wartime and post-war experiences. His final writings were marked by strong denunciations of 'spiritualist evasion' in Christian religiosity. Often this was in the framework of an attack on the Greek influence on Western culture – and on his own intellectual development: he ascribed the mind-body or spirit-matter dualism in the West to Greek origins. In the Middle Ages it had fostered 'the long Platonic aberration' which hampered a full reaffirmation of matter and human personality. This had been transmitted from century to century down to modern times under false Christian credentials.[56] Hellenism taught Christians to scorn 'the temporal, the body, matter, even when these are at the heart of the mystery of the Redemption.'[57]

Spiritual escapism in the Greek tradition had undermined the equilibrium of the human personality. The true Christian attitude towards the body and matter, in Mounier's view, contrasted with this Greek aberration; the Christian who spoke of the body or matter with contempt did so against his own most central tradition. The Christian personalist realized that 'Man is a body to the same degree that he is a spirit, wholly body and wholly spirit':

My moods and my ideas are shaped by the climate, by geography, by my situation upon the crust of the earth, by my heredity and perhaps ... by indiscernible currents of cosmic rays. In these influences, the supervening psychological and collective determinants are interwoven: there is nothing in me that is not mingled with earth and blood.

Mounier noted that the great religions spread along the same routes as the great epidemics. The Christian personalist had no reason to be shocked: 'Missionaries also go on legs and have to follow the contours of the landscape.'[58] In sum, Mounier sought to describe most modern 'flesh-hating' or 'world-hating' as originating with Plato, not St Paul. This theme was not completely new to his thought – in *L'affrontement chrétien*, during the war, he had attributed idealistic alienation to the Greeks – but it underlined the ever-increasing extent of his anti-Hellenism. The Athenians and the bourgeoisie were personalism's historical adversaries, both responsible for the 'idealist alienation' which Marx condemned.

Mounier's excoriation of Platonism enabled him to insist that his Nietzschean, life-affirming personalism was in the central Christian tradition. In any case, the 'measured and contemplative wisdom' mixed with a general 'contempt for the material' of the Greeks ran against his revolutionary instincts and the new existentialist current in his thought.[59]

Mounier's condemnation of philosophical idealists reinforced his antipathy for a Church corrupted by them. The first generation of the French Catholic intellectual revival had been anti-bourgeois; Mounier's urging of the younger generation to be anti-Greek as well was to have far-reaching effects.

There were philosophical implications to Mounier's anti-Hellenism that were not immediately apparent. He found fault with the Catholic bourgeoisie, then with Christian culture, and, by the end of his life, with the very bases of that culture. Since he believed that every culture had metaphysical roots he began to critically examine those of the West. In Germany, Heidegger, whose association with Nazism Mounier did not mention in his history of existentialism, was engaged in a similar enterprise on a more formally philosophical level. Mounier ended up strongly 'anti-metaphysical.' He was no longer, if he had ever been, a student of Jacques Maritain. He had been on the fringes of Catholic philosophical, political, and social thought since his youth. He had been outside the prevailing tradition of Christian spirituality since the efforts of Uriage to discover a new, Nietzschean relationship between action and contemplation. By 1950 he had completely abandoned the traditional intellectual formation of the Christian intelligentsia for a Christian existentialism he had derived, for the most part, from German thought.

Mounier's new anti-metaphysical bent brought frequent references to the importance of the will and of 'action,' and a rejection of various 'uncommitted' philosophical positions. He attacked philosophical absurdists who thought there was 'no sufficient reason for engaging in one action rather than another.' People of this sort were characterized by 'aesthetic dilettantism, ironic anarchism, a maniacal advocacy of everything non-party, abstentionist, protestant or libertarian.' With these men 'an almost visceral repugnance to commit themselves, an inability to accomplish anything, betrayed the dried-up sources of feeling underlying their sometimes highly-coloured eloquence.' Mounier also had harsh words for the apolitical abstentionist who 'took flight from the vital zone of political action ... upwards to meditation and character-formation, as a "spiritual deserter".'[60] As above, the strong language here has an urgency born, in no small part, of self-criticism.

Mounier professed to have drawn this new appreciation for the value of commitment from Marx as much as Nietzsche. However, when forced to defend the personalist stance against the absurdists, Mounier could affirm only one principle valid for action that could always be maintained: 'Do what you will, it matters not what, so long as your action is intense and you are vigilant about its consequences.'[61] Even in his fellow traveller phase, the political agnosticism in Mounier's thought kept him closer to Nietzsche and Malraux than to Marx.

Mounier's new notion of commitment inspired fresh reflections on the subject of violence. He claimed that there was no society which did not originate in 'a struggle between forces' or was not 'sustained by some force.' It was hypocrisy to be against class struggle or to be against violence 'as though we were not taking advantage of "white violence",' as if we were not always living in a society which, in exploiting the poor or the disadvantaged, did not have us 'participating at a distance in a sort of diffused murder of mankind.'[62] Mounier's conclusion was that 'there is no value that is not born of conflict or established without struggle, from political order to social justice, from sexual love to human unity or, for Christians, to the Kingdom of God. Violence must be condemned, but to evade it at any cost is to renounce the principle tasks of mankind.'[63] At the time, Mounier's exhortation to struggle and his qualified apology for violence seemed unusual, if not bizarre, positions for a man who had seen World War II while professing to be a Christian intellectual. Only twenty years later would revolutionary activism and violence be significant themes among radical Catholics, with priests joining guerilla bands in the mountains of Latin America.

There was another issue in the late forties which set Mounier off from his contemporaries and made him appear, in retrospect, as a prophet of the attitudes of European Catholics in the sixties and seventies. His alienation from the bourgeoisie eventually led him to be more critical of the United States. He had never paid much attention to the New World until after the war, when he had sided with the French communists against the Atlantic Pact, as a special critic of the religious war element that had crept into American anti-communist policies. His distinctive notion of 'Christian civilization' in modern times reinforced these political judgments.

In April 1948, Mounier had warned: 'It is not the pope who equates Christianity with America. It is the Americans, all day long and with all their propaganda, who equate the American block with Christian civilization.'[64] In the papal decree against communism on 13 July 1949, Mounier saw continuation of the success of the American effort and imagined 'all the world's social egoism ... that monstrous coalition ... of money, dancing a victory dance' around it. He thought that in capitalists, 'in their ideas, in their acts, in their hearts of hearts,' there was far more materialism than in a worker from Belleville. Mounier thought that many of them idolized in God 'a selfish projection of their own interests.' The Americans had justified their selfish anti-communism on religious grounds and dragged the Church with them.[65]

Mounier remarked that the Catholic Church since the time of Pope Gregory the Great and Constantine had intervened excessively in worldly affairs. Therefore some Catholics were struggling against 'a certain "defence of Christian civilization," a certain lumping together of the Church and the capitalist and American West.' He warned that that 'blasphemous temptation' influenced the attitude of the Church towards communism.[66] He observed that it was extremely difficult to 'link the Sermon on the Mount to the perspectives of capitalism' and that if the Church was going to condemn atheistic materialisms it might begin with the United States.[67]

Thus, Mounier not only rejected the concept of the struggle of the 'Christian West' against the 'materialistic East' but actually looked to the east, notably Poland, for Christian renewal, over thirty years before the election of Pope John Paul II. Berdyaev had foreseen a post-communist spiritual surge in the East, but Mounier may have been a singular prophet when he foresaw that the long-term interests of the Roman Catholic Church might better be served by compromise with communist régimes in eastern Europe than by close ties with the United States. Thirty years after Mounier's prediction the prospect of a tacit alliance between 'law and order' communist bureaucrats and the Catholic hierarchy against the materialism of the masses seems far more conceivable than it did when he formulated it.[68] Mounier was a living prototype of a new-style Catholicism, and felt an instinctive aversion for American culture and foresaw its inevitable clash with Catholic values.

Mounier's rejection of traditional Catholic metaphysics, his political activism, his criticism of the United States, and his sympathy for communism and long-range prophecies of its providential role have caused him to be remembered as a Christian progressive, a man with a firm faith in an apocalyptic future, in a humanity transformed by the Christian religion. The popularity of Teilhard de Chardin after Mounier's death, the influence in the Church of ideas common to both, at the Second Vatican Council and after it, has led to inevitable comparisons especially in their views of Christianity and history. The historian of ideas Madame Madeleine Barthélémy-Madaule in her study of Teilhard's personalism found a strong parallel. Both men were devotees of progress but both were 'determined, at each stage, to preserve human liberty and never to drift into a dogma of progress.' Both men, she thought, struggled against pessimism regarding technology but both were convinced of 'the rapport between historical progress and the coming of the Kingdom.'[69] Both also saw the prospect of a great spiritual leap forward for mankind after the French defeat in 1940, but she did not mention that.[70]

Did Emmanuel Mounier have Teilhard de Chardin's faith in historical evolution? Not long before his death, Mounier pondered the future of Western civilization while on an extended visit to Sweden, a country enjoying technological progress, a form of socialism, and neutrality from the great international rivalries. But he was disappointed with the lack of spiritual life he found there, blamed prosperity for the country's 'general enervation,' and wondered if the Swedes were concealing 'some hidden fire which would be able to rekindle the spiritual flame of the country.' He found 'stiffness, formalism, friendly or ceremonious emptiness' – although sometimes the 'ancient undercurrents of poetry,' which remained the basis of resistance to Americanization, broke through. But his final observations were pessimistic for the future of abundance and security promised by scientific organization: 'the few bridgeheads which have been established on the far side of poverty at least invite us to ask the question: is man made for happiness? Is he able, in prosperity, to preserve the passion of Prometheus, the divine kindness of compassion?'[71] Mounier's questioning of technological society led him to ask if a Christian civilization was, ideally, a well-ordered and happy civilization. He asserted that if men could establish 'an orderly, satisfied civilization ... with the moral virtues deriving from health and strength,' they would enjoy 'a sort of animality of superior conditioning' – but not necessarily a Christian civilization, for that entailed 'faith, hope and charity, and their reverberations in all of life.' Mounier warned that a prosperous and balanced civilization could become so confining that the true destiny of man would find no place to take root. Such a world would not be 'human' and 'the thunderous powers deposited in us by the Holy Ghost would burst forth there someday.' What was the providential purpose of the countries leading the way to this future? Some nations, large and small, had enjoyed a prosperity and relative peace which enabled the new technological world to 'delineate itself and reveal its spiritual poverty.'[72]

At the end of his life, therefore, Mounier had serious doubts about the future of the West whether communist, socialist, or capitalist. Did he retain a hope that some future marriage of religion with socialism would inspire Christian renewal? He ultimately professed agnosticism on the relationship between 'civilizations' and the Christian faith. He said that theologians did not shed more light on these problems than anyone else: 'no one today would pretend to decide peremptorily whether the conversion of Constantine was a good or an evil for the Church, or whether a socialistic type of economic structure is better suited to the progress of the kingdom of God than a capitalist economy.'[73] His remarks on the role of particular cultures in the designs of God displayed an agnosticism not found in most of his earlier writings.

Madame Barthélémy-Madaule, after analysing Mounier's most historically progressive essays, concluded that he, like Teilhard de Chardin, believed in a 'rapport between historical progress and the coming of the Kingdom.' But did Mounier believe this or adopt this position for rhetorical purposes? In a 1947 *Esprit* article, he remarked that Teilhard, 'like all the spirits of his school, tends to accentuate the old theme of the co-operation of Evil in the divine plan, and he feels repugnance for theologies that are too conspicuously tormented.' Theological optimism, Mounier concluded, threatens 'to remove the sense of tragedy from our condition, to hide the abysses of sin and grace: a counterweight for it is useful.'[74]

Mounier's counterweight was evident in what he called his 'tragic optimism.' A few weeks before his death, he wrote to a young associate: 'I know that there is no paradise on earth. I consider dangerous the tendency of many of our contemporaries to want to find an absolute in a political régime. I am Christian, and therefore consider the Church more important than all political régimes. ... History is neither a diagram nor a fairy-tale....'[75] Mounier's optimism for the Church's future became more guarded as he became more agnostic philosophically and politically. In 1949 he wrote: 'There is no more a Christian philosophy than there is a Christian social doctrine or a Christian political program. There is a Christian inspiration, which runs through all of history ... from which a shower of glittering philosophies descends.' Certainly Mounier was happy to see Christians rediscovering 'the sense of the earth' and 'the value of history,' against a religion become 'too subtle, sophisticated, and confined.' This tendency responded to a need of the epoch while also rejoining a primary inspiration of Christianity.[76] But here Mounier's hopes were certainly far less 'progressive' than in 1945 or even 1940.

In the end, Mounier's sense of the future of Christianity was grounded less in a perception of linear historical progress than in a feeling of mystery regarding the activity of the Spirit of God:

Whoever seeks the continuity of the Kingdom had better turn his attention away from the statistics of Massachusetts or the Ubangui, away from the epaulettes of Franco and from the prestige of Cardinal Spellman in the *Reader's Digest*. He will find ... in the workers' quarter of Montreuil, ... three priests living in community, in shabby clothes, and around them an obscure, stammering and shocking reality. ... The Church of the year three-thousand will place these solitaries on pedestals when Franco ... will not even leave a trace in the pitiless books of History. Before burying the Christian tradition, one had better direct a little attention to its avant-gardes.[77]

Mounier, despite the frustration of so many of his projects, may not have died completely disillusioned. His religious sense inspired an attachment and detachment from the world, a love and hatred for it. He projected religious hope into a succession of revolutionary initiatives and each in succession failed him. Still, the hope that an avant-garde would someday unlock the mystery of history and 'make straight the way of the Lord' remained with him.

The election of Pope John Paul II, an intellectual who was an essayist and a poet in a milieu in Poland strongly influenced by Mounier, was an event that went beyond Mounier's most grandiose hopes for the influence of his ideas in the Church. Not only had the new pope, like Mounier, studied the possibilities of reconciling the community-oriented philosophy of Max Scheler with Christian values, but he had also done his other major research on a mystic – John of the Cross. Like Mounier, the new pope was both an intellectual and an effective administrator concerned with the relationship between action and contemplation. Like Mounier, John Paul II had a long-standing interest in educating adolescents. Like Mounier, the new pope did not believe that the 'American way of life' was necessarily the best for Christians, and, while fighting for the liberty of the human person, sought to reconcile Catholicism with the most positive aspects of socialist régimes.

12

Epilogue

No clerical-fascist dictatorship can claim *Esprit*'s founder.

However, it would take only an inventive demon to turn Mounier's dream into a nightmare. Imagine the communist society of the future Christianized, *concordataire*, not at all liberal, communitarian but not personalist, suffocating under the double patronage of the Church and the Party! The veil of the sacred would cover its technocratic organization, its directed culture, and its proletarian virtues reinforced by Catholic austerity. Virtuous families, modestly prosperous and piously expurgated of humour, fantasy, taste, voluptuousness, and thought, would reverently depose red wreaths on Mounier's tomb, without a hint of that metaphysical passion, that fervour for liberty, which consumed him.[1]

Emmanuel Mounier was not driven to rebellion because he saw a privileged minority living in richness and comfort while the masses lived in poverty and suffering. He did not condemn the very rich nor did he promise the poor that the world would be healed if property were distributed more equally, or abolished altogether. Rather he attacked the bourgeoisie because they were decadent and in need of a revolution to save themselves from themselves. He also attacked them to save himself from his own background. Salvation could only come through a revolution that would make proletarians of everyone while preserving 'personhood,' whether theirs or his.

There were problems with a middle class French Catholic calling for a revolution to make personalist proletarians of the members of a middle class that had become the backbone of the French Catholic Church, while the working class was religiously indifferent, if not militantly atheist. Thus a 'Catholic revolution' had to have another dimension: there had to be a means to 'spiritualize' the proletarian uprising. If not, that day of reckoning would see the eclipse of the Catholic Church, as in France in the 1790s.

This Quixotic, uniquely personal, search for a simultaneous spiritual and social revolution was behind the sinuous course of Mounier's political enthusiasms. He turned with hope to the Right and then to the Left; he was disappointed by both, but tried again. It is noteworthy, but not surprising, that he was invited to join both Vichy's National Revolution and the French Communist party. How were such contradictions possible? Briefly, to Mounier there was no contradiction. He was convinced that his Christian duty was to be visible in the age in which he lived whatever the political setting. He did not have the patience for ideological purity or consistency. He found his age inhuman and oppressive, and thought his generation was perishing from spiritual asphyxiation. Rather than denounce his times from a hermit's cave he threw himself, in so far as his nature allowed, into revolutionary activity. He thought one could not endure as a Christian in his culture; for that reason he thought that the social equation had to be altered.

The peculiar roots of Mounier's fascination for revolutionary initiatives explain that curious mixture of political fervour and indifference to politics that characterized his life. He never could become completely immersed in politics because his sense of God was at the centre of his experiences. He believed that death would liberate him in the eternal sense, so he never took the promise of an earthly kingdom, or even the mundane world, with unreserved seriousness. In addition, he was certain that grace and God's love transformed men far more than political structures ever could, even when he found more grace in Third Force revolutionaries or Marxists than in Christians. The successful revolution had to be spiritual and he saw the infusion of spirituality as more the work of God than of politicians. This vision of revolution was, of course, not widespread among revolutionaries and, accordingly, Mounier often judged them one-sided and cruel. The strictly political hopes of many of Mounier's allies were less restricted and allowed them to have unreserved political commitments, and less sensitive political consciences. Thus, while Mounier was a very convincing religious personality for a generation highly sophisticated in that area, he was far less convincing as a revolutionary to those who judged him on political acumen alone.

An unreserved faith in political change would seem to require a firm sense of the direction of history. Mounier, however, believed in an eternity that dwarfed whatever worldly vision he might embrace, and he could not reconcile the two. It is true that when he thought French

Catholicism needed someone to interpret confused events in a broader historical context, he did so: in the Popular Front, under Vichy, in the euphoria of the post-war period. In each case he tried to put a revolutionary élan into a framework that allowed for the supernatural, but in each case he had private reservations about the soundness of his public rhetoric. He was certain of the importance of the eternal, but never seemed completely convinced of the appropriateness of any particular incarnation of it in the temporal.

When Mounier was drawn to revolutionaries, above all to the 'super-revolutionaries' at Vichy and the communists, he was himself warmed by the fire that burned within them. It was Marxists who attracted him, not Marx; the revolutionary élan more than the revolution; the personal qualities more than the practical plans of action; the persons more than the politics. He hailed any violent contrast to the bourgeois Christians he despised; he admired vigorous, heroic, community-oriented, and selfless men, like the communists or the new élites which the Ecole Nationale Supérieure des Cadres d'Uriage tried to form.

Mounier's olympian gesture to the French Marxists was not recipro-cated. He offered a spiritual dimension to a communist philosophy of politics that he thought incomplete and one-sided. From a Marxist point of view it was Mounier who was so. They viewed his revolutionary position like Péguy's, wholly lacking at least in two essential ingredients: he did not embrace the concept of class struggle; and he was blind to historical determinism, to the dictum that the dialectic in history was leading inevitably to a classless society. It further vexed the Marxists that he had a history of holding back at the decisive moment or, as Paul Nizan had pointed out early in Mounier's career, or engaging in a final defence of some aspects of bourgeois culture. While Mounier had generous words for the communists when they were a party of opposition, he waffled when there seemed to be a genuine possibility of their coming to power, in France or elsewhere, especially before the war. He had difficulty overcoming his mistrust of their rigid discipline and the threat they posed to the 'human person.' He also had some difficulty believing that the 'people' could, on their own, transcend the materialism of the Marxists and middle classes unless they were guided by 'spiritual' men.

Thus Mounier was never a Marxist; at most he had a certain moral solidarity with French communists. This is why he sometimes cited the young Marx – Marx the philosopher, Marx the moralist condemning the dehumanizing effects of alienation. When Marx went beyond speculation about modern 'man' and his alienated condition Mounier did not follow.

In his more mature writings, Marx, rejected abstract speculation about 'man' as a metaphysical holdover, the concern of bourgeois moralists, while the true concern of communists was changing the world, not speculating about it – the liberation of all men, not 'man.' For Mounier, however, there was a certain permanence and consistency to the structure of the human person; his sense of the eternal demanded there be something unchanging in men. Concern for 'man' (or, from Nizan's point of view, concern for the bourgeois personality) made him doubt the transformation of all men which Marx had demanded, or even the likelihood of the proletariat liberating itself along personalist lines as he himself had hoped. Mounier went along with Marx as long as the latter was diagnosing the faults of the modern bourgeois, but he balked when Marx proposed a remedy whereby the proletariat would be the purging instrument. It was the humanist side of Marx and the inner flame of some of his disciples that attracted Mounier; he had an instinctive aversion to most of what Lenin and Stalin represented.

Mounier's reservations about Marx and Marxism are a partial explanation for the use of his personalism, despite his intentions, by movements on the Right and the anti-Marxist Left. Vichy France and South Vietnam under the Catholic Ngo Dinh Diem both claimed that they drew upon the principles of Mounier's personalism in creating their 'national revolutions.' In present-day France Vie Nouvelle, a left-wing movement which partly grew out of the scout movement under Vichy, makes more frequent reference to Mounier's revolutionary principles than did the new *Esprit* under Jean-Marie Domenach's direction. Mounier, after all, never seemed enthralled by the vision of a classless society or the abolition of private property. There was always the danger, as he recognized, that personalism would become the movement of a bourgeois élite interested in 'spiritualizing the revolution' at the expense of much of what the working class demanded. Mounier's personalism could prove a useful alibi to a bourgeoisie with a bad conscience: it could justify their 'yes, but...' attitude to the communists. Comfortable intellectuals could claim they were revolutionaries with serious reservations about the revolution. These reservations could be sufficiently important as to rationalize the usual aggrandizement of property, or to divorce themselves from concrete, practical programs to aid the poor materially. The property question is sometimes embarrassing for spiritual and moral revolutionaries.

Then, too, what if the proletariat were not immediately receptive to the spiritual dimension of the revolution? What if its revolutionary ambitions became vulgarly materialistic? The 'spiritualization' of medieval Europe had often required a certain pressure exerted by an élite. While revolutionary passions had often spread like fire through dry grass among the peoples of Europe, Mounier was not anticipating this to be the case for spirituality. Although the personalists, like Péguy, believed in 'the people,' they were always tempted by the authoritarianism that Mounier so often denounced as incompatible with personalism.

Thus Mounier could be committed to revolution and indifferent to politics, an enthusiastic admirer of the Marxists and an anti-Marxist, a communist sympathizer and an anti-communist, a purist democrat and an authoritarian. In his plethora of paradoxes he prefigured the new style of the Catholic Left after the Second Vatican Council. He had wanted, with his personalist formulae, to restore perspective to the political passions of his day. Revolutions, he thought, should be made for people and not for abstractions and parties; when they were not made for people above all, they degenerated into destructive, fanatical aberrations.

Mounier was obliged by his own chequered political career to justify his evolving engagement and disengagement from different political régimes and movements. His humanism, and concern for mankind, was at the base of his various political sympathies. He could work within various political contexts as long as they served humanity's interests. Thus he kept rewriting his history and practising his own brand of moral pragmatism. He judged any political régime according to the benefits it provided to the person; he relegated its rhetoric and abstract political principles to an inferior plane of consideration. In this effort he created a political 'method' for 'spiritual' men who wanted to engage in political action but who could never see an absolute in any political régime. Several contemporary Christians found something valuable in his example.[2]

After the war, Mounier was finally satisfied that he was both a Catholic and a man of the Left without compromising either commitment. This was constant struggle but by the end of his life he felt in the main that he was living, while constantly recreating, an equilibrium he had sought since his youth. In finding his own way Mounier created formulae and tactics that served a generation of French Catholics. He was able to lead many of them out of an intellectual and political ghetto, away from the rearguardism of the Action Française, and into the centre of French political life. While they sometimes replaced old political dogmas with new ones, many, like Mounier, oscillated politically, while the French Church became more and more pluralistic. Mounier always said he wished to divorce his religious and political hopes, to transcend that ancient confusion. In this aim neither he nor his followers were particularly successful, but the effort remained part of his political legacy.

To the end Mounier freely admitted that religion was more important to him than politics and, fittingly, he had more impact on the history of French Catholicism than on the history of philosophy, French politics, or political theory. He did not see the traces of God in the created universe. Rather, like his spiritual master Pascal, he sought and found evidence of the supernatural in himself and other human beings. Specifically, with his personalist focus, he was moved by the love that men exhibited for their fellow humans. However rarely it manifested itself, it unlocked the secret of the universe for him. For him, love of neighbour was the essence of the spirit of Christ at work and the highest proof of the love of God. Like his friend Raymond de Becker and the Chrétiens Progressistes, the mutual love that Christians exhibited when they lived selflessly in community was his most profound experience of the supernatural. This formed the core of his faith and the source of its paradoxes.

A great source of consolation and hope for Mounier was the personalist community which he founded at Châtenay-Malabry. In the white house at the centre of the park there were three floors: Mounier and his wife and children had the top floor, the Fraisse family the second floor, the Domenachs the first. The community also created a personalist library and conference halls in the old coach house. Six or seven intellectuals and their families could live comfortably in Les Murs Blancs. At first they all ate meals in common but this was soon abandoned in favour of periodic, optional, common meals. A happy balance was achieved between privacy and community life, intellectual and spiritual collaboration, and the pursuit of individual careers. This community can be seen as the best expression and symbol of his spiritual life. Here Mounier and his family, some of his close associates such as Henri Marrou, Paul Fraisse, Jean-Marie Domenach, Paul Ricœur, and Francis Jeanson and their families, established a personalist 'family' after the war.

For several decades, some of France's leading intellectual figures have lived in friendship and harmony at Châtenay-Malabry, living in community according to Mounier's inspiration. Self-conscious avant-garde Christians, they have welcomed visitors from around the world and sought to demonstrate by example that their personalism is more than an intellectual position.

Mounier created Les Murs Blancs to be a microcosm of the personalist civilization of the future and also with a specific, practical purpose: it was to be a nursery of that Catholic avant-garde he described in the thirties as pioneers in exploring the Christianity of the future. Christianity, too, needed an élite of guides to determine its future. He wanted to aid Christianity to be in the 'line of history' because he feared for its survival if it were not. Thus he thought Christianity had to be *modified* to suit the times and required individuals of superior intelligence – and, he hoped, wisdom and virtue – to lead. The personalists and their like were to fulfil this role in France.

Mounier's calm assurance of his avant-garde role in French Catholicism contributed to his unusual religious perspective. He assumed that the personalists were playing a part in the twentieth century like that played by the great Christian spiritual writers of the twelfth and thirteenth and fourth and fifth centuries: leading the more simple Christians of their time to adapt to a radically new intellectual and political universe. Most frequently he thought of himself in a setting similar to St Augustine in the latter days of the Roman empire, a period on which his friend Henri Marrou was a great authority. Mounier refused to join the mass of his fellow Christians in condemning the pagan hordes that were overrunning Christian civilization; like St Augustine, he tried to make sense of the collapse and discern how the new barbarians were to be Christianized.

This view led Mounier to become a 'mandarin' of modern French Catholicism and he felt more affinity for other, non-Christian, mandarins, or the new barbarians, than for most fellow Christians. Sometimes he thought of the Christian cosmology as more an ideology in need of revision than as the best explanation of the universe. He was convinced that future Christians had to profit from the relevations of Nietzsche and Marx as, after St Thomas Aquinas and St Augustine, they had drawn upon the genius of Plato and Aristotle. Unfortunately, the vast majority of Christians had yet to read either Nietzsche or Marx, if they ever would. It was the duty of the few Christian intellectuals to renew the spirits of the many with the new synthesis. In the meantime Mounier did not condemn the mass of believers, the Church hierarchy, or Rome, few of whom had yet had the chance to live the Christian renewal. But he could hardly conceal his pleasant surprise when, in a remote mountain village or at a conference in the provinces, he would meet a Christian of superior virtue who had read the personalists or Nietzsche and had some experience of communists. One might expect to find such a person among the 'Christians of the future,' the community of intellectuals in Les Murs Blancs, but in the hinterlands where there were no intellectuals it was always rather unexpected.

Mounier was determined that the personalist community live as Christians of the future because he had a profound loathing for the middle class Christians of the present. The basis for this alienation from his co-religionists evolved during his lifetime. When he was twenty, it was sparked by Jacques Chevalier's ardour for mystical purity. At twenty-five Mounier had turned critically against his own Christian background in the effort to remedy his vulnerability and over-sensitivity. At thirty he saw not only his background but a whole culture doomed by brutal and insensitive historical forces. At forty he realized that, from many points of view, the Nietzschean and the Marxist had a decided superiority over the Christian. Accordingly, his criticism of the Christian personality became more critical and penetrating. He viewed excessive concern for religious purity as based upon a 'flight from reality' ascribed to psychosis or neurosis that was not unconnected with an 'incompetence in ordinary affairs,' but was rooted in a Christian education directed towards 'scruple and evasion.'

Just as Mounier became more critical of the Christian personality and influenced more and more by Nietzsche and Marx, he also turned even further from the literal imitation of Christ as the centre of Christian life. Like his master Péguy he began to identify himself with saints more than with Jesus, especially with soldier-saints. Like Péguy he was impelled by his rhetoric to a peculiar use of hero figures from Christian history, as well as extracting passages from scripture that supported his views.

Mounier was driven to this position by his elevation of 'concern for the human person' as the prime means of reforming Christianity. This personality reform of Christianity led to a difficult problem Mounier had not foreseen: were all Christian beliefs salvageable on personalist terms? He had assumed that this was so. Nietzsche, before him, had argued that all Christian views were vestigial. Mounier made a great effort to prove Nietzsche wrong and in the process become an inverted Nietzsche. Nietzsche tried to demonstrate that the Christian religion corrupted and sapped the strength of the human personality; Mounier tried to demonstrate that Christianity provided a wide variety of priceless gifts to the human person unavailable elsewhere. Nietzsche tried to demonstrate that there was a strong pragmatic justification for abandoning the Christian faith; Mounier tried to demonstrate that there was a strong pragmatic justification for adhering to it; that Christianity was a superior 'way of life' for all people even if they did not share its supernatural beliefs.

Thus there was little place for sin, redemption, and resurrection in this debate; the central acts of the Christian drama were set aside. Mounier was certain that the superior quality of the love that inspired Christians would convert a sceptical but pragmatic age. Everyone agreed that the world needed love and, if Christians demonstrated that they had more than anyone else, their fellow humans would flock to them, would beg to be kindled by that fire of love that burned within them.

Here was the root of Mounier's deepest dilemma: did Christians demonstrate this superior love? He thought that in the present bourgeois culture they did not. He placed his hope in the Christianity of the future that was being born amid the ruins of old Christendom. Someday it would renew all mankind. His torment, however, lay in the fact that in the contemporary world charity seemed to be strongest among professed atheists and Marxists. It was Mounier himself who proposed that Christianity could and should be judged pragmatically on its ability to call forth altruism, moral heroism, and selflessness.

In the end, Mounier's perceptions forced him into a public stance that differed greatly from his personal temperament, a rhetorical position that included some intellectual and spiritual gymnastics. Christ had warned his disciples that he was sending them out as lambs among wolves. In a strictly personalist perspective this seemed an unjustifiable folly in an age dominated, on all sides, by wolves. Mounier responded by trying to create a Christian that would be a higher type of revolutionary, a superior sort of wolf. Such a super-Christian would no longer be a stumbling block to the Jews, a scandal to the Greeks, or a bourgeois to Friedrich Nietzsche and Karl Marx. The new Christian, the Christian super-revolutionary, would fulfil the long overdue promise to renew the face of the earth.

Mounier's personalism was partially born in an antithetical response to his own religious background. He soon discovered that young men totally lacking his own rich and complex spiritual dimensions were willing to follow his call to revolution, with little of that religious dimension that he always insisted was essential. Their charity was not fueled by spiritual ardour and thus, like St Paul, he could not consider their selflessness to be genuine.[3]

Despite the infidelity of several of his disciples to his whole synthesis, Mounier remained a symbol of its viability to his admirers, a man who balanced contemplation and action, deep religiosity and political commitment. If Mounier's religiosity was, in the end, far more convincing than his political side, that explains his impact among religious people. He was a rigorous critic of Christian faults and a sophisticated religious reformer. He and his review did much to draw a generation of young French Christians away from nostalgic reaction, authoritarian royalism, and militant nationalism, as well as from bourgeois culture and Christian democracy. Mounier was determined to guard his religiosity from these 'impurities' and his example inspired both those in his immediate circle and others beyond it.

At a time in which Catholic priests are calling for armed insurrection in Latin America, Mounier's call to revolution, so audacious in its day, seems relatively tame. He was the prophet of a new kind of Christianity but, in retrospect, he was also cautious and prudent. His personalism had a tangible influence on the spirit of the Second Vatican Council and its reforms. This does not mean that Mounier necessarily would have been enthusiastic about the direction the Catholic Church has taken since then. He always tried to balance extremes: despite his attacks upon the excessively contemplative Christianity of his day he always insisted that it had an essential role in Christian life. He was always a vigorous champion of the spiritual dimension of revolution when he found it lacking among revolutionaries. He might well have joined his old friends Henri de Lubac, Jean Daniélou, and Jacques Maritain – and John Paul ii – in their recent counterattack against the irreligious politically activist spirit that has inspired some younger elements in the Church since the death of Pope John.

Most biographers have portrayed Mounier as a man completely identified with his public positions. Examining his career from the perspective of his post-war writings, they have represented him as an archetypal avant-garde Catholic, a stolid and consistent man of the Left. Many of the battles in which he was engaged at his death have continued unabated, and he remains an important symbolic figure in them. It is easier to recall a Mounier who was as convinced as he was convincing, as revolutionary as he sometimes said he was. His name has been emblazoned on the banner of the French Catholic Left; he lends prestige to it, and much of his writings offer philosophical support. Since he was one of the first of the 'new Christians,' it has been useful to make something of a saint out of him.

Mounier may have been a saint, as François Mauriac, his old critic, suggested when he died, but he acted according to a host of complex impulses. A large part of Mounier's reforming righteousness was based on his deep hatred of his own background. There was a masochistic element in this. He bitterly rejected a softness and vulnerability that was an element in his upbringing. His childhood and adolescence were Christian, so he punished Christianity. He was unsparing in his attack on the elements of bourgeois Christianity that he found in himself.

Mounier was genuinely concerned about the living conditions of the poor in France, but what he described as his love of the working class often resembled a guilt complex about them. He sometimes seemed caught up in an exagerated expiation, an atonement for the sins or the egoism of the bourgeoisie among whom he had been raised. He was not alone in this attitude; it is a phenomenon which he himself recognized as common to the sons of the French bourgeoisie in his generation. Some of Mounier's 'Christian charity' seemed rooted in what he aptly called 'a bad bourgeois conscience'; but perhaps genuine Christianity gives a bad conscience to the bourgeoisie. In any case many of the left-wing intellectuals of Mounier's generation also seemed determined to prove that they were as vigorous and tough as the strongest French proletarian.

A more disturbing aspect of Mounier's career is evident in those instances when the 'truth' of the cause he represented was more important to him than the simple truth. Most obvious was his later reconstruction of the history of his role at Vichy. This duplicity is not excused by the fact that he was not alone in it. Many French Leftists did the same thing, at the same time, for much the same reasons. In his case he seemed to think that the strength and prestige of the Catholic revolution-ary Left in the post-war period was more important than intellectual probity, and so denied his former hopes and friends. To be frank about Vichy was unsafe after the Liberation, so he was not. He rewrote his own history and his admirers have carried on in this tradition. Accordingly, most remember Mounier as a simple and consistent man of the Left, as a link between the 'spirit of the Resistance' and Vatican II. They are understandably vague about his complex political evolution and persis-tent self-doubts.

Mounier has had his critics, but even the most virulent has never questioned the genuineness of his religious concern, which impressed friend and foe alike. His detractors have seen his religion as hot-headed, misguided, or warped but have never questioned its deep roots. He shared neither the despairing activism of Malraux or Drieu nor Sartre's severe lucidity. His intentions fed on that impulse that drove him as a young man to 'construct his life against his temperament.' He never abandoned this effort, even when it required the sacrifice of his comfort, consolation, and peace of mind. He severed himself from an ancient tradition at the expense of personal happiness. His admirers have hailed the nobility and moral heroism in this sacrifice. He could not accept middle class Christian civilization as the city of God and so became a prophet of Christianity as the most radical of counter-cultures, a herald of a vast mutation in contemporary Catholicism.

Another factor explaining Mounier's influence on his own generation was his personal magnetism; all his old friends attest to his directness, warmth, openness to strangers, and sensitivity. Since he was the linchpin of both a review and a movement, his ideas had much more opportunity to shape ideas than those of most. And since, before the war, the review attracted some of the most talented writers of the younger generation in France, particularly from among Catholics, Mounier had far more opportunity to express his opinions, sound or not, than most men. To adopt personalism, to be published in the review if you were young and unknown, a certain method, vocabulary, and style of life had to be affected that was very close to that of the editor.

Despite the fact that Mounier was haunted by secularization and sometimes longed for a new Middle Ages, he lived in an extraordinarily religious time, the time of the cathedrals of light at Nuremberg, the emergence of the cult of Stalin, surrealism, 'frontism', 'le fascisme, immense et rouge,' and the rebellion of the existentialists. Mounier, with admirable or disquieting flexibility depending on one's point of view was open to each new 'secular religion' as it came along. More often than not he had genuine empathy for a new arrival, while always retaining Christian belief as the centre of his own life. There was not great novelty in a Catholic Christian being seduced by Gandhian pacifism in the nineteen-thirties, or the promise of the Popular Front, or the cause of the Republic in Spain, or Italian fascism, or authoritarian, corporatist schemes for transforming France. There were many other prominent Catholics, too, who got swept up by Pétain's National Revolution, and then by the mystique of the Resistance. Mounier was not alone, either, in his fascination with Christian-communist dialogue after the war. What was unique about him was his capacity for embracing these successive mystiques while always consciously, and in good conscience, basing his actions on Christian belief. If Mounier sometimes seemed a hesitant, even confused, 'revolutionary' – an unsatisfactory Marxist and an unconvincing fascist – one must recall the surprise of his contemporaries that a man like him addressed these things at all. For those who see a fundamental contradiction between the message of Christ and all other religions, between the Christian gospels and the great secular religions that dominate modern times, Mounier was a chimerical living synthesis of a set of fundamentally irreconcilable antitheses. To those who try to be both Christian and contemporary he was, and remains, an extremely attractive prototype.

Notes

CHAPTER ONE: INTRODUCTION

1 Jacques Ellul to the author, 30 Jan. 1976; my translation
2 Jean-Louis Loubet del Bayle, *Les non-conformistes des années 30* (Paris 1969) 415
3 H.-I. Marrou, 'L'action politique d'Emmanuel Mounier,' *Les Cahiers de la République* II (1956) 96
4 Jean Lacroix, *Le personnalisme comme anti-idéologie* (Paris 1972)
5 Paul Ricœur, 'Une philosophie personnaliste,' *Esprit* 174 (Dec. 1950) 861–2
6 Cf. Jean-Marie Domenach, *Emmanuel Mounier* (Paris 1972). This formula comes from Mounier's *Personalist Manifesto* (New York 1938) 271.
7 See the chapter on 'the person' in Jacques Ellul, *Exégèse des nouveaux lieux communs* (Paris 1966).
8 Particularly Eileen Cantin, csj, in *Mounier: A Personalist View of History* (New York 1973)
9 R. William Rauch, Jr, *Politics and Belief in Contemporary France: Emmanuel Mounier and Christian Democracy, 1932–1950* (The Hague 1972); Joseph Amato, *Mounier and Maritain: A French Catholic Understanding of the Modern World* (University of Alabama 1975). The peasant of the Garonne would not have been pleased with this title.
10 'Sur un certain front unique,' *Europe* (Jan. 1933), reprinted in Paul Nizan, *Pour une nouvelle culture*, Susan Suleiman, ed. (Paris 1971) 53
11 *Esprit*, and its sister review *Ordre Nouveau*, had fairly important affiliated groups in Belgium, Germany, Italy, Switzerland, and Spain and smaller groupings through the French Empire and North and South America.
12 Cf. Cantin, *Mounier.*
13 Nicholas Berdyaev (Russian Orthodox), Alexandre Marc (Russian Jew),

Paul-Louis Landsberg (German Jew), Henri de Man (German-educated Belgian socialist), Arnaud Dandieu (French non-believer)

14 The Church historian Daniel-Rops and the architect of European federalism, Marc converted to Catholicism.

15 On this matter the testimony of Denis de Rougemont is valuable. See his essay 'Alexandre Marc et l'invention du personnalisme' in *Le Fédéralisme et Alexandre Marc* (Lausanne 1974) 51–69. A careful dating of early personalist texts also demonstrates this.

16 *Esprit* 4–6 (Jan.–Mar. 1933)

17 Jacques Maritain to Emmanuel Mounier, 2 Nov. 1932, in *Maritain/Mounier, 1929–1939*, ed. Jacques Petit (Paris 1973) 59. Professor Amato's study does not go into the important divergences revealed in these letters.

18 For a general survey of this criticism see W.R. Rauch, Jr, *Politics and Belief in Contemporary France*.

19 For a general survey of French and Soviet Marxist analyses of personalism see below 71–3, 86, 104–5, 134, 227, 236–8, 293n49, 330.

20 Mounier, 'Was ist der Personalismus?' *Deutsch-Französische Monatshefte* I, 11 (1936)

21 Eg, Martin Hieronimi, 'Der Personalismus: Eine Geistige Ernuerungsbewegung in Frankreich,' *Monatshefte* II, 1 (1937)

22 Eg, Paul Distelbarth, *Neues Werden in Frankreich* (Stuttgart 1938)

23 Loubet del Bayle, *Les non-conformistes*; François Goguel, 'Positions politiques,' *Esprit* 174 (Dec. 1950) 797–819. Michel Winock, *Histoire politique de la revue 'Esprit,' 1930–1950* (Paris 1975)

24 Pierre de Senarclens, *Le mouvement 'Esprit' 1932–1941: Essai critique* (Lausanne 1974)

25 See his *Vichy France: Old Guard and New Order, 1940–1944* (New York 1973)

26 *Essais sur la France* (Paris 1974)

27 Cf. Jean-Marie Domenach and Robert de Montvalon, *The Catholic Avant-Garde* (New York 1967).

28 Winock, '*Esprit*.' Cf. Rauch, Jr, *Politics*; Amato, *Mounier*.

29 Eg, Jacques Marteaux, *L'Eglise de France devant la révolution marxiste* I, II (Paris 1958–9)

30 Cf. John Hellman, 'Vichy Background: Political Alternatives for French Catholics in the Nineteen-Thirties,' *The Journal of Modern History* XLIX, 1 (Mar. 1977) D1111–D1144; 'French Left Catholics and Communism,' *Church History* XLV, 4 (Dec. 1976) 1–17.

31 Candide Moix, *La pensée d'Emmanuel Mounier* (Paris 1960) 331; Etienne Borne, *Emmanuel Mounier ou le combat pour l'homme* (Paris 1972) 50; Michel

Barlow, *Le socialisme d'Emmanuel Mounier* (Toulouse 1971); Moix, *Mounier* 331; Cantin, *Mounier*; Amato, *Mounier* 9

32 Cantin, *Mounier*

33 'Le Bloc-Notes d'Eugène Ionesco,' *Arts* (24 Feb.–1 Mar. 1960)

34 *L'Express* 16 Mar. 1956

35 See, most recently, Bernard-Henri Lévy, *L'Idéologie française* (Paris 1981) and the subsequent polemics in *Le Monde* during January 1981.

CHAPTER TWO: THOSE YEARS 'TOO HAPPY, TOO CALM'

1 Letter to Xavier de Virieu, 1 Mar. 1950, *Œuvres* IV (Paris 1963) 413

2 See, for example, *ibid.*, and letters to Paulette Leclercq of 30 Apr. 1933 and 18 May 1933 in *Oeuvres* IV, 414, 415.

3 As a child Mounier had otitis, which had a series of after effects. He also developed necrosis of the knuckles, which provoked a series of painful accidents and was only cured by a Parisian specialist when he was twenty. An ulcer of the cornea of the right eye made him squint and be wall-eyed. At thirteen the same eye was pierced by a stone thrown by a friend during recess at the lycée; fragments of Mounier's shattered glasses wounded it and it was left with less than one-tenth normal vision. It exempted him from front-line military service.

4 Letter to Jacques Lefrancq, 27 Aug. 1933, *Esprit* 174 (Dec. 1950) 939. Mounier later described this retreat as 'decisive' for his development, but did not refer to it at all at the time. He later seemed to prefer to remember a host of influences on his youth other than his intellectual and spiritual *maître*, Jacques Chevalier.

5 Albert Béguin, 'Une Vie,' in *ibid.* 941; interview with Jean Lacroix, 2 Aug. 1973

6 'Journal of Jacques Chevalier,' 15 Mar. 1924, *Esprit* 174 (Dec. 1950) 941

7 Cf. Mounier to Maritain, 7 Mar. 1930, in *Maritain/Mounier, 1929–1939*, ed. Jacques Petit (Paris 1973) 23.

8 On this last point: Mounier, 'Entretiens I,' 26 Jan. 1927, 43, unpublished. The first two volumes of Mounier's unpublished diaries contain a sensitive and admiring description of Chevalier's teaching methods. For Chevalier's own view of his teaching goals, see his *Cadences* II (Paris 1951).

9 'Entretiens II,' 9–13 July 1929, 47, unpublished. His Bergsonianism and intellectual collaboration with Father Pouget, one-time colleague of the modernist leader Father Alfred Loisy, seemed to place him in the modernist camp among Catholics. Before World War I, Loisy had wanted to employ the most advanced techniques of historical scholarship in biblical studies, but

came to doubt the inerrancy of the Bible. Like Loisy, Chevalier's friend Father Pouget wanted to reconcile the Catholic faith and modern intellectual developments, especially new research into mysticism by Bergson. The 1907 encyclical *Pascendi gregis* had loosely fixed the name 'modernism' on several new movements of thought, particularly those associated with Loisy. The philosophical doctrines of Bergson, too, were 'modernism' in so far as they led Catholics to alter some of their religious perceptions.

10 *Lamentabili sane exitu*, 3 July 1907; *Pascendi gregis*, 8 Dec. 1907

11 'Entretiens I,' 16 Feb. 1927, 47, unpublished. Blondel's philosophy was particularly important to Chevalier. Blondel thought that philosophy and theology erred in considering the supernatural like a 'church steeple' coming, from outside, to cap the natural; he thought they interpenetrated in the way the arch of a vault only holds thanks to the *vinculum*. The supernatural was that substantial *lien*, that keystone, without which the natural would not hold. Blondel searched in the very structure of concrete man for signs showing that man could go beyond himself: the traces of a preordination to a superior life, the exigencies of the spiritual. This Blondelian perspective, as we shall see, shaped Chevalier's entire pedagogical effort.

12 There are references to the essay for Chevalier in Mounier's unpublished correspondence. It seems to have been lost.

Rivière had died at thirty-nine the previous year. His wife Isabelle, the sister of Rivière's close friend, the novelist Alain-Fournier, who had gone to live at the gates of their daughter's convent, published some of Rivière's diary excerpts as *A la trace de Dieu* (Paris 1925).

The militantly Catholic poet Paul Claudel had helped convert Rivière in a confrontation similar to that of the young Jacques Maritain with the self-styled poet-prophet Léon Bloy in the same period. In both cases, a brilliant intelligence passionate for certitude was converted by someone of essentially simple, violent opinions. See Richard Griffiths, *The Reactionary Revolution: The Catholic Revival in French Literature, 1870–1918* (London 1966) 33–4.

13 Cited on the front page of Paul Beaulieu, *Jacques Rivière* (Paris 1956). Rivière shared a passion for psychological self-analysis with his friends Proust and Gide.

Mounier's excitement over Rivière coincided with his first effort to spread to his friends his enthusiasm for his 'maître incomparable,' Chevalier. Letter to Abbé x, 2 May 1925, unpublished.

14 Letter to Madeleine Mounier, 1926, *Œuvres de Mounier*, IV (Paris 1963) 424. *Esprit* 174 (Dec. 1950) gives 1925–6 for this letter. A fellow student of Grenoble days remembered Mounier studying Rivière, along with Péguy and Gide's plays.

15 Letter to Jacques Lefrancq, 25 Aug. 1933, *Œuvres* IV, 421

16 'Entretiens II,' 7 May 1926, *Œuvres* IV, 421
17 Letter to Jacques Chevalier, 8 Dec. 1925, unpublished section
18 *Ibid.*
19 Letter to Madeleine Mounier, 19 Dec. 1925, *Esprit* 174 (Dec. 1950), 940
20 Chevalier later insisted that he had resigned from his important post in the Vichy government over its failure to properly recognize Bergson's achievements on the latter's death in 1941. Chevalier was Bergson's literary executor.
21 'Jacques Chevalier: un penseur français,' *La Vie Catholique* 79 (Apr. 1926) 1
22 This 'double movement' was basic to the historical analysis of Henri Bremond (1865–1933), a brilliant literary stylist, admirer of the quietist mystic Fénelon, and friend of the modernist leader Alfred Loisy.
23 (Paris 1926). Cf. letters of Madeleine Mounier, Nov., Dec. 1926, *Œuvres* IV, 421, 423.
24 Journal of Jacques Chevalier, 22 Nov. 1926, *Esprit* 174 (Dec. 1950) 943; testimony of L. Maggiani; *ibid.* 948; letter to Jean Guitton, 26 Nov. 1926, *Œuvres* IV, 421
25 Catholic Action, of largely middle class membership, was founded by 'Social Catholic' Albert de Mun in 1886. At this time, under the leadership of Charles Flory, it was a controversial organization. Flory had participated in the January 1924 meeting in Paris where he, Gaston Tessier (for the Christian trade union, the CFTC, established in 1919), and Adéodat Boissard of the Semaines Sociales (annual conferences of Catholic employers, trade unionists, and teachers, founded in 1904) had decided to form a Christian Democratic party in France.
26 'Entretiens II,' 21 Nov. 1926, unpublished
27 Recollections of L. Maggiani, a young professor from Paris who joined Chevalier's circle in the fall of 1926. *Esprit* 174 (Dec. 1950), 947
28 Pierre Barral, *Le Département de l'Isère sous la Troisième République, 1870–1940* (Paris 1962) 404
29 Prior to his election as Pius XI in 1922, Cardinal Ratti had been denounced in the *Action Française* as a member of the 'liberal clan,' the 'Italian candidate' for pope, 'an eminently political man ... partisan of collaboration between Italy, Germany, and Bolshevist Russia – The Holy Catholic Empire.' Harry W. Paul, *The Second Ralliement: The Rapprochement between Church and State in France in the Twentieth Century* (Washington, DC 1967) 150
30 This charge was levied despite the fact that Sangnier and his followers displayed little interest in the scriptural exegesis of Loisy or the theories of Le Roy or Laberthonnière. Cf. Henri Daniel-Rops, *A Fight for God* I (Garden City, NY 1967) 278; André Latreille and René Rémond, *Histoire du Catholicisme en France* III, 2nd ed. (Paris 1962) 524

31 *Une opinion sur Charles Maurras et le devoir des catholiques* (Paris 1926)
32 Cited in Paul, *Second Ralliement* 153, 155
33 *Ibid.* 156–9
34 'Entretiens I,' 15 Dec. 1926, unpublished
35 'Entretiens II,' 20 Nov. 1926, unpublished
36 'Entretiens I,' 15 Dec. 1926, unpublished
37 Cf. 'Entretiens I,' 5 Jan. 1927, unpublished. Chevalier suggested that 'the long and tenacious search, by life, for the human form gives a sort of dignity to evolution.'
38 Chevalier's resentment extended to the nationalist novelist Maurice Barrès, whom he blamed for once slighting Bergson as 'a dirty little Jew who makes compliments to the ladies.' 'Entretiens II,' 23 May 1929, *Œuvres* IV, 447
39 Emmanuel Mounier, 'Le conflit de l'anthropocentrisme et du théocentrisme dans la philosophie de Descartes' (unpublished DES thesis, University of Grenoble 1927). The conclusion was published under the same title in *Etudes philosophiques* 3 (July-Sept. 1966) 319–24. Mounier also became interested in the Catholic philosopher Ernest-René Le Senne at this time, and in his pioneering study of caractérologie and 'existential spiritualism.' Testimony of Abbé René Cadiou, *Esprit* 174 (Dec. 1950) 946. See J. Paumen, *Le Spiritualisme existentiel de René Le Senne* (Paris 1949). Le Senne (1882–1954) and Louis Lavelle launched the important philosophical collection Philosophie de l'Esprit in 1934 and contributed to the study sessions held for Mounier's review, *Esprit*.
40 'Entretiens I,' 7 May 1927, unpublished
41 Georges Dumas (1866–1946), professor of psychology at the Sorbonne, was one of the foremost scientific psychologists in France at the time.
42 'Entretiens I,' 25 May 1927, unpublished. Chevalier provided his students with a capsule definition of Maine de Biran's effort: 'He conceived of a metaphysics which would rise higher and higher, towards the spirit in general, to the degree the conscience would descend deeper into the depths of the interior life.' *Ibid.*, 5 Jan. 1927, unpublished
43 'A propos d'une thèse sur Maine de Biran: la leçon d'une vie,' *La Vie Catholique* 153 (3 Sept. 1927)
44 The examination for the recruitment to lycée and certain university level teaching posts in France
45 'Réflexions et souvenirs de J. Chevalier,' *Esprit* 174 (Dec. 1950) 944–5
46 Testimony of L. Maggiani, *ibid.* 948
47 *Time and Eternity in Plotinus and Saint Augustine* was published in 1933. Many unpublished letters of Guitton to Mounier in this period reveal a close

bond between the two young men, who later were among France's most prominent Christian intellectuals.

48 Letter to Jacques Lefrancq, 27 Aug. 1933, *Esprit* 174 (Dec. 1950) 949

49 Letters to Madeleine Mounier, 30 Oct. 1927, Nov. 1927, *Œuvres* IV, 428

50 Under the Vichy régime, Chevalier and Mounier helped to create their own kind of Ecole Normale Supérieure.
Letter to Paulette Leclercq, 25 June 1933, *Œuvres* IV, 426

51 Pouget was the son of a peasant family, a shepherd and autodidact until he was in his teens, when he went to the seminary and began a teaching career in mathematics, physics, geology, and above all, botany. In the scholasticate of Dax his research with the microscope began to ruin his eyesight. He eventually was sent to the headquarters of his order in Paris where he undertook biblical studies with Alfred Loisy, and geology (to study the geology of the Bible), as well as Hebrew, Greek, and Latin to analyse scriptural texts, which he eventually knew by heart. When Mounier met him, Pouget was unknown save among the Bergsonians – Jean Guitton and Chevalier made him famous after his death. Each time he was in Paris, Chevalier visited Pouget, who was by this time almost completely blind. The austere Lazarist left his tiny room only to converse with Henri Bergson, whom he was leading closer and closer to the Catholic faith. See Jacques Chevalier, ed., *Bergson et le Père Pouget* (Paris 1954). See also *Le Père Pouget: Logia*, presented by Jacques Chevalier (Paris 1955) and Jean Guitton, *Portrait de M. Pouget* (Paris 1941), *Dialogues avec M. Pouget* (Paris 1954), and *Monsieur Pouget* (Paris 1954).

52 Testimony of Jean Daniélou, *Esprit* 174 (Dec. 1950) 959; editor's note, *Œuvres* IV, 429

53 Testimony of Jean Guitton, *Esprit* 174 (Dec. 1950) 959. In May 1934 Mounier obviously had not forgiven Chevalier's old nemesis when he wrote: 'Nous n'avons pas encore fini, on le voit, de compter les victimes de la mentalité néo-prélogique de M. Brunschvicq qui pendant vingt ans aura empêché un certain nombre de bons esprits de concevoir la transcendance autrement que comme un rapport spatial et une violence faite, à l'immanence qu'en réalité elle achève et soutient.' 'Tentation du Communisme' (May 1934), in *Œuvres* I (Paris 1961) 233

54 Letter to Jacques Chevalier, Nov. 1927. *Œuvres* IV, 428

55 Letter to Madeleine Mounier, 8 Jan. 1928, *Œuvres* IV, 429

56 His published letters contain at least ten which analyse his friendship with Barthélemy in this spiritual perspective.

57 Letter to Madeleine Mounier, 12 Jan. 1928, *Œuvres* IV, 430

58 Letter to Jacques Chevalier, 27 Aug. 1933, *Esprit* 174 (Dec. 1950) 949; letter to Jacques Chevalier, 25 May 1928, *Œuvres* IV, 433–4

59 Letter to Madeleine Mounier, June 1928, *Œuvres* IV, 418

60 Editor's note, *Esprit* 174 (Dec. 1950), 953; letter to Jean Guitton, 20 July 1928, *Œuvres* IV, 435

61 These figures and a description of the relatively exclusive status of the educated Catholic élite in this generation are given in Georges Hourdin, *Dieu en liberté* (Paris 1973).

62 Editor's notes, *Esprit* 174 (Dec. 1950), 953

63 Testimony of L. Maggiani, *ibid.* 948

64 Letters to Jean Guitton, 5, 10, 18 Aug. 1928, *Œuvres* IV, 435–7

65 Letter to Jean Guitton, 17 Oct. 1928, unpublished. The Maison de la Jeunesse belonged to the Paulins, a religious group of priests and laymen founded by Cardinal Ferrari in Milan; Daniélou represented the group in France.

66 Even after he became a noted patristic scholar and cardinal in the Roman Catholic church in 1969, Jean Daniélou carried on free-for-all debates with Communist Roger Garaudy on the French television network.

67 Apparently he meant that he was considering entering the religious life; letter to Renée Barbe, 10 Nov. 1928, *Œuvres* IV, 440. Letter to Jean Guitton, 17 Oct. 1928, *ibid.* 439

68 'Entretiens II,' 17 Dec. 1928, unpublished

69 Maritain described her to Mounier as a 'non-believer.'

70 Raissa Maritain, *Les Grandes Amitiés* (Paris 1949), translated by Julie Kernan as *We Have Been Friends Together* (Garden City, NY 1961) 61, 97, and various interviews.

71 Bergson published his essay 'Introduction to Metaphysics' in 1903, thus marking the passage from a critical to a constructive stage of his philosophy. For a more detailed discussion of Bergson's philosophical influence and Maritain see Joseph Amato, *Mounier and Maritain: A French Catholic Understanding of the Modern World* (University of Alabama 1975) 40–7.

72 Raissa Maritain, *Friends* 72, 80, 97–8

73 'Entretiens II,' 9 Feb. 1930, unpublished

74 Raissa Maritain, *Friends* 316

75 'Réponse à Jean Cocteau' (1926) in Jacques Maritain, *Œuvres (1912–1939)*, ed. Henry Bars (Paris 1975) 363

76 Raissa Maritain, *Friends* 183

77 Raissa Maritain's memoirs pass over Jacques' pre-World War I sympathy for the *Action Française* but they were published in 1941 when the Maritains had other concerns.

78 In his book *La philosophie bergsonienne: Etudes critiques* (Paris 1914). Cf. Raissa Maritain, *Friends* 343

79 Jacques Maritain, *Carnet de notes* (Paris 1965) 179

80 For a view of Jacques Maritain's relationship with the *Action Française* that somewhat contradicts Raissa Maritain's see Henri Massis, *Maurras et Notre Temps* I (Paris 1951) 156–77.

81 'Politics First' was the famous headline of the *Action Française* which explained its defiance of Pius XI. 'The spiritual first' comes from *Primauté du spirituel* (Paris 1927).

82 *Religion et culture* (Paris 1930). The translation of this work into English, *Religion and Culture* (London 1931), had a laudatory preface from English Catholic historian Christopher Dawson, whose *Progress and Religion* preceded it by three years and also drew heavily from Joseph de Maistre. Dawson never expressed the enthusiasm for Maurras of his compatriot T.S. Eliot, but the historical perspective of all three was similar.

83 In his 'Entretiens'

84 Letter to Madeleine Mounier, 17 Mar. 1929, *Oeuvres* IV, 444

85 Letters to Jéromine Martinaggi, 1 Feb. 1929, and to Madeleine Mounier, 20 Feb. 1929, *ibid.* 442, 443

86 Letters to Madeleine Mounier, 6, 17 May 1928, *ibid.* 445–6; Jean Daniélou, 'La mort d'Emmanuel Mounier,' *Etudes* CCXV (May 1950) 250

87 Letter to Jacques Chevalier, 11 May 1929, *Œuvres* IV, 446

88 'Then Péguy intervened. It was during the Christmas vacation of 1928–1929. I remember reading his prose works with enthusiasm. Then I understood why I was hesitating so much on the threshold of the well-regulated machinery which led directly from the Ecole Normale to "superior" education. He crystallized all the extra-university part of my life....' Letter to Jéromine Martinaggi, 1 Apr. 1941, *Œuvres* IV, 452. If Péguy crystallized the 'extra-university' part, it is hard to say what was the 'intra-university' part of Mounier's life at this time. There seems to have been more hesitation on the part of the 'machinery' than on Mounier's.

89 'Entretiens II,' 23 May 1929, *Œuvres* IV, 446–7

90 This was evident in a clash on this point between Chevalier and A. Dubarle recorded by Mounier, 'Entretiens I,' 16 Feb. 1927, unpublished.

91 'Entretiens II,' 19 June 1929, *Œuvres* IV, 448

92 'Entretiens II,' 19 June 1929, unpublished section

93 Not to be confused with his very different nephew, novelist Hervé Bazin

94 See Jean Guitton, *Les Davidées: Mouvement d'apostolat laic, 1916–1966* (Paris 1967).

95 'L'idée d'irrationnel,' 20 Mar. 1929, 'L'Intuition bergsonienne,' 20 July 1929, *Après ma classe*

96 François Chauvrières, 'Une amitié spirituelle: Les Davidées,' *La Vie spirituelle* 27 (Apr. 1931) 66–91, reprinted in Guitton, *Les Davidées* 82–108

97 'Entretiens II,' 29–31 Aug. 1929, *Œuvres* IV, 449

98 Letter to Madeleine Mounier, 18 Apr. 1929, *Œuvres* IV, 444

99 It is in the masses that one finds the élite,' was one of her sayings recorded by Mounier. 'Entretiens II,' 9–13 July 1929, in *Esprit* 174 (Dec. 1950) 963

100 'Entretiens II,' 29–31 Aug. 1929, *Œuvres* IV, 449

101 Jean Sylvestre (pseud.), 'De l'esprit philosophique,' *Aux Davidées* (Nov. 1929) 83–9

102 Jean Sylvestre (pseud.), 'L'étranger,' *Aux Davidées* (May 1930) 470

103 'Entretiens II,' 9–13 July 1929, unpublished sections

104 Letter to Madeleine Mounier, 20 Apr. 1929, *Œuvres* IV, 445

105 Testimony of Madame Paul Vignaux, *Esprit* 174 (Dec. 1950) 955. Jean Lacroix, 'Les trois conversions d'Emmanuel Mounier,' *Témoignage Chrétien* (30 Mar. 1950), reprinted in *Bulletin des Amis d'Emmanuel Mounier* 16–17 (Apr. 1961) 12

106 Letter to Madeleine Mounier, 5 Nov. 1929, 'Entretiens II,' 15 Nov. 1929, *Œuvres* IV, 452–3

107 Baruzi later became professor of the history of religions in the Collège de France. His great work was *Jean de la Croix et le problème de l'expérience mystique* (Paris 1942).
    'Entretiens II,' 17 Nov. 1929, *Œuvres* IV, 453–4

108 Letter to Jean Guitton, 10 Dec. 1929, *Œuvres* IV, 455; 'Entretiens II,' 20 Dec. 1927, unpublished

109 'Entretiens II,' 5 Mar. 1930, unpublished. According to Mounier the first vote on 12 Jan. 1929 had split 20–20. The summer vote had 24 for Mauss, 17 for Chevalier, and 5 for Etienne Gilson, who was teaching at the University of Toronto and not campaigning for the post. Letters to Jéromine Martinaggi, 13 Jan., 4 July 1929, unpublished. Gilson was elected to the Collège de France in 1932, but later abandoned the post for the Medieval Institute at the University of Toronto.

110 Henri Gouhier was a student of Gilson who was an expert on medieval philosophy, Maine de Biran, and Malebranche and who became professor at the Sorbonne in 1941.

111 'Entretiens II,' 30 Sept. 1929, unpublished

112 'Entretiens II,' 3 Nov. 1929, unpublished. During the Vichy period Marshal Pétain assisted at a ceremony here.

113 Jacques Madaule, *L'absent* (Paris 1973), 11–14

114 'Entretiens II,' 2 Dec. 1929, *Œuvres* IV, 454

115 'Entretiens II,' 20 Dec. 1929, unpublished

116 Hauviette was a character in Péguy's *Jeanne d'Arc*. 'Entretiens II,' 2 Feb. 1930, *Œuvres* IV, 459–60
117 'Entretiens II,' 2 Feb. 1930, unpublished section
118 *Ibid.*, in *Œuvres* IV, 460
119 Letter to Mounier, 4 Feb. 1930, *Œuvres* IV, 22
120 'Entretiens II,' 5 Mar. 1930, unpublished
121 *Ibid.*
122 Cf. Mounier to Maritain, 7 Mar. 1930, in *Maritain/Mounier* 23–4. Jacques Mersennes, 'Méditations dans la forêt,' *Vie Catholique* (5 July 1930)
123 'Rapport sur les projets de thèse adressé à M. Le Directeur de la Fondation Thiers,' 22 Mar. 1930, *Œuvres* IV, 467
124 'Entretiens III,' 1–75, unpublished
125 Letter to Jéromine Martinaggi, 18 May 1930, *Œuvres* IV, 468
126 Jean Sylvestre, 'Mon garçon: Visite à la mère de Péguy,' *Aux Davidées* (May 1930), in *Œuvres* IV, 456–9
127 'Entretiens II,' 23 June 1930, unpublished. The version of this passage in Mounier's *Œuvres* IV, 469–70, concludes with the phrase: 'Copeau read some pages on work while they, hands behind their ears, listened, with religion....' It adds colour but raises questions about the accuracy of the *Œuvres*.
128 'La Pensée de Charles Péguy,' reprinted in *Œuvres* I, 21–2
129 *Ibid.* 27–8
130 *Ibid.* 57
131 *Ibid.* 82
132 *Ibid.* 2, 878
133 *Ibid.* 112
134 *Ibid.* 119
135 Letter to Jéromine Martinaggi, 28 Nov. 1930, *Œuvres* IV, 472
136 Letter to Mounier, 15 July 1930, *Maritain/Mounier* 26–7
137 Letters to Maritain, 20 June, 21 July 1930, *Maritain/Mounier* 26–7; letter to Jacques Chevalier, 7 Nov. 1930, *Œuvres* IV, 471–2.
138 Reflections of Jacques Chevalier (July 1950), *Esprit* 174 (Dec. 1950) 945
139 Albert Béguin, 'Une Vie,' *ibid.* 937–9
140 Letter to Jacques Lefrancq, 27 Aug. 1933, *ibid.* 939
141 See Mounier, 'Un penseur français: Jacques Chevalier,' *La Vie Catholique* (6 Apr. 1926) 22–38.
142 Henri Marrou, 'La signification religieuse de la pensée d'Emmanuel Mounier,' *Bulletin des amis d'Emmanuel Mounier* XXVIII (Aug. 1966) 28
143 Cf. *L'affrontement chrétien* in *Œuvres* III, (Paris 1962), translated by Katherine Watson as *The Spoil of the Violent* (West Nyack, NY, nd) 30.

144 L'action politique d'Emmanuel Mounier,' *Les Cahiers de la République* II (1956) 90–1

CHAPTER THREE: THE FOUNDING OF 'ESPRIT'

1 Emmanuel Mounier, 'André Déléage,' *Esprit* 107 (Feb. 1945) 476–7; 'Souvenirs d'André Déléage,' *Esprit*, 340 (July–Aug. 1965) 189–208; Louis Galey and Georges Izard in 'Qu'as-tu fait de ta jeunesse? Une grande enquête de Gilbert Ganne sur les mouvements intellectuels d'avant-guerre,' *Arts* 561 (8 Mar.–3 Apr. 1956); Michel Winock, *Histoire politique de la revue 'Esprit,' 1930–1950* (Paris 1975) 43

2 'L'événement et nous,' *Aux Davidées*, Dec. 1930. This article was rewritten to form 'Refaire la renaissance,' Mounier's lead article in the first *Esprit* review (Oct. 1932).

3 Arland was literary critic at, and has since become director of, the NRF.

4 Letter to Georges Izard, 26 Dec. 1930 (partially unpublished)

5 Jean Daniélou, *Et qui est mon prochain?* (Paris 1974) 77

6 Cf. Mounier to Jacques Chevalier, 18 Feb. 1931 (unpublished)

7 Maritain to Mounier, 21 Feb. 1931 in *Maritain/Mounier, 1929–1939*, ed. Jacques Petit (Paris 1973) 31

8 Letter to Jéromine Martinaggi, 27 Feb. 1931, *Œuvres* IV, 474

9 Letter to Madeleine Mounier, 27 Feb. 1931, *ibid.*, 478

10 Letter to Jacques Chevalier, 14 Mar. 1931 (unpublished). In fact Mounier received a prize from the conservative Académie Française for the study.

11 Letter to Jacques Chevalier, 21 Apr. 1931 (unpublished)

12 Letters to Jacques Chevalier, 29 Apr. 1931 and 7 May 1931 (unpublished sections).

13 'When you are established,' Maritain told Mounier, 'perhaps you should go and see Cocteau. It will be good to keep in contact with everything which is germinating – even on the manure pile.' 'Entretiens IV,' 29 Apr. 1931 (unpublished)

14 'Entretiens IV,' 23 May, 4, 6 June 1931 (unpublished); Letter to Georges Izard, 13 June 1931 (unpublished)

15 Mounier hoped for something by the young André Malraux. Mauriac promised 'something' to Maritain, 'though not a novel, I live off them.' 'He said that so ingenuously,' Maritain commented, 'that we have to forgive him.' But returning from a meeting of Maritain's protégés with a young friend, the novelist rasped out a brusque judgment of them: 'no talent,' he lamented. Letter to 'Diverse Personalities,' 8 July 1931 (unpublished)' 'Entretiens IV,' 24 June 1931 (unpublished); recollection of the late Bernard Guyon

16 Letter to Nicolas Berdyaev, 27 June 1931 (unpublished section); letters to Georges Izard, 13 June, 31 July 1931 (unpublished); Jean Guitton, *Ecrire comme on se souvient* (Paris 1975)

17 Letters to Madeleine Mounier, 17 Apr. 1931, *Œuvres* IV, 479; to Georges Izard, 31 July 1931 (unpublished), 11 Aug. 1931 (unpublished section)

18 Letter to Georges Izard, 31 July 1931 (unpublished); to Jacques Maritain, 8 Aug. 1931, in *Maritain/Mounier* 40

19 Letter to Georges Izard, 31 July 1931 (unpublished); Jacques Lefrancq, *Oser Penser* (Neuchâtel 1961) 149–50, 155; 'Entretiens IV,' 14 May 1932 (unpublished); Winock, *'Esprit'* 95

20 'Entretiens III,' 30 Nov. 1930 (unpublished)

21 'Entretiens IV,' 21 Dec. 1930, 1 Feb. 1931 (unpublished)

22 Including Mounier cf. 'Entretiens III,' 30 Nov. 1930 (unpublished)

23 Cf. 'Entretiens IV,' 4 June 1931 (unpublished); Maritain to Mounier, 3 Aug. 1932, *Maritain/Mounier* 50

24 For example, see the *Gulag Archipelago*

25 For an interesting account of Berdyaev's relationship with *Esprit* in the nineteen-thirties, see the mémoire of *Esprit* group member Hélène Iswolsky, daughter of the last czarist ambassador to France: *Light before Dusk: A russian Catholic in France, 1923–1941* (New York 1942).

26 Mounier to Berdyaev, 8 Sept., 16 Oct. 1931 (unpublished)

27 Cf. letter to Jacques Chevalier, 29 Apr. 1931 (unpublished).

28 'Entretiens III,' 18 June 1930 (unpublished)

29 *Ibid.*, 15 May 1930 (unpublished)

30 'Entretiens IV,' 21 Apr. 1931 (unpublished)

31 'Entretiens III,' 30 Nov. 1930 (unpublished); 'Entretiens III,' 21 Dec. 1930 (unpublished)

32 'Entretiens III,' 30 Nov. 1930 (unpublished); 'Entretiens V,' 20 Aug. 1932 (unpublished)

33 'Entretiens IV,' 2 July 1931 (unpublished). Ramon Fernandez later evolved towards the extreme right and collaboration with the Nazis.

34 'Entretiens III,' 15 May 1930 (unpublished). Henri Daniel-Rops, on the eve of the war, sponsored young Colonel Charles de Gaulle and his ideas in the intellectual salons of Paris.

35 Borne collaborated on the Dominican review *Vie Intellectuelle*. Maritain signalled the 'judiciousness' of Borne's philosophical analysis of the relationship of action to contemplation. Borne had also worked with the Davidées. Letter to Mounier, *Maritain/Mounier* 55

In a letter to Georges Izard, 24 Dec. 1931 (unpublished), Mounier described his efforts to involve Vignaux and Lacroix.

36 He undertook two major theses: *Vie ouvrière en France pendant le Second Empire* (Paris 1946) and *La pensée ouvrière sur l'éducation*. Among his other distinguished historical studies was *1848* (Paris 1965).

Four other historians of French revolutions or French labour in the nineteenth century also were later associated with *Esprit*: Edouard Dolléans, Henri Guillemin, Georges Lefranc, and Maxime Leroy. The young men around the review were trying to rethink French society against a background of the 'errors' of the nineteenth century.

37 'Entretiens v,' Nov.–Dec. 1931 (unpublished)

38 *Ibid.*, 8 Dec.

39 Reported by Jacques Madaule, *L'Absent* (Paris 1973) 88–9

40 Mounier to Izard, Jan. 1932 (unpublished)

41 Letter to Maritain, 11 Dec. 1931, *Maritain/Mounier* 42–3

42 Recollections of Jacques Madaule, *Esprit* 174 (Dec. 1950) 974–5

43 'Entretiens v,' 3 Jan. 1932 (unpublished)

44 Letters to Georges Izard, 13 July 1931, Feb. 1932 (unpublished); 15, 19, and 19 February 1932, cited in Winock, '*Esprit*' 54

45 *Esprit* [brochure] (Dec. 1931/Jan. 1932). These passages are from the copy which may be found in the archives of the Archdiocese of Paris. Certain extracts are in *Œuvres* IV, 489–91.

46 On Garric as a teacher see Simone de Beauvoir, *Mémoires d'une jeune fille rangée* (Paris 1958) 251. The young Mlle de Beauvoir was an admirer of Garric. For an example of a Garric attack on *Esprit* see 'Pourquoi nous acceptons,' *La Revue des Jeunes* (15 Feb. 1933).

47 The group was called the Société St-Louis. 'Entretiens v,' 20 Feb. 1932, unpublished

48 Guitton to Mounier, 3 Mar. 1932, unpublished. This letter is cited extensively in Winock, '*Esprit*' 52.

49 Letter to Robert Garric transcribed in 'Entretiens v,' 16 Jan. 1932, in *Œuvres* IV, 488

50 Letter to Marcel Primard, transcribed in 'Entretiens v,' 20 Feb. 1932, *Œuvres* IV, 480–1

51 Letter to Georges Izard, 19 Feb. 1932, *Œuvres* IV, 489. He singled out André Gide and Julien Benda for criticism. See 'L'action intellectuelle ou l'influence,' *Revue de Culture Cénérale* I–v (20 Oct. 1931–20 May 1932)

52 The encyclical's references to property were cited early in the essay. On 20 Jan. 1932, Mounier wrote Maritain for a brochure on 'the right to property according to St Thomas' which contained the references to the relevant texts in the 'Angelic Doctor.' He hoped to have Maritain's comments on his effort one month later. 'Entretiens v,' 20 Feb. 1932, unpublished. In later years

the personalists tended to downplay instances of Maritain's influence on the origins of their positions.

53 'Entretiens v,' 9–10 Nov. 1931, 13 Jan. 1932, unpublished

54 Cf. Mounier's essay 'Péguy, médiateur de Bergson' in *Henri Bergson*, ed. A. Béguin and P. Thevanez (Neuchâtel 1941) 319–28. Maritain regularly tried to encourage Mounier to read works, including his own, that gave a Thomist approach to this problem. Eg, letter to Mounier, 27 Oct. 1932, *Maritain/Mounier* 55

55 Letter to Madeleine Mounier (1932) in *Esprit* 174 (Dec. 1950), 956. A letter to Jéromine Martineggi, 8 Apr. 1932, asked: 'Avez-vous lu l'émouvant Bergson? Il me l'a envoyé, et ce soir-là, si vives furent la surprise et l'émotion que j'en eus la fièvre.'

56 Bergson died on 4 Jan. 1941 without having been baptized a Catholic, out of fidelity to his fellow Jews suffering persecution.

57 'Testimony of Madame Duhameaux,' *Esprit* 174 (Dec. 1950) 956

58 Bernard Guyon, the *Esprit* representative in Ghent and an expert on Péguy and Balzac, was one. He could not accept the bond with non-believers as articulated in the discussions in the period. (interview with the author)

59 See below 67–9, 94, 103, 111–12.

60 Winock, '*Esprit*' 58. Professor Winock's study of the Déléage-Izard correspondence revealed their side of *Esprit*'s founding.

61 'Entretiens v,' 25 Feb. 1932, unpublished

62 Cited in Winock, '*Esprit*' 58

63 Jean Daniélou, who kept in contact with the project with the Jesuit seminary, was surprised to observe Mounier's leadership qualities assert themselves. Jean Daniélou, *Et qui est mon prochain? Mémoires* (Paris 1974) 77. See Mounier's letter to Déléage, transcribed in 'Entretiens v,' 4 Apr. 1932, *Œuvres* IV, 494

64 Letter to Jéromine Martinaggi, 8 Apr. 1932, *Œuvres* IV, 494–5

65 At this time he mentioned Glasgow, Oxford, Brussels, Gand, Milan, Palermo, Cracow, Prague, Vienna, and Salamanca. Letter to André Déléage, 17 Apr. 1932, *Œuvres* IV, 498

66 Letter to Francisque Gay, 2 June 1932, *Œuvres* IV, 481

67 'Entretiens v,' 2 July 1932, unpublished

68 'Entretiens v,' 17 July 1932, unpublished

69 Maritain to Mounier, 21 July 1932, *Maritain/Mounier* 49

70 Maritain to Mounier, 3 Aug. 1932, *ibid.* 51

71 See Jean-Louis Loubet del Bayle, 'La jeune Droite,' in *Les non-conformistes des années 30* (Paris 1969) 37–77.

72 On the history of this review see Pierre-Marie Dioudonnat, *Je suis partout, 1930–1944* (Paris 1973).

73 'Entretiens v' 9–10, 16, 17, 20 July 1932, unpublished. On 20 July Mounier recorded: 'we are unanimous on eliminating Luchaire and on creating an occasion to do so as soon as possible.'

74 The foundation of *Esprit* in the context of the formation of a 'New Left' runs through Mounier's unpublished diary in 1932. This private perspective conradicted *Esprit*'s public claim to be 'neither Right nor Left.' It also runs counter to the later charge by some Marxists that *Esprit* was cryptofascist.

75 'Entretiens v,' 15, 18 Aug. 1932, *Œuvres* IV, 499–501. In 1976 the villas were still there but surrounded by the urban sprawl of what was no longer a peaceful resort village. The larger Villa St-Paul was a public hotel catering to older people and its chapel was disused. There was no plaque to mark the birth of personalism.

76 Some of the others present – Georges Duveau, L.-E. Galey, Mademoiselle Péchegu, Gabriel Marty, and Pierre Doat – also contributed regularly. Sometime contributors to the discussions or 'spectators more than actors' were Merlant, Bouyx, Father Maxime Gorce, mesdemoiselles Marty, Arduin, Déléage, and the other Mademoiselle Péchegu – along with Catherine Daniélou Izard, who only dropped in from time to time.

77 The only person working around *Esprit* since before the Font-Romeu congress who stayed close to Mounier until the latter's death in 1950 was Maritain's protégé Etienne Borne, the self-appointed link between the *Esprit* project and the Christian Democrats. Jean Lacroix was interested in it by the summer of 1932, but it was only at the end of that year, after *Esprit* had published three issues, that he decided to 'commit himself to the movement and the review.' Mounier to Georges Izard, 29 Dec. 1932 (unpublished)

78 'Entretiens v.' Most of this description is unpublished except for sections in Winock, '*Esprit*' 61–7.

79 During the occupation of France, 1940–4, Gorce wrote for several collaborationist publications including *L'Emancipation nationale* of Jacques Doriot. Fleeing to Switzerland after the war, he abandoned the Roman Catholic Church for that of the 'Old Catholics.'

80 Georges Izard, *L'Express*, 29 Mar. 1960

81 'Entretiens v,' 22 Aug. 1932, *Œuvres* IV, 501. Just before catching the train, as the final copy of the Manifesto was being written, a phrase was modified without Déléage's approval. Furious, threatening to resign from the movement and hold a new congress, he forced the others to back down. Mounier to Jéromine Martinaggi, 1 Apr. 1941, *Œuvres* IV, 499

82 'Entretiens v,' 22 Aug. 1932, *Œuvres* IV, 501

83 On the congress see the recollections of Georges Izard, *Esprit* 174 (Dec. 1950). 979

Izard won out over Jacques Isorni, defence lawyer of Marshal Pétain, in a contest described by Isorni in his book *La Fièvre verte* (Paris 1975). The election of Isorni, who had no fascist connections before defending Pétain, was considered as a gesture which would be a symbolic rehabilitation of 'Pétainism' in France. Izard was known to be the founder of the left-wing review *Esprit*, at the opposite end of the political spectrum from 'Pétainism.'

For the claim of fidelity, see the recollections of Georges Izard in 'Qu'as-tu fait de ta jeunesse?,' *Arts* 561. In the same article, Louis Galey, who became an executive at Pathé Cinéma after having been director of Cinéma at Vichy, also cited his lasting debt to Font-Romeu.

84 Letter to Georges Izard, 24 Aug. 1932, *Esprit* 174 (Dec. 1950) 980

85 Letters from Déléage to Christian Lacour, 19 Sept. 1932, and to Georges Izard, 9 Feb. 1933, cited in Winock, '*Esprit*' 66

86 Mounier's essay is reprinted as 'La vision des hommes et du monde,' in *Œuvres* I (Paris 1961) 77. Letter to Izard, 24 Aug. 1932, *Esprit* 174 (Dec. 1950) 980

87 Mounier sent the report to 'Delaisi, Chabrun, Valois, De Man, Dubreuil, Dulot, B.I.T., etc.' Letter to Georges Izard, 30 Aug. 1932, unpublished

88 Letter to Jacques Chevalier, 20 Sept. 1932, *Œuvres* IV, 503

89 The Mystical Body theory would not be a defined Roman Catholic doctrine until 1943.

90 *Vie intellectuelle*, xv, 1 (10 Apr. 1932), 20–3. The importance of Father Congar's article in introducing this doctrine into France is underlined by Roger Boisvert in 'La théologie de l'Eglise en France de 1918 à 1939,' unpublished thesis, Institut Catholique (Paris 1966–7).

91 Recollection by Marie-Dominique Chenu, OP (interview with the author, 7 Apr. 1976)

92 'Entretiens VI,' 23 Sept. 1932, *Œuvres* IV, 503–4

93 'Entretiens IV,' 9 Oct. 1932, *ibid.* 504–6

CHAPTER FOUR: 'ESPRIT' LAUNCHED

1 Galey, Izard, and Alexandre Marc were without clear job prospects. Denis de Rougemont wrote his *Journal d'un intellectuel en chômage* (Paris 1937) in this period. The report on *Esprit* to the archbishop of Paris referred to the large number of the educated unemployed around the review. Mounier, Déléage, Izard all had academic problems. Although Ulmann was in the pay of the 'political bureau' of the police, he wrote violent articles against them in *Esprit*. According to a Parisian police archivist who wished to remain unidentified and Jean Lacroix, Ulmann was probably a police spy.

2 Jean Lacroix had been appointed to the lycée in Dijon.
3 Although the ascension of members of the *Esprit* group after World War II
was remarkable. Among individuals associated with the founding of *Esprit*
several were later elected to the 40 'immortals' of the Académie Française
(Robert Aron, Jean Daniélou, Jean Guitton, Georges Izard) along with other,
later, *Esprit* contributors (Pierre Emmanuel, Pierre-Henri Simon, Eugène
Ionesco).
4 An interesting example is Janet Flanner, who regularly presented a colourful portrait of French artistic and intellectual life for *The New Yorker*.
Although she was uninterested in politics she presented a sympathetic portrait of the young rioters of 6 Feb. 1934 who sought to bring down the
'rotten' Republic which sustained the liberty Miss Flanner valued so highly.
She seemed to reflect a common sentiment of disgust with the French
'politicians' among the expatriate literary colony and an attendant sympathy
for young French anti-Republicans of several stripes. See Janet Flanner,
Paris was Yesterday, 1925–1939 (Toronto 1972).
5 Cf. 'Rupture entre l'ordre chrétien et le désordre établi,' *Esprit* 6 (Mar. 1933).
A thin dossier of press commentary remains in the Bibliothèque E. Mounier
in Châtenay-Malabry, near Paris.
6 Interview of Alexandre Marc with the author, 7 Aug. 1973
7 Berdyaev's 'Vérité et mensonge du communisme' was noted, for example, by André Gide in his *Journal, 1889–1939* (Paris 1948) 1154:
'Remarquable, l'article de Berdiaeff ... que je lis dans le premier numéro
d'*Esprit*.'
8 Thus it would be inaccurate to situate the new review exclusively in a French/
Catholic context, as has been the tendency among historians.
9 'Refaire la Renaissance' (Oct. 1932), *Œuvres* I (Paris 1961) 137–74
10 Jean Lacroix, 'Individualisme et socialisme,' *Esprit* 1 (Oct. 1932) 156–7
11 Pabst, Lang, and Sternberg were the figures he cited. See André Déléage,
'Films de 1932,' *ibid.* 179
12 'Ce ne sont pas ceux qui disent: Esprit, Esprit' (Dec. 1932), *Œuvres* I, 845–7
13 See Mounier's comments on the early *Esprit* in 'Les cinq étapes d'*Esprit*,'
Bulletin des amis d'Emmanuel Mounier XXIX (Mar. 1967) 10–15
14 *La nouvelle revue française* (Dec. 1932) 801, 838, 845
15 The clippings remain in the aforementioned dossier in the Bibliothèque
E. Mounier. *Esprit* had only 500 subscribers in Jan. 1933
16 'Sur un certain front unique,' *Europe* (Jan. 1933), reprinted in Susan
Suleiman, ed., *Pour une nouvelle culture* (Paris 1971) 51, 53, 58–65
17 André Ulmann, 'Les fondements humains de la révolution,' *Esprit* 4
(Jan. 1933) 580

18 Mounier noted that Thierry Maulnier's definition of a spiritual revolution was one 'we would countersign almost from one end to the other.' 'Chronique du monde barbare,' *ibid.* 669

19 Figures taken from F.L. Carsten, *The Rise of Fascism* (Berkeley 1971) 139–40

20 Hitler announced the party program on 24 Feb. 1920 and beyond the demands of a greater Germany and for the annulment of the Versailles Treaty they called for the abolition of income not earned by work, the 'breaking of the shackles of interest,' the nationalization of all businesses and trusts which had already been amalgamated, the communalization of department stores, confiscation of land for the commonweal without compensation, the prohibition of speculation in land, and so on. These 'twenty-five points' were published for the first time in French in *Esprit* 16 (Jan. 1934) 640–50.

21 *Das Tagebuch von Joseph Goebbels, 1925–26*, ed. Helmut Heiber (Stuttgart 1961) 27, 30, cited in Carsten, *Fascism* 125

22 Himmler was formerly secretary to Gregor Strasser.

23 Goebbels, *Vom Kaiserhof zur Reichskanzlei* (Munich 1934) 191–2, 199, cited in Carsten, *Fascism* 149–50

24 On French attitudes towards National Socialism see Charles Micaud, *The French Right and Nazi Germany, 1933–1939* (New York 1972).

25 Denis de Rougemont, 'Alexandre Marc et l'invention du Personnalisme,' in *Le fédéralisme et Alexandre Marc* (Lausanne 1974) 52–4. Heidegger rejected 'existentialism' as a descriptive term for his philosophy.

26 Jean-Louis Loubet del Bayle, *Les non-conformistes des années 30* (Paris 1969) 94

27 Having adopted the 'nationalist corporatist' ideas of Mussolini, Lagardelle was named 'counsellor for social questions' of the French embassy in Rome by Henri de Jouvenel in Jan. 1933 and he remained there until 1940. In Apr. 1942 he succeeded René Belin as minister of labour in the Vichy government.

28 Cited in Edmond Lipiansky [Marc], 'L'"Ordre Nouveau" (1930–1938)' in *Ordre et démocratie: Deux sociétés de pensée – de l'Ordre Nouveau au Club Jean-Moulin* (Paris 1967) 14–15

29 Denis de Rougemont, in his *Journal d'une époque (1926–1946)* (Paris 1968) 92, described the meeting. The Manifesto of the Black Front was published in *Plans* (10 Dec. 1931) and a long exposition of Strasser's positions was later published by Mounier in early 1933 in three consecutive issues of *Esprit*.

30 The text is cited in Lipiansky, *Ordre* 43.

31 Schulze-Boysen later was active in *Die Rote Kapelle*, a German Communist resistance group, and was decapitated by Hitler during the war.

32 For more detail on *Plans* see Loubet del Bayle, *Les non-conformistes* 97–101.

33 *Ibid.* 102–3; Lipiansky, *Ordre* 17

34 Interview with the author, 7 Aug. 1973. On the origin of *Esprit*'s ideas see Marc's introduction to 'Misère et grandeur du spirituel' by Dandieu and Marc, *Documents du CIFE*, nouvelle série, no. 34.

35 Letter to Georges Izard, 8 Sept. 1932, unpublished

36 Interview with the author, 7 Aug. 1973; Marc, introduction in *Documents*, no. 34

37 Robert Aron and Arnaud Dandieu, *Décadence de la nation française* (Paris 1931), *Le cancer américain* (Paris 1931)

38 Marc and Dandieu, 'Misère et grandeur,' *Documents*, 9–10. This essay was still being used, at this writing, for the philosophical formation of students in Alexandre Marc's Centre de formation européenne in Nice, France and Aosta, Italy.

39 'Entretiens VI,' 18 Oct. 1932, *Œuvres* IV, 507–9

40 Mounier, 'Réponse à l'*Ordre Nouveau*,' *Esprit* 19 (Apr. 1934) 199–203

41 Denis de Rougemont, a pastor's son himself, in his *Journal*, 55–6, later signalled the importance of these discussions, which included figures such as W. Visser 't Hooft and a host of men who later were prominent Catholic theologians, for the ecumenical movement.

42 'Entretiens VI,' 12 Oct. 1932, *Œuvres* IV, 506; letter from Maritain to Mounier, Oct. 1932, in *Maritain/Mounier, 1929–1939*, ed. Jacques Petit (Paris 1973) 54

43 Maritain to Mounier, 27 Oct. 1932, in *Maritain/Mounier* 55–7

44 5 Nov. 1932, *ibid.* 61–2

45 Maritain to Mounier, 8 Nov. 1932, *ibid.* 63

46 Mounier to Martiain, 5 Nov. 1932, *ibid.* 61–2; 'Entretiens V,' 5 Nov. 1932, *Œuvres* IV, 510

47 Here Maritain mentioned Jacques de Monléon, Etienne Borne, and Olivier Lacombe as possibilities. Letter to Mounier, 10 Nov. 1932, *Maritain/Mounier* 66–8

48 Letter to Maritain, 11 Nov. 1932, *ibid.* 64–5

49 'La misère et l'espérance (1832–1932),' *Esprit* 3 (Dec. 1932) 483–92

50 'Chronique de la vie privée,' *ibid.* 475–7. Mounier noted the reception of a letter from a young man who had founded 'a revolutionary order' on 20 Oct. This idea persisted in the personalist movement. 'Entretiens VI,' 20 Oct. 1932, *Œuvres* IV, 509

51 'Les jeunes radicaux et nous,' *Esprit* 3 (Dec. 1933) 493–5

52 Mounier to Georges Izard, 29 Dec. 1932, unpublished; editor's note, *Esprit*, 174 (Dec. 1950), 982. Chevalier, we must recall, was the son of an army officer and firmly anti-German. Mounier wrote several letters to Chevalier in early 1933 in an effort to mollify him.

53 Mounier to Izard, 29 Dec. 1932, unpublished; Jean Lacroix, interview with

the author, 2 Aug. 1973. Lacroix was never a member of the *Action Française*, but while he was a student in the law faculty at Lyon he was an enthusiastic reader of the conservative daily *L'Echo de Paris* and secretary of the local Cercle Joseph de Maistre.

54 Lacroix and Simon later became prestigious and influential in their own right as prolific authors and, respectively, the chief philosophy and literature critics of the daily *Le Monde*. In Nov. 1966 Simon was elected to Daniel-Rops' chair in the Académie Française.

55 'Religion et culture II,' *Esprit* 4 (Jan. 1934) 523-45

56 More recently a conception close to Maritain's idea has been eloquently reaffirmed by Jacques Ellul, *Trahison de l'Occident* (Paris 1975). Ellul, working with *Esprit* and *Ordre Nouveau*, was an interested observer at the original debate. His social thought, particularly influential in North America, has been strongly influenced by personalism as shall be seen.

57 'Religion et culture II,' *Esprit* 4 (Jan. 1934) 523-45

58 Cited by Pierre Bertaux, 'Préoccupations de part et d'autre,' *Esprit* 5 (Feb. 1933) 717. Alexandre Marc, 'Jeunesse allemande,' *ibid.* 726

59 'Le désordre établi' was employed by Mounier in the title of the subsequent issue of *Esprit* and became a cliché at the review to describe what *Esprit* was against. At this writing the term is used now and then in *Le Monde* and, like personalism, attributed to Mounier, never to Marc.

60 This title was taken over by Jean-Louis Loubet del Bayle in his study of La Jeune Droite, Ordre Nouveau, and Esprit, *Les non-conformistes des années 30* (Paris 1969). He described these groups as distinctively French, unprecedented, and in search of a 'new politics' which they never found.

61 Marc, 'Jeunesse allemande,' *Esprit* 5 (Feb. 1933) 722-30. The other groups or organs which Marc mentioned were Hans Ebeling's *Der Vorkämpfer*, Ernst Niekisch's *Der Widerstand*, Karl O. Paetel's *National bolschewistische Blätter*, and Fritz Kloppe's *Der Wehrwolf*. Harro Schulze-Boysen, 'Lettre ouverte d'un jeune Allemand à la France,' *ibid.* 731-4

62 'Lettre ouverte d'un jeune Français à l'Allemagne,' *ibid.* 735-43. Both Raymond Aron and his close friend Jean-Paul Sartre were studying German philosophy in Berlin at this time. Sartre had even less interest in politics than Mounier. His *Temps modernes* and Mounier's *Esprit* spread existentialism and phenomenology in France after World War II.

63 Extant histories of *Esprit* seem to assume, in their brief discussions of the review's ties to the 'oppositionists,' that these groups were a sort of liberal or left-wing resistance to Nazism, instead of a radical current within the movement. Cf. Winock, '*Esprit*' 83; Pierre de Senarclens, *Le mouvement 'Esprit,'* 1932-1941 (Lausanne 1974) 95.

64 Otto Strasser, *Aufbau des deutschen Sozialismus* (Leipzig 1932)
65 Ernst Nolte, *Three Faces of Fascism* (New York 1966) 336
66 Maritain to Mounier, 6 Mar. 1933, *ibid.* 75–6. Maritain sent Mounier, for the French side, an article from the Montréal daily *Le Devoir* of 'a young Canadian lawyer on capitalism'; for the English side he called Mounier's attention to a young writer called Morley Callaghan. By the eve of World War II Mounier tended to think of the liberal Catholic review *Commonweal*, published in New York, as a sort of American *Esprit*. In 1950, the year of Mounier's death, a 'French-Canadian *Esprit*,' *Cité libre*, was founded by a young professor of law, Pierre Elliott Trudeau, and his friends, while that same year *Cross Currents* began to introduce new European religious thought to Catholics of the United States with a long essay from its chief *maître*: Emmanuel Mounier.
67 A. Dandieu, 'Le travail contre l'homme' *Esprit* 10 (July 1933) 571. In the same letter Mounier asked Izard to get Déléage to write an article on Hitler. This would hardly have mollified Maritain either. Mounier to Izard, 'Friday,' Apr. 1933, unpublished
68 'Entretiens VI,' 26 Nov., 10 Dec. 1932, 6 Jan. 1933, in *Œuvres* IV, 513–14, 518–19
69 'Entretiens VI,' 16 Mar. 1933, unpublished. 'Carnets VII' (1 Apr. 1933) in *Œuvres* IV, 525, gives a somewhat different and abridged version of this same passage.
70 Letter to Paulette Leclercq, 1 Apr. 1933, in *Œuvres* IV, 525
71 'Entretiens VI,' 3 Jan. 1933, 516–17
72 'Confessions pour nous autres chrétiens,' in *Œuvres* IV, 373, 379, 382–3, 374–5, 378, 390–2
73 *Ibid.* 381
74 'Esprit,' *Politique*, VIe année, 11 (Nov. 1932) 1034–6
75 'Pourquoi nous acceptons,' *La revue des jeunes* (15 Feb. 1933) 159
76 'La jeunesse intellectuelle' (dossiers), *La documentation catholique*, 15e année, t. 30, no. 666, 15 July 1933, 95–115. This dossier presented pro and con articles about *Esprit*.
77 Nonciature apostolique de France to the Vicaire général de Paris, Communication #22610, 19 Apr. 1933, in the archives of the Archdiocese of Paris. Unfortunately the theologian's report seems to have been lost.
78 Letter to Georges Izard, 11 Apr. 1933, unpublished section
79 Bergery's political line was unusual. J. Plumyène and R. Lasierra in *Les fascismes français, 1923–63* (Paris 1963) 89–91, qualify Bergery's 'Frontisme' as a 'fascism of the Left' similar to the 'neo-socialism' of Marcel Déat. Drieu la Rochelle later proposed to the Vichy government and to the German authorities the creation of a single French political party under the leader-

ship of Bergery or Jacques Doriot during the occupation. Cf. Alastair
Hamilton, *L'illusion fasciste* (Paris 1975) 269.

80 'Entretiens VII,' 27 May 1933, *Œuvres* IV, 89. This phrase embarrassed Izard
   when Mounier confronted him with it.

81 'Certitude de notre jeunesse' (May 1933) in *Œuvres* IV, 11, 15–16

82 In *Maritain/Mounier* 78–81

83 'Entretiens VII,' 23 May 1933, in *Œuvres* IV, 531

84 Mounier recorded these themes, passed onto him by Father Plaquevent, in
   'Entretiens VII,' 16 May 1933, unpublished.

85 Cf. Letters of Plaquevent to Mounier, Feb. 1932; Mounier to Plaquevent,
   2 Mar. 1932, 24 Jan. 1933, archives of the Archdiocese of Paris.

86 Coquelle-Viance was a prominent corporatist, former partner of Georges
   Valois, and apparently influential in such matters. He defended *Esprit* in
   La Croix.

87 24 May 1933, in *Maritain/Mounier* 86

88 'Entretiens VII,' *Œuvres* IV, 23 May 1933, 531

89 Minutes, Conseil de Vigilance de l'Archidiocèse de Paris, 23 May 1933

90 Maritain to Mounier, 25, 29 May, 7 June 1933, in *Maritain/Mounier* 87–8,
   91–2

91 Letter to Paulette Leclercq, 7 June 1933, *Œuvres* IV, 532

92 Canon Dupin to His Excellence Luigi Maglioni, 13 June 1933, archives of the
   Archdiocese of Paris

93 'Cinquante Mille,' *Esprit* 8 (May 1933) 147; 'Entretiens VII,' 30 June 1933,
   in *Œuvres* IV, 533; Mounier to Maritain, 30 June 1933, *Maritain/Mounier*
   94–5

CHAPTER FIVE: THE FASCIST CHALLENGE

1 Among French Catholic 'intellectual' publications *Etudes*, the scholarly review
  of the Jesuits, was publishing 13,000 copies by 1936. *Sept*, the high quality
  Dominican weekly (Mar. 1934–Aug. 1937), published up to 100,000 copies,
  while their erudite *La vie intellectuelle* was publishing 5–6,000 in 1934. René
  Rémond, *Les catholiques, le communisme et les crises, 1929–1939* (Paris 1960)
  271, 273–4

  On the Left, the Popular Front weekly *Vendredi*, founded in Nov. 1935,
  published 100,000 copies, while the centre-Left *Marianne* attained 120,000.
  Claude Estier, *La gauche hebdomadaire, 1914–1962* (Paris 1962) 264, 266

  On the Right, *Gringoire*, the extreme right weekly favourable to fascist
  Italy, published 640,000 copies in Nov. 1936. *Candide*, a bit more moderate
  than *Gringoire*, published 150,000 in 1930 and 340,000 in Mar. 1936. Pierre-
  Marie Dioudonnat, *Je suis partout, 1930–1944* (Paris 1973) 15

Sept and its successor, *Temps Présent*, seemed closer to Maritain's idea of a Catholic *Nouvelle revue française* than *Esprit* and published 70–100,000 copies. But *Esprit* and *La vie intellectuelle* articulated the new ideas, which the others popularized.

2 'Déclaration,' *Commune* 3 (Nov. 1933) 257

3 Paul Nizan, 'Jeune Europe,' *ibid.* 314–15

4 Gérard Servèze, 'Notes sur la revue *Esprit*,' *Commune* 1 (July 1933) 84

5 Georges Sadoul, 'Quelques études "objectives" du fascisme,' *Commune* 2 (Oct. 1933) 114; Nizan, 'Jeune Europe,' *Commune* 3 (Nov. 1933) 313

6 Nizan, *ibid.* 311, 314–15

7 Jacques Bartoli, 'Crise de croissance et révolution de l'esprit,' *Commune* 3 (Nov. 1933), 467

8 Servèze, 'Notes' 84–5

9 'Les enfants de la lumière,' *Commune* 2 (Oct. 1933) reprinted in J.J. Brochier, ed., *Paul Nizan, intellectuel communiste, 1926–1940: Ecrits et correspondance inédite* (Paris 1967) 219, 221–2, 224–5

10 'Alexandre Marc et l'invention du personnalisme,' in *Le fédéralisme et Alexandre Marc* (Lausanne 1974) 57, 61

11 See, for example, Marc and Dupuis, *Jeune Europe* (Paris 1933) 125–6, where it was asserted that the Nazi régime would dissolve 'in despair, chaos, mud, and blood' if it did not 'transcend itself,' 'surpass itself' by adopting some of the ideas of the élite of German youth (eg, *The Opponent*) such as 'the primacy of the human person, federalism, and regional corporatism.'

12 According to Denis de Rougemont, Ribbentrop and Abetz took the term 'New Order' to describe the Nazi ideal for Europe from Marc's review. Cf. Denis de Rougemont, *Journal d'une époque (1926–1946)* (Paris 1968) 371.

13 The French homologue of this orgnization was the Comité France-Allemagne directed by Jules Romains and Fernand de Brinon.

14 In England, for example, T.S. Eliot, who had moved away from Maurras at the same time as Maritain, called attention to Esprit and Ordre Nouveau (along with the Jeune Droite) as groups offering a precious defence of the individual while avoiding liberalism. *The Criterion* (Apr. 1934), 454. Cited in Alastair Hamilton, *L'illusion fasciste* (Paris 1973) 297

15 Georges Friedmann, *Problèmes du machinisme en URSS et dans les pays capitalistes* (Paris 1934) 79

16 'Des pseudo-valeurs spirituelles fascistes: prises de position,' *Esprit*, 16 (Jan. 1934), in *Œuvres* I (Paris 1961) 223–8

17 'Entretiens II,' 2 Feb. 1930, unpublished

18 'Des pseudo-valeurs,' in *Œuvres* I, 228

19 Marcel Martinet, 'Le chef contre l'homme: Nécessité d'un nouvel indi-

vidualisme,' *Esprit* 16 (Jan. 1934) 541–58; Edmond Humeau, 'Le Fascisme et le sens de l'honneur,' *ibid.*, 589–603; Georges Duveau, 'L'esprit fasciste et la mystique de la jeunesse,' *ibid.* 583–8

20 Henri-L. Miéville, 'L'aventure Nietzschéenne et le temps présent,' *ibid.* 604–31
21 'La mystique de la vie dans la révolution nationale allemande,' *ibid.* 634
22 Eugène Meves, 'Les vingt-cinq points d'Adolphe Hitler,' *ibid.* 640–50
23 Otto Strasser, 'L'Allemagne est-elle un danger ou un espoir pour l'Europe?', *ibid.* 651–70; Heintz Berg, 'Traits de la nouvelle Allemagne,' *ibid.* 706–13
24 'Die Volkische Idee,' *Esprit* 17 (Feb. 1934) 765, 769
25 *Ibid.* 779
26 Mounier's private reaction is difficult to ascertain because his *Entretiens* for this period were lost a few years after his death.
27 Paul Archambault, 'La démocratie et la révolution! Lettre ouverte à M. Emmanuel Mounier,' *L'Aube* (21–2 Jan. 1934); 'Destin d'un mot,' *Politique*, 8e année, 2 (Feb. 1934) 154–9
28 'Lettre ouverte sur la démocratie, 20 Feb. 1934,' *L'Aube*, 27 Feb. 1934, reprinted in *Œuvres* IV, 292–7
29 'Leçons de l'émeute ou la révolution contre les mythes,' in *Œuvres* I, 361–9
30 Letter to Paulette Leclercq, 6 Sept. 1933, *Œuvres* IV, 538
31 For attacks on anti-Semitism, see Wladimir Rabinovitch, 'La tragédie du peuple juif'; René Schwob, 'Protestation d'un chrétien,' *Esprit* 8 (May 1933) 154–65, 166–72. *Esprit*'s consistent opposition to anti-Semitism in general and Nazi persecution of the Jews in particular is one of the proudest themes in the history of the pre-war *Esprit*. It is, however, another thing to interpret this position as a 'liberal' political stance as the review's historians have done. There was a considerable disdain for anti-Semitism among Nazi dissidents or SA leaders such as Erich Rohm. It is inaccurate to see anti-Semitism as the *sine qua non* of Nazism or fascism.
   'Entretiens VII,' 11 May 1933, unpublished; letter to Paulette Leclercq, 14 May 1933 and 'Entretiens VII,' 30 June 1933 in *Œuvres* IV, 529–30, 533; Michel Winock, *Histoire politique de la revue 'Esprit,' 1930–1950* (Paris 1975) 163. The secretary of *Esprit* was Angèle Touchard, the wife of P.-A. Touchard, editor of the Third Force's *Front social* and theatre critic at *Esprit*.
32 See Georges Zerapha, 'La mission d'Israel,' *Esprit* 11–12 (Aug.–Sept. 1933) 794–800. Zerapha maintained: 'Je ne dois rien au judaisme, ou plutôt je ne dois rien aux Juifs, moralement, culturellement et à bien d'autres points de vue. Nous sommes des milliers en France qui devons notre formation morale et culturelle au christianisme et à la France.' Cited by Mounier in 'Judaisme: La conscience des Juifs,' *Esprit* 20 (May 1934) 309

Maurice Schumann was another prominent Jew, close to the *Esprit* group but a contributor to Dominican and Christian Democrat publications, who converted to Christianity in this period.

33 'Constitution des amis d'*Esprit*,' *Esprit* 10 (July 1933) 461–2

34 'Deuxième année,' *Esprit* 11–12 (Aug.–Sept. 1933) 663–7. The tone indicated that there was a considerable amount of frustration with the review's vagueness.

35 Arnaud Dandieu, 'Le travail contre l'homme,' *Esprit* 10 (July 1933); E. Mounier, 'Mort d'Arnaud Dandieu,' *Esprit* 11–12 (Aug.–Sept. 1933) 841; Mounier to Edmond Humeau (29 Aug. 1933), unpublished. For Alexandre Marc, over forty years later, Dandieu's death deprived 'the generation of 1930' of one of its great geniuses. Marc named a son after him.

36 Letter to Georges Izard, 20 Aug. 1933, *Œuvres* IV, 535–6

37 Letter to Izard, 6 Sept. 1933, *ibid.* 537–8

38 'There is no value above the Person, no essential occupation outside of his interior life. ... Two beings who love one another ... end up forming, with their two persons a true new Person. ... A community is a new Person which unites persons by their heart of hearts.' 'Argent et vie privée,' *Esprit* 3 (Oct. 1933), in *Œuvres* I, 236. Cf. introduction to 'travail et prolétariat,' *Esprit* 14 (Nov. 1933) 179

39 Letter to Nicholas Berdyaev, 15 Feb. 1934. This letter is misdated 15 Feb. 1936 in *Œuvres* IV, 580 and has helped persuade a generation of historians that Mounier's public quarrel with the *Ordre Nouveau* group in early 1934 constituted a definitive break between *Esprit* and that movement. In fact the dispute lasted only a few months and, according to Denis de Rougemont, was probably conducted largely for the benefit of Berdyaev and Jacques Maritain. *Esprit* and *Ordre Nouveau* worked closely together through most of the nineteen-thirties and when this letter was published, *Ordre Nouveau–Esprit* veterans, such as de Rougemont, could not recall any tension between the two movements in 1936. Cf. Denis de Rougemont, 'personnalisme,' in *Alexandre Marc* 57.

40 Letter to Nicholas Berdyaev, 15 Feb. 1934, unpublished section

41 Besides Mounier's essay, noted above, there was Jean Lacroix's charge of a 'mystique of aggressiveness' and a 'second-rate Nietzscheanism.' Jean Lacroix, 'De la "révolution nécessaire" au "plan" d'Henri de Man,' *Esprit* 17 (Feb. 1934) 811

42 Mounier, 'Réponse à l'*Ordre Nouveau, Esprit* 19 (Ap. 1934) 199–203

43 'Entretiens VIII,' 13, 16 May 1934, in *Œuvres* IV, 548; 'Chronique des amis d'*Esprit*,' *Esprit* 21 (June 1934) 518–20

44 Jacques Ellul and Father M.-D. Chenu have both told the author that the influence of Berdyaev dominated the discussions. Philosopher Paul Ricœur

has argued that Landsberg was the most important philosophical influence on the pre-war *Esprit*.

45 'De la propriété capitaliste à la propriété humaine,' *Esprit* 19 (Apr. 1934) in *Œuvres* I, 419–77; 'Tentation du communisme: Pour un certain sang-froid spirituel,' *Esprit* 21 (June 1934), in *ibid.* 229–5; 'Y-a-t-il une politique chrétienne?,' *ibid.* 344–408; 'Nos positions: Anticapitalisme' (feuillet détachable), *ibid.* 270–6; 'Lignes de positions: Le travail' (feuillet détachable), *Esprit* 23–4 (Aug.–Sept. 1934) in *Œuvres* I, 277–83; 'Préface à une réhabilitation de l'art et des artistes,' *Esprit* 25 (Oct. 1934) in *Œuvres* I, 255–69

46 'Manifeste au service du personnalisme,' *Esprit*, 49 (Oct. 1936), 7–216. Reprinted with additions and the same title (Paris 1936) and in *Œuvres* I, 481–647

47 'De la propriété capitaliste,' in *Œuvres* I, 419–77

48 'Y-a-t-il une politique chrétienne?,' *Œuvres* I, 401, 403–4

49 'Nos positions: Anticapitalisme,' *ibid.* 275

50 'Préface à une réhabilitation de l'art et de l'artiste,' *ibid.* 256, 260, 264, 266

51 'Qu'est-ce que le personnalisme?,' *Esprit* 27 (Dec. 1934), in *Œuvres* I, 175; *ibid.* n4

52 *Ibid.* 177, 179

53 *Ibid.* 178

54 *Ibid.* 181–2

55 *Ibid.* 182

56 'Révolution communautaire,' *Esprit* 28 (Jan. 1935), in *Œuvres* I, 184

57 *Ibid.* 190–1

58 *Ibid.* 195

59 *Ibid.* 190

60 *Ibid.* 199

61 'Révolution communautaire,' *Œuvres* I, 199, 194 n11, 202

62 *Ibid.* 202–3

63 These generalizations are gleaned from the recollections of several former 'friends of *Esprit*' in interviews cited elsewhere in the text.

64 Mounier's 'Entretiens VIII,' 20 June 1935, *Œuvres* IV, 572

65 'Révolution communautaire,' *Œuvres* I, 208

66 *Ibid.* 209 n23, 891

67 'Les événements et les hommes,' *Esprit* 6 (Mar. 1933) 1027

68 Raymond de Becker, *Le livre des vivants et des morts* (Brussels 1942) 1–162

69 Mounier, 'Révolution spirituelle,' *Esprit* 11–12 (Sept. 1933) 791–2

70 Mounier to Izard, 18 Nov. 1933, unpublished

71 'Révolution spirituelle d'abord?,' 'Le problème des moyens,' *Esprit* 16 (Jan. 1934) 673, 675, 678, 688

72 R. de Becker, 'La lutte de l'église contre l'hitlérisme,' *Esprit* 20 (May 1934) 288–9

73 'Entretiens VIII,' 9, 31 May 1934, in *Œuvres* IV, 546–7, 551

74 'Entretiens VIII,' 9 May 1934, unpublished section

75 *Ibid.*, in *Œuvres* IV, 547; *ibid.*, 31 May 1934, 551

76 *Ibid.*, 29 May 1934, 550

77 *Ibid.*, 29 May 1934, unpublished section

78 *Ibid.*, 9 May 1934, unpublished section

79 Jacques Maritain to Mounier, May 1934, in *Maritain/Mounier, 1929–1939*, ed. Jacques Petit (Paris 1973) 110–11

80 'Entretiens VIII,' 5 June 1934 in *Œuvres* IV, 552

81 *Ibid.*, unpublished section. Jacques Maritain was still alive when the *Œuvres* were published, so the omission of passages such as this from Mounier's Entretiens was not so surprising.

82 'Entretiens VIII,' 8 June 1934, unpublished

83 'Entretiens VIII,' 27 June 1934, unpublished. Mounier did not make much of this visit, or of Strasser, in his diary.

84 'Faut-il passer à l'action?,' *Esprit* 22 (July 1934) 604

85 See 'Entretiens VII,' 31 May 1934, in *Œuvres* IV, 550 and n33, 886

86 'Entretiens VIII,' 8 June 1934, *Œuvres* I, 552; Mounier to Izard, Aug. 1934, unpublished; de Becker to Mounier, Sept. 1934, unpublished

87 For a good brief summary of Bergery's role as an 'unfaithful precursor' of the Popular Front, along with Marcel Déat and Jacques Doriot, see Jacques Delperrie de Bayac, *Histoire du Front Populaire* (Paris 1972) 67–83

88 Mounier to Izard, 16 Oct. 1934, in *Œuvres* IV, 557; 'Entretiens VIII,' 22 Nov. 1934, in *ibid.* 557–60

89 'Entretiens VIII,' 22 Nov. 1934, in *Œuvres* IV, 559–60; Mounier to Izard, 18 Oct. 1934, 6 Nov. 1934, in *Œuvres* IV, 559

90 'Pour une technique des moyens spirituels,' in *Œuvres* I, 314, 328–30, 334–6, 351, 357

91 At the end of his series of essays on 'spiritual means' Mounier said there were 'new movements animated by the very orientation which inspired these pages,' *ibid.* 360. These were the Friends of *Esprit*, La Croisade of L.-E. Galey, and Communauté of de Becker. See *ibid.* 893n70

92 'Communautés chrétiennes,' *Esprit* 29 (Feb. 1935) 781

93 Cf. 'Chronique des amis d'*Esprit*,' *Esprit* 27 (Dec. 1934) 534

94 'Les jeunes catholiques belges et le plan de Man,' *Esprit*, 30 (Mar. 1935) 952–3, 958. Spaak was well known in Belgium for his prowess in tennis but was still some years from political prominence.

95 'Chronique des amis d'*Esprit*,' *Esprit* 30 (Mar. 1935) 1020; Mounier to Maritain, 5 Mar. 1935, in *Maritain/Mounier* 118

96 'Entretiens VIII,' 26 Feb. 1935, *Œuvres* IV, 566–7; R. de Becker, *Livre des vivants* 186. Mounier recorded that the Dominicans of Juvisy, near Paris, were 'excited and proud' when the French police came to investigate de Becker's activities. 'Entretiens VIII,' 26 Feb. 1935, unpublished section

97 Review of *L'idée socialiste* of Henri de Man, *Esprit* 31 (Apr. 1935) 90–3

98 De Becker frequently referred to the necessity for the Catholic party in Belgium to sever itself from clerical influences. *Esprit* was always carefully 'ecumenical.' Even Communauté, Mounier feared, was too Catholic.

While the Order was explicitly Catholic, it was to be linked, from the outset, with La Croisade, a short-lived movement created by L.-E. Galey for members of the Third Force who did not want to join Bergery.

99 Maritain to Mounier, Dec. 1934, *Maritain/Mounier* 117

100 Maritain to Mounier, 'Friday,' 'very probably 1935' (ed.), *Maritain/Mounier* 120–1

101 'Entretiens VIII,' 26 Feb. 1935, unpublished

102 Maritain to Mounier, Apr. 1935, and editor's notes, *Maritain/Mounier* 121

103 Mounier to Maritain, 12 Apr. 1935, *ibid.* 123; Maritain to Mounier, April 1935, *ibid.* 124

104 'Entretiens VIII,' 23 Apr. 1935, *Œuvres* IV, 567

105 'Centre de liaison des mouvements de recherche et d'action pour une cité personnaliste,' *Esprit* 32 (May 1935) 335

CHAPTER SIX: 1935–7: CONTROVERSIES, RESTRUCTURING, DISCIPLINE

1 'La course à la guerre,' *Esprit* 31 (Apr. 1935) 142–5

2 For texts of this controversy see René Rémond, *Les Catholiques, le communisme et les crises, 1929–1939* (Paris 1960) 79–88.

3 'La course à la guerre,' *Esprit* 31 (Apr. 1935) 142, 145, 148

4 'Les catholiques et la défense nationale,' *ibid.* 134

5 'Entretiens VIII,' 17 May 1935, *Œuvres* IV, (Paris 1963) 568

6 The Jeune République called for a great effort at Franco-German reconciliation after Hitler's proclamation of military conscription, declared antifascism an inadequate basis for French foreign policy, condemned the arms race as a major cause of war, and called for revision of the peace treaties and complete moral and material disarmament. The party's two deputies voted against the two-years' law. The Christian Democrat daily, *L'Aube*, also opposed the law, although with less vehemence than did *Esprit* or the Jeune République, and in the Chamber all sixteen members of the Parti Démocrate Populaire supported it. On the pacifism of the Christian Democrats at this time see R.W. Rauch, Jr, *Politics and Belief in Contemporary France* (The Hague 1972) 160–1.

7 'Notre patrie, déclaration collective,' *Esprit* 33 (June 1935) 344
8 'Servitude et grandeur militaires, 1935, Note,' *Esprit* 32 (May 1935) 164–5
9 Eg, editor's note for 'La course à la guerre,' *Esprit* 31 (Apr. 1935) 146; 'Correspondance,' 'Notre Patrie,' *Esprit* 33 (June 1935) 339–54. Mounier also wrote two letters to de Gandillac affirming his solidarity with him in the face of 'nationalist' attacks (27 Mar., 15 May 1935, unpublished).
10 Charles Micaud, *The French Right and Nazi Germany, 1933–1939* (Durham, NC 1943) traces the evolution of right-wing attitudes towards Hitler. Jacques Delperrie de Bayac's *Histoire du Front Populaire* (Paris 1972) describes the Left's 'pacifism' as an important factor in the background of Vichy.

General de Castelnau insisted that the bulletin *Chantiers* of the youth branch of French Catholic Action, directed by Lalande, retract a page sympathetic to *Esprit*. 'Entretiens VIII,' 29 May 1935, unpublished; Mounier to Maurice de Gandillac, 15 May 1935, unpublished
11 'Note,' *Esprit* (new series) (Apr. 1971) 928. Pacelli, known to be more sympathetic to the *Action Française* than Pius XI, became Piux XII on the eve of the war.
12 *Esprit* 32 (Mar. 1935) 310–11
13 The next year Marion was an official in the Parti Populaire Français of the renegade communist Jacques Doriot. Later, as an official in the Vichy government, he worked against the influence of Catholics in the National Revolution.

'Entretiens VIII,' 29 May 1935, *Œuvres* IV, 570–1. Jean de Fabrègues, a devout Catholic, at first was faithful to the *Action Française* after the condemnation while retaining relations with Maritain's circle. Although he had been Maurras' secretary he broke with the *Action Française* in 1930 and began to work at a series of 'New Right' reviews.
14 See Pierre Milza, *L'Italie fasciste devant l'opinion française, 1920–1940* (Paris 1967) 115–49. Henri Marrou, 'L'action politique d'Emmanuel Mounier,' *Les Cahiers de la République* II (1956) 94
15 L. Rozenstock-Franck, 'Le Corporatisme fasciste,' *Esprit* 23–4 (Sept. 1934) 774
16 'Esprit au congrès franco-italien sur la corporation,' *Esprit* 33 (June 1935) 35–8. According to Mounier the fascists' reaction to his personalism was 'a vaguely courteous and respectful boredom.' 'Entretiens VIII,' *Œuvres* IV, 571. According to another observer, the personalism of the French delegates seemed a 'curiosity' to the fascists: 'lofty considerations without a close relationship to the realities of human life,' 'abstract ... a general and sterile

critique.' Georges Viance, 'Fascisme et liberté,' *Vie Intellectuelle*, XXXVII 4 (25 Sept. 1935) 650–3.

17 'Entretiens VIII,' 29 May 1935, unpublished section

18 Recollections of Marie-Dominique Chenu, OP (7 Apr. 1976)

19 The historians of *Esprit* describe Leenhardt as having been an employee of the 'political office' of the Prefecture when he joined *Esprit*. An archivist at the Prefecture, who did not wish to give his name, told me that there was no such thing as a 'political office' of the Prefecture and that Ulmann and Leenhardt, neither of whose names is on the list of employees of the Prefecture in the nineteen-thirties, were probably paid informers. Jean Lacroix told me he suspected this of Ulmann. There are references in Mounier's unpublished diaries to police suspicions of Raymond de Becker and, on the eve of the war, *Esprit*, for their attitudes towards Germany.

Both Labrousse's parents had been killed in World War I and, with Goguel, he contributed essays to *Esprit* during the Munich crisis strongly recommending a pacifist line on Germany.

20 *Destin de la personne* (Paris 1935)

21 'Les paternalistes contre la personne humaine,' 'La personne ouvrière et le droit du travail,' *Esprit* 42 (Mar. 1936). This is the judgment of Henry W. Ehrmann in *Organized Business in France* (Princeton 1957) 51

22 Cf. Marrou, 'L'action politique.'

23 Cf. the *Maritain/Mounier* correspondence for this period. Mounier published two non-personalist essays by Maritain in the fall of 1935, but they had been written for *Etudes Carmélitaines*, not *Esprit*. For the rest of the decade Maritain gently put off Mounier's several entreaties to publish essays in *Esprit*, or a monograph in the Collection Esprit. Madame Mounier recalls that when they first became engaged, Mounier hurried to take her to meet Maritain. After that she only saw Maritain once or twice for the rest of his life. Interview with the author, 12 June 1976

24 See the letter from M. de Gandillac to Mounier in *Esprit* 33 (June 1935) 349.

25 This review reflected the 'vastness of Christianity,' drew contributions of Christians from all sides of the political spectrum, and had a much larger circulation than *Esprit* – there being over 100,000 copies of some of its issues. On *Sept*, see Aline Coutrot, *Un courant de la pensée catholique, l'hebdomadaire 'Sept'* (Paris 1961).

26 The original slogan of this influential review, 'From André Gide to Jacques Maritain; had to be dropped when Maritain had to leave *Vendredi* under threat of losing his teaching position at the Institut Catholique.

27 The subsidy had been 10,000F per year. Cf. Mounier to Maritain, 29 Apr. 1936 in *Maritain/Mounier, 1929–1939*, ed. Jacques Petit (Paris 1973) 142.

28 Emmanuel Mounier, 'Les cinq étapes d'*Esprit*,' *Dieu Vivant*, 16 (1950), 37–53
29 'Entretiens VIII,' 1 July 1935, *Œuvres* IV, 575
30 'Deux Journées Esprit,' *Esprit* 37 (Oct. 1935) 25–6
31 This is the figure given by Michel Winock, *Histoire politique de la revue 'Esprit' 1930–1950* (Paris 1975) 164. Most of the records of the review were lost during the war. Jean Lacroix recalled a circulation of c3000 before the war. Interview with the author, 2 Aug. 1975

The distinguished intellectual historian Father M.-D. Chenu recalled that *Esprit* was learned and relatively difficult to read. Its positions were later vulgarized in reviews like *Sept* and *Temps Présent* and a host of books. He considered its influence decisive. Interview with the author, 7 Apr. 1976
32 'Deux journées *Esprit*,' *Esprit* 37 (Oct. 1935) 246
33 'Notre humanisme, Déclaration collective,' *ibid.* 246; E. Mounier, 'Faisons le point,' *Esprit* 38 (Nov. 1935) 278–9
34 'Entretiens VIII,' 24 Oct. 1935, *Œuvres* IV, 576. Two years later Loustau was one of the directors of Jacques Doriot's Parti Populaire Français, but he resigned the next year. Along with Gibrat he held responsible positions in the Vichy government; he helped draft some of the key documents of Pétain's 'National Revolution.'
35 'Chronique Permanente,' *Esprit* 38 (Nov. 1935) 280
36 'a complete system of doctrine and of life. ... It is a religion ... certain that it is called to replace all other religions, an atheistic religion for which dialectical materialism is dogma and of which Communism as a way of life is the ethical and social expression. Atheism is presupposed as the principle of this system. It is the starting point. And that is why Communist thought holds so ardently to it, as to the principle which stabilizes its practical conclusions and without which these would lose their necessity and value.' *Humanisme intégral* (Paris 1936) 44–6.

To the objection of a French Marxist intellectual that atheism should be considered the consequence and not the starting point of Marxism (George Sadoul, *Commune*, Dec. 1935), Maritain cryptically noted: 'It is not easy to see how one passes from the recognition of the fact that class war exists to the conclusion that God does not exist....'
37 Nicolas Berdyaev, 'Vérité et mensonge du communisme,' *Esprit* 1 (Oct. 1932) 104–28
38 'Entretiens VIII,' 29 June 1935, *Œuvres* IV, 572–3
39 *Ibid.* 573–4
40 See Mounier's review of Malraux, *Le Temps du mépris*, in *Esprit* 35–6

(Aug.–Sept. 1935) 805; and 'L'infiltration sentimentale,' *Esprit* 34 (July 1935) 632–4.

41 Eg, Brice Parain, review of *Socialisme fasciste* by Drieu la Rochelle; P.A. Touchard, review of 'Le Chef' by la Rochelle, *Esprit* 27 (Dec. 1934) 491; Touchard review of *Beloukia* by la Rochelle, *Esprit* 47–8 (Aug.–Sept. 1936) 732.

42 'Entretiens VIII' (unpublished)

43 Cited in Jean Lacroix, 'De la "Révolution nécessaire" au "Plan" de Man,' *Esprit* 17 (Feb. 1934) 840

44 In Aug. 1933, Mounier encouraged Izard to study Marx for the sake of personalism and promised: 'I will also put myself to that one day.' Letter to Georges Izard, 20 Aug. 1933, *Œuvres* IV, 536

45 Marcel Moré, 'Notes sur le marxisme,' *Esprit* 21 (June 1934) 461

46 Jean Daniélou, *Mémoires: Et qui est mon prochain?* (Paris 1974) 150–4; Winock, *Histoire politique* 149; Pierre de Senarclens, *Le mouvement 'Esprit,' 1932–1941* (Lausanne 1974)

47 See David Caute, *Communism and the French Intellectuals, 1914–1960* (London 1964).

48 This was readily apparent in the Catholic reaction to the 'outstretched hand' of Maurice Thorez in Apr. 1936. See John Hellman, 'French "Left-Catholics" and Communism in the Nineteen-Thirties,' *Church History* XXXXV, 4 (Dec. 1976) 1–17. Cardinal Jean Daniélou recalled that in 1937–8, when he was immersed in Marx, the only prominent French Catholic intellectuals who had engaged in a serious study of Marx were Fessard and Moré. Interview with the author, 14 June 1973

49 Cornu himself thought Mounier and the Personalist enterprise intellectually bankrupt. Interview with Robert Hellman, East Berlin 1971

50 '"Les années d'apprentissage de Karl Marx": A propos d'un livre récent,' *Esprit* 31 (Apr. 1935) 19

51 'Vers le matérialisme historique: l'humanisme communiste,' *Esprit* 37 (Oct. 1935) 70

52 Reported in the 'Chronique des amis d'*Esprit*,' *Esprit* 40 (Jan. 1936) 664

53 'La pensée de Marx et nous,' *Esprit*, 40 (Jan. 1936), 567–8. One thinker whom Moré particularly recommended was Max Scheler, whose analyses of community, as we have seen, had been so important in the articulation of *Esprit*'s 'communitarian personalism.' The future Pope John Paul II also studied Scheler on community.

54 The young Jesuit Jean Daniélou was an exception. Cf. his *Mémoires* 85.

55 Review of Souvarine, *Staline*, in *Esprit* 40 (Jan. 1936) 645–53

56 Daniélou, *Mémoires* 77

57 *Esprit* 31 (Apr. 1935) 90
58 'Les cinq étapes d'Esprit' (1945), in *Bulletin des amis d'Emmanuel Mounier* XXIX (Mar. 1967) 10–14
59 'Tentation du communisme' (Mar. 1934), *Œuvres* I, 231
60 In this line of reasoning Mounier assumed that Marx had formulated a 'philosophy of man.' 'Manifeste au service du personnalisme,' in *Œuvres* I, translated by St John's Abbey as *Personalist Manifesto* (New York 1938) 52–3
61 Letter to Guy Malengrau, 24 Oct. 1936, in *Œuvres* IV, 600
62 *Personalist Manifesto* 63
63 *Esprit* 5 (Mar. 1936) 6. These mimeographed *Journaux intérieurs*, most of which remain in the Bibliothèque E. Mounier, are an important record of the central doctrines of personalism until the war. *Esprit* was more pluralistic in what it published.
64 *Personalist Manifesto* 52–3
65 Marie-François (pseudonym of Maurice Laudrain), 'Vers un marxisme catholique,' *Terre Nouvelle* VIII (Jan. 1936) 12
66 'Réflexions d'un étudiant catholique,' *Terre Nouvelle* II (June 1935) 8
67 'Réflexions d'un étudiant protestant,' *ibid.* 8–9. Paul Ricœur later became Mounier's philosophical heir at *Esprit* and one of France's most prominent philosophers. He became active at *Esprit* after the war and at this writing lives in the personalist community at Châtenay-Malabry and remains a militant Christian socialist/communist.
68 'Croix-faucille-marteau,' *Terre Nouvelle* III (July 1935) 17
69 Marcel Dupont, 'Pour vaincre sans violence,' *Terre Nouvelle* XIII (May 1936) 12
70 *Terre Nouvelle* claimed a circulation of 10,000 in the fall of 1935 ('En Avant,' *Terre Nouvelle* V [Oct. 1935] 3), a figure three or four times that of *Esprit*. But *Terre Nouvelle* was proscribed by the Roman Catholic church in the summer of 1936 (see below 113–14), and thereafter declined in influence among Catholics.
71 See above 196.
72 'Chrétiens et révolutionnaires,' *Esprit* 33 (June 1935) 423–4
73 After its condemnation, *Terre Nouvelle* printed some bitter criticism of Pius XI's 'fascist sympathies' and continued undaunted. Its 'spirituality' and some of its properly theological reflections are remarkably similar to those of certain Catholic theologians since the Second Vatican Council. Also, like the 'anti-theologians' in the Jansenist community at Port-Royal, the *Terre Nouvelle* group seems to have been 'as pious as angels and as proud as devils.'
74 See José Streel, *Les Jeunes Gens et la politique* (Brussels 1932).

75 Robert Brasillach, *Léon Degrelle et l'avenir de Rex* (Paris 1936) 19, 21
76 See Pierre-Marie Dioudonnat, *Je suis partout, 1930–1944* (Paris 1973) 143–7.
77 Elie Baussart, 'Libérons le spirituel,' *Esprit* 41 (Feb. 1936) 699
78 J. Parfait, 'Troisième Force et Jeunesse Belge,' *ibid.* 787–91
79 Cf. André Ulmann, 'Chronique politique,' *Esprit* 39 (Dec. 1935) 473.
80 Max Liebe, 'Hendrik de Man's Arbeitsplan'; H.N., 'Die Presse in Belgien,' *Deutsch-Französische Monatshefte* iv–v (1936) 161–4, 165–7
81 See Mounier, 'L'Après-Guerre: Tableau des Responsabilités (introductory pages), *Esprit* 34 (July 1935). N.D.L.R., 'Encore de la révision des traités,' *Esprit* 42 (Mar. 1936) 1000–3
82 'Manifeste pour la Justice et la Paix,' *Esprit* 38 (Nov. 1935) 306–8
83 Cf. H.D., '... Italie prolétaire et fasciste!' *Esprit* 39 (Dec. 1935) 493; C.G. Paulding, 'Sur les Italiens,' *Esprit* 44 (May 1936) 236–8; Henri Davenson (Marrou), 'Pour l'honneur national,' *ibid.* 260–3.
84 See Aldo Dami, 'Sur la mort des traités,' *Esprit* 34 (July 1935) 501–49.
85 'Adresse des vivants à quelques survivants,' *Esprit* 43 (Apr. 1936) 2–16
86 'Amis d'*Esprit*, plébiscitez la paix,' *Esprit* 44 (May 1936) 259–60
87 'Adresse des vivants,' *Esprit* 43 (Apr. 1936) 2, 8, 15, 16
88 Aldo Dami, 'Election?,' *Esprit* 43 (Apr. 1936) 29–34
89 'Our revolution,' Mounier continued, 'will be profoundly other.' 'Les deux grandeurs,' *Esprit* 44 (May 1936) 152
90 Cf. Mounier, 'Infiltration sentimentale?,' *Esprit* 34 (July 1935) 633–4; André Ulmann, 'Lettre à un camarade de province sur le Front populaire,' *ibid.* 635–9; 'L'émeute contre la révolution,' *Esprit* 33 (June 1935) 460–2; 'Chronique politique,' *Esprit* 40 (Jan. 1936) 636–42.
91 Mounier's presentation to 'Le Congrès international des écrivains pour la défense de la culture,' *Esprit* 35–6 (Aug.–Sept. 1935) 793–8, set off the personalist view of man from the Marxist. Mounier and Jacques Madaule joined Ulmann and Maritain in contributing to the early issues of the review *Vendredi* but, as *Esprit* pointed out, this review was expected to be 'neither Right nor Left.'
    Two articles could be considered exceptions to the general *Esprit* 'line' on the Popular Front before the elections. Roger Labrousse seemed to raise the possibility of personalist participation in, or sympathy for, the Popular Front in an article in which he asked for a clear definition of *Esprit*'s 'revolutionary non-conformism' ('Panorama de l'hérésie révolutionnaire,' *Esprit* 40 [Jan. 1936] 588–91), as did André Philip's note, 'Et après?' (*Esprit* 43 [Apr. 1936] 35–8). Two political historians of the review entitled their analysis of *Esprit* in this period 'Critical Adhesion to the Popular Front' (Michel Winock) and 'The Fear of the Popular Front' (Pierre de Senarclens)

respectively. M. de Senarclens, in this instance, provides much more documentation.

92 'Esprit 1936,' *Esprit* 40 (Jan. 1936)

93 François Perroux, 'La personne ouvrière et le droit du travail,' *Esprit* 42 (Mar. 1936) 881

94 *Œuvres de Maurice Thorez*, t. 11 (Paris, 1950–6) 215–16

95 See the issues of the important Popular Front review *Vendredi* in this period.

96 See, for example, Abbé Desgranges, *Journal d'un prêtre député, 1936–1940* (Paris, Geneva 1960) 27; Jean Guiraud, 'La Révolution dévore ses pères,' *La Croix*, 22 Apr. 1936; A.M., 'Les élections législatives du 26 avril manifestent une importante poussée communiste,' *La Croix*, 28 Apr. 1936.

97 This was even the interpretation of many politically moderate Catholics, including Christian Democrats in the Chamber of Deputies. See Degranges, *Journal* 23, 41, 125–6.

98 On the electoral fortunes of the left-wing Christian Democrats in 1935 see R. William Rauch, Jr, *Politics and Belief in Contemporary France* (The Hague 1972) 176–7.

99 See Rauch, *Politics* 172–4.

100 See the interview with Martin-Chauffier by Hubert Forestier, 'Catholiques et communistes: Notre enquête au Quartier Latin,' *Sept* 109 (27 Mar. 1936) 14, and Martin-Chauffier's *Catholicisme et Rébellion* (Paris 1936). Martin-Chauffier had been a member of the literary committee of Jean Luchaire's *Notre Temps*, but strongly disapproved of continuing the Sohlbergkreis initiatives after Hitler came to power in early 1933. His career illustrates once again, as in the case of Drieu la Rochelle, how an interest in early national socialism coincided with an interest in Christian Marxism. Martin-Chauffier later became a prominent Resistance author and, with Mounier, a proponent of Christian-Marxist dialogue after the war.

101 *Terre Nouvelle*, 11 (Apr. 1936)

102 Mounier led the attack against *Terre Nouvelle* in *Esprit*. He also sympathetically described Paul Nizan's violent criticism of that review. 'Entretiens IX,' 3 July 1936, *Œuvres* IV, 596–7

103 Maritain to Mounier, 30 Dec. 1935, in *Maritain/Mounier* 138.
  The abbé Journet later became a cardinal and an influential theologian considered the spokesman of Jacques Maritain's ideas at the Second Vatican Council. Letter from C.G. Paulding to Mounier, 'January,' 1936, unpublished

104 'Lignes de positions: Chrétiens et incroyants' (detachable pages), *Esprit* 41 (Feb. 1936) 1–12

105 Cf. Roger Leenhardt, 'Panorama de l'hérésie révolutionnaire,' *Esprit* 40

(Jan. 1936) 583–91; André Philip, 'Et Après?,' *Esprit* 43 (Apr. 1936) 35–8.

106 Victor Serge, 'L'impasse Saint-Barnabé,' *Esprit* 43 (Apr. 1936) 68–84; *Esprit*, 44 (May 1936) 178–98

107 See Mounier's review of Pierre-Henri Simon, *Les Catholiques, la politique et l'argent* in *Esprit* 44 (May 1936) 225–8.

108 Maritain to Mounier, 23 May 1936, *Maritain/Mounier* 146–7

109 'Carnets, IX,' 30 May, 9 June 1936, unpublished

110 *Ibid.*, unpublished

111 'Rassemblement Populaire,' *Esprit* 45 (June 1936) 441–9

112 *Journal Intérieur des groupes d'amis d'Esprit* 89 (June–July 1936) 6

113 'Extraits du rapport privé sur "Esprit" à l'usage de Mgr Courbe et de l'Archevêque de Paris,' *Œuvres* IV, 592–4

114 'Entretiens IX,' 9 June 1936, unpublished

115 Respecting the constitutional tradition, the socialist leader allowed a delay until the expiration of the mandate of the preceding chamber before taking the reins of government.

116 On 5 June, the 'red archbishop' of Paris, Cardinal Verdier, summoned French Catholics 'to turn, immediately and courageously, to the construction of the new order which all desire.' Pastoral letter to the archdiocese of Paris, 5 June 1936, reprinted in *Documentation Catholique* XXXV, 800 (13 June 1936) 1492. The editor of *La Croix*, Father Merklen, thought that after the solidarity of the Christian trade unions with the strikes and Verdier's appeal, 'the true visage of the Church has finally been manifested in the working class milieu where it has been misunderstood for seventy years' and he predicted that 'the Catholic Church and Christian society will emerge revivified and renewed from the experience.' Léon Merklen, 'Où en sommes-nous?' *La Croix*, 18 June 1936

117 'Carnets IX,' 11 June 1936, unpublished

118 Reprinted in J. Brugerette, *Le Prêtre français et la société contemporaine* III (Paris 1938) 678

119 'Journal de l'Allemagne,' edited and reprinted in Denis de Rougemont, *Journal d'une époque, 1926–1946* (Paris 1968), 320. The relevant book of Mounier's *Journal* has been lost since his death. This is unfortunate, as he always kept vivid descriptive records of his trips and I have never found any other published allusion to this trip to Germany.

120 'Entretiens IX,' 3 July 1936, *Œuvres*, IV, 596–7

121 For more on the Didier salon and 'Jeune Europe' see J. Gérard-Libois and José Gotovitch, *L'An 40: La Belgique occupée* (Brussels 1971), 44–7.

122 'Un programme des Revendications des Jeunes dans l'Ordre international,'

Sohlbergkreis, 7 (Apr. 1935); *Esprit* 41 (Feb. 1936) 791; 'Tentation,' *Jeune Europe* 3 (1936). This article is not included in the complete bibliography of Mounier's writings in *Œuvres* IV, but may be found in the folder Documents sur *Esprit* (1936) in the Bibliothèque E. Mounier.

123 'Rencontre de Jeunesse,' *Esprit* 46 (July 1936) 631

124 F.L., 'Le Groupe Esprit de Bruxelles et la politique internationale,' *L'Avant Garde*, 6 May 1936

125 It is curious that the personalist argument, if accurately reported here, was close to the personalism of *Ordre Nouveau*, against which *Esprit* had worked out its 'personnalisme communautaire.'

126 'Le camp international de Zoute,' *L'Avant-Garde*, 16 July 1936. Nowhere else have I found any reference to these discussions. They were not reported in *Esprit* or the *Journal Intérieur* of the *Esprit* groups.

127 Cf. Charles Micaud, *The French Right and Nazi Germany* (New York 1972) 85–106.

128 Letter to Madame Guittet, 15 Aug. 1936, *Œuvres* IV, 597

129 'Notre Manifeste,' *Esprit* 49 (Oct. 1936) 4

130 Cf. 'Manifeste au service du Personnalisme' in *Œuvres* I, 513.

131 For a discussion of these developments in a larger context see Jacques Delperrie de Bayac, *Histoire du Front Populaire* 99–244. M. Delperrie de Bayac cites interesting sections of his interview with René Belin. Georges Lefranc also had ties with *Jeune Europe* and the 'Didier salon.'

132 Victor Serge, 'Choses de Russie' (notes), *Esprit* 47–8 (Sept. 1936) 700–3

133 The writer Charles Plisnier, of the Belgian *Esprit* group, had joined Magdeleine Paz in bringing up the 'Serge affair' at the Congress for the Defence of Culture, chaired by André Gide, in June 1935 – after which Gide successfully intervened for Serge.
      In many respects, this testimony recalled that of Alexandre Solzhenitsyn forty years later when the French Left was reunited for the first time since 1936.

134 Z.V. Pesis, 'Fascism and the french Intelligentsia: Notes on the *Esprit* Group,' *International Literature* 8 (Aug. 1935) 54–71

135 The *Action Française* linked *Esprit* with *L'Aube* and *Sept* in Oct. 1935, and then with *Terre Nouvelle* and *Vendredi* in July 1936. Cf. A.F., 'Ni réaction, ni révolution,' *Action Française*, 2 Oct. 1935; 'Et après "Terre Nouvelle",' *Action Française*, 26 July 1936.

136 'L'Internationale de la haine,' *Le Figaro*, 25 July 1936. Albert Lebrun, President of the French Republic, also warned Blum of the danger of civil war in France at this time. Cf. Delperrie de Bayac, *Front Populaire* 284.

137 Mounier, 'Espagne, signe de contradiction,' *Esprit* 49 (Oct. 1936) 1–3

138 On the autonomy of national *Esprit* groups see 'Bref historique des groupes "Esprit" en Suisse,' *Esprit* 61 (Oct. 1937) 133.

139 The prominent Catholic Ossorio Y. Gallardo to Brussels and the 'socialist personalist' Fernando de Los Rios to Washington. *Journal Intérieur* 11 (Dec. 1936) 7

140 J.M. Semprun y Gurrea, 'Un programme de reconstruction des Amis d'*Esprit* en Espagne,' *Esprit* 52 (Jan. 1937) 595–601

141 'La Question de l'Espagne inconnue,' *Esprit* 50 (Nov. 1936) 291–319; (Alfred Mendzibal Vilalba), 'Double Refus,' *ibid.* 320–3

142 Cf. 'Terre Libre,' *ibid.* 286–90. Mounier to Chevalier, 24 Oct. 1936, *Œuvres* IV, 597–8; Maritain to Mounier, 17 Nov. 1936, *Maritain/Mounier* 155–7

143 Notably Georges Bernanos, Maritain, Mauriac, the Christian democratic daily *L'Aube*, and most essayists in *Sept*

144 Mounier to Chevalier, 24 Oct. 1936, *Œuvres* IV, 597–8

145 René Belin, 'Du côté de la CGT,' *Esprit* 54 (Mar. 1937) 871–80; Paul Vignaux, 'Du côté du syndicalisme chrétien,' *ibid.* 881–92

146 'Introduction,' *ibid.* 865–70

147 Her letter is cited extensively in Simone Pétrement, *La Vie de Simone Weil* II (Paris 1973) 124–9.

148 Mounier, review of Victor Serge, *Destin d'une révolution*, *Esprit* 54 (Mar. 1937) 991

149 G. Fédotov, 'La Stalinocratie,' *Esprit* 56 (May 1937) 243

150 'Le destin spirituel du mouvement ouvrier: Anarchie et personnalisme,' *Esprit* 55 (Apr. 1937) 109–206. On its composition, see Mounier's letter to E.A . Niklaus, *Œuvres* IV, 618.

151 Mounier's review of *Itinéraire spirituel* by Jean Lacroix in *Esprit* 56 (May 1937) 306. Conspicuously absent is any reference to the young German Hegelian anarchist Max Stirner.

152 Jean Lacroix, *Itinéraire spirituel* (Paris 1937) 158

153 Michel Winock, *Histoire politique de la revue 'Esprit', 1930–1950* (Paris 1975) 100

154 'Guernica ou la technique du mensonge,' *Esprit* 57 (June 1937) 449–73

155 'L'Espagne victorieuse de soi,' *Esprit* 57 (June 1937) 497–501

156 This at least was Jacques Maritain's impression in reading the issue. Maritain to Mounier (July 1937), *Maritain/Mounier* 157–8

157 Chevalier cited its paragraph 20. Chevalier to Mounier, 25 May 1937, unpublished

158 Mounier to Chevalier, 26 May 1937, *Œuvres* IV, 605

159 Maritain to Mounier, July 1937, *Maritain/Mounier* 158

160 Mounier to Maritain, 8 July 1937, *Maritain/Mounier* 158–9

161 'N.D.L.R.,' *Esprit* 65 (Feb. 1938) 680

162 'Sur l'Espagne,' *Esprit* 67 (Apr. 1938) 153–7

163 J.M. Semprun y Gurrea, 'Lettre ouverte à Emmanuel Mounier et aux Amis d'*Esprit*,' *Esprit* 68 (May 1938) 235–43; Mounier to Semprun, *ibid.* 243–51

164 Cf. 'Notre action,' *Esprit* 73 (Oct. 1938) 40–1.

165 Francis Bertin, *L'Europe de Hitler* I (Paris 1976) 142

166 According to the bulletin of *Communauté*. Cited in J. Gérard-Libois and José Gotovitch, *L'An 40: La Belgique occupée* (Brussels 1971) 45, 474

167 Cf. Raymond de Becker, 'Les tendances des jeunes intellectuels français,' *La Cité chrétienne* (20 Nov. 1936) 44; 'Une conférence E. Mounier,' *Le Soir* (Brussels), 30 Jan. 1936

168 All these groups had also attended the Italian corporatism congress together. Cf. Raymond Millet, 'Jeunes Français et jeunes Italiens,' *Le Temps*, 30 June 1935.

169 Raymond de Becker, *Le Livre des vivants et des morts* (Brussels 1942) 197, 199, 219; 'Die Entwicklung des Nationalen Bewusstseins in Belgien,' *Deutsch-Französische Monatshefte/Cahiers Franco-Allemands* 8–9 (1936) 311–17

170 André Falk, 'Un camp des jeunes à Winkelmoos,' *Monatshefte* I (1937) 26. Remember that Emile Hambresin had worked with de Becker at *L'Avant Garde* and, as a Belgian collaborator of *Esprit* contributed to Mounier's review essays critical of extant corporatism. Vercruysse was an alumnus of de Becker's *Esprit Nouveau* group. Dr Liebe was Otto Abetz's man in Brussels.

171 *Monatshefte* II (1937) 78–9; 'Henri Nicaise,' *Esprit* 86 (Nov.–Dec. 1939) 109. Nicaise died in 1939.

172 De Becker, *Livre des vivants* 203, 207, 209

173 Mounier to Guy Malengrau, 24 Oct. 1936, *Œuvres* IV, 599–600

174 Mounier to Malengrau, 24 Oct. 1936, unpublished section

175 'Manifeste au service du personnalisme,' *Indépendance belge*, 21 Jan. 1937

176 *Livre des vivants* 166

177 'Was ist der Personalismus?', *Monatshefte* XI (1936). This essay should be added to the Mounier bibliography in *Œuvres* IV.

178 Martin Hieronimi et Hugo Rheiner, 'Der Personalismus, eine Geistige Ernuerungsbewegung in Frankreich,' *Monatshefte* II (1937) 58–63

179 'Aber was ich vor allem aus dieser Zweisprache festhalten will, das ist, dass zwischen den verschiedenen europäischen Jugenden ein gemeinsamer Bereich besteht, das mir mindestens ebenson bedeutend erscheint wie unsere Verschiedenheiten,' *Monatshefte* III–IV (1937) 120

180 Commentary on 'Les Cahiers Franco-Allemands' (Mar.), in *Esprit* 59 (May 1937) 299–300.

181 Cf. Bertin, *L'Europe* 149–50.
182 R. Piron, 'L'élection du 11 avril à Bruxelles,' *Esprit* 56 (May 1937) 340–3
183 'Chronique des amis d'*Esprit*,' *Esprit* 58 (July 1937) 654; *Journal Intérieur* xx (Nov. 1937) 9
184 *Journal Intérieur, Mensuel des Groupes Esprit de Belgique* 1 (Dec. 1937) (mimeographed); *Journal Intérieur* [France] xxi (Dec. 1937) 11
185 Max Liebe, 'Belgischer Sozialismus?' *Monatshefte* v (1937) 152–4
186 R. Piron, 'Lettre de Belgique,' *Esprit* 64 (Jan. 1938) 641–5
187 *Journal intérieur belge* 3 (Feb. 1938) (mimeographed); 'Revue des revues,' *Esprit* 65 (Feb. 1938) 745–6
188 Gérard-Libois, *L'An 40* 474; *Journal intérieur belge* 5–6 (Apr.–May 1938)
189 *Journal intérieur belge* (Feb. 1938); 'Revue des revues,' *Esprit* 65 (Feb. 1938)
190 *Journal intérieur belge* 4 (Mar. 1938)
191 Ivo Rens and Michel Brelaz, 'Préface,' Henri de Man, *Au delà du Marxisme* (Paris 1974) 14
192 '"Esprit" et l'Action Politique,' *Esprit* 73 (Oct. 1938) 54, 58–9
193 Mounier to Guy Malengrau, 14 Nov. 1938, unpublished. For example, according to de Becker, Maritain, disturbed about his Nazi sympathies, would not see him after 1937 (*Livre des vivants*, 161); Alexandre Marc recalls breaking with de Becker after the latter's involvement with Spaak. Interview with the author, 7 Aug. 1973
194 'Où va la Belgique?' *Esprit* 75 (Dec. 1938) 471–6
195 *Terre Wallonne*, a formally Catholic review, fused with *Esprit* in the spring of 1938. Beaussart sent the review's subscription lists to *Esprit*. Mounier to Madame Hélin, 'January' 1938, 'January' 1939, unpublished; *Journal intérieur belge* (Apr.–May 1938); Gérard-Libois, *L'An 40* 65; de Becker, *Livre des vivants* 229
196 Otto Abetz, *Histoire d'une politique franco-allemande, 1930–1950* (Paris 1953) 105; Bertin, *L'Europe* 153; Léon Degrelle, *La Cohue de 1940* (Lausanne 1949) 176
197 Gérard-Libois, *L'An 40* 46
198 Rens and Brelaz, 'Préface' 14
199 Bertin, *L'Europe*, 154; Gérard-Libois, *L'An 40*, 48
200 Mounier to Mlle Martineggi, 25 Oct. 1936, unpublished. François Perroux and classics professor Jacques Perret worked to spread *Esprit*'s influence in Brazil. Cf. Winock, *Histoire 'Politique'* 136. In Montréal the prominent journalist and publisher Claude Hurtubise was trying to found a 'groupe des amis d'*Esprit*' in early 1937. *Journal Intérieur* xiv (Apr. 1937) 8 *Journal Intérieur* vi–vii (Apr.–May 1936) 3
201 'Notre Action: Clubs de Presse,' *Esprit* 53 (Feb. 1937), 789–801.
202 Cf. *Journal Intérieur* xi (Dec. 1936) 2–3.

203 *Journal Intérieur* x (Oct. 1936) 5–6; *Journal Intérieur* xi (Dec. 1936) 2
204 'Chronique des amis d'*Esprit*,' *Esprit* 54 (Mar. 1937) 1007–8
205 *Journal Intérieur* xvi (June 1937) 8; 'Le Théâtre des "Quatre-Saisons",'
  Esprit 58 (July 1937) 627–31. During the Vichy period Barbier received
  government support for a similar program when he was director of
  Jeune France.
206 Cf. 'Chronique des amis *d'Esprit*,' *Esprit* 54 (Mar. 1937) 1007–8; François
  Perroux, 'Questionnaire sur l'Etat,' *Journal Intérieur* xviii (July 1937) 3–7
207 'Chronique des amis d'*Esprit*,' *Esprit* 55 (Apr. 1937) 216
208 Roger Labrousse, 'Front Populaire, An ii,' *Esprit* 58 (July 1937) 636
209 Roger Leenhardt, 'Le vin nouveau et les vieilles outres,' *Esprit* 54 (Mar.
  1937) 983, 986
210 *Journal Intérieur* xviii (July 1937) 2
211 'Programme pour quelques années,' *Esprit* 60 (Sept. 1937) 690
212 This 'strictly private' notice appeared on the masthead for the first time
  on number 18 (Aug.–Sept. 1937). 'Le Congrès Esprit 1937,' *Esprit* 60 (Sept.
  1937) 823
213 Cf. *Journal Intérieur* xii (Dec. 1937) 7. Mounier commended that 'alert discipline' observed by the *Esprit* groups of Geneva, Lausanne, Neuchâtel,
  and Berne when their members met him in Geneva on his arrival.
214 'Le Congrès Esprit 1937,' *Esprit* 60 (Sept. 1937) 824
215 'Programme pour quelques années,' *ibid.* 694, 696
216 The complete list included, in Paris: Berdyaev, François Berge, Bergamin,
  Charles Blondel, Duveau, Iswolsky, Madaule, Lacombe, Maritain, Merleau-
  Ponty, Mendzibal, Moré, Mounier, Touchard, Vignaux. Correspondents
  out of Paris: Borne, Chastaing, Ellul, Gandillac, Jean Grenier, Abbé
  Journet, Lacroix, Lefrancq (circular letter, Oct. 1937, unpublished; letter to
  Jean Gosset, 29 Oct. 1937, in *Œuvres* iv, 607).
217 'Pierre Teilhard de Chardin: "La crise présente. Réflexions d'un natura-
  liste",' *Esprit* 63 (Dec. 1937) 459
218 The study group included 'Charles Blondel, Reinach, Labrousse, Maxime
  Leroy, Duveau, Laurat, Schorderet, Philip.' Maxime Leroy, a distinguished
  historian of ideas, had recently become interested in *Esprit*.
219 *Journal Intérieur* xx (Nov. 1937) 4; *Journal Intérieur* xviii (Aug.–Sept.
  1937) 5
220 *Journal Intérieur* xxi (Dec. 1937) 4, 6
221 Mounier to Jean Gosset, 29 Oct. 1937, unpublished; *Journal Intérieur* xxi
  (Dec. 1937) 2 On Merleau-Ponty see Barry Cooper, *Merleau-Ponty and
  Marxism; From Terror to Reform* (Toronto 1980).
222 Recollections of Alexandre Marc (7 Aug. 1973); Jacques Ellul to the

author (30 Jan. 1976); 'Chronique des amis d'*Esprit*,' *Esprit* 55 (Apr. 1937) 216

223 'Le Congrès Esprit 1937,' *Esprit* 60 (Dec. 1937) 824; *Journal Intérieur* XXII (Jan. 1938) 1–3, 6

224 Jacques Ellul to the author, 30 Jan. 1976

225 *Journal Intérieur* XXIV (Mar. 1938) 6

226 *Journal Intérieur* XVIII (Aug.–Sept. 1937) 5

227 *Journal Intérieur* XXII (Jan. 1938) 5

228 Dautry was singled out for praise in the *Cahiers Franco-Allemands* for promoting contact between French and German youth. The dynamic Jardin later held responsible positions in the Vichy government. He was recently portrayed in *La bête à bon Dieu* (Paris 1980) the fourth book consecrated to him by his novelist son, Pascal. Daniel Villey, 'Les "Nouveaux Cahiers",' *Esprit* 65 (Feb. 1938)

229 'La situation du socialisme,' *Esprit* 61 (Oct. 1937), 122–6

230 *Journal Intérieur* XVIII (Aug.–Sept. 1937) 1

231 Jacques Perret, *Journal Intérieur* XXI (Dec. 1937) 11

232 *Journal Intérieur* XXIV (Mar. 1938) 5. Humeau was also connected with Trotskyists and the *Révolution prolétarienne* element of the CGT.

233 *Journal Intérieur* XXIV (Mar. 1938) 5

234 Roger Gal, 'L'évolution syndicale.' *Esprit* 65 (Feb. 1938) 788. In Feb. 1938 Mounier asked Izard for an essay on the 'uselessness of parties.' Mounier to Izard, 3 Feb. 1938, unpublished

235 Cf. Mounier's review of *Bataille de la France*, *Esprit* 76 (Jan. 1939) 621–2.

236 They were reported in the 'private and confidential' *Journal Intérieur* and not the 'Chronique' in *Esprit*, where even Oprecht's visit was kept quiet.

237 *Journal Intérieur* XXIII (Feb. 1938) 1

238 Cf. the report of the group in Grasse in *ibid.*

239 'Chronique des groupes français,' *Esprit* 67 (Apr. 1938) 158–60

240 'Et maintenant?,' *Esprit* 66 (Mar. 1938) 803–4

241 Noël Régis, 'Bilan économique du Front Populaire,' *ibid.* 827; Jacques Madaule, 'Bilan et avenir politique et parlementaire,' *ibid.* 855; Bernard Serampuy, 'Vers de nouvelles valeurs françaises?,' *ibid.* 921–37

242 'Bilan spirituel: Court traité de la mythique de Gauche,' *ibid.* 873–920 in *Œuvres* IV, 40–75

CHAPTER SEVEN: 'ESPRIT' AND THE ONSLAUGHT OF HITLER

1 Otto Abetz, 'A la recherche de l'Occident,' *Sohlbergkreis* 4–5 (Jan.–Feb. 1935) 117

2 Cf. *ibid.*, and Hugo Rheiner, 'Das Germanentum und der Untergang des Abendlandes' 6 (Mar. 1935) 208–9

3 This thesis is developed very well in Francis Bertin, *L'Europe de Hitler* I (Paris 1976)

4 Mounier review of 'Le service social et la communauté' by G. Braun, Karlsruhe, in *Esprit* 51 (Dec. 1936) 474

5 Mounier, 'Revue des revues,' *Esprit* 56 (May 1937) 299–300

6 Pierre Cherny, 'Jeunesse française en Allemagne,' *Sohlbergkreis* 1–2 (Oct.–Nov. 1934) 39–40

7 'Französischer Frontkampfführer spricht zu H-J Führern,' Sohlbergkreis 4–5 (Jan.–Feb. 1935) 123. Cf. romantic photograph of Savoyard peasant woman inserted in *Sohlbergkreis* 6 (Mar. 1935) np. Cf. Henning Schlottmann, 'Deutsch-Französischer Akademikerbund,' *Sohlbergkreis* 8–9 (May–June 1935) 244–5

8 'Plus de querelle d'Allemand,' *Deutsch-Französische Monatshefte* II (1937) 79. The chateau of Uriage became an important institution for personalism under Vichy.

9 François Berge, 'Les Germains en France,' *Monatshefte*, VI (1937), 199. Berge, who was involved in an *Esprit* study group in Paris, also strongly criticized the anti-Semitism of *Mein Kampf*. Cf. François Berge, 'Bilan de l'ethnologie: Le problème des races,' *Esprit* 64 (Jan. 1938) 536

10 Raymond Millet, *Le Communisme ou quoi?* (brochure, nd) 101

11 Paul Distelbarth, *Neues Werden in Frankreich* (Stuttgart 1938) 180–3; 'Massstab unseres Handelns,' *ibid.* 183–90

12 Distelbarth reintroduced himself to Mounier after the war. Distelbarth to Mounier, 8 Nov. 1947, unpublished

13 It remains in the Bibliothèque E. Mounier at Châtenay-Malabry.

14 'Au sujet du socialisme/Eine Aussprache über den Sozialismus,' *Sohlbergkreis*, 8–9 (May/June 1935), 237–43

15 Cf. 'Auberges de la jeunesse'; Yves Arvestour, 'Qu'est-ce que la centralisation hitlérienne?', *A nous la liberté*, I 2, 3 (Mar. 1937). The second issue urged young Frenchmen to meet young Germans through the Auberges de la jeunesse program and sympathetically described the efforts of Frick, German minister of the interior, to decentralize the internal administration of his country along federalist lines, 'on the basis of ethnic, linguistic, and cultural realities.'

16 Cf. Joseph Rovan, *Le Catholicisme politique en Allemagne* (Paris 1956) 234–5.

17 Cf. René Dupuis, 'Les gouvernements totalitaires,' *Ordre Nouveau* 40 (1 May 1937) 1–22.

18 A group of German Catholics (anonymous), 'Mémoire sur la situation des catholiques dans le troisième Reich,' *Esprit* 58 (July 1937) 593–609

19 Review of A. de Chateaubriant, *La Gerbe de Forces* in *Esprit* 59 (Aug. 1937) 687–8

20 *Journal Intérieur* XXI (Dec. 1937) 2. I found no other reference to this report.

21 Review of *La Gerbe de Forces* 688

22 Philippe Wolf, 'Problèmes autrichiens,' *Esprit* 30 (Mar. 1935) 1004–19; 'Dernières cartouches,' *Esprit* 67 (Apr. 1938) 1–4

23 Aldo Dami, *Esprit* 67 (Apr. 1938) 25–50

24 Jacques Madaule, 'L'Europe et la France au carrefour,' *ibid.* 5–24

25 'Dernières cartouches,' *ibid.* 4

26 François Perroux, 'Limites et dépassement de la notion de classe, *Esprit* 68 (May 1938) 161–80

27 Mounier, *Journal Intérieur* XXVI (June 1938) 1; 'Situation de la France,' *Esprit* 70 (July 1938) 469, 471

28 Paul Vignaux, 'Réflexions sur les relations du travail,' *Esprit* 70 (July 1938) 474–87; Claude Le blond [Blondel], 'Le Droit et la grève,' *ibid.* 488–99. Georges Lefranc, 'La CGT et l'arbitrage,' *ibid.* 526–34; François Perroux, 'Notes pour l'emploi de textes à tout faire,' *ibid.* 535–41. Cf. E.M., 'Grève et arbitrage,' *ibid.* 472–3

29 H. Thomas, 'L'arbitrage et le tarif forcé dans l'Allemagne weimarienne,' *ibid.* 521–5

30 *Journal Intérieur* XXVII (July 1938) 7

31 See *ibid.* 7, and François Goguel, 'La Flèche, le Frontisme,' *Esprit* 72 (Sept. 1938) 736, 738, 740, 742–6.

32 *Journal Intérieur* XXVII (July 1938) 10

33 Mounier, '*Esprit* et l'Action Politique,' *Esprit* 73 (Oct. 1938) 39, 42, 49, 54–5

34 Cf. 'Le Voltigeur Français,' *ibid.* 65–6.

35 'Revue des revues,' *Esprit* 72 (Sept. 1938) 752. As if to demonstrate this, Denis de Rougemont referred to 'hopeful signs' from the young Right such as Thierry Maulnier's rejection of Anti-Semitism. *Esprit* signalled Maulnier's joining Denis de Rougemont at *Ordre Nouveau, ibid.* 747, 750

36 Mounier to E.A. Niklaus, 1 Oct. 1938, *Œuvres* IV, 621; 'Enquête sur les partis,' *Esprit* 73 (Oct. 1938) 104–6

37 Roger Labrousse, 'Le tournant tchécoslovaque,' *Esprit* 67 (Apr. 1938) 149–52; 'Autour de la négociation franco-italienne,' *Esprit* 68 (May 1938) 303

38 Editor's note, 'La guerre pour la Tchécoslovaquie?'; Madaule, 'Nous jouons la paix,' *Esprit* 69 (June 1938) 422, 427. Essays by Edith Bricon and Dami in the same issue supported this view.

39 'Comment le fascisme vient aux nations,' *Esprit* 72 (Sept. 1938) 645–51
40 'Revue des revues,' *ibid.* 749; 'Des monts des sudètes aux Pyrénées,' *ibid.* 781–5
41 Cf. Adrien Miatlev, 'Par delà la guerre et la paix,' *Esprit* 73 (Oct. 1938) 16–19; Max-Pol Fouchet, 'La guerre n'est pas la mobilisation,' *ibid.* 27–8; Brice Parain, 'Campagne,' *ibid.*, 27–8; Georges Bonnefoy, *ibid.* 30–1. Jacques Lefrancq, 'A mes amis,' *ibid.* 19–27
42 Daniel Villey, 'L'honneur qui se moque de l'honneur,' *ibid.* 31–3; Jean Lacroix, 'L'inacceptable dilemme,' *ibid.* 134–8
43 Review of André Fribourg, *La victoire des vaincus, ibid.* 139
44 'Lendemains d'une trahison,' *ibid.* 1, 10
45 Cf. Geneviève Vallette and Jacques Bouillon, *Munich 1938* (Paris 1964) 154–6
46 'Lendemains d'une trahison,' *Esprit* 73 (Oct. 1938) 13–14
47 *Ibid.* 15
48 Maritain to Mounier, 30 Sept. 1938, in *Maritain/Mounier, 1929–1939*, ed. Jacques Petit (Paris 1973) 163
49 Cf. Mounier to Maurice de Gandillac, 10 Oct. 1938. This letter – 'to a friend' in *Œuvres* IV, 621–2 – is incorrectly described as 'to E.A. Niklaus' in Michel Winock, *Histoire politique de la revue 'Esprit,' 1930–1950* (Paris 1975) 184. This is an important error, as the letter reveals the moderate tone of the disagreement between Mounier and M. de Gandillac, when the latter's pacifism was denounced as *lâche* by Georges Bernanos. See Winock, *Histoire politique*, 180.
50 *Esprit*, 74 (Nov. 1938) 295–9; *ibid.* 299–301
51 Mounier, 'L'Europe contre les hégémonies,' reprinted in *Œuvres* IV, 201, 204, 206–207; 'Essai d'une politique française,' *Esprit* 74 (Nov. 1938) 166–79; Jacques Madaule, 'Il faut passer à l'acte' *ibid.* 289–93
52 Cf. Vallette and Bouillon, *Munich* 199.
53 'Autour de la Flèche,' *Esprit* 74 (Nov. 1938) 311–19
54 Schumann's firm anti-Nazi stand in the 10 Oct. *Vie intellectuelle* was noted in 'Revue des revues,' *ibid.* 279. J.-M. Semprun de Gurrea, 'Sens et contresens de l'honneur,' *ibid.* 303–6
55 *Journal Intérieur* xxx (Dec. 1938) 3–4
56 Hélène Iswolsky, *Light before Dusk: A Russian Catholic in France, 1923–1941* (New York 1942) 200–1
57 '26–27 novembre,' *Esprit* 77 (Feb. 1939) 780
58 'Appel à un rassemblement pour une démocratie personnaliste,' *Esprit* 75 (Dec. 1938) 425–6, 429, 431
59 Jacques Madaule, 'Le préfascisme français,' *ibid.* 342; François Perroux,

'Intelligence de la nation,' *ibid.* 353, 355; P.-H. Simon, 'Equivoque de l'anti-parlementarisme,' *ibid.* 401; Jean Lacroix, 'D'une méthode de penser,' *ibid.* 437

60 'Les deux sources du préfascisme,' *ibid.* 324

61 Eg, 'Revue des revues,' *Esprit* 76 (Jan. 1939) where an article by Hans Geschke in *Geist der Zeit* (Dec. 1937) is noted. Geschke admired Denis de Rougemont's conception of man but faulted personalist understanding of 'Blutsverwandtschaften' and 'Schicksalsgemeinschaften.'

62 'Responsabilités de la pensée chrétienne,' in *Œuvres* III (Paris 1963) 593. For the circumstances in which this essay was composed see E.M. to Paulette Mounier, 16 Nov. 1939, *Œuvres* IV, 647.

63 *Ibid.*

64 Most of Mounier's generation whom I interviewed thought this book of key importance for French Catholic thought before the war.

65 American writer Flannery O'Connor borrowed this phrase from Teilhard, whom she admired, for the title of a collection of her short stories. But she also admired the very different Simone Weil.

66 I use 'metahistorical' in the sense in which it was employed by the late Christopher Dawson.

67 Cf. the documentaries on the conditions of women and workers in the Third Reich in *Vie intellectuelle* (25 Dec. 1938, 10 Jan. 1939) by François Perroux and Robert Pitrou, mentioned in *Esprit*, 77 (Feb. 1939) 761. Cf. Mounier's comments on the incorporation of Czechoslovakia into the Reich. 'Le jouer à terme,' *Esprit* 79 (Apr. 1939) 1–2

68 'Pogroms 1938,' *Esprit* 76 (Jan. 1939) 1–2

69 He published his views in the *Nouveaux Cahiers* but they were cited in *Esprit*. 'Revue des revues,' *Esprit* 80 (May 1939) 301

70 Vignaux's denunciation of French pacifism was published in *Vie intellec-tuelle* (25 Mar.) and recorded in *Esprit, ibid.* 302.

71 Cf. his essay *Pacifistes ou Bellicistes?* (Paris 1939), in *Œuvres* I, 837.

72 'Péguy, prophète du temporel,' *Esprit* 77 (Feb. 1939) 631.

73 'Essai d'une politique française,' *Esprit* 74 (Nov. 1938) 166–79; 'Réflexions sur la crise ou petit traité de tactique,' *Esprit* 76 (Jan. 1939) 523, 548; 'Les grandes puissances et la poussée vers l'Est,' *ibid.* 549–70; 'L'Italie et nous,' *ibid.* 617–20

74 'L'Europe contre les hégémonies,' *Esprit* 74 (Nov. 1938) 867

75 Cf. Mounier to Jacques Lefrancq, 16 Mar. 1939, *Œuvres* IV, 629; Mounier's review of Robert Aron, *La fin de l'après-guerre* in *Esprit* 79 (Apr. 1939), 151.

76 Letter to Edith Bricon, 13 May 1939, in *Œuvres* IV, 630. For a more detailed treatment of *Esprit*'s position see Pierre de Senarclens, *Le mouvement 'Es-*

prit,' 1932–1941 (Lausanne 1974) 221–5. This perspective was not necessarily or self-consciously personalist and so is not of central concern here.

77 Mounier to 'some collaborators,' 8 June 1939, *Œuvres* IV, 630. Those invited were Charles Blondel, Georges Duveau, Paul Fraisse, Edouard Frick, François Goguel, Jean Gosset, de Guneberg, Isambert, V. Jahier, Ionesco, Landsberg, Leenhardt, J. Madaule, Brice Parain, François Perroux, J. Reinach, J.B. Rivain, de Semprun, Spoulberg, P.-A. Touchard, and Paul Vignaux.

78 Mounier, 'Le problème dit "idéologique",' *Esprit* 83 (Aug. 1939) 661; Jacques Delperrie de Bayac, *Histoire du Front Populaire* (Paris 1972) 459

79 'Le problème politique,' *Esprit* 83 (Aug. 1939) 692

80 'Conditions de paix pour l'été,' *ibid.* 687–92

81 *La Flèche* published as many as 60,000 copies; Claude Estier, *La Gauche hebdomadaire, 1914–1962* (Paris 1962) 262. Recollections of historian Henry Ehrmann, who visited their offices.

82 Jean Maze, 'Autour de la Flèche,' *Esprit* 74 (Nov. 1938) 311–17

83 Cf. Mounier's warm review of J.P. Maxence, *Histoire de dix ans, Esprit* 79 (Apr. 1939) 129. Maxence was literature critic of *Gringoire* and a prominent figure of the 'Young Right.'

84 'Journal des groupes,' *Journal Intérieur* XXIV (Nov. 1938) 5. He also lauded the effort of *Ordre Nouveau*'s Joseph Voyant and Boutet, in Lyon, in publishing *Fédération française* to bring together the personalist groups.

85 'Victoire de la paix ou trahison,' *Politique* (Oct. 1938)

86 'Revue des revues,' *Esprit* 80 (May 1939) 302–3, included extensive citations of Beuve-Méry's article in the April *Politique*.

87 Cf. Vallette and Bouillon, *Munich 1938* 295, 298.

88 Other contributors included *Esprit* supporter Robert Delavignette, head of the Ecole Nationale d'Outre-Mer, whose 'progressive' view of the French Empire (cf. his *Les vrais chefs d'empire* [Paris 1939]) appeared in the Collection Esprit with books by Perroux and Gabriel Marcel. Also the planist Robert Lacoste of the CGT, Léo Lagrange, Brice Parain, and the conservative anti-Hitlerites Pertinax and Henri de Kerillis. Special issue: 'Eléments d'une génération,' *Courrier de Paris et de la province* (20 July 1939)

89 Préhistoire de la "troisième France",' *Courrier de Paris et de la province, ibid.* 30

90 Letter to Dr Vincent, 15 Aug. 1939, in *Œuvres* IV, 632

91 Eg, Georges Lefranc, 'La CGT et le problème de la représentation,' *Esprit* 78 (Mar. 1939) 810–30; letter from Lefranc, *ibid.* 931; editor's note, *ibid.* 933–4.

92 'Appel à un rassemblement pour une démocratie personnaliste,' *Esprit* 75 (Dec. 1938) 426–9, 432

93 'Quelques conclusions,' *Esprit* 78 (Mar. 1939) 878

94 *Capitalisme et communauté de travail* (Paris 1938); 'La représentation comme fiction et comme nécessité,' *Esprit* 78 (Mar. 1939) 808–9

95 'Quelques conclusions,' *ibid.* 876–7; 'Lignes de structures d'un pouvoir politique,' *ibid.* 886

96 *Journal Intérieur* XXI (Dec. 1937) 4. André Philip analysed the SFIO, Jean Lacroix the Radical party, Jacques Madaule Christian Democracy. *Journal Intérieur* XXIX (Nov. 1938) 2

97 Mounier to Edith Bricon, 13 May 1939, *Œuvres* IV, 630

98 Cf. 'Le Parti Socialiste,' *Esprit* 80 (May 1939) 203; Raymond Millet, 'Notes sur les partis modérés,' *ibid.* 207–8

99 See *Esprit* 84 (Sept. 1939)

100 'Fondation des "Groupes Esprit" de Paris,' *Esprit* 76 (Jan. 1939) 622–3

101 *Journal Intérieur* XXXI (Jan. 1939) 8; XXXIV (May 1939)

102 Cf. *Journal Intérieur* XXXII (Mar. 1939) 2, 8.

103 *Le Voltigeur* had only 900 subscribers, 400 of whom already subscribed to *Esprit. Journal Intérieur* XXXI, 3

104 Cf. Mounier to Maritain, Jan. 1939, in *Maritain/Mounier* 167.

105 'Pour une maison Esprit,' *Esprit* 77 (Feb. 1939) 784. Jean-Marie Soutou became the other member of the community.

106 *Journal Intérieur* XXXV (June 1939). Mounier himself had very little money at the time.

107 'Une nouvelle réalisation *Esprit,' Esprit* 81 (June 1939) 414–18

108 'The régime of Salazar is the one for which I have the most sympathy: it is the régime which tries to free the human personality. It is the contrary to a totalitarian régime. It is a régime of authority. It is the model Christian state.' Michel Liais, 'En écoutant M. Gonzague de Reynold, l'auteur de l'Europe tragique,' *Je suis partout*, 8 May 1937, cited in Dioudonnat, *Je suis partout, 1930–1944* (Paris 1973) 150

109 After the war, Roger Garaudy accused Mounier of having been a supporter of Salazar, but Mounier's only comment on the Portuguese régime that I have been able to find is an apparently sympathetic brief note written under the peculiar conditions of the Vichy period. Mounier, 'Pour une charte de l'unité française,' *Esprit* 103 (Aug. 1941) 691

Perroux had more right-wing connections than any other prominent contributor to *Esprit*. He even contributed to the French 'fascist' review *Je suis partout*'s analysis of the failure of the Popular Front. Dioudonnat, *Je suis partout* 150

110 Cf. letter to Paulette Mounier, 4 Sept. 1939, in *Œuvres*, IV, 633.

111 See his novel *Siegfried et le Limousin*, in which a young amnesic living in

Germany is unaltered in his deep affection for German culture after the discovery that, in fact, he is French. *Pleins pouvoirs* (Paris 1939) 31–101

112 Alfred Fabre-Luce, *Vingt-cinq années de liberté*, I, *Le grand jeu 1936–1939* (Paris 1942) 167

113 See *Pleins pouvoirs*, 66, where Giraudoux laments the effect of 'des centaines de milles askenasis, échappés des ghettos polonais ou roumains.'

Julien Reinach, 'Du code de la famille à la nomination de M. Giraudoux,' *Esprit* 84 (Sept. 1939) 793–5. Reinach later tried to secure a post for Mounier in Giraudoux's office.

114 Mounier to Jacques Lefrancq, 6 Sept. 1939, *Œuvres* IV, 635

115 Letter to Paulette Mounier, 23 Sept. 1939, *Œuvres* IV, 639; letter to Paul Fraisse, 28 Oct. 1939, unpublished

116 Letter to Paulette Mounier, 9 Sept. 1939, *Œuvres* IV, 636

117 Letter to Jacques Lefrancq, 10 Sept. 1939, *Œuvres* IV, 637

118 Letter to Paulette Mounier, 31 Oct. 1939, *Œuvres* IV, 644. This was a problem for this entire generation of intellectuals in France. It was a veritable agony for devout Catholics.

119 Cf. Jean Lacroix, *et al.*, 'Journal des témoins de guerre,' *Esprit* 86 (Nov.–Dec. 1939) 73–9.

120 'Un mois qui a transformé le monde,' *Esprit* 85 (Oct. 1939) 23

121 'Par tous les temps,' *ibid.* 5–6

122 'Journal des témoins de temps de guerre,' *Esprit* 86 (Nov.–Dec. 1939) 73–9

123 Landsberg, 'Réflexions pour une philosophie de la guerre et de la paix (suite et fin),' *Esprit*, 86–87 (Nov.–Dec. 1939) 54; Touchard, 'Les buts de la guerre,' *ibid.* 33–6

124 Mounier to Berdyaev, 11 Nov. 1939, unpublished. Also in *Œuvres* IV, 646, with the date 13 Nov. 1939; Mounier to Berdyaev, 16 Nov. 1939, unpublished. The same letter is in *Œuvres* IV, 649 dated 26 Nov.

125 Emmanuel to Paulette Mounier, 20 Nov. 1939, *Œuvres* IV, 648; Mounier to Paul Fraisse, 24 Nov. 1939, *ibid.* 648

126 Mounier to Jacques Lefrancq, 7 Oct. 1939, *Œuvres* IV, 642

127 Mounier to Paul Fraisse, 5 Dec. 1939, unpublished. Most of this letter, dated 3 Dec., is in *Œuvres* IV, 649–50.

128 Mounier to Paul Fraisse, 8 Dec. 1939, unpublished

129 Cf. letter to E.-A. Niklaus, 14 Dec. 1939, *Œuvres* IV, 651. Mounier made a special trip to Paris in this effort to join Giraudoux. His friend Reinach told him that he would be named to the information ministry in a matter of days. Mounier to Paul Fraisse, 19 Feb. 1940, unpublished. But in early

March he still had no news. Mounier to Jéromine Martineggi, 3 Mar. 1940, unpublished

130 Mounier to Paul Fraisse, 8 Mar. 1940, unpublished
131 Cf. *Journal Intérieur* XXXVII (Jan. 1940) 4.
132 'Gardons-nous de notre ennemi l'Ennemi,' *Esprit* 88 (Jan. 1940) 119
133 Mounier to Paul Fraisse, 5 Dec. 1940, unpublished
134 Cf. *Esprit* 88 (Jan. 1940) 103. A social/psychological study of alpinism in this period should be done. It was an important factor in the mentality of some personalists.
135 Francisque Gay, 'Pour une anthologie de la misère spirituelle: Une page de M.P.-Aimé Touchard,' *L'Aube*, 18 Jan. 1940
136 Letter to Francisque Gay, 25 Jan. 1940, unpublished
137 Letter to Etienne Borne, 8 Feb. 1940, unpublished
138 Letter to Francisque Gay, 9 Feb. 1940, *Œuvres*, IV, 655–6
139 'Des deux Allemagnes aux deux traités,' *Esprit* 89 (Feb. 1940) 219
140 'Radio-reportage,' *ibid.* 332–3. See Maurice de Gandillac, 'Aimer comme une brute,' *Esprit* 89, 335–6.
141 'Lettre de rédaction,' I, 1 (30 Jan. 1940); 2 (25 Apr. 1940), unpublished
142 Mounier to Berdyaev, 30 Jan. 1940, unpublished; Mounier to Berdyaev, 18 Feb. 1940, unpublished
143 Cf. 'A la recherche de l'Europe,' *Esprit* 91 (Apr. 1940) 1–3.
144 Karl Barth, 'Lettre aux protestants de la France,' *ibid.* 73–80. Along the same lines as Barth see the essays of Landsberg and Berdyaev in the Jan. 1940 *Esprit*.
   For example Mounier, 'Personnalisme catholique' (fin), *ibid.* 66
145 'Lettre de rédaction,' I, 1, 30 Jan. 1940, unpublished, 4–5
146 See Yves Simon, *La grande crise de la République* (Montréal 1942) 192–3. Interviews with various Catholic intellectuals also substantiated this resentment.
147 In *L'Emancipation nationale*, 4 Oct. 1938, cited in Paul Serant, *Le Romantisme fasciste* (Paris 1959) 155
148 *Ibid.* 164, 166
149 P. Drieu la Rochelle, 'L'explication du coup,' *Esprit* 90 (Mar. 1940) 413–14. For Mounier's review see *Esprit* 91 (Apr. 1940) 87–90
150 'A nos lecteurs,' *Esprit* 89 (Feb. 1940) 335–6
151 Mounier to Paul Fraisse, 25 Feb. 1940, *Œuvres* IV, 658
152 Mounier to Paul Fraisse, 15 Mar. 1940, unpublished. This article was later published by *Esprit* in the context of Vichy's national revolution. *Esprit* 95 (Dec. 1940) 18–30

153 'Sur le décombre du communisme,' *Esprit* 90 (Mar. 1940) 428–30
154 Cf. Maxime Chastaing, 'Témoins de guerre (lettre des armées),' *ibid.*
425–8; Jacques Sthenel, 'La fin de la guerre,' *ibid.* 410–12.
155 'Pour un examen de conscience,' *ibid.* 337–45
156 Mounier to Jéromine Martineggi, 5 May 1940, unpublished
157 'Lettre de rédaction,' I, 2 (25 Apr. 1940)
158 Cf. Valois, *Prométhée vainqueur* (Paris 1940) 126; *Nouvel Age*, 7 Mar. 1940,
cited in Yves Guchet, *Georges Valois* (Paris 1975), 239.
159 Mounier review of *Gilles*, *Esprit* 91 (Apr. 1940) 90
160 Mounier, 'Nous autres Français,' *ibid.* 110–11
161 But Maxence's essay was lost. Editor's note, *Esprit* 92 (June 1940), 213.
162 'Changer les hommes; changer les méthodes' (éditorial), *ibid.* 213, 215–16
163 *Ibid.* 217; 'Bilan de notre socialisme.' *ibid.* 231–4
164 'Pour une paix totale,' *ibid.* 225–30; La France et les Européens,' *ibid.*
224
165 'L'Allemagne et l'Europe,' *ibid.* 241–51
166 'Prière pour nos ennemis,' *ibid.* 237–40
167 'Autour d'une trahison,' *ibid.* 262

CHAPTER EIGHT: PERSONALISM IN POWER

1 Touchard to Mounier, 29 May 1940, 31 May 1940, unpublished
2 Mounier to Touchard, 4 June 1940, unpublished
3 Mounier to Chevalier, 5 June 1940, unpublished
4 *La France nouvelle: Appels et messages*, 17 juin 1940–17 juin 1941
(Montrouge 1941) 20
5 The appeal of 26 June 1940 is cited in Edouard Bonnefous, *Histoire politique de la Troisième République* VII (Paris 1967) 299.
6 This phrase was borrowed from Ordre Nouveau by German foreign minister Joachim von Ribbentrop who, like the wartime German ambassador in Paris, Otto Abetz, was a regular reader of French reviews. It was utilized in Nazi propaganda. Denis de Rougemont, *Politique de la Personne* (Paris 1946) 8
7 Emmanuel to Paulette Mounier, 19 June 1940, in *Œuvres* IV (Paris 1963) 664
8 Mounier to Touchard, 4 July 1940 and 6 July 1940, unpublished
9 'D'une France à l'autre,' *Esprit* 94 (Nov. 1940) 7
10 Francis Bertin, *L'Europe de Hitler* (Paris 1976) 155
11 Cited in Ivo Rens and Michel Brelas, preface to Henri de Man, *Au delà du Marxisme* (Paris 1974) 14
12 Henri Pirenne, *Dossier du roi Léopold III: Livre blanc* (Brussels 1970); Els de

Bens, 'La presse au temps de l'occupation de la Belgique (1940–1944),'
Revue d'Histoire de la Deuxième Guerre Mondiale (Oct. 1970) 15

13 J. Gérard-Libois, and José Gotovitch, *L'An 40: la Belgique occupée* (Brussels
1971) 47; Bertin, *L'Europe, ibid.*

14 *Ibid.* 158–63; Raymond de Becker, *Livre des vivants et des morts* (Brussels
1942) 89; Gérard-Libois, *L'an 40* 468–73

15 Léon Degrelle, *La cohue de 1940* (Lausanne 1949) 388; Peter Dodge, *Beyond
Marxism: The Faith and Works of Hendrik de Man* (The Hague 1966) 209

16 Cf. T.J. Knight, 'Belgium Leaves the War, 1940,' *Journal of Modern History*
XLI, 1 (Mar. 1969) 62–3.

17 Robert Paxton, *La France de Vichy* (Paris 1973) 56–7

18 See the statements reprinted in Jacques Marteaux, *L'Eglise de France devant
la révolution marxiste,* I (Paris 1958), 478–515. The many statements of the
episcopacy in favour of the National Revolution are remarkably similar to
those few enthusiastic episcopal exhortations to Catholics to support the
Popular Front in June and July 1936. See *ibid.* 252–69.

19 'La France en cellule,' quoted in *ibid.* 459–550.

20 As Olivier Wormser noticed at the time. See Olivier Wormser, *Les ori-
gines doctrinales de la 'Révolution Nationale'* (Paris 1971). Indeed, one historian
of political thought has suggested that 'Vichy is much more understandable in
'terms of themes developed in the small reviews of the thirties than in terms
of the themes developed by movements of the traditional Right.' Raoul
Girardet, quoted in Jean-Louis Loubet del Bayle, *Les non-conformistes des
années 30* (Paris 1969) 405

21 Mounier to Touchard, 12, 22, 23 July 1940; Mounier to Edmond Humeau,
24 July 1940, unpublished; *Entretiens* x, 4, 20 Aug. 1940, in *Œuvres* IV (Paris
1963) 668–9

22 Paxton, *Vichy* 160

23 Jacques Duquesne, *Les Catholiques français sous l'occupation* (Paris 1966), 200.
According to Robert Paxton, Chantiers de la Jeunesse was the only Vichy
youth organization that touched an important number of adolescents but,
he said, they devoted much of their time to making charcoal. *Vichy* 163

24 *Un an de Révolution Nationale, juin 1940–juillet 1941* (Lyon 1941) 52

25 Cf. Duquesne, *Les Catholiques* 67, 197–200.

26 Quoted in Etienne Borne, *De Marc Sangnier à Marc Coquelin* (Toulouse
1953) 97

27 *Ibid.* 83

28 Duquesne, *Les Catholiques* 201

29 *Un an de Révolution Nationale* 53

30 Quoted in Duquesne, *Les Catholiques* 203

31 Quoted in Paxton, *Vichy* 160
32 André Deroo, *L'épiscopat français dans la mêlée de son temps, 1930–1954* (Paris 1955) 83–5. For the fate of Catholic youth organizations during the Nazi régime, see Guenter Lewy, *The Catholic Church and Nazi Germany* (New York 1964) 116–33.
33 Loubet del Bayle, *Les non-conformistes* 410–11; Duquesne, *Les Catholiques* 205
34 *Gouvernement de Vichy* 289; Duquesne, *Les Catholiques* 205; R. William Rauch, Jr, *Politics and Belief in Contemporary France* (The Hague 1972) 219; and 'Entretiens x' (10 Aug. 1940), *Œuvres* IV, 668–70
35 As well as into Catholic parishes from one end of the world to the other
36 According to the Robert Paxton, the German secret service estimated that the Compagnons numbered only 8,000 in Mar. 1941 and only 3,350 in June 1942, *Vichy* 160
37 Letter to Xavier Schorderet, 15 Oct. 1940, *Œuvres* IV, 674
38 'L'éducation nationale' 250
39 'La politique sociale de l'avenir,' *Revue des deux mondes* (15 Sept. 1940) 113, 115–16
40 Message of 11 Oct. 1940 reprinted in David Thomson, ed., *France: Empire and Republic, 1850–1940* (New York 1968) 297–303
41 The speech of 13 Aug. 1940 and 'L'éducation nationale,' by René Gillouin; 'La politique sociale de l'avenir,' and the message of 11 Oct. 1940 by Gaston Bergery. On the fabrication of Pétain's speeches and essays see Robert Aron, *Histoire de Vichy* I (Paris 1954) 286–7; Robert Paxton, *La France de Vichy* (Paris 1973) 142–208; Jean-Louis Loubet del Bayle, *Les non-conformistes des années 30* (Paris 1969), 406–8.
42 H. Dumoulin de Labarthète, *Le temps des illusions* (Geneva 1946) 161
43 Mounier's *Œuvres* IV, 576. Loustau and Gibrat were the contacts between the X-Crise group of the Centre polytechnicien d'Etudes économiques and *Ordre Nouveau*. They joined the Croix de Feu in an effort to convert it to *Ordre Nouveau* ideas but left in frustration in July 1935, taking other young intellectuals such as Pierre Pucheau along with them. Pucheau then founded Travail et Nation, a study group, with the 'neo-socialist' Paul Marion, Louis-Emile Galey, Georges Izard, Loustau, and Gibrat. Pucheau and Marion aided Jacques Doriot to found the Parti Populaire Français in 1936. Loustau was on the comité directeur of the PPF from 1937 to 1938. Loustau, Gibrat, Pucheu, and Marion all had important positions at Vichy. Philippe Rudaux, *Les Croix de Feu et le PSF* (Paris 1957), 129; Edmond Lipiansky, 'L'"Ordre Nouveau" (1930–1938),' in Lipiansky and Bernard Rettenbach, *Ordre et démocratie* (Paris 1967) 76; Paxton, *Vichy* 242; Loubet del Bayle, *Les non-conformistes* 467
44 On the formulation of the Charte du Travail, see Jacques Juillard, 'La

Charte du Travail,' in Fondation Nationale des Sciences politiques, *Le Gouvernement de Vichy, 1940–1942* (Paris 1972) 157–210, and Paul Vignaux, *Traditionalisme et syndicalisme* (New York 1943). Perroux founded *Renaître* to give 'homogeneous and coherent doctrinal interpretation' to the principles of the National Revolution and emphasized the pre-war positions of *Esprit* and *Ordre Nouveau* in this effort. René Belin also had personalist connections before the war and the head of his staff, the historian Georges Lefranc, contributed an essay on syndicalist reform to the last pre-Vichy issue of *Esprit* (June 1940). Loubet del Bayle, *Les non-conformistes* 408–9

45 Robert Aron has suggested that was so in his *Vichy* I, 279.

46 Chevalier's father was an army officer, as was Philippe de Gaulle's, another godson of Pétain.

47 Robert Paxton prefers to call devout Catholics 'traditionalists.' When Pétain tried to counter Laval's pressure in the spring of 1942, he again turned to prominent Catholics. See Paxton, *Vichy* 134.

48 Cf. Karl R. Popper, *Open Society and Its Enemies* (London 1951). Popper argues that to 'see' a direction in history is to invite slavish acceptance of what merely happens to occur.

49 'Entretiens IX,' Aug. 1940, in *Œuvres* IV, 668

50 'Information contre x,' *Marianne*, 1 Aug. 1940. Alexandre Marc, for one, was shocked at the essay. Interview with the author (7 Aug. 1973).

51 Letter to Jéromine Martineggi, 6 Sept. 1940, *Œuvres* IV, 672

52 'Lettre de France,' *Cahiers protestants* (Sept.–Oct. 1940) 423–9

53 'Letter from France,' *The Commonweal*, XXXIII, 1 (25 Oct. 1940) 11

54 Ie, a figurehead who would be pushed aside by more determined 'revolutionaries.' Letter to Edmond Humeau, 24 July 1940, unpublished

55 'Entretiens x,' 26 Aug. 1940, in *Œuvres* IV, 670

56 François Perroux to Mounier, 11 Sept. 1940, unpublished

57 Cf. 'Entretiens x,' 9 Nov. 1940, *Œuvres* IV, 676–7.

58 Letter to Jacques Chevalier, 14 Sept. 1940, unpublished

59 'Entretiens x,' 25 Sept. 1940, cited in Michel Winock, *Histoire politique de la revue 'Esprit,' 1930–1950* (Paris 1975) 212

60 'Entretiens x,' 29 Sept. 1940, *Œuvres* IV, 209

61 'D'une France à l'autre,' *Esprit* 94 (Nov. 1940) 2–3

62 'Entretiens x,' 19, 28 Oct. 1940, in *Œuvres* IV, 675–6

63 Cf. Mounier to Landsberg, 12 Nov. 1940, unpublished. Victor Serge to Mounier, 21 Sept. 1940, unpublished; Delavignette to Mounier, 18 Oct. 1940, unpublished

64 'Entretiens x,' 10 Nov. 1940, *Œuvres* IV, 677

65 Mounier had been invited to the foundation meeting of *Temps nouveaux* on 29 Sept. 'Entretiens x,' 29 Sept. 1940, cited in Winock, *Histoire politique* 211

66 'Entretiens x,' 30 Nov. 1940, *Œuvres* IV, 680. Cf. 'Entretiens x,' 28 Oct. 1940, in *ibid.* 675–6.

67 See Paxton, *Vichy* 96–103.

68 'Entretiens x,' 20 Dec. 1940, *Œuvres* IV, 682–3

69 'Ceci se passait autrefois en des temps plus misérables que ceux d'aujourd'hui, mais plus riches d'espoir' (Pierre Dunoyer de Segonzac, in 1956, recalling the 1940–2 Uriage school). Extract from an article published in *La vie intellectuelle* on the death of Father Maydieu. Reprinted in *Pierre Dunoyer de Segonzac: Le vieux chef. Mémoires et pages choisies* (Paris 1971) 86

70 'L'éducation nationale,' *Revue des deux mondes* 252

71 *Le vieux chef* 80

72 W.R. Rauch, Jr, *Politics and Belief in Contemporary France* (The Hague 1972), 222; *Le vieux chef* 82–3

73 Raymond Josse, 'L'école des cadres d'Uriage (1940–1942),' *Revue d'histoire de la deuxième guerre mondiale*, 61 (Jan. 1966) 55

74 *Le vieux chef* 97–8

75 Gilles Ferry, *Une expérience de formation des chefs* (Paris 1945) 33. On the Ordensburgen in the larger context of the Reich, see W.L. Shirer, *The Rise and Fall of the Third Reich* (New York 1960), 352; David Schoenbaum, *Hitler's Social Revolution* (New York 1966) 269–71, 279, 284.

Professor Schoenbaum minimizes the importance of the Ordensburgen as the source of the Third Reich's élites, but most of the Ordensburgers were still young men when the Reich collapsed. According to H. Höhnen, Heinrich Himmler, whom Hitler often referred to as his 'Ignatius of Loyola,' modeled the ss after the Jesuits. The ss 'Order' had a sort of novitiate and a personal oath of fidelity to Hitler was its ordination rite. (Heinz Hohne, *L'Ordre Noir: Histoire de la SS* [Paris 1968] 95–7) Emmanuel Mounier's former friend, the Belgian personalist Raymond de Becker, who had tried to create the Communauté movement as a secular order with the aid of Mounier and Maritain in 1934 (see above 92–3) was later fascinated by the Ordensburg of Sonthofen:

'J'eus également l'occasion de visiter l'Ordenburg de Sonthofen et de converser avec ses dirigeants. Partout je rencontrai la volonté de créer une nouvelle aristocratie, à base socialiste. Le style en était à la fois purement allemand, en ce qu'il cherchait à continuer la tradition de l'officier prussien, et européen, en ce qu'il s'efforçait de renouer avec l'idéal grec de l'équilibre du corps et de l'esprit.

Je recueillis notamment une impression fort profonde de ma visite à l'Ordenburg de Sonthofen. Cette école de chefs tient à la fois du monastère et de l'académie antique. C'est une puissante et massive construction dotée

d'une tour trapue, du haut de laquelle de vraies cloches de monastère
égrènent calmement le chapelet des heures. Tout, d'ailleurs, y concourt à
renforcer cette impression monastique: nos modernes chevaliers teutoni-
ques s'entendent, comme les anciens moines, à choisir l'endroit où il con-
vient de s'installer; comme eux aussi, ils savent construire en harmonie
avec le paysage et s'intègrent dans les lieux. Le burg domine ainsi un gros
village situé dans la vallée et face auquel se profilent les hauts sommets des
Alpes bavaroises; les bâtiments déjà grandioses mais encore inachevés à
l'époque, sont principalement construits avec des matériaux de la région,
mœllons et bois. A l'intérieur, ce ne sont que longs couloirs sonores, salles
voûtées, dortoirs, chambres de réunions; le tout d'une sobriété austère et
pleine de goût. Plus de 500 élèves y séjournaient alors, ainsi que 150
professeurs à leur service; les constructions définitives devaient abriter une
immense salle de gymnastique ainsi qu'un vaste bassin de natation; dès ce
moment, l'Ordenburg possédait son champ d'aviation et vingt-cinq appa-
reils. La bibliothèque, les salles de jeux, les laboratoires, l'admirable salle de
musique blanc et or étaient tous d'un goût parfait. L'on devine, par l'atmos-
phère des lieux, le genre d'éducation donnée aux jeunes gens qui y sont
reçus. Ceux-ci, dépistés souvent dès l'école par les dirigeants nazis de leur
région, sont entretenus aux frais du parti. Des jeunes gens d'origine ouvrière
et paysanne ont ainsi la possibilité de faire partie de la nouvelle aristocratie du régime s'ils en ont vraiment la capacité. Dans l'éducation qui leur est
donnée, le sport possède une grande importance. Et l'on estime même
que l'éducation sportive ne peut être complète si le milieu physique ne lui
apporte sa collaboration; c'est pourquoi chaque Ordenburg est construit
dans une région dont les caractéristiques géographiques et climatologiques
sont différentes et l'on veillera à faire passer les jeunes gens de l'un à
l'autre afin que leur personnalité physique s'adapte autant au climat et aux
sports de montagne qu'au climat marin et aux sports nautiques, etc. Alors
que l'après-midi est consacrée aux sports, la matinée est occupée par des
conférences et des travaux de séminaire. La formation scientifique y est
particulièrement soignée de façon que chacun puisse posséder des notions
élémentaires de géopolitique et de biologie, d'anthropologie, d'ethnologie
et de raciologie; l'histoire du peuple allemand et de sa culture, l'histoire
des principaux peuples étrangers, l'histoire de l'Art constituent également
des branches importantes de cet enseignement. Vers la troisième année
d'étude, l'élève choisit la branche du parti à laquelle il consacrera son activité
et, dès lors, sa formation théorique alternera avec une occupation pra-
tique dans le parti ou l'Etat; il deviendra ainsi führer à son tour et s'en
retournera dans la masse dont il est issu et où il formera cette aristocratie

nouvelle sur laquelle compte le régime pour durer et mener à bien la révolution totale qu'il a l'ambition de réaliser. Le but même de cet enseignement nous était indiqué par un des chefs de l'Ordenburg dont je viens de parler: "L'Eglise a d'abord voulu soigner les âmes, nous disait-il, l'humanisme de la Renaissance a voulu développer l'Esprit; le matérialisme marxiste s'est préoccupé du corps et du bien-être matériel. Nous, nous voulons faire la synthèse de ces trois préoccupations et former des hommes complets qui soient à la fois des idéalistes désintéressés, des lutteurs âpres au combat, des athlètes vigoureux et des êtres cultivés." Et il ajoutait: "Ici, nous bâtissons le Reich pour plusieurs siècles...".' Raymond de Becker, *Livre des vivants et des morts* (Brussels 1942) 226–8

76 *Le vieux chef* 103. An oath to the leader was a normal practice in 'Orders.' The Jesuit élite made a special vow of obedience to the pope. The ss made a personal oath of fidelity to Hitler.

'Ecole d'Uriage. Projet de formule d'engagement. Projet de règle.' Reprinted in *Le vieux chef* 241–2

77 *Le vieux chef* 103. 'One Christmas evening' is the only date given for Dunoyer de Segonzac's renunciation of his oath. Was it before or after he entered into the Resistance against the Nazis? He never discussed 'resisting' Pétain.

78 Josse, 'L'école des cadres' 56–60

79 *Le vieux chef* 82–3. Beuve-Méry had lost his position at *Le Temps* over his uncompromising opposition to the Munich agreements. He had his revenge after the war when he used the confiscated facilities of *Le Temps* to build *Le Monde* into one of the world's great newspapers.

80 *Le vieux chef*, 93–5. Msgr de Solages later became a prominent Catholic resistor. Père de Lubac contributed to the resistance journal *Témoignage chrétien*.

81 Interview with Jean Lacroix, 2 Aug. 1973. Later when Guitton returned to France he contributed to *Demain*, a review founded to rally French Catholics to the National Revolution. His philosophy courses in a prison camp were markedly Bergsonian. They were published as *Regards sur la pensée française, 1870–1940* (Paris 1968).

82 *Le vieux chef*, 93–5, 85, 102. According to Dunoyer de Segonzac, Pétain seemed to know little about Uriage. Alain-Gérard Slama, one of the few scholars to have been granted access to the Vichy archives, confirms a lack of information on Uriage at Vichy. Interview with the author, 8 July 1974. Hubert Beuve-Méry recalled Uriage's chief contact at Vichy to be a young woman who later became Madame Georges Bidault. Interview with the author, 9 July 1974

83 *Le vieux chef*, 102. Frenay later founded Combat a resistance movement

which until late 1942 professed to act in the name of Pétain. Paxton, *Vichy*, 48–9

Domenach had been a Catholic student leader of right-wing leanings. He later became director of *Esprit*. Dru, like Frenay, became a Resistance hero.

84 *Le vieux chef* 88
85 Msgr Beaussart, co-adjutor of the archbishop of Paris, had interceded in Rome for *Esprit* when condemnation had been threatened in 1936. Bœgner was president of the Fédération protestante de France. Lafont was head of the Scouts.
86 *Le vieux chef* 104
87 Josse, 'L'école des cadres' 60
88 See Rauch, *Politics*, 224 and Pierre Dunoyer de Segonzac, 'Réponse: Le christianisme a-t-il dévirilisé l'homme?' *Jeunesse de l'Eglise* 2 (1943) 78–82.
89 'Entretiens x,' 30 Mar. 1941, in *Œuvres* IV, 699 Beuve-Méry recalled the horror at Uriage over tales of the Ecole des Cadres in the Nazi zone, interview with the author, 9 July 1974.
90 'Aux jeunes Français,' *Esprit* 96 (Jan. 1941) 130–1
91 'Programme pour le mouvement de jeunesse française,' *ibid.* 161–5, 167
92 'Aux jeunes Français,' *ibid.* 129
93 Robert Aron, *The Vichy Régime*, translated by Humprey Hare (London 1958) 267; Dumoulin de Labarthète, *Les temps des illusions* (Geneva 1946) 266; Mounier, letter to George Zérapha, 9 Mar. 1941, *Œuvres* IV, 697
94 *Œuvres* IV, 685
95 'Jeune France,' *Esprit* 97 (Feb. 1941) 261–4; 'Entretiens XII,' 25 Sept. 1941, *Œuvres* IV, 715
96 'L'école nationale des cadres d'Uriage,' *Esprit* 99 (Apr. 1941) 430–1
97 Letter to Etienne Borne, 22 Feb. 1941, *Œuvres* IV, 694. In response to an inquiry from the author as to why he did not explore his differences with Mounier over Vichy in his *Mounier* (Paris 1972), M. Borne replied:

'Je sais bien que les ennemis de Mounier utilisent contre lui ce qui ne fut qu'une brève hésitation dans les tout premiers commencements du régime de Vichy. Je n'ai pas manqué de faire allusion à un désaccord entre lui et moi à ce moment, puisque, et je le dis, je n'ai pas approuvé la parution d'*Esprit* après l'armistice. Divergence mineure et qui n'a pas tardé à s'effacer, puisque de 41 à 44 nous avons l'un et l'autre combattu dans la Résistance.

Aussi je ne vois pas ce que vous voulez dire lorsque vous écrivez: "Les divergences entre lui et vous à cette époque semblent capitales pour bien comprendre les différences entre les traditions personnalistes et démocrates chrétiennes." Croyez bien que je n'ai aucune tentation de majorer l'importance de ce que je peux représenter, mais qui signifie, au contraire de ce que vous dites, un accord en profondeur du personnalisme et de la démocratie chrétienne.' Letter to the author, 14 June 1973

98 'Entretiens XII,' 14 Apr. 1941, *ibid.* 706

99 'Entretiens XI,' 30 Mar. 1941, *ibid.* 700

100 'Entretiens XI,' 18 May 1941, *ibid.* 709

101 'Entretiens XI,' 30 Mar. 1941, *Œuvres* IV, 701

102 Hubert Beuve-Méry, *Réflexions politiques, 1932–1952* (Paris 1951) 128

103 'Entretiens XI,' 30 Mar. 1941, *Ibid.* 701

104 Report to the secretary general of the police, *Œuvres* IV, 747. According to one account, the JFOM's essential activities consisted in shouting slogans like 'à bas de Gaulle' or 'Les Juifs à la porte.' See *Le Gouvernement de Vichy* 279.

105 'Entretiens XII,' 11 Aug. 1941, *ibid.* 712

106 'Entretiens XIII,' 17 Nov. 1941, *ibid.* 718

107 *Esprit*, 102 (July 1941), 647–51. For a balanced assessment of *Esprit*'s 'openly clandestine' criticism of Vichy see Pierre de Senarclens, *Le mouvement "Esprit" 1932–1941* (Lausanne 1974) 290–300.

108 Josse, 'L'école des Cadres' 56, 70

109 'C'est ainsi qu'on en a avec ceux dont on répète du matin au soir les formules.' Mounier to Jéromine Martinaggi, 1 Nov. 1941, unpublished

110 'Entretiens X,' 9 Jan. 1941, in *Œuvres* IV, 687–8; Winock, *Histoire politique* 229

111 Cf. Mounier to Silbermann, 13 Dec. 1940, unpublished; Winock, *Histoire politique* 228.

112 'Réponse de M. Gabriel Marcel,' *Esprit* 97 (Feb. 1941) 238

113 'Entretiens X,' cited in Winock, *Histoire politique* 230

114 'Entretiens X,' 21 Jan. 1941, in *Œuvres* IV, 690

115 'Entretiens X,' 18 May 1941, *ibid.* IV, 21

116 For Mounier's view, see 'Entretiens XI' 4 Apr. 1941, *ibid.* 704

117 'Entretiens XII,' 28 July 1941, *ibid.* 711

118 Loubet del Bayle, *Les non-conformistes* 409; Henri Massis, *Maurras et notre temps* (Paris 1961) 350

119 Letter to Xavier Schorderet, 5 Oct. 1941, *Œuvres* IV, 718

120 *Temps Nouveau*, directed by Stanislas Fumet, was forbidden on the same day as *Esprit*, and for the same official reasons, by Admiral Darlan. *Temps Nouveau* was the wartime version of *Temps Présent*, the journal on which General de Gaulle's friend Henri Daniel-Rops had worked before the war. Gaullist emissaries from London secretly conveyed 'Les amitiés de Charles de Gaulle' to Stanislas Fumet in this period. Jacques Duquesne, *Les Catholiques français* 143

121 'De l'usage du mot catholique' (May 1949), *Œuvres* III (Paris 1962) 653

122 Henri de Man published *Après coup* and *Cahiers de ma montagne* in this period, in which Edouard Didier also lived in La Clusaz.

123 Bertin, *L'Europe* 163; Gérard-Libois, *L'An 40* 47; Rens, preface 15, Jon Braun, interview with the author, 7 Oct. 1980.

124 Bertin, *L'Europe* 164–5

125 See Jacques Fauvet, *Histoire du parti communiste français*, II (Paris 1965) 66. The controversial copies of *L'Humanité* have disappeared from the Bibliothèque Nationale but may be consulted, I am told, in various private libraries of the French Jesuits.

126 See Paxton, *Vichy* 215–16.

127 Cited in *ibid.* 218

128 *Ibid.* 225

129 *Ibid.* 144

130 See *ibid.* 258, and *Gouvernement de Vichy* 275.

131 Pélorson had his own brand of personalism: 'Lorsque je dis unité je ne dis pas seulement union. Je veux dire communion absolue, définitive, dans une seule foi, sous un même drapeau, aux ordres d'un seul chef ... c'est dans la mystique du chef que la personne humaine trouve sa meilleure école et sa plus grande exaltation ....' Cited in *ibid.*, 272

132 See *Gouvernement de Vichy*, 275.

133 Cf. Duquesne, *Les Catholiques*, 200–4.

134 René Rémond, *The Right Wing in France from 1815 to de Gaulle*, trans. James M. Laux (Philadelphia 1966), 318

135 See Jean-Marie Domenach, *Gilbert Dru, celui qui croyait au ciel* (Paris 1947).

136 Bertrand D'Astorg, 'Mémoire,' *Revue des deux mondes*, 326

137 See G.E. Soley, 'General de Gaulle and Participation' (unpublished MA essay, McGill University 1972), and E. Michelet, *Gaullisme, passionante aventure* (Paris 1962). Albert Ollivier, colleague of Mounier at Jeune France, later became political director of the weekly *Rassemblement*, organ of the Rassemblement du Peuple français, created by General de Gaulle in 1949.

CHAPTER NINE: WAR AND TRANSITION 1941–4

1 'Entretiens XII,' (25 Sept. 1941), in *Œuvres* IV (Paris 1963), 716

2 Letter to Henri de Lubac, Dec. 1941, *ibid.* 722

3 See 'Entretiens XIII' (23 Dec. 1941), *ibid.* 722–3.

4 *Ibid.* 725–6, and 'Journal d'un acte fragile,' *Esprit* 174 (Dec. 1950) 731–75

5 'Journal d'un acte fragile,' *Esprit* 174 (Dec. 1950) 744

6 Jacques Duquesne, *Les Catholiques Français sous l'occupation* (Paris 1966) 144–5

7 Letter to Robert Schmidt, 9 Nov. 1942, and 'Journal de Dieulefit,' 6 June 1944, Œuvres IV, 766, 792
8 Traité du caractère (Paris 1946), re-edited as Œuvres II (Paris 1962)
9 Henri Marrou's term for L'affrontement chrétien (Neuchâtel 1945), Œuvres III (Paris 1962) 7–66
10 L'affrontement chrétien in Œuvres III, 32, 11, 10
11 Ibid. 34, 36
12 Ibid. 35–6
13 Ibid. 39, 33
14 Traité du caractère, in Œuvres II, 336–65, 562
15 L'affrontement chrétien, Œuvres III, 20
16 Ibid. 38
17 Ibid. 12
18 Mounier's conviction that only an 'anti-bourgeois,' anti-capitalist Christian spirituality could appeal to the working classes was shared by the abbés Godin and Daniel, who saw the hope for the re-Christianization of France through the conversion of the élites of factory workers to a Christian spirituality stressing adherence, in a new community spirit, to the Mystical Body of Christ. Since the late 1930s Godin had been seeking a middle way between 'prolétarisation générale' and 'embourgeoisement général à l'américaine.' Godin was enthusiastic about Vichy's social and economic initiatives, which he analysed in his book La Charte du Travail (Paris 1943). Godin, with Jesuits such as fathers Desbuquois and Dillard, had a vision of a new 'revolutionary Christianity of the future, transcending bourgeois Christianity,' which they effectively instilled in the new worker priest movements created during the war. The Mission de Paris, under the patronage of Cardinal Suhard, Archbishop of Paris, was an organization of missionaries to the working classes which was 'inspired by the theological movement, which had severed itself from the religious individualism that dominated Catholic thought.' The Mission de Paris generated such fervour among its missionaries that during the winter of 1943–4 they felt they were living through a 'new Pentecost.'

The worker priests, during and after the war, drew special inspiration from the communalistic theorizing during the Vichy period of the Esprit group's François Perroux and Jacques Madaule, Gustave Thibon, and Father Henri Desroches. New forms of communal life, such as the 'communautés de base,' were to be the key to a new Christian spirituality, and a new Christianity. See Emile Poulat, Naissance des prêtres-ouvriers (Paris 1969) 48–9, 67–74, 95–6, 322–8, 429.
19 Ibid. 32

20 *Ibid.* 11
21 I owe the term to Avery Dulles, sj.
22 'Fixiste' is employed by Jean Onimus to distinguish metaphysical, ahistorical Christians from Christians with more sensitivity to and faith in modern historical progress: *Pierre Teilhard de Chardin* (Paris 1963) 38.
23 *L'affrontement chrétien, Œuvres* III, 22
24 *Ibid.* 21, 24
25 *Ibid.* 22, 24
26 *Ibid.* 66
27 Eg, it was the first essay published by the American Catholic review *Cross Currents*, founded in 1950, which introduced much modern European religious thought to North America. It was an essay which particularly touched the young Pierre Elliott Trudeau (conversation with the author).
28 *L'affrontement chrétien, Œuvres* III, 11

CHAPTER TEN: A MARXIST REFORMATION OF CHRISTIANITY 1944–8

1 In 1940–1, Mounier had noted the tendency of Christian Democrats to opt for the Resistance. See above 170, 173, 180.
2 Many Vichy 'technocrats' remained firmly in place at the Liberation, while the 'traditionalists' were purged. See Robert Paxton, *La France de Vichy* (Paris 1973) 309–52.
3 The granting of the vote to women was also an important factor. 'We will build the MRP with women and curés,' said Bidault. See William Rauch, Jr, *Politics and Belief in Contemporary France* (The Hague 1972) 244–8. Rauch outlines the influence of Mounier's personalism on the post-war MRP as does Etienne Borne in *De Marc Sangnier à Marc Coquelin* (Toulouse 1953).
4 'Les cinq étapes d'*Esprit*,' *Bulletin des amis d'Emmanuel Mounier*' XXIX (Mar. 1967) 22
5 'Esprit, nouvelle série' (éditorial), *Esprit* 105 (Dec. 1944)
6 To between 15,000 and 19,000 in 1964. See Rauch, *Politics* 305
7 'Esprit '40–'41,' *Esprit* 106 (Jan. 1945) 303–4
8 'Qu'est-ce que le Personnalisme?' in *Œuvres* III, 242
9 In contrast to Christian Democrats such as Jacques Maritain and Etienne Gilson, who had taught in, and seen good qualities in, the United States
10 *Bulletin des amis d'Emmanuel Mounier* VII–VIII (Dec. 1955) 35, 58–9
11 See Pierre Dunoyer de Segonzac, *Le Vieux Chef* (Paris 1971) 13: 'Les Américains constituent un véritable danger pour la France. C'est un danger bien différent de celui dont nous menace l'Allemagne ou dont pourraient éventuellement nous menacer les Russes. Il est d'ordre économique et d'ordre

moral. Les Américains peuvent nous empêcher de faire une révolution nécessaire et leur matérialisme n'a même pas la grandeur tragique du matérialisme des totalitaires. S'ils conservent un véritable culte pour l'idée de liberté,
ils n'éprouvent pas un instant le besoin de se libérer d'un capitalisme plus
important chez eux qu'ailleurs. Il semble que l'abus du bien-être ait diminué
chez eux la puissance vitale de façon inquiétante.' Dunoyer de Segonzac,
Mémoires, c1943

12 'L'homme américain,' *Esprit* 127 (Nov. 1946) 739–40
13 On the Charter of the resistance see Henri Michel, *Les Courants de pensée de la
Résistance* (Paris 1965) 400–5.
14 'Qu'est-ce que le Personnalisme?', in *Œuvres* III (Paris 1962) 226
15 'L'agonie du Christianisme,' *ibid.* 542
16 'Les mauvaises raisons,' *Esprit* 108 (Mar. 1945) 619
17 See Rauch, *Politics* 256, 294–5, 328–32.
18 'Le casse-cou occidental,' *Esprit* 115 (Nov. 1945) 10
19 'L'ordre règne-t-il à Varsovie?' *Esprit* 123 (June 1946) 97–103
20 'Qu'est-ce que le Personnalisme?', in *Œuvres* III, 208
21 *Ibid.* 227
22 *Ibid.* 211, 212
23 *Ibid.* 212
24 *Ibid.* 214
25 *Ibid.* 236, 231, 233
26 See Rauch, *Politics* 257.
27 'Qu'est-ce que le Personnalisme?', *Œuvres* III, 216–17
28 *Ibid.* 221–2
29 *Ibid.* 224
30 'Réponse à une enquête,' in *Œuvres* III, 618
31 Especially in 'La petite peur du XXe siècle,' in *Œuvres* III, 216–17
32 *Ibid.* 154
33 *Ibid.* 368–9
34 *Ibid.* 375
35 *Ibid.* 393
36 *Ibid.* 396
37 *Ibid.* 391–2
38 *Ibid.* 400–1
39 *Ibid.* 403, 416
40 *Ibid.* 420
41 The old mimeographed, privately circulated, essays of Teilhard remain in
the Bibliothèque Emmanuel Mounier, Châtenay-Malabry, France. *Œuvres* III,
402

42 *Ibid.* 419
43 *Ibid.* 425
44 Mounier thought that his wife's nerves were at the breaking point in this period. Letter to Paul Fraisse, 5 Sept. 1945, unpublished correspondence, Folio I, Bibliothèque E. Mounier.
45 'Les cinq étapes,' *Bulletin* XXIX, 22
46 'A nos lecteurs,' *Esprit* 110 (May 1945) 920
47 See David Caute, *Communism and the French Intellectuals* (New York 1964) 164.
48 'Le discours de clôture de Maurice Thorez à la Conférence Nationale du Parti Communiste Français (Montreuil, 10 avril 1949),' *L'Humanité*, 12 Apr. 1949
49 As we have seen, this glorification of the young Marx had been introduced into *Esprit* by Marcel Moré in 1935. See above 102–3. This seems to be another instance of Mounier half-digesting and then popularizing the insights of an *Esprit* colleague. Nicolas Berdyaev's personalist critique of Marxism before the war seems clearer and more tightly reasoned than anything by Mounier. It called for a humanist socialism. For example, see Berdyaev's essay 'Personne humaine et marxisme,' in François Mauriac *et al., Le Communisme et les chrétiens* (Paris 1937) 178–202.
50 David Caute, *Communism* 212

CHAPTER ELEVEN: A NEW DISORDER 1948–50

1 'Petkov et nous' (Sept. 1947), in *Œuvres* IV (Paris 1963) 613–15
2 'Prague' (Feb. 1948), in *ibid.* 154
3 See Roger Garaudy, 'Lettre à Emmanuel Mounier, homme d'"*Esprit,*' *La Nouvelle Critique,* pamphlet, 1950; Jean Desanti, 'Scrupules et ruses d'Emmanuel Mounier,' *La Nouvelle Critique* 9 (Oct. 1949) 56–70; Jean Kanapa, 'Gendarmes et sirènes ou violences et ruses des Versaillais,' *La Nouvelle Critique* 12 (Jan. 1940) 19–41; Victor Leduc, '*Esprit* et une certaine manière de tromper le peuple,' *Cahiers du Communisme* 12 (Jan. 1950) 112–14.
4 R. William Rauch, Jr, *Politics and Belief in Contemporary France* (The Hague 1972) 245
5 See *ibid.* 287
6 See 'Le dossier de la quinzaine. Un Centre d'Etudes: Economie et Humanisme,' *Informations catholiques internationales* 67 (1 Mar. 1958); Jean-Louis Loubet del Bayle, *Les non-conformistes des années 30* (Paris 1969) 420; Emile Poulat, *Naissance des prêtres ouvriers* (Paris 1965) 415–16, 525, 420; Jacques Duquesne, *Les catholiques français sous l'occupation* (Paris 1966) 393–4.

7 On the Chrétiens Progressistes and Mounier's relationship to them, see Rauch, *Politics* 285, 289–91, 300–1, 314, 330.

8 Henri Marrou, 'L'action politique d'Emmanuel Mounier,' *Les Cahiers de la République* II (1956) 96

9 The Holy Office condemned *Quinzaine*, the journal of the Chrétiens Progressistes, in 1955.

10 'Introduction aux existentialismes' (1947), in *Œuvres* III (Paris 1962) 70

11 *Ibid.* 111, 113

12 *Ibid.* 85, 86

13 When Mounier used the term 'medieval philosophy' in this context, he seemed to mean Thomism.

14 'Introduction aux existentialismes,' *ibid.* 128

15 *Ibid.* 126–8

16 *Ibid.* 155, 156, 127

17 *Ibid.* 111

18 *Ibid.* 106

19 'Réponse à une enquête' (1947), in *Œuvres* III, 613–15

20 'Communistes chrétiens?' (July 1947), *ibid.* 621–2

21 The Jesuit Hegel scholar, Gaston Fessard, wrote the most penetrating critique of Mounier's position. See 'Lettre à Emmanuel Mounier,' in Gaston Fessard, *De l'actualité historique*, II (Paris 1960), and his 'Réponse à E. Mounier,' *Etudes* CCLX (Mar. 1950) 394–9.

22 'Délivrez-nous' (Jan. 1948), in *ibid.* 626–8

23 *Ibid.* 632

24 'Prague,' *Œuvres* IV, 160

25 'Le personnalisme' (1949), *Œuvres* III, 435–8

26 Henri Marrou, 'L'action politique,' *Les Cahiers* II, 90

27 'Le personnalisme,' *Œuvres* III, 445–6

28 *Ibid.*, 468

29 Jean Lacroix, *Panorama de la philosophie française contemporaine* (Paris 1966) 100

30 Paul Ricœur, 'Une philosophie personnaliste,' *Esprit*, 174 (Dec. 1950) 861–2

31 See the bibliographical note below.

32 'Devant nous,' *Esprit* 140 (Dec. 1947) 940–2. All Mounier's friends of the older generation at *Esprit* followed his line on this issue.

33 'Réponse à quelques critiques,' *Esprit* 143 (Mar. 1948) 460

34 In the speech to the communist congress at Montreuil which is reprinted in Mounier's *Œuvres* IV, 173 and *L'Humanité* (12 Apr. 1949)

35 'Le procès du Cardinal Mindszenty' (1949), in *Œuvres* IV, 161

36 'L'avilissement ne rend pas' (Mar. 1950), in *ibid.* 187

37 'Nouvelle lettre à *Esprit*,' *La Nouvelle Critique* 15 (Apr. 1950) 24
38 'Le pacte atlantique' (May 1949), with Jean-Marie Domenach and Paul Fraisse, in *ibid.* 217
39 'Déclaration de guerre' (Nov. 1948), in *ibid.* 254
40 *Ibid.* 255, 257
41 To employ Stanley Hoffmann's general distinction in 'Collaborationism in France during World War II,' *Journal of Modern History* xxxx, 3 (Sept. 1968) 375–95
42 'Lettre à Emmanuel Mounier,' *La Nouvelle Critique* 13
43 *Ibid.* 13–14
44 *Ibid.* 17
45 'L'avilissement ne rend pas,' *ibid.* 185
46 'Fidélité' (Mar. 1950), *ibid.* 17
47 'L'avilissement ne rend pas,' *ibid.* 188
48 'Fidélité,' *ibid.* 20
49 *Ibid.* 19; 'L'avilissement ne rend pas,' *ibid.* 189
50 'Fidélité,' *ibid.* 20
51 'L'avilissement ne rend pas,' *ibid.* 181
52 'Fidélité,' *ibid.* 20
53 *Ibid.* 21
54 'L'avilissement ne rend pas,' *ibid.* 188
55 'Dernier dialogue,' *Esprit* 12 (Dec. 1950) 780–1
56 'Le personnalisme,' *Œuvres* III, 434, 442
57 'Feu la chrétienté' (1950), *ibid.* 694
58 'Le personnalisme,' *ibid.* 434, 441–2
59 *Ibid.* 501
60 *Ibid.* 499–500
61 *Ibid.* 499
62 *Ibid.* 473
63 *Ibid.* 489
64 'Prière pour les abandonnés,' *Esprit* 144 (Apr. 1948) 668
65 'Le décret du Saint-Office' (July 1949), in *Œuvres* III, 660
66 Letter to André Dumas (9 Oct. 1949), *Œuvres* IV, 820–1
67 'L'histoire chrétienne' (May 1949) *Œuvres* III, 607
68 The controversy surrounding Cardinal Mindszenty's departure from Hungary comes to mind, as well as the present situation in Poland.
69 Madeleine Barthélèmy-Madaule, *La Personne et le drame humain chez Teilhard de Chardin* (Paris 1967) 306–8, 319. See also Henri de Lubac, SJ, *The Religion of Teilhard de Chardin* (Garden City, NY 1968), ch. 13, 'Personalism' 167–76.
70 'We never could have imagined a parallel opportunity and atmosphere

for the great humano-Christian resurrection of our dreams. I constantly think that my place should perhaps be in Europe with you.' Letter from Teilhard de Chardin in Peking to Bruno de Solages, 11 July 1941. *Lettres intimes de Teilhard de Chardin* (Paris, 1974) 336

71 'Du bonheur' (Feb. 1950), in *Œuvres* IV, 273, 276, 280–1
72 'Feu la chrétienté,' *ibid.* 710
73 *Ibid.* 707
74 'Optimisme et pessimisme chrétiens,' *Esprit* 131 (Mar. 1947) 483–5
75 Letter to a young contributor (14 Mar. 1950) *Œuvres* IV, 830
76 'Perspectives existentialistes et perspectives chrétiennes' (1949), *ibid.* 360, 365
77 'L'histoire chrétienne,' *ibid.* 608

CHAPTER TWELVE: EPILOGUE

1 Micheline Tison-Braun, *La crise de l'humanisme: le conflit de l'individu et de la société dans la littérature française moderne*, II (Paris 1967) 429
2 Mounier's influence was particularly noticeable on the Left Catholic 'Znak' group in Poland, which nurtured the future Pope John Paul II and became the largest non-communist group in the Polish parliament, the avant-garde Catholic review *Cross Currents* in the United States, which was founded in 1950 to be an American *Esprit* and which pioneered in introducing European religious thought into North America in the 1950s, and the review *Cité Libre* in Québec, which was founded in 1950 to be a Canadian *Esprit* by a number of people who later became prominent in Canadian political life such as Gérard Pelletier and Pierre Elliott Trudeau.
3 See 1 Corinthians 13.

Bibliographical Note

When Emmanuel Mounier tried to explain his lack of gratitude to the Christian Democratic tradition he wrote: 'gratitude is a virtue of historians. Youth, life, creation are ungrateful. ... The Person who preoccupies himself with references at age twenty or thirty begins to dig his own grave.'[1] Indeed, most biographers of Mounier have been extraordinarily grateful to him, without interring themselves in footnotes. At several stages in his career Mounier reconstructed the history of *Esprit*, and his own history, with 'youth, life, and creation' firmly in mind and a somewhat less resolute regard for the facts.[2] Nonetheless, the incomplete nature of extant studies of Mounier required interested scholars to place unwarranted stock in his 'official version' of his own history. At his death more camouflage was added by a special issue of *Esprit* (XII, December 1950) in which a number of Mounier's old friends, including some of France's most distinguished historians such as François Goguel and Henri Marrou, generously helped to edit the history of the man and his work.[3] Nothing in that issue contradicted Mounier's earlier efforts to define the history of the *Esprit* movement as the history of a movement of the Left – 'in that tradition of human socialism peculiar to France since 1830' – which had 'always' been sympathetic to the Popular Front, the Spanish Republic, the Resistance, and Marxism and consistently hostile to capitalism, the Nazis, fascism, Vichy, and the Right in general.[4]

One might have thought that when the *Œuvres de Mounier* (Paris 1961–3) were published there would be some tensions between the documents and the legend, but the works were arranged without a strict regard for chronology and were incomplete: 288 of Mounier's *Esprit* articles and 102 of his *Esprit* book reviews, were not included, not to mention a wide range of his essays in other publications.[5] Nonetheless, even partial accessibility to his assembled work produced several books which combined the exposition of his thought with brief biographical information.[6] With inadvertent wisdom, one of these biographers, an editor of *La Croix*, observed that 'the worst punishment for [Mounier's thought] would be to submit it to the kinds of analyses that Mounier found abhorrent among a certain kind of academic.'[7]

There were a few cautious notes sounded after Mounier's death. *Esprit* dissident Marc Beigbeder avoided the general elegiac tone. Mounier, he insisted, had been 'innocent and not at all innocent, angelic and cunning, pure and a tactician.'[8] Jean Daniélou warned that 'Mounier ... although a disciple of Péguy, did not share the latter's conception of a Christianity of masses. ... He wanted a Christianity of élite Christians ...' and that there was, in Mounier, the danger 'of reducing Christianity to a religion of élites, who would refuse Church baptism or marriage to the masses of good people who are not mystics.'[9] Jacques Maritain, who kept a discrete silence about his views on Mounier both during and after the war, nevertheless commented in his 1966 attack on neo-modernism in the Church that the communitarian spirit of Mounier seemed to have swept up many modern Catholics at the expense of personalism.[10] Such views notwithstanding, Maritain was linked to Mounier's memory more often than not, and one right-wing Catholic broadside against 'Red Christian' Mounier even reported an alleged conversation with Pius XII in which the Holy Father condemned French Catholics for 'that detestable "sociological" Christianity' which came 'from the lessons of Maritain and Mounier.'[11]

The French Communist party made no pretense of embracing the noble Christian ideal to speak only well of the dead. While the obituary in *L'Humanité* recalled the times when Mounier had 'very warmly affirmed his attachment to the working class,' it added that when a number of French communists had tried to make him 'face his responsibilities' and 'bring his actions into accord with his declarations of principle,' he had 'balked each time.'[12] Completing the confusion, Mounier's most bitter communist critic completely reversed himself: Roger Garaudy, has been expelled from the party, returned to the Christian faith, and now praises Mounier as a great pioneer in Christian-Marxist dialogue.[13]

In more recent years precise questions began to emerge about the accepted notion of the history of *Esprit*. In 1969 Jean-Louis Loubet del Bayle published a vast study on what he called the 'non-conformists' of the nineteen-thirties in which he analysed the Young Right, *Ordre Nouveau*, and *Esprit* groups.[14] The uncritical disciple of Mounier would be surprised, first, at the multiplicity of groups in the 'generation of 1930' which embraced views Mounier had implied were unique to *Esprit*. The disciple also would be surprised to see Mounier's review associated with groups of intellectuals who were not in any known tradition of humanist socialism. At the end, in a flourish of footnotes, Loubet del Bayle cautiously notes certain unholy links between familiar personnel and the élites at Vichy. His book casts doubt on a reconstruction of Mounier's position made through an exclusive reliance on the Œuvres and Mounier's own outline of Esprit's history.[15]

R. William Rauch, Jr, studying the history of Mounier's relationship with Christian democracy, went back to the sources, and, as a frank admirer of Mounier, sought to reconstruct this particular thread of his career. Rauch sided with his criticisms of Esprit's more moderate opponents, saying that 'Mounier performed a necessary, though inevitably thankless task.'[16] However, Rauch's effort to reconcile the accepted version of Mounier's history with the data was challenged by Pierre de Senarclens' study of the entire Esprit group before the war from an antithetical point of view. De Senarclens, professedly nauseated by Mounier and his friends, carefully reconstructed Esprit's position on thirties' issues and put forward a psychological explanation for the group's impotence and 'constant flights from reality' (unhappy childhoods, hatred of fathers, and so on).[17] Although some of the psychohistorical themes do not fit Mounier as well as some of his friends – Mounier rather liked his father, for example – de Senarclens' book offered a novel corrective to the plethora of Mounier hagiographies.

In 1975 Michel Winock, a young professional historian living in the Esprit community in Châtenay-Malabry, produced a 'political history' of Esprit from 1932 until 1950.[18] It is a witty and colourful study which fosters the impression that Esprit generally has always been what it is in the nineteen-eighties: a multifaceted, pluralistic, tolerant, and good humoured organ for a set of French intellectuals with a diversity of philosophical and religious views. Unfortunately he devotes a mere four paragraphs to the review's doctrine – what he calls its socialisme personnaliste – yet presumes to slap de Senarclens, whom he accuses of being sans-barbe, for suggesting that there had been something Vichyiste about Esprit and its ideology. Curiously, Winock also finds fault with Mounier and Esprit, but for naïveté about Stalinism in the late nineteen-forties. He thereby has irritated some older members of the Esprit group, not to much for his analysis as for being a painful reminder that the younger generation around Mounier's review fail to understand the old personalist commitment. What in fact was a powerful mystique has been experienced, and described, as a politique by Winock. Esprit is showing its fifty years.

In my book I have tried to supplement, and correct, the picture of Mounier and his generation presented in the *Œuvres*. It is the first study of Mounier based upon his unpublished diaries, the unpublished letters to and from him, and the full range of other sources in Madame Mounier's collection.[19]

NOTES

1 Open letter to Paul Archambault. Quoted in R. William Rauch, Jr, *Politics and Belief in Contemporary France* (The Hague 1972) 121
2 Notable in this regard are his essays 'Les cinq étapes d'*Esprit*,' reprinted in the *Bulletin des Amis d'Emmanuel Mounier*, XXXIX (Mar. 1967), and 'Quelques réflexions sur le personnalisme,' *Synthèses* 4 (1947) 25–30. These seem to be the essays most historians have used to reconstruct the history of *Esprit*. But all Mounier's post-war books on personalism reiterate themes articulated with greater precision in the historical essays.
3 François Goguel, 'Positions politiques' 797–819; Henri Marrou, 'Un homme dans l'Eglise' 888–905
4 See above 207–8.
5 See the bibliography in his *Œuvres* IV, (Paris 1963) 835–72.
6 In the hagiographical exposition category are the books of Barlow, Borne, Cantin, Chaigne, *et al.*, Charpenteau, Conilh, Domenach, Guissard, Lestavel, and Moix. The studies of Borne and Domenach are more subtle than the others but they, too, are written to 'turn people on' to Mounier.
7 Lucien Guissard, *Mounier* (Paris 1962) 119
8 Marc Beigbeder, *Lettre à 'Esprit'* (Paris 1951) 176
9 Daniélou, 'Un chrétien dans le monde,' *Le Cri* (Jan. 1966) 13
10 *Le Paysan de la Garonne* (Paris 1966) 82
11 Jean Calbrette, *Mounier, le mauvais Esprit* (Paris 1957) 112. Joseph Amato, concentrating on the intellectual backgrounds of both, found that Mounier and Maritain shared a common 'understanding of the modern world.' *Mounier and Maritain* (University of Alabama 1975)
12 'Mort d'Emmanuel Mounier,' *L'humanité* (23 Mar. 1950)
13 'Christianisme et marxisme,' lecture at the Université de Québec (Montréal), 14 Apr. 1975
14 *Les non-conformistes des années 30* (Paris 1969)
15 A final heroic attempt to follow Mounier's outline was made by Roy Pierce in 'Emmanuel Mounier: Tragic Optimist,' chapter 3 in his *Contemporary French Political Thought* (London 1966) 48–88.
16 R. William Rauch, Jr, *Politics and Belief in Contemporary France* (The Hague 1972) 335
17 Pierre de Senarclens, *Le mouvement 'Esprit,' 1932–1941* (Lausanne 1974)
18 Michel Winock, *Histoire politique de la revue 'Esprit,' 1930–1950* (Paris 1975)
19 Although Winock had access to the diaries and letters for his study of *Esprit*'s politics

Bibliography

PRIMARY SOURCES

Writings by Emmanuel Mounier

A bibliography of the writings of Emmanuel Mounier, compiled by Madame Paulette Mounier and others, is printed in Mounier's *Œuvres*, IV (Paris 1963), 835–76. The publications most important for the present book are listed below.

Œuvres, I–IV. Paris 1961–3
  A collection of Mounier's writings chosen and arranged by his widow, Madame Mounier. It includes all but one of Mounier's books, most of which originally appeared as a series of articles in *Esprit*. The system of arrangement is not strictly chronological.
La Penséé de Charles Péguy, with Marcel Péguy and Georges Izard. Paris 1931. In *Œuvres* I (Paris 1961) 13–109
Révolution personnaliste et communautaire. Paris 1935. In *Œuvres* I, 129–409
Manifeste au service du personnalisme. Paris 1936. In *Œuvres* I, 481–648
Pacifistes ou bellicistes? Paris 1939. In *Œuvres* I, 785–834, without the introduction
L'affrontement chrétien. Paris 1948. In *Œuvres* III (Paris 1962) 14–66
Montalembert, collection of texts with preface. Paris 1945
Liberté sous conditions. Paris 1946. In *Œuvres* I, 419–71, 653–76, 729–67
Traité du caractère. Paris 1946. Reprinted as *Œuvres* II (Paris 1962)
Introduction aux existentialismes. Paris 1946. In *Œuvres* III, 69–175
Qu'est-ce que le personnalisme? Paris 1947. In *Œuvres* III, 179–245
L'éveil de l'Afrique Noire. Paris 1948. In *Œuvres* III, 257–338
La petite peur du XXe siècle. Paris 1948. In *Œuvres* III, 341–425

Le personnalisme. Paris 1949. In *Œuvres* III, 179–245

Feu la chrétienté. Paris 1950. In *Œuvres* III (Paris 1962)

Les certitudes difficiles. Paris 1951. In *Œuvres* IV, 7–282

L'espoir des désespérés. Paris 1953. In *Œuvres* IV, 283–406

Mounier et sa génération. Letters, private journals, etc. Paris 1956. Augmented, in *Œuvres* IV, 407–831

Esprit 1 (Oct. 1932)–103 (Aug. 1941); 105 (Dec. 1944)–166 (Apr. 1950). These issues of *Esprit* contain 288 articles and 102 book reviews that were not reprinted in book form or included in the *Œuvres*. These are of central importance in tracing the chronological development of Mounier's thought and in determining his attitudes towards fascism, Vichy, and French and Soviet communism.

Bulletin des amis d'Emmanuel Mounier (Feb. 1951). The *Bulletin* prints previously unpublished Mounier material such as texts of his radio lectures and articles about him by various authors.

Le Voltigeur I–XVIII. 29 Sept. 1938–12 July 1939. Mounier wrote a number of articles in this journal edited by P.-A. Touchard which attempted to embody *Esprit*'s principles in political action.

Unpublished correspondence. Folio I–III. Bibliothèque E. Mounier, Châtenay-Malabry, France

Unpublished sections of the Mounier diaries

Other Sources Consulted

L'Aube	*L'Humanité*
Cahiers d'Uriage	*Nouvelle Revue Française*
La Croix	*Sept*
Documentation Catholique	*Temps Présent*
Dossiers de l'Action Populaire	*Terre Nouvelle*
Etudes	*Vendredi*
Jeune République	*La Vie Catholique*
Jeunesse ouvrière	*La Vie Intellectuelle*

Interviews and Correspondence

Among the individuals with whom this book was discussed particular gratitude is due to: the members of the community Les Murs Blancs, especially Madame Emmanuel Mounier for her hospitality, and, in alphabetical order:

François-George Barbier	Jon Braun
Hubert Beuve-Méry	M.-D. Chenu, OP

Martin J. Corbin
Aline Coutrot
Donald Baker
Cardinal Jean Daniélou
Charles Davis
René Dupuis
Henry W. Ehrmann
M. and Mme Bernard Guyon
Robert Hellman
Stanley Hoffmann
Georges Hourdin
Dick Howard
Guy Hoyon
H. Stuart Hughes

M. and Mme Jean Lacroix
Edmond Lipiansky
Alexandre Marc
Francis J. Murphy
Jean Onimus
Jean-Louis Onimus
John W. Padberg, sj
Simone Pétrement
Emile Poulat
R. William Rauch, Jr
Maurice Schumann
Alain-Gérard Slama
René Thoreval
Rt Hon. Pierre Elliott Trudeau

Among those kind enough to provide information by correspondence, particular gratitude is due to:

Etienne Borne
Gaston Fessard, sj
Jacques Ellul

Etienne Gilson
Louis Martin-Chauffier

SECONDARY WORKS

Books about Mounier

Amato, Joseph *Mounier and Maritain: A French Catholic Understanding of the Modern World* University of Alabama 1975

Barlow, Michel *Le Socialisme d'Emmanuel Mounier* Toulouse 1971

Borne, Etienne *Mounier* Paris 1972

Calbrette, Jean *Mounier, le mauvais Esprit* Paris 1957

Cantin, Eileen *Mounier: A Personalist View of History* New York 1974

Chaigné, Hervé, *et al. Emmanuel Mounier ou le combat du juste* Bordeaux 1968

Charpentreau, Jacques, *et al. L'esthétique personnaliste d'Emmanuel Mounier* Paris 1966

Conilh, Jean *Emmanuel Mounier* Paris 1966

Domenach, Jean-Marie *Emmanuel Mounier* Paris 1972

Guissard, Lucien *Emmanuel Mounier* Paris 1962

Lestavel, Jean *Introduction aux personnalismes* Paris 1961

Moix, Candide *La pensée d'Emmanuel Mounier* Paris 1960

Zaza, Nureddine *Etude critique de la notion d'engagement chez Emmanuel Mounier* Lausanne 1955

Books about 'Esprit' or the Personalist Movement

Loubet del Bayle, Jean-Louis *Les non-conformistes des années 30* Paris 1969
Rauch, R. William, Jr, *Politics and Belief in Contemporary France* The Hague 1972
Senarclens, Pierre de *Le mouvement 'Esprit,' 1932–1941* Lausanne 1974
Winock, Michel *Histoire politique de la revue 'Esprit,' 1930–1950* Paris 1975

Index